# DRY SPRING

## THE COMING WATER CRISIS
*of*
## NORTH AMERICA

## CHRIS WOOD

RAINCOAST BOOKS
*www.raincoast.com*

Raincoast Books gratefully acknowledges the financial support of the Province of
British Columbia through the BC Arts Council and the Book Publishing Tax Credit and
the Government of Canada through the Canada Council for the Arts and the Book
Publishing Industry Development Program (BPIDP).

Edited by Naomi Wittes Reichstein
Cover and interior design by Five Seventeen

**LIBRARY AND ARCHIVES CANADA CATALOGUING IN PUBLICATION**

Wood, Chris, 1953–
Dry spring : the coming water crisis of North America / Chris Wood.

Includes index.
ISBN 13: 978-1-55192-814-2
ISBN 10: 1-55192-814-0

1. Water-supply.   2. Water quality.   3. Water conservation.   I. Title.

HD1691.W65 2008          333.91          C2007-904381-X

Library of Congress Control Number: 2007932325

Raincoast Books
9050 Shaughnessy Street
Vancouver, British Columbia
Canada v6p 6E5
www.raincoast.com

*In the United States*:
Publishers Group West
1700 Fourth Street
Berkeley, California
94710

Raincoast Books is committed to protecting the environment and to the responsible use of
natural resources. We are working with suppliers and printers to phase out our use of paper
produced from ancient forests. This book is printed with vegetable-based inks on 100%
ancient-forest-free, 100% post-consumer recycled, processed chlorine- and acid-free paper.
For further information, visit our website at www.raincoast.com/publishing/.

Printed in Canada by Transcontinental

10   9   8   7   6   5   4   3   2

# DRY SPRING

*for*
Harold Wood,
*in memoriam*

# Contents

# Thanks

I am a reporter before I am a writer. I like to see the story with my own eyes, walk its ground and feel its bones in my hand. Wherever possible, therefore, I have rooted this story in places I have seen and the lives of people I was privileged to meet face-to-face. More than 160 interviews, the majority in person and a smaller number over the phone, are at the heart of this book. My first thanks must go to the many who generously gave me their time and a glimpse of the changes they've witnessed in their world. In this connection, my particular gratitude to Francisco Zamora Arroyo and Guadalupe from the *Asociación Ecológica de Usuarios del Río Hardy-Colorado*, who made it possible for me to meet a few of the people of the Colorado Delta.

Inevitably I have also consulted other sources. As far as possible I have sought those closest to the raw experience or the scientific observations: first-hand reports from around the world, published and unpublished original research, and major studies that have either aggregated scholarly research or delved deeply into particular issues. The United Nations Environment Programme (UNEP) Millennium Ecosystem Assessment (MA) and Intergovernmental Panel on Climate Change (IPCC) reports were particularly key resources of this last kind.

Among the many scientists who have given me their time, I would like in particular to thank Andrew Weaver, whose lucid imagery and vital engagement with the importance of the subject caused me to start watching the weather with a closer eye. I also wish to thank Tom Fennell, formerly managing editor at *The Walrus*, whose encouragement first allowed me to bring my ideas about water to print. In the preparation of this book for publication, I am hugely indebted to the patience, candour and care of Naomi Wittes Reichstein at Raincoast Books.

This book would not have been written, however, without the immeasurable support, moral and practical, that I receive daily from my wife, Beverley Wood. To her I owe a life's worth of gratitude.

# Prologue
## The Marble and the Bowl

Waist-deep in work on the manuscript that would become *Dry Spring*, I began that late August morning as I do most days, scanning the internet for news about water and climate. One headline caught my eye: "Drought to Shut Down Canadian Rain Forest Resort." I clicked and my interest spiked as I read the linked report: "A well-known resort town in a Canadian Pacific rain forest must shutter its hotels and businesses this week because a prolonged drought has slashed water supplies. 'We just don't have the water,' Tofino mayor John Fraser told CBC television."[1]

I know Tofino. The picturesque village on the remote west coast of Vancouver Island is a popular jumping-off spot for eco-tourists exploring the UNESCO-designated Clayoquot Sound Biosphere Reserve. Surfers seek it out for the mighty waves that roll in from the Pacific to break on kilometres of sandy beach. From my home in the Island's more settled Cowichan Valley, you can drive in under four hours the 90 corkscrew kilometres of two-lane blacktop to the Crab Dock at the foot of a short street of surf shacks and art galleries. So this international story struck close to home.

But not nearly so close for me as for Maré Bruce Dewar. Rosy-cheeked, affable and sporting a spiky blond 'do that cuts a couple of decades off her real age, which is north of 50, Maré is a rarity among

Tofino's 1,800 souls: someone who actually grew up there. Back in the 1960s, the settlement was little more than a work camp on the edge of nowhere. Maré's dad drove a "belly-dump" truck at a mine up the road. Her mother ran the only restaurant, in a house barged in after World War II from a semi-abandoned air station. At 18 Maré fled the sticks for big-city Vancouver, entering university just as Tofino began to attract the first young counter-cultural types and Americans dodging Vietnam. Soon she was living as far away as possible, married to a welder and raising kids in New Zealand. Then, in 1987, her mother phoned to ask whether she'd come home, buy the restaurant and run it. "I told her if I did, it would be the end of the marriage," Maré recalls. "But I did. And it was," she adds without visible regret.[2]

Much dressed up, Tofino's oldest restaurant is still the busiest eatery around, its fine cellar and elegantly authentic local cuisine attracting diners from the luxury resorts south of town. Still, not even the Schooner's fresh oysters drizzled in truffle oil and lime juice were a match for the "man-bites-dog" story of the rainforest resort closed down by lack of rain. Breaking into the international media just before the last long weekend of summer, it almost screamed, "Stay away." Bookings plunged.

It hardly mattered that the reports weren't entirely accurate. True, there *was* a drought, the worst in memory along North America's wettest coast. And when a pump that pushes water from an underground creek into Tofino's mains began to suck air, town officials *did* warn local businesses that they would be left dry before residents were. Yet redoubled conservation efforts and emergency deliveries from the rival tourist town of Ucluelet, 43 kilometres away, kept taps flowing and business doors open. It barely mattered. "It was presented as 'Tofino's closed,'" Maré gripes from behind her desk in a small, peach-toned office high under the Schooner's eaves. "We kept hoping the business would come back, but it didn't. We went $50,000 in the hole to be open in September."

Botanists describe Tofino's setting as "rain forest" for good reason. In most years the place gets roughly three and a half metres of rain, enough to fill the average suburban room to the ceiling and then some, roughly seven times what the continent of Australia gets and nearly 20 times what falls on Arizona. The wettest spot in all of Canada is just inland, where enough rain falls at Henderson Lake each year to drown three Michael Jordans, each standing on another's head, beneath nearly three more feet of water.[3] As Maré and I spoke, six weeks after the damaging news reports, fog drifted past the windows. Beyond them, hedges of shiny holly, sprays of pampas grass, bamboo and a few sheltered yucca palms gleamed a lush green. Back down the highway, moisture clung to the drooping skirts of cedar and hemlock in Pacific Rim National Park. It was difficult to reconcile the visible dampness with the knowledge that Tofino was still beset by drought. But this startling contrast lay at the very heart of the subject I had been studying for a year and a half with growing fascination and concern.

It's a paradox that all of us will become increasingly acquainted with in the present century. Around the entire world, reliable weather patterns are breaking down. Snow is falling where it was rarely seen before—and vanishing from where it was once a familiar presence. Seasons that once set farm calendars for sowing and reaping are falling out of step. Streaks of days with searing hot temperatures—or chilling cold ones—are breaking through old records like storm tides over levees. With the weather, past is no longer prologue.

The Tofino of Maré Dewar's childhood has vanished in more ways than one. "When I was growing up, it snowed every winter. There were always about 10 days when you couldn't get out and there'd be 20 feet of snow beside the road [over the mountains]." On one memorable class trip across the island, the school bus in which she was riding became jammed against an oncoming truck, the two vehicles unable to pass each other in a snow canyon. "Now, there's maybe six inches of snow in the mountains. I have pictures of the carpenters putting in the dormers [to expand the restaurant] in February. They were wearing T-shirts and shorts."

What in heaven's name is happening?

In brief, the heavens are changing.

The precious balloon of air and cloud that fills the space between land and sky, our planet's atmosphere, is where climate happens. It is inherently dynamic, as the great oceans and flowing currents of air weave their circulatory rhumba around the world. To say that it is changing is thus to state the obvious. But climate as we experience it is *weather*: the daily warming and cooling of the air, the gale or the stillness of the wind, the rain that soaks our streets or fields and forests—or not. And evidence makes it all too clear that the weather is changing far beyond the range of predictable variety to which we've become accustomed. Observations from Scotland to Texas, from spring and fall, from forests to savannahs, confirm that the patterns of the last century are shifting in this one. Much longer records, derived from sources as disparate as the ancient ice of glaciers, the rings of fossil trees and the sediments beneath the sea, lead many scientists to conclude not only that the weather is changing, but that it is changing on a scale and pace unlike anything nature has experienced in the last 100 million years.

That much had become clear to me long before my conversation with Maré Dewar.

My journalistic familiarity with weather initially extended no further than the detailed meteorological summaries that chattered across the pre-web news wire into the radio newsrooms where I worked in the 1970s. Later, however, I spent a great deal of time reporting to newspapers and magazines on stories that reflected the impact of weather on human lives: freezing rain that brought down a powerful airliner, killing 256 U.S. servicemen on their way home for Christmas; flood waters that destroyed the hopes of small businesses along the Mississippi River; droughts that drove families from rural farms to city slums in Brazil; insubstantial air that scattered bricks like plastic Lego pieces when a hurricane struck suburban Florida.

Just as the last millennium was closing, an ice storm marched across the eastern Great Lakes like some monster from Norse mythology. Days on end of freezing rain and high winds turned entire counties into skating rinks, splintered full-grown hardwood trees like matchsticks and brought huge steel electrical transmission towers to their crumpled knees. Editors at the newsmagazine for which I was working at the time assigned me the task of explaining to readers where this storm had come from. To gain a deeper understanding of its genesis, I visited one of the world's leading centres of climate study, coincidentally also on Vancouver Island, at the University of Victoria, and interviewed one of that institution's top specialists. Over wild mushroom soup and a green salad, amid the polite hum of academic conversation in the faculty dining room, Andrew Weaver described what he thought was going on.

"Imagine a bowl," he told me, "with a marble in it. The marble is in constant motion, running up the side of the bowl and falling back down to the bottom and running up the side again. That's the normal variability of climate: hot ... cold ... wet ... dry. Well, now imagine that the marble is gaining energy, running higher up the side of the bowl at the top of each roll. That's what's happening with the climate; it's becoming more energetic, more extreme." I could picture that: as the energy in the atmosphere amps up, the weather manifests that greater energy by becoming more pronounced. Rainy days get rainier. Hot days get hotter. Wind, windier. Droughts, drier.[4]

"What we don't know," Weaver said next, "is what happens when the marble goes right over the edge of the bowl. We know that sometimes in the past, the climate has changed from one more-or-less stable regime to another that may be quite different. We think that the closer the marble gets to the rim of the bowl, the closer we are to that kind of change. But we don't know how close we are or what will happen when the marble goes over. We just know that the marble is going higher and higher up the side of the bowl as time goes on."

In the decade that followed that conversation, I made a point of keeping tabs on the evolving science of climate. I also looked with a new eye at the increasingly common reports from around the world of increasingly uncommon weather. As time passed, these changes moved from the margins of public consciousness to centre stage. Debate continues over the precise extent of human responsibility for them, although doubt is now concentrated among right-wing economic and political interests. In scientific circles, only the most stubborn contrarians and a few vocal dissenters bankrolled mainly by the fossil fuel industry persist in skepticism.

There is a more vigorous and authentic debate over the *forecast*: which way the wind is blowing over any given part of the globe, where it is taking us and precisely how fast. The more long-range the out- look, the less the certainty. But for the most reliable current report, just step outside your door and look around. The record of actual weather, and of the innumerable natural events that tick-tock from the piping of frogs in spring to the falling of snow in winter, is un- ambiguous. Climate change isn't an abstract scenario for the distant future. It is upon us *now*. We feel its impact in each new departure from the familiar vagaries of the weather we are used to.

"The term 'global warming' is inadequate to describe the changes we can expect," wrote the British authors of one of the most compre- hensive surveys to date of climate science.[5] "We should focus not only on temperature but also on anticipated shifts (perhaps rapid) in the full range of climate variables, their variability and extremes." Our hottest heat waves are getting sweatier, our chilliest cold snaps icier, our strongest winds, heaviest downpours and driest droughts all more extreme, and the weather swings from one manifestation to the next with disorienting swiftness.

Global warming itself is now palpable. During March of 2005, I was taking a plane from southern Florida to the Pacific Northwest. This was during late winter in the mountains, yet, as the plane cruised over the northern Rockies and I gazed down at the peaks and ranges of the continent's western spine, I was struck by the extent of brown and absence of snowy white. Much of what is written, broadcast, or posted on the internet about climate change continues to address global averages in the century ahead or even further into the future. Failure to arrest warming, we read, could "by the end of the century" push the planet's average temperature two or three degrees Celsius over its pre-industrial average. Melting ice-caps may "over millennia" leave the Statue of Liberty knee-deep in New York's harbour. We'd like to dismiss these forecasts as irrelevant to our own lives or too marginal to make a difference. What, after all, are two degrees, even in Celsius?

But science tells us what a difference even a single degree can make, if it happens to be the degree that melts ice or snow into liquid water. Precipitation that collects on mountains in the winter as snow may remain there into the following summer, melting in a timely way to fill rivers in July and August when farmers rely on their flow to irrigate crops, and when fish make an upstream dash to create another generation. Moisture that falls in the winter months as rain instead of snow, or snow that quickly melts and runs off, is available to neither farmers nor fish come August or September.

By the time our plane made its final descent over the great, grey, snow-fed Fraser River into Vancouver International Airport, the seed of this book was planted.

If climate displays itself in weather, it is through water, above all, that we notice both. This is most evident when it rains or snows. But it is equally true when day after day of clear, dry, sunny skies draw the last beads of moisture out of soil, bodies and plants. Wind may do damage on its own, but the wreckage is far greater when wind drives sheets of rain before it, or pushes waves into storm surges that overwhelm beaches and dikes. Both wind and rain (or snow) are, moreover, creations of heat distributed unevenly through the atmosphere. Water's capacity to absorb, hold and release enormous quantities of that heat is central to the forces that keep the clouds and breezes in perpetual motion. The physics that drive all of these also determine whether there will be enough water—or too little, or too much—to meet the needs of ecology and humanity on any day in any given spot on earth.

An extreme enough change in the climate could alter almost everything we know about our planet. But we'll feel even a very small degree of change most personally and acutely in its effect on the distribution of fresh and ample water.

You often hear that water is life. And if water in its molecular essence—a pair of hydrogen atoms bonded to one of oxygen—is not itself life, it is, nonetheless, essential to it. We can find simple life in a remarkable range of environments. We've found bacteria in the deepest oceans, sustained by sulphurous exhalations from volcanic vents. Microbes endure and replicate at temperatures approaching absolute zero in the frozen crevices of Antarctic glaciers. We've found life on the highest mountains and beneath deserts that get only millimetres of rain annually. The only place we've never found it is in the absolute absence of water.

That fact seems to reside in the pre-conscious memory of our species. It emerges in the many ways that water is enlaced in the sacred. A practitioner of no particular religion, I've always found it easier to feel a Creator's presence when I visit the shore and watch the waves come in. Christians exercise the sacrament of baptism by immersing believers in pools or streams, or anointing them with water made holy by prayer. Hindus are called to bathe at least once in their lives in the sacred Ganges River. "We made from water every living thing," Allah reveals in the Qur'an, which further instructs the faithful to wash with water before each daily prayer.[6] Jews seek ritual purification in the *mikvah*, a specially built pool of natural water.

If life and the sacred strike you as insufficiently pragmatic considerations, then look at the economy. Nothing—absolutely *nothing*—is made, sold, traded or supplied without water. That is most obviously true for food. The 11,000 litres of water used to grow the ingredients of a single hamburger (bun, beef and condiments) would fill more than 75 bathtubs.[7] This is less evident but just as true for every other product. It would require two large tanker trucks to deliver the 33,000 litres of water needed to manufacture an ordinary desktop computer.[8] Now picture a convoy of 22 such tankers and you have the 400,000 litres that go into the average new car.[9] Many policy analysts describe the trading of the invisible but necessary water that goes into farm and factory products as the sale of "virtual" water. By this thinking, Canada sends between two and five *Exxon Valdez*-size shiploads of virtual water to the United States every day in the form of synthetic crude oil, which takes up to four-and-a-half barrels of water for each barrel of crude extracted from boreal "tar" sands.[10]

Toward the end of the 1990s, the same newsmagazine assigned me to write a story about the breathtaking new gadgets promised by the era's frenzied technology boom. As my research looked into the future, however, I became aware of an uncomfortable disconnect. At the same time that technophiles were imagining breathtaking capabilities for new developments in computing, nanotechnology and genetic science, other forecasts, no less rigorous and in some cases much more firmly footed on present-day trends, called attention to a variety of rising threats to our society's optimistic trajectory. Among them were the depletion of the world's oceans and an impending peak in oil production. How to feed the world's increasingly urbanized and prosperous billions of inhabitants from diminishing acres of farmland was another. A fourth was the water crisis looming in some of the planet's least stable regions, notably in Africa and the Middle East.[11]

Those pressures have only increased in the years since. It was mid-October 2006 when I negotiated the cliff-hanging curves of the mountain highway to Tofino. A few days earlier, an American group calling itself the Global Footprint Network had announced a gloomy precedent: the earliest-ever World Overshoot Day. The idea was a twist on "Tax Freedom Day," that date when the average taxpayer has earned enough income to satisfy all the various taxes he or she will pay during the year, and after which she or he gets to keep anything earned over the rest of the year.[12] World Overshoot Day is when the human economy is estimated to have consumed all the ecological resources the earth can renew within the same year, and after which our species, in effect, borrows from future years of planetary productivity.[13] The Global Footprint Network calculates that humanity first went into "overshoot" in late December, 1987. By 1995, the day was arriving in late November. It crept into October around the turn of the millennium and is now heading toward September, as it takes the ecosystem about 15 months to produce all the natural services—food, fresh air, clean water—that the human economy consumes in 12.

Plainly, this cannot go on without end. And, as economist Herb Stein memorably observed, "If something cannot go on forever, it will stop."[14] If we don't change our "business as usual" voluntarily, events will change it for us, probably painfully. Gregg Easterbrook, a writer on climate policy and visiting fellow at The Brookings Institution in Washington, D.C., envisions a future decade when "huge numbers of people die, while chaos render[s] social progress impossible in many developing nations and armies of desperate refugees c[o]me to the borders of wealthy nations."[15] Even darker prospects condemn *Homo sapiens* to the fate of the woolly mammoth, put out of commission by a wave of extinctions that he himself unleashed. The bleakest forecasters even seem perversely to welcome this outcome.

The mountain rocks of Vancouver Island are over 80 million years old in places. If you look, you can find fossils of palm forests and alligator-like reptiles that flourished here then. Should humankind not survive, doubtless something else will be along in a millennium or two, with or without the faculty of intelligence.

That is not an inevitable outcome. There *are* things we can do to prevent these dystopic visions from becoming our future. And there is time to do them. But not limitless time.

Much of the literature of climate change looks to the end of the present century and beyond. That's too long a frame. I focus instead on a more relevant window: the next 25 years. Why? Because that's a span through which the great majority of us today can be reasonably assured of living. Whether we have enough water to sustain our diets, livelihoods and styles of life over that period isn't an academic question. It will largely determine whether we'll prosper, encounter adversity or—let us be candid—end disastrously.

Another reason to dwell on the next 25 years is that we're beginning to understand what kind of weather to expect, as a growing weight of real-world, real-time observations bolsters increasingly comprehensive and powerful climate models to reinforce our confidence that some trends will continue over this forecast period.

A third reason is that if we continue our current habit of environmental overshoot, we'll quite simply run out of key resources within the next quarter century. Consider that by every measure, China is the emerging colossus of our new century. If business-as-usual continues uninterrupted, China should enjoy by 2031 a per-capita income and style of living equal to those of the United States in 2005. But Lester Brown of the Earth Policy Institute in Washington, DC, has pointed out the actual impossibility of this. If it comes about, he has said,

"China would be consuming two thirds of the current world grain harvest. Their consumption of paper would be double current world production. It would have a fleet of 1.1 billion cars; the current global fleet is 800 million. And they would be consuming 99 million barrels of oil a day. The world is currently producing 84 million barrels a day and will probably never produce much more than that."[16] All of that takes no account of the rising lifestyle of India, close behind China in population, or of the continuing increase in material wealth that North Americans and Europeans expect to enjoy in the same period. To paraphrase Stein, what cannot go on forever will stop before the next 25 years are out.

But there would be little point in sounding an alarm if there were nothing to be done. So a fourth reason for thinking about the next quarter-century is that it's a time in which we *can* do something. We know too little about our circumstances in 2040 or 2050 to plan usefully for then. Our time is now. Indeed, actions we take or fail to take in the next few years will largely determine whether circumstances later leave us with any choices at all.

And the final reason to think about the 25 years in front of us may be the most urgent of all. Response takes time. Just as water runs through everything we do, everything we do affects our water. Factories and farms aren't replaced or retooled overnight. Investments in communities, housing and utilities can't easily be abandoned. Habits, policies, laws and societies possess inertia: changing them takes a great deal of effort.

To provide enough water for our future, we must choose between two fundamental strategies. We can *build more things*: more dams and reservoirs, more impoundments and river diversions, more aqueducts and canals and pipelines, more wells, and more recycling plants or desalination facilities. Or we can *change how we use what we have now*: we can manage our watersheds differently, choose more ecologically sound appliances and irrigation techniques, and change how our markets, bookkeeping and laws treat the one asset that underwrites every other. Assuming hopefully that we will choose to do anything at all, we'll probably choose some of both. But either strategy takes time.

Utility planners estimate that at least 15 to 20 years, but often many more, pass from the day they decide to build a new reservoir to the day when water starts filling it. To change rules and attitudes takes just as long: health advocates worked more than two decades to convince North American society to ban smoking from public places, and in much of the rest of the world, offices and restaurants are as smoky as ever. Whatever we may need to build or change to assure ourselves of water by 2031, we must start soon: preferably within the next five years, certainly within 10.

There is no time to waste.

Tofino feels like a town at the end of the world. It is, quite literally, the town at the end of the Trans-Canada Highway. Beyond here there is nothing but ocean all the way to Japan. Tourists seek the place out for the very qualities that set it apart from the congested freeways and pressured calendars of their workaday lives. Here, a blackberry is a fruit, not an electronic tether to the office. A large part of Tofino's year-round population has sacrificed conventional careers in order to live under the eaves of a primeval forest within the sound of the wild Pacific surf. Among the surfers and kayak guides, the artists and aging hippies and occasional leftover draft dodger, it is easy to find critics of the rest of the continent's all-consuming appetite for *more*.

There are many reasons to be apprehensive about the quarter-century ahead. Many things could go terribly wrong: religious and ideological fanaticism; militarization; poverty; material self-absorption; ultimately ecological overshoot and habitat collapse. Water, however, is at the heart of solving all of these other problems. If we can get the water part right, we will have the chance to apply our astonishing collective ingenuity and adaptive capacity to all the rest.

Fail on water, as individuals and communities, and little else we get right will matter much.

# Chapter 1
### Eden Ablaze:
## Why the World's Forests Are Burning

Walled by dry hills and high plateaus to east and west, the Okanagan Valley is a sliver-shaped Shangri-La set about a long Zen brush stroke of blue lake. Warmer and drier than California's Napa region, and about the size of Long Island, the Valley was a fruit-growing centre in the last century. Now aerospace companies encroach on premium-label wineries, condos colonize the lakeshore, and million-dollar houses command the views above.

Among the Valley's many successful transplants are brothers Leo and Andy Gebert. Born in southern Switzerland and married there to two sisters, Barbara and Suzanne, the Geberts moved with their wives to Canada in 1984, choosing the Okanagan as the place to chase their dreams. Together, the two couples acquired 75 acres of land near Kelowna with heart-stopping views out over Okanagan Lake. Two-thirds of the acreage was planted in maturing grapevines. In 1992, after eight years of growing grapes for established wineries, the two families made the risky jump into producing wine themselves. Named for the patron saint of hunting, the favourite pastime of the brothers' late father Franz, the new winery's "St. Hubertus" German-style whites and refined reds soon earned a good reputation among discerning oenophiles.

Close to where the Geberts' vineyard runs down to the shore of Okanagan Lake, the narrow lace of blue water doglegs sharply west. Off toward the sunset, a vast thrust of bare, grey-brown rock rises sheer from the waves. When the Geberts first laid eyes on Okanagan Mountain, an open forest of tall lodge-pole and ponderosa pine softened its stony slopes. Woodland extended to the very edge of the new landowners' grape fields. The brothers appreciated the trees' presence for reasons both aesthetic and practical: owls and hawks· residing in the forest helped control the rodents and smaller birds that liked their grapes.

Then came the summer of 2003. Through July and August that year, day followed day of blue skies, unbroken UPF-40 sunshine, dry breezes and afternoon temperatures that soared into the high 30s C.

As night fell on August 15, 2003, thunderheads began to thicken over the Valley. Toward midnight, a strong wind came up from the southwest. Lightning flickered in the velvet dark. Shortly before 2:00 a.m., a blue-white flash split the sky. A hundred million volts of electricity struck the forested mountain a little north of an area known as Wild Horse Canyon. Grey lichen and rust-red pine needles sent up small bright tongues of flame.

Within 10 minutes a phone rang at the nearest fire-control centre. An officer drove out to examine the reported red glow on Okanagan Mountain from across the lake. The lightning had struck a steep slope far from the nearest house. In any case, the fire centre had other worries. Nearly 900 fires were already burning across Canada's third-largest province. The latest alarm was only one of two dozen the centre would receive that day. Fire commanders put off any response until first light.[1]

Some 20 kilometres away on the far side of the mountain, Leo and Barbara and Andy and Suzanne Gebert and their five children slumbered peacefully in the two houses they occupied, one on either side of the main winery building. The coming day, a Saturday, would be busy at the growing family business. There were wine-tasting tourists to welcome at the tent pavilion, protective netting to be spread over ripening grapes, and the contents of the last barrels remaining from the previous season—the tenth-anniversary vintage for St. Hubertus—to ready for bottling.

Dawn broke clear and cloudless once again. A faint haze staining the blue sky beyond the mountain was the only sign of anything out of the ordinary. Andy Gebert thought nothing of it: "I remember looking out and seeing one single helicopter piddling about."[2] Even when radio news reports mentioned the newest fire among the many then burning across the province, he never thought it would pose an imminent danger to his family's property.

Neither did the first fire crew to reach the remote mountainside shortly after daybreak. Fuelled by dry mosses and fragrant sage, the flames ignited overnight had quickly run uphill into standing pine. Trees were burning across nearly 40 acres of forest. Still, fire bosses were confident they could contain what looked like a run-of-the-mill burn. They called in helicopters to bucket hot spots with water, and for an hour, three fixed-wing planes spread bright red chemical retardant along the fire's northern front. When those efforts seemed to check the advancing flames, the aircraft returned to base. Within minutes they refuelled and were aloft again to attack other fires.

But the young monster on Okanagan Mountain had only been thrown back, not defeated. Weeks of drought had left the forest exceptionally dry. Around noon the wind freshened. Hot gusts picked up glowing embers and blew them out ahead of the main fire front, igniting new blazes. Soon flames leapt uphill faster than the helicopters, returning every two or three minutes, could douse them. The Incident Commander radioed for aircraft to drop more fire retardant, but with every available plane already in action elsewhere it was an hour before the first water bomber came free. For the rest of that long, hot afternoon, it and the helicopters continued to assault the fire. But the flames proved stronger, consuming even branches stained the colour of blood by retardant. With two hours of daylight left, the smoke from the burning forest became too thick to fly into. The fire crews withdrew and flames leapt forward unchecked. The monster had broken out of its cage.

Back at the St. Hubertus winery, Andy and Suzanne's son and daughter, both under 10, had spent the day splashing in the family pool. Leo's three teenagers, two sons and a daughter, had joined in winery chores or spent time with their grandmother Gebert, who was visiting Canada for the summer. Apart from the faint tang of smoke in the hazy air, the fire burning in a remote corner beyond the mountain still seemed nothing to be concerned about.

The following day was a Sunday, another day of summer tourists for the winery and frustration for the firefighters. As the flames burned through rugged ravines and cliffs inaccessible to heavy equipment, commanders again called in helicopters and water-bombers. But heavy smoke blunted their effectiveness. By nightfall, the fire front had come within six kilometres of Kelowna's city limits. Police evacuated the half-dozen houses closest to the fire and warned the occupants of another 40 to be ready to leave. The Geberts were not among them. In fact, Kelowna's emergency planning officials considered their green expanse of irrigated vines part of the city's protection against the fire burning up from the south.

The next day firefighters from Kelowna and several surrounding communities joined the battle. But not even these reinforcements could prevail against continuing strong winds and the almost unlimited dry fuel available on the mountain. Over the next 48 hours, flames and flying embers repeatedly leapt over fire breaks, extending the blaze to a front more than 10 kilometres long. On Wednesday afternoon, an emergency-response officer appeared at the winery gate to warn the Gebert families that they should be prepared to evacuate on short notice. Still, Andy considered the warning "an absolute non-event. You could see flames and little white puffy spots of smoke miles away, but it was nothing too serious."

The next day, Thursday, dawned "absolutely gorgeous," Andy remembers. "The fire was going away to the northwest. The kids were in the pool, playing. The winery was going like crazy, preparing for harvest. We were serving wine to tourists." That evening, Andy lingered with a neighbour over a plate of cheese and a bottle of the family's

Northern Summer red. Leo drove into town to attend the weekly meeting of his Rotary Club.

Partway through the meeting, Leo's cell phone trilled. It was Barbara, urging him to come home. A nervous-looking police officer had just been to the door, warning everyone to get out—*now*.

By the time Leo turned into the winery's drive, choking smoke obscured the hill beyond the vineyard. Orange light flickered and glowed eerily in the murky air. Together the brothers ran up the hill to open the gates in the fence along the tree line so that any animals fleeing the fire could get through. Smoke stung their eyes. Flames burst from treetop to treetop across the entire hillside. The ground fire disappeared to either side in swirling smoke. White ash fell like warm snow, and even from a distance the heat on their skin was unbearably intense. The roar of the fire surrounded them. "It was like a 747," Leo remembers.[3]

Back in the winery drive, Andy's wife Suzanne had their two youngsters and a suitcase of clothes for each in their Blazer. Andy had his laptop beside him in the passenger seat of his Mustang; three cases of wine filled its back seat. Leo ran into the house and spotted his own laptop and new video camera. Grabbing those he raced back out to rejoin his family in their camper and second car. As the little convoy pulled out, the first flames reached the vineyard fence.

That night you might have thought the gates of Inferno had opened and the Devil himself was stalking Eden. Viewed from across the lake, a terrifying arc of flame and glowing smoke seemed to march across a vast darkness glimmering with secondary fires. By dawn the heat of the conflagration, consuming incalculable volumes of air, drew winds into the firestorm at over 70 kilometres an hour. Great gusts of flame leapt to the height of 40-storey buildings. Burning debris the size of dinner plates rode the roaring winds to ignite fresh fires as much as eight kilometres away from the main front.

Most house fires burn at around 1,000°c. On that day temperatures more than twice that hot ignited wooden structures even before the flames could reach them. In the forested hills on Kelowna's southern fringe, where nearly 4,000 families had fled their homes, firefighters poured water on any house they could reach until the tanks in their trucks ran dry, embers burned through their hoses or the heat simply became too fierce. By nightfall over 200 houses lay in ashes. One-third of Kelowna's population slept in cars or camped with friends, in motels or emergency shelters.

At last, long after midnight, the wind finally dropped. The monster was far from extinguished—flames would continue to flicker here and there for another three weeks—but for the first time since lightning struck Okanagan Mountain above Wild Horse Canyon, the inferno was contained. The worst was over.

Two days later, troops allowed Leo Gebert back to inspect the family property. With ferocious caprice the flames had bypassed Andy and Suzanne's house entirely. But of the building in which the brothers had turned grapes into St. Hubertus wine, only a few scorched and twisted metal tanks remained. Of Leo's own Tudor-style house, filled with old-country furniture inherited from his and Barbara's grandparents, nothing was left but an ash-filled grave marked by two bare masonry chimneys.

Why begin a conversation about water with an account of fire? The two are opposites, after all, in symbol and experience. One ignites only where the other is not. The first quenches the second.

Yet the Promethean nightmare that roared down off Okanagan Mountain embodies the very extremity of the danger we face. Dry forests burn. Wet ones don't. And more forests are burning now than in the past, even the recent past. They're burning longer and more violently. And they're burning all over the world.

A month after fire destroyed the St. Hubertus winery, grassland fires swept Southern California for weeks. Their flames killed more than a dozen people, destroyed hundreds of houses and reduced an area three times the size of San Francisco to ashes.[4] That same pitiless season, fires in Europe blazed across nearly half of Portugal.[5] The next year, fires blackened an area of Alaska as big as Massachusetts. Other monster outbreaks have consumed thousands of acres of forest and grassland in Saskatchewan and Northern Ontario, in Florida, Texas and Oklahoma. The same fiery plague has visited wildlands from Sweden to Siberia, Indonesia to the Amazon. The early onset of the southern hemisphere summer late in 2006 helped ignite what Australian firefighters described as "the worst spring bushfire in living memory," near the Tasmanian capital of Hobart. One survivor, teenager Teegan Speakman, described howling winds that sent flames spiralling through dry gullies around her family's farm: "I couldn't breathe. I couldn't see in front of me, and the tractor blew up in the shed."[6]

Forests burn every year. Humans start many forest fires, either accidentally or intentionally. Lightning causes more. In some areas, fire suppression in years past has built up a larger stock of unburned fuel than nature might have allowed. Still, those factors cannot explain the full extent of the pandemic of flame. Never in human memory have so many fires burned for so long over so much terrain. The area ablaze every summer around the Arctic Ocean in North America and Russia in the 1990s was more than twice what had burned there 30 years earlier.[7] Alaska's 7,600 fires in 2004 were 10 times the seasonal average over the previous decade.[8] Overall, the American West has experienced four times as many large wildfires each year in the new century as in the years of the 1970s; the fires typically burn four to five times longer and destroy six times more woodland.[9] The acreage burned in Portugal, Spain, Italy and Greece has similarly quadrupled in the new century compared to the 1960s.[10]

The violence of these blazes has staggered even firefighters of long experience. Jesús Abad, the only survivor of a 12-person crew trapped while fighting a monster blaze near Guadalajara, Spain, in 2005, described a "hurricane of fire" that seemed almost demonic in its malice. "I think it saw us and said, 'You, you're mine,'" he recalled from his hospital bed, his arms and face swaddled in white bandages.[11]

New megafires sometimes stretching across hundreds of kilo-metres overwhelm the best-equipped firefighters. After a shift in the wind finally checked a raging California wildfire in 2006, veteran San Bernardino fire chief Mat Fratus said in awe, "Everything we had to throw at it, we did, and it just seemed to burn right through us."[12]

It's been the same experience down under and everywhere else the globe is burning, finds Australia's Bushfire Cooperative Research Centre. "These fires can't be controlled by any suppression resources that we have available anywhere in the world," the Centre's chief ex-ecutive Kevin O'Loughlin says. "They basically burn until there is a substantial break in the weather, or they hit a coastline."[13]

The increase in number, extent and ferocity of fires burning worldwide is no coincidence. It reflects unprecedented periods of dry weather. Hot, dry days, often accompanied by wind, act on grassland and forests exactly as a household blow-dryer does on hair, drawing out every possible molecule of moisture. Leaves, living twigs and the vegetation decaying beneath them transform into spark-ready fuel. Such days, formerly exceptional in many places, are now becoming the norm. Weeks of them preceded the Okanagan fire, as well as those that blazed before and after it across Southern California, Europe, Africa, South America, Southeast Asia, Russia and Australia.

Perched on a bluff overlooking a sand beach north of San Diego, the Scripps Institution of Oceanography has been a world-ranked re-search centre since 1903. As the Scripps celebrated its centennial in 2003, grey columns of smoke were visible from its windows, rising over the hills to the east. At night, the darkness flickered with red flames fanned by what are known locally as Santa Ana winds, blowing down from the dry plateau beyond the Sierra Nevada. The connec-tion spurred scientists at the venerable institution to compare decades of weather records with fire data from the U.S. Forest Service. They found that temperatures over the western Sierras had become steadily warmer, with the result that upland snow melted earlier each spring. That gave forests longer to dry out and fires more opportunities to start.[14] By the dawn of the new century, the fire season in California had become *more than two months* longer than it had been 40 years earlier. "People think climate change [is] 50 to 100 years away," says Scripps researcher Thomas Swetnam. "It's not. It's happening now in forest ecosystems through fire."[15]

As it has often been for humanity, fire is merely a messenger. Consuming forest and savannah and scarring innumerable lives, it races across landscapes to bear a warning: the weather is changing. Not in some distant decade at the end of the century, but now, today, all around us. In the next few chapters we'll explore the manifestations of that change. Inferno, we will find, wears many faces.

The most ominous shifts over North America are taking place where its society is experiencing its most exuberant growth: in the American Southwest, the western Canadian Prairies, and our shared Great Lakes heartland. Later chapters will examine each of these more closely. Around the entire globe, the forces that bring us wind and rain, snow, and hot, drying days are undergoing a realignment; we'll explore that in Chapter Eight. One shift in particular will stand out: what are known as the sub-tropics, the latitudes occupied by most of the continental United States, are getting drier, while higher latitudes where Canada lies, are getting wetter.

As we explore these changes in the air, we will also come to appreciate a great flaw in much of what is written about weather and climate. Climate forecasts couched in *average* global temperatures too often conceal the increasing severity of the *real* weather we get. This is a defect of arithmetic means: to a mathematician, a glass that is full to the brim and one that is bone-dry are, on average, each half full. While climate's marble zips higher and higher up first one side of the bowl then the other, its average position may still place it resting somewhere on the bottom. It's not the averages we have to fear, but the extremes.

Someone with the eyes of an eagle might stand between the rows of the St. Hubertus vineyards, look north across the dogleg reach of Okanagan Lake and pick out the modest white house that serves as an office for the Okanagan Nation Alliance. The Alliance is a common front of seven Aboriginal bands that claim the Valley as traditional territory. Its small staff is overstretched in representing the varied interests of 3,000 constituents. Perpetually multi-tasking, Deana Machin is the Alliance's fisheries manager and also its voice on the Okanagan Water Stewardship Council, a volunteer forum created to advise municipal leaders.

"We were here before Europeans came," Deana told me. "That gives us a more long-term perspective. Elders talk about what is good for our grandchildren's children, and I hear a lot of them say we're not doing a good job of keeping our water clean."[16] In particular, Deana says, "I'm very concerned about how rapidly development is happening." After bursting through every growth forecast of the last 40 years, the Okanagan's population of fewer than 300,000 at the turn of the millennium is expected to grow by a third within a dozen years. Deana wonders how the land will take it. "Every natural habitat has its carrying capacity."

"To the Okanagan Nation," Deana tells me, "water is sacred," inseparable from her people's sense of spirit and identity. At the same time, she regards water as just another asset seized from her people without so much as a shotgun treaty in the 19th and 20th centuries. It riles her greatly to see it "given away for free," to Valley residents. "The Okanagan Nation has never given up title over our territory. We don't view water as any different from trees, any different from fish. The Nations are getting a pittance for resources leaving their land."

The liquid asset flowing so freely off what Deana considers unceded First Nation territory is what the Valley's booming new society runs on. Forty-five minutes south down Okanagan Lake from Westbank is a community optimistically named Summerland. A narrow paved road winds away from the water up onto a bench of land. There I found Lorraine Bennest early one morning, spading a trench along a line of matchstick-thin saplings. Her two dogs—Jack, a namesake Jack Russell terrier, and Sarah, a standard poodle—chased scents and small animals among the newly planted rows. A second-generation orchardist, Lorraine bought her 15 acres of Eden more than a decade ago against the advice of her parents. "They thought it was a dumb business to be in," she says. "They wanted us to get an education and go into a real business." Instead, Lorraine now tends her own apple groves with a fierce pride.[17]

These aren't just any apple trees, mind you. Fastidiously cloned and cared-for, these are precision growing machines for what Lorraine calls a "premium-price, fresh market eating experience," producing fruits whose names are as embedded with promise as the town below: Ambrosia, Silken, and Aurora. They don't come cheap. An acre of newly planted saplings ordered a year in advance, along with the plastic drip lines buried at their roots, costs $30,000 to install. Lorraine must carry that debt for at least six years before the trees begin to generate enough fruit for her to start paying it down. Actual profit hovers a decade away.

It rests, moreover, on perpetual defiance of an unhelpful fact of nature that few visitors here stop to consider. Green, despite appearances, is not the Okanagan's natural colour. That colour is brown. "Look up at the hills," Lorraine told me on a June day. Above the emerald landscaping of the lower slopes, the hills around us were a dull tan, the colour of dry foliage. This popular valley is in fact one of the driest places in Canada. According to botanists, the Okanagan's native vegetation reveals a climatic kinship with that of the distant Sonoran Desert in the American Southwest. "We get ten inches of rain a year here," Lorraine tells me. "I can't grow anything on ten inches of rain."

What makes this Shangri-La bloom, bear fruit and seduce so many visitors into putting down roots is plumbing: a hidden network of reservoirs, creeks, canals and pipes. Out of sight in the hills above Summerland is a community reservoir. Scores just like it are concealed up and down the length of the Valley. When rain falls, or snow melts in spring, the reservoir fills. Through the rainless weeks of summer, it supplies the water that flows to Lorraine's trees in amounts calibrated to the ounce by a small computer in a shed at the foot of her property. "We're spoon-feeding our plants," she says, but during the most critical months from June through September, "We fucking well need it."

So do we all. It wasn't the wheel that made civilization possible. It was plumbing. From the earliest Mesopotamian city-states to the plains empires of southeast China to Southern California's 20th-century metamorphosis from desert to shimmering oasis, our species owes its successes largely to the capture, storage and controlled distribution of water. Irrigated fields produced the food surpluses that allowed early societies to increase in number and afforded the spare time and specialized manpower that led to further inventions. Sanitation lets many of us live together in densities that otherwise would invite lethally epidemic infections (and that, before widespread urban plumbing, did). Where irrigation and sanitation are lacking today, as in sub-Saharan Africa, humanity's condition is most miserable and our societies are most vulnerable.

On this score the Okanagan is very well served. Despite their semi-arid circumstances, the residents of Kelowna, Westbank and Summerland enjoy clean, fresh water for drinking, washing, growing and making things in more lavish volumes than almost any other humans on the planet. They pay less for it than the residents of many Developing World shantytowns do for jerry cans of water teeming with parasites, and they seldom worry that their taps may run dry. Still, even here, the pipes have gurgled an early warning once or twice. In the same month that flames raced up the opposite side of the Valley, Lorraine's drip lines were nearly shut off in order to keep enough water in nearby Trout Creek that the namesake game fish would stay alive. Now Lorraine sits with Deana Machin on the Water Stewardship Council, trying to forestall a similar Hobson's choice in the future. The two women share much the same fear. "My community has added residents in anticipation of more water being available," Lorraine says. "The thinking is, 'It'll all be okay in the future.' Why will it be okay in the future? It's not okay now." She surveys a row of newly planted trees. "I don't know what we're going to do."

The conundrum facing the Okanagan faces the wider world. Several books have catalogued the water shortages stalking many breadbasket regions. Although few listened, a warning bell sounded in 2006 when for the sixth time in seven years, humanity harvested less food than it consumed, and grain reserves hit their lowest point in decades.[18]

Particularly in Asia, populations are growing in expectation of ever-expanding harvests from these crucial plains, even as they are hardly "okay now." In China, some 140 million rely on the Huang He (Yellow) River for drinking water, for water to irrigate an area the size of South Carolina, for water to flow in wells for miles on either side, and for water to help people realize Western-influenced lifestyle aspirations in scores of large industrial cities. These combined demands on the river already add up to 10 percent more than the Huang He typically provides, and yet economic expectations for the Chinese heartland imply that by 2030 withdrawals from the river will somehow rise by nearly half.[19]

This perfect brew, of growing populations, rising material demands and mounting calls for water, threatens developing regions from India to Egypt to Mexico. But it's not only the poor who are pinning their futures on impossibly optimistic expectations of water availability. Water tables beneath the American high plains have been falling for decades. So has the Colorado River, whose water keeps Southern California in bloom.

With so much depending on the water in the pipes, I wanted to know more about where the Okanagan's water comes from. To answer that question I drove back north to the top of the Valley and the town of Vernon. There I called on an engineer named Bob Campbell. A comfortably rumpled fellow in jeans and a plaid camp shirt, Campbell takes a boyish pride in the century-old water system under his charge. To show me its source, he bundled me into a four-wheel-drive Jeep for the bone-rattling ascent up a rough track into the hills above the Valley.

It's true that the Okanagan gets very little summer rain. Its southern half, moreover, is drier in general than its north. But in most years the Valley as a whole receives plenty of precipitation: more than enough, on average, to fill a dozen ocean-going tankers every day. But that generous water "income" doesn't come in regular paycheques, so much every week. In fact, as much as nine-tenths of the Valley's precipitation falls in the late autumn, winter and early spring when fields and vineyards are idle. And much of it falls as snow. Water *consumption*, by contrast, peaks between June and September. On some days during those months, Vernon homes and businesses and the area's farmers consume *four times* as much water as they do in wet January.[20]

More than simply moving water from source to tap, Campbell's great challenge is to budget it between months of surplus and months of deficit. In that task, his main assets are three small artificial lakes named Aberdeen, Grizzly and Haddo, nestled out of sight of the Valley in upland cedar and pine forest. When filled to the brim, their low earthen dams hold nearly 20 billion cubic metres of water: enough, in theory, to supply everyone downstream for over a year. "That's our money in the bank" is how Campbell puts it. But theory is just that. The reality is that unlike bank accounts, the lakes can't ever be drained completely dry. Also unlike bank accounts, the reservoirs don't pay interest; instead, they all lose some volume to evaporation before the water can get to fields or houses. In some rainless summers, the water they contain barely lasts through the season.

Campbell's problem is a pocket-size version of humanity's. Viewed as a global whole, our species and planet aren't running short of water in an absolute sense. Our impending water crisis is not one of world scarcity: to the contrary, there is *more* water circulating through the atmosphere now than for a very long time past. Rather, the crisis we face is one of water's *distribution*: its surplus or deficit relative to our needs at particular times and places.

It's often pointed out that most of the blue on a world map doesn't represent water our species can actually use. This is true: 97 percent of it is salty. Nearly three-quarters of the fresh remainder is buried too deep underground to be reached or is frozen (for now) in polar ice-caps. Less than four-fifths of one percent of all the water on earth is fresh, liquid and available for human and other terrestrial life. That's still a very great deal, more than five times the water contained in all of the earth's rivers combined.[21] Averaged across the planet's entire human population, it's more than enough for each of us to guzzle down even on the gluttonous scale that North Americans do.

We don't live in the world of averages, however. We live, increasingly, at the extremes. Consider China's Huang He River again. Sixty percent of its water flows down between July and October, rainy months in north China when farmers don't need the water to irrigate their fields. When they do need it, in the year's driest quarter between March and June, the river is at its lowest ebb. The same asynchronism afflicts the world's second most populous country: India gets 90 percent of its rain during the four monsoon months of June to September, little in the rest of the year.

Water falling at the "wrong" time for human convenience is one side of the distribution problem. The other is water's unequal allotment across the map. In this, Canadians are the outsize winners. With less than one percent of humanity, Canada enjoys 20 percent of all the world's liquid fresh water and seven percent even of its renewable supply. Yet here too, nearly two-thirds of our renewable surface fresh water flows across the relatively unpopulated north, while the vast majority of us do our drinking, bathing and farming in the far south.[22]

America's water divide is between east and west rather than north and south. Water studies of the United States divide the country along the 100th degree of longitude, a line running vertically through the middle of the Dakotas and almost directly over Abilene, Texas. Most places east of that line get 51 centimetres or more of rain a year, enough to grow crops on most soils without additional irrigation. Those to the west (apart from the Pacific Northwest) typically get much less. The most intensely irrigated acreages in America, in consequence, are all west of that line. So are 11 of the 15 fastest-growing cities in the United States.[23] Four are in the two driest states, Arizona and Nevada.[24]

The same mismatch of people and water holds true everywhere else. Mexico's three largest cities and three out of four of its citizens are located in central and northern states that possess only a third of the country's water; the southeast and Yucatan, with less than a quarter of Mexico's people, are amply supplied. Most of Australia's rain falls in the north; most Aussies live in southern coastal cities. Nearly a third of Africa's water flows in the Congo River Basin, which only one African in 10 calls home.[25] Collectively, the lands where two-thirds of humanity live—four billion people—get only about a quarter of the globe's precipitation.

We are most reliant on water in its liquid state. Water frozen into snow or ice, or water suspended as airborne vapour, carry significantly different implications for both human and wild life. This turns out to be surprisingly important.

More than half the water the Okanagan Valley receives comes as snow, in most years blanketing the high-altitude plateau by January and piling up through March. When it eventually melts under the returning spring sun, the liberated water fills the Valley's creeks over many weeks. The more snow, the better Bob Campbell likes it. Two dates dominate his calendar: the last early-summer day when melting snow overflows his three reservoir spillways—his last chance to capture and save it—and the first day in the fall when it rains in earnest. Each year lately, the first seems to come sooner and the second later. Half a century of records kept by his predecessors back up this impression: the snow in southern British Columbia is melting at least three weeks earlier today than it did in the 1950s. At the other end of the season, the cold spells that usher in autumn are arriving up to a week later than they did in the past.[26] That means Campbell's water "in the bank" has to last longer too. Even were the Valley's population not growing, he observes, "When you start taking water out earlier and your users are wanting it longer, you've got a real potential for shortages."

Not only the timing but the very qualities of the seasons are changing in the Okanagan. The same detailed records that show the slow recession of spring reveal that the water contained in winter snow (what scientists call "snow water equivalent") has declined by about 10 percent a decade for half a century. Summer days more often test the upper end of the thermometer while summer nights cool off less than in the past. Like that blow-dryer's "high" setting, warmer days and nights increase the speed at which water evaporates from lakes and reservoirs, from forest underbush and the Okanagan's fertile soil, as well as the rate at which plants "transpire" moisture into the air (together called "evapotranspiration," or ET).

The person who has studied most closely what these changes mean for the Okanagan doesn't live there. He is a reedy, bespectacled academic with an office off the broad green avenue that divides the campus of the University of British Columbia in Vancouver into faculties of arts and science. Stewart Cohen works on the science side. A geographer, he and a team of specialized associates have put the Okanagan under the microscope since the late 1990s, as a kind of living experiment in how changes in the climate may affect societies. They have reached two disturbing conclusions: that the Valley is already near the limit of its annual water income, and that the fiery summer of 2003 was merely a foretaste of what is to come.

"If we don't do anything," Cohen warns, the Okanagan will inevitably hit a tipping point when its residents' rising demands for water collide with dwindling supplies carried over from winter, and taps go dry. And given that averages are not real-life, that some winters are drier than others and some summers hotter, that rain and snow fall unevenly around the Valley and that some communities are growing faster than others, some parts of the Valley, "could pass that balance in the next 10 years."[27]

Getting water is never so simple as turning on a tap. Every North American city and acre of irrigated cropland relies on some version of Bob Campbell's upland reservoirs, as do every other developed and most of the developing regions of the world. In some cases those reservoirs are natural underground aquifers. In other places, large rivers serve the same purpose. And it is an under-appreciated fact that many of the world's warmest places, including populous parts of central Africa, the state of California and major cities in India, China and Australia rely as much as the Okanagan on snow and ice for their year-round supply of water. But the changes observed in southern British Columbia are happening elsewhere too. Around the entire globe the familiar cadence of precipitation and clear skies, of seasons themselves, is changing. The sky is releasing ample—sometimes too ample—supplies of water when it is least expected and withholding it at times when once it could be counted on. Campbell's reservoirs were designed to bank and budget the reliable water income of a vanished century. Like others around the world, they're straining now to accommodate unpredictable new extremes of precipitation.

To a casual observer, the lake that sparkles down the length of the Okanagan Valley embodies a pristine beauty. Housing developments springing up around its shores strive for the same unblemished image with names like Lakeshore Gardens, Pinnacle Point and Greata Ranch Vineyard Estates. But this postcard image of bucolic perfection is carefully staged. The Okanagan watershed is one of the most hydraulically enhanced in Canada. In addition to the hidden reservoirs on virtually every stream running into the Valley, levees confine the rivers that used to wind freely between the lakes, turning them into straight-line culverts. Gated spillways precisely control the water released from each lake to the next.

The rise and fall of the Okanagan lakes are choreographed from an industrial building just off the highway in the city of Penticton. "I'm the guy with his hand on the tap," Brian Symonds says as he introduces himself. Tall, with a ready grin, he manages a plumbing system that has evolved over nearly a century. The first dam in the chain was installed at the outlet of Okanagan Lake at the turn of the last century, holding back and later dispensing enough water to ensure that paddlewheel steamers on the river below would stay afloat all summer long. After a devastating flood in 1942, the governments of Canada and British Columbia built more dams to prevent similar disasters in the future. Now, while controlling floods remains his top mandate, Symonds says the system "is managed for multiple objectives." That means balancing the competing demands of waterfront condo-dwellers, homeowners proud of their kelly-green lawns in July, fruit-growers and vintners, and the Valley's expanding secondary industry and vital tourist trade—all while trying to keep a little water in the creeks for struggling trout and Kokanee salmon. "We have 300,000 'experts' watching us," Symonds jokes.[28]

"The lifestyle people come here for relies on water," he tells me. The trends in Bob Campbell's records and Stewart Cohen's forecasts alarm him deeply. "At the snowline, a single degree [of warming] can make a big difference," Symonds says. "If climate change affects evaporation off the lake, we won't be able to control that. In the future, the same storage may not be sufficient." Another summer like the one of 2003 is a certainty, and similar seasons will strike more often. Those dry years will confront his neighbours with hard options, he says: learn to use less water, find a way to bring more of it from somewhere beyond the Valley or watch their treasured lifestyle shrivel up. "It comes down to which trade-offs people are willing to make. I don't think people appreciate some of the hard choices."

We can do a great deal to be ready for what is coming down the wind. If our reservoirs are too small, we could build larger ones. As we shall see, though, we probably don't want to: there are countless other, more inventive and Earth-kindlier ways of making the water go around. Some of these ways are pedestrian, but necessary. Many are neither rocket science nor expensive; they are simply choices we need to make. Others will challenge us to think about water and nature in an altogether new relationship to our economy. We'll meet them all in later chapters.

✦

Fire didn't extinguish the Gebert family's dreams. Most of their grapevines survived being scorched to the roots. The brothers and their wives rebuilt their winery, bigger and better than before the monster visited. On the hill above, fresh green shoots rose within a season through black ash. "Nature regenerates," says Andy Gebert, but never exactly as before. "The forest is gone. I know I will never see those trees again."

Our species has built a society and economy on the experience—and in the anticipation—of seasons and weather patterns that have passed into history. New seasons are upon us. There is one more thing Brian Symonds thinks his resident "experts" are missing. "'Do nothing' costs too," he says. "People need to understand that." What he means is that it takes time to prepare for a change in the weather. If the storm blows in before we're ready, our society is vulnerable. "It's coming," he says, "sooner than you think."

# Chapter 2
## Running Dry:
## Drought, Thirst and the Spread of Deserts

Early in the 1990s I lived for a time in Texas, covering news events in the United States from a base near the vast Dallas-Fort Worth air hub. After rejecting several houses for rent in the area's interchangeable suburbs, my wife and I agreed on a ranch house that sat in a working pasture in view of a pretty lake. As he handed us the keys, our landlord, a charming JR knock-off in hand-tooled boots and outsize belt buckle, drawled, "And y'all can use the tanks as well."

A good Canadian who entertained the usual stereotypes of Americans, I instantly imagined armoured vehicles concealed in the property's several barns. But no. It turned out he meant several murky pools scooped out of the red Texas clay that were intended to water livestock but in which lived fat grey catfish that we were free to catch.

More mental adjustments followed as I got to know a region that, in water as in much else, differed so greatly from my Canadian home. Countless wild lakes sprinkle Canada's countryside with blue. The second-largest state in the Union can claim precisely one: Caddo Lake, on the Louisiana border. All the other 200-plus bodies of water on the Texas map, I discovered, are as artificial as its cattle tanks. A dearth of natural lakes has not prevented Texans from swaddling their cities in emerald lawns, dotting their interstates with water-themed amusement parks or harvesting America's third-largest acreage of irrigated farmland.[1] Even so, a string of years at the start of the new century began to erode even the Lone Star State's unassailable confidence in the capacity of money and engineering, when applied in sufficient quantities, to overcome all natural obstacles.

Since we left, the Dallas-Fort Worth Metroplex has continued to colonize the north Texas plains. Its housing developments, commuter arteries, arena-size retail outlets and low-rise industrial campuses now extend over parts of a dozen counties, with more land area than the entire state of New Jersey. With six million inhabitants, it's the fourth-largest urban concentration in the United States. The cattle and coyotes that once lowed and yipped beyond our rented ranch windows were long ago pushed aside to make room for more SUVs and appliance-stuffed single-family dwellings.

An hour south of our vanished catfish tanks, an unincorporated community of older bungalows and threadbare trailers, sheltered by tall cottonwoods and gnarled live oaks, is slowly giving way to trophy mansions on acreage lots. Off a back road there, tucked between a shooting range and land owned by a breeder of illegal fighting cocks, you can find Jim Stegall's lovingly kept six acres patrolled by a flock of grey guinea fowl. Texan to the colourful depths of his anti-establishment opinions, Jim is nonetheless a local anomaly: a professional art conservator. Trained in oil and watercolour painting in the 1960s (in the Pennsylvania city he scornfully calls "Filthydelphia"), Jim has repaired Goyas and Rembrandts for wealthy collectors and instructs students in an airy studio where light streams through north-facing windows.

For two decades, however, Jim has supplemented his fitful artist's income with a second career as a nurseryman. A file of humpbacked greenhouses leads away behind the studio. There, under plastic roofs dripping with condensation, Jim and his hired hands annually start some 130,000 bedding plants, from petunias and marigolds to hibiscus and peonies. When the larger plants have rooted, he moves them in their black plastic containers out to the shade of the property's full-grown trees to harden in the open air. He sells his plants mostly to local towns, business campuses and golf clubs. It's a water-intensive enterprise that relies on his two wells. It's also weather-sensitive: he counts on moderate weather in spring, when the young plants are first exposed to the outdoors.

Then came the new century. First, there was a summer when the thermometer shot above 100°F (38°C) and stayed there for a month straight. Then came two years when day followed unbroken day of cloudless, mid-90°F (mid-30°C) heat for months on end. Even in the years when no single baking blast lasted more than a week or so, soggy humidity, unrelieved by rain, made even normally sweltering temperatures unbearably oppressive. Soon climatologists and farm bureaus up and down America's heartland were calling it the worst drought in 70 years. "Plants get stressed," Jim explained. "When you have 90, 100-and-some [°F] days and you don't get clouds, you don't get rain, you don't get a cool day for three months, you can water them all day long and if they never get a break from the sun they're still not going to survive. You do two years of that, they die."[2]

It wasn't just young plants struggling to become established that died. So did a score of what Jim refers to as "big stuff," the mature oaks and cottonwoods that provide critical shade for his stock. "That's what worries me more. We're talking about 70-foot trees that are 50, 60, 70 years old. Those trees were older than I am. They've been through droughts before. And that's happening everywhere. [Golf] clubs lost hollies, which are one of the hardiest plants in Texas. And it's not because they don't water and take care of them, because they're very good at that. It's stress." When Jim's shade trees died, soon the plants beneath their bare branches did as well, as the heat of the sun baked the air near the ground.

What little break Jim's plants got from the relentless heat came from the water he used to mist the air in his greenhouses and moisten the roots of his outdoor stock. Miraculously, it seemed, his two wells continued to flow, though not in gushes. By pumping all night, he was able to fill a tall grey cistern with 5,000 gallons each morning, enough to keep his plants hydrated for another day. "Then one morning," he says, "I went to the tank and the tank was dry." After three of the hottest and driest years in Texas memory, his wells had finally given out.

A series of panicked calls to local drillers revealed that his weren't the only ones. So many other luckless home and business owners were calling to have their wells deepened or new ones drilled that the waiting time for service had stretched to six months or more, and prices had spiked. Reaching down to a deeper aquifer would have set Jim back at least $40,000 CDN. The water down there was also different from the shallower water he'd been using: so salty that before using it for plants, he'd have to inject caustic sulphuric acid down into the well just to neutralize the salinity.

Forced into a corner, Jim turned to the municipal main that supplied drinking water to his house. He was able to buy enough water to nurse the last of his plants through to sale that autumn, but at a cost that ate up most of his profit. Over the winter that followed, water returned to Jim's wells, although not with the previous abundance. Other wells belonging to neighbours nearby remained dry. "I don't know what my situation is," Jim admitted. But with a new growing season approaching, "I'm scared to death."

Drought lacks the drama of a forest fire. It sets in little by little, taking its victims by stealth. Yet ultimately it poses the greater danger to wealth, health and communities. Losses to drought cost the world economy at least $42 billion U.S. a year.[3] Famine brought on by drought affects scores of millions of people each year, taking an incalculable toll in death, suffering and the lasting effects of malnutrition. Relief agencies reckon it the most socially destructive natural disaster of all, with a corrosive effect on the ties of family and community greater than that of fire, flood, earthquakes, tsunamis or windstorms. Historically, droughts that endured over decades brought down entire civilizations.

+

Jim Stegall's fear had plenty of company in Middle America early in the new century. The whole heartland thirsted.

In South Dakota, America's corniest tourist attraction was left without a new suit of cobs. The 114-year-old tradition (heavily advertised from one end of the South Dakota Interstate to the other as the "Mitchell Corn Palace") of decorating a community centre with mosaic murals assembled from different colours of corn, had to be abandoned for lack of ears. That had never happened before, even in the dry depths of the 1930s.[4] Ranchers culled their herds. Over a period of three months more than 27,000 cattle passed through Herman Schumacher's sales ring at Herreid, seven times his usual traffic. "I've been here 25 years," Schumacher said, "and I can't compare this to any other year."[5] For many cattlemen it was the end of the trail. "Some of them just trimmed off their herds," Schumacher said. "But a third were complete dispersions. They'll never be back."

Down on the flatlands of the Gulf Coast near Corpus Christi, Texas, Charlie Ring's eight tall grain silos stood mostly empty after both his corn and his sorghum harvests came in two-thirds below normal. Three-quarters of his cotton harvest was similarly lost to weeks on end of rainless heat sucking the moisture out of leaves and soil. "We lost any sort of buffer we had built up over several years," he agonized. "We're back to square one. We can't [afford to] stub our toe in the coming year."[6] That year again started out dry, threatening to leave his seed lifeless in the dusty ground.

Those whose livelihoods depended on serving the farm sector were often worse off. Trey Williams, a fertilizer distributor also in the Corpus Christi area, faced bankruptcy. "I've been in business 11 years," he said. "I expected bad years, but this has been terrible. Ag[riculture] will survive because of insurance programs, government assistance. But the independent business people will not survive this."[7]

The year 2005 saw Phoenix, Arizona, set a record of 142 days without rain, far outstretching the old mark of 101. Ominously for a state that relies on winter snow from its mountains to green its desert lawns, surveyors from the water department scouting highlands north of the city reported "nothing but dead leaves and parched pine trees."[8] Never since record-keeping began in 1898 had there been a winter without at least some snow in those areas.

By 2006, states from the southern Mississippi Valley to the upper Great Lakes and even into the Pacific Northwest were recording their longest periods on record without meaningful rainfall. The Colorado River, whose flow is life to nine American and Mexican states—including parts of California, Arizona, and Nevada and Mexico's Sonora and Baja California—fell to less than half its low level recorded during the Dust Bowl years. The National Drought Mitigation Center declared 60 percent of the continental United States to be "abnormally dry or [in] drought."[9] The following year the drought marched east and west, more than doubling the extent of its grip on the southwest while the most intense dry spell ever recorded in Alabama sucked the life from fields there and much of the rest of the southeast.[10] Researchers studying the human and natural record through proxies extracted from tree-rings called the drought easily among the most severe in five centuries.[11]

As seasons passed into years, alarm spread to water and power utilities. West of Fort Worth, the small town of Aledo took the decidedly un-Texan step of ordering emergency water rationing, explaining to its citizens that dozens of private wells had dried up and its municipal wells threatened to do the same. Lubbock and Amarillo took similar steps after Lake Meredith, a large reservoir on the Canadian River that supplies both cities and nine others in the Texas panhandle, shrivelled to half its usual size.

Along with water tables and reservoirs, America's most important waterways began, literally, to evaporate. Hydro-electric production at dozens of dams along the Missouri River fell by nearly half. America's longest navigable river is also part of a vital marine transportation system. Barges plying it and other Midwestern rivers—in good times lashed together five hulls wide and eight long, covering the area of

five football fields—carry half the United States' corn and most of
its soybean crop on the first stage of their journey to world markets,
returning upstream with bulk cement, asphalt, coal and chemical
feedstocks. After years of below-average rainfall, stretches of the
Missouri, Mississippi, Ohio and Illinois rivers dropped to shallow
riffles and sandbars. Barge captains had to cut back the size of their
rafts and lighten their loads by half. Outright closures of parts of the
strategic waterways became common.[12]

Compounding the lack of rain, the same record days of summer
heat that blighted Jim Stegall's plants oppressed much of the continent. Over one fortnight in California, unrelenting heat that topped
46°C on some days led to more than 140 deaths. In St. Louis and New
York City, overworked air conditioners and electrical transformers
brought down power mains, causing blackouts that lasted for days.
Equally significant was something that *didn't* happen. The overnight
cooling that normally provides respite for overheated bodies never
came. Instead, hot, humid nights hovered at levels that matched the
hottest 10 percent of "daily low" temperatures ever recorded.

Canada has experienced extreme droughts as well. The Dust Bowl
of the 1930s devastated many Prairie communities. More recently
in 2001–2002, the arid triangle of southwestern Saskatchewan and
southeastern Alberta named for John Palliser, the early surveyor
who declared it too dry to farm, saw moisture levels drop lower than
any recorded in 110 years. The region's economy lost well over a billion dollars.[13] Central parts of the country are familiar with steamy
summers. Still, the worst droughts and heat waves more often strike
elsewhere. And in the new century drought has become more frequent, more persistent and more extreme over much of the world.

Europe's worst heat wave since instrumental records began around
1780—and likely its hottest in 500 years—claimed as many as 27,000
lives in 2003.[14] Britain recorded its hottest day ever when the mercury soared above 38°C at Gravesend that August, a record that was
itself broken barely 36 months later. Germans feared their country's

most important river might dry up entirely after some stretches of the Rhine shrivelled to a stream little more than ankle deep. Hundreds of Rhine barges lay idle. Yet more barges were stranded on the Danube when that storied river, relied on by 10 countries from Germany to the Black Sea, fell to a quarter of its customary depth. "Never in my life have I seen the river this low," marvelled Danail Nedialkov, a veteran ship's pilot who plied the Danube for 20 years before joining the international commission that manages river navigation.[15] Economic losses from the 2003 Euro-sizzle closed in on $15 billion.[16] Within three years extreme drought returned to the continent, in places exceeding even its experience in 2003.

Europe's heat waves are lasting twice as long now as in the 1880s. The number of very hot days has tripled.[17] When the largest reservoir in England fell below half-full, authorities in Kent and Sussex contemplated importing water by tanker from Norway. Gardeners who turned on their water hoses faced penalties of up to £5,000 (about $10,700 CDN), and even clowns were ordered to stop the "wasteful" prank of throwing buckets of water at one another. France curtailed nuclear generation, the mainstay of its electricity supply, when depleted streams became too warm to cool reactors. Rain in Spain stayed away from the plain and almost everywhere else. Forests burned and hydro-electric production fell to levels last seen in the 1950s.[18] Next door in Portugal, authorities declared more than 80 percent of the country under drought.

Similar conditions have seared Asia in the new century. Nearly two-thirds of China's 660 cities, home to a third of a billion people, were chronically short of water; one in five suffered "severe water shortages," according to officials.[19] In the far northwestern city of Yinchuan, a young truck-driver interviewed in the spring of 2006 couldn't remember the last time it rained: "I think it rained once or twice last year. But I'm not sure. It definitely rained the year before that."[20] Across the northern provinces of Shanxi, Hebei and Inner Mongolia that year, nearly 600 reservoirs went dry. Two-thirds of the rivers in central Chongqing province were reduced to sand. At mid-summer, Szechuan's government begged farmers to plant extra beans and sweet potatoes to make up for five million tons of grain that wouldn't be harvested from parched fields.

South America's Amazon isn't the world's longest river (the Nile is), but in normal years it discharges more water at its mouth than any other on Earth. The first years of the 21st century were anything but normal, as the Amazon experienced its worst drought in half a century. By mid-decade the river's headwater reaches had fallen below any previous low-water record. Downstream, more than a thousand towns and villages that relied on the river for communication with the outside world found themselves cut off, forcing Brazil's government to fly in supplies of food and medicine.

Australia, already the world's driest continent, got even drier in the new century. In Goulburn, a regional centre two hours by car northeast of the national capital, schools put their playing fields off-limits for fear that students would hurt themselves on surfaces baked to the hardness of cement. With the town reservoir reduced to a muddy puddle containing less than one-tenth its normal volume, Goulburn bars started serving beer in paper cups to save washing. Most families installed cisterns to save any rain that did fall, and the town council considered spending the equivalent of $26 million CDN on a recycling plant to turn sewage into drinking water. "It's heartbreaking," said Ken May, surveying a dozen dead trees in his formerly prize-winning garden. "We can't do anything. I don't want to plant a thing."[21]

Goulburn's troubles were duplicated across most of southern Australia as watershed after watershed recorded unprecedented high temperatures and low rainfall. The Murray-Darling river system in the southeastern state of New South Wales, which even in good years gets only about four percent of Australia's rain and snowfall but supplies three-quarters of its population, saw precipitation drop by a staggering 95 *percent* from averages of the last century. Water levels in the rivers that supply Sydney dropped to barely half of previous record low flows. In a sorry echo of Goulburn's closed playing fields, Victoria's once internationally competitive rowing association contemplated throwing in the towel when its course at Lake Wendouree dried up. Even farm-raised Murray River cod disappeared from menus, after fish farms lost their water allowances to any fish left in the wild.[22] At reservoirs around the country, the receding water revealed a rusty harvest of abandoned weapons, prompting police to re-open a rash of old cases.[23]

Among Australia's farmers, what plant and geological records revealed to be the worst drought in a thousand years went beyond a mere lifestyle inconvenience. For many it proved an economic catastrophe, to some even deadly. As the long dry deepened over southeastern sheep country, desperate farmers seeking to unload herds before their animals starved to death found no one willing to buy them, at any price. On one day before Christmas 2006, nearly 1,000 sheep went up for auction in Cowra without attracting a single bid. Heartbroken herders broke down and wept at the side of the ring. "One paid $360 to get his sheep to the market and then had to pay another $360 to truck them home again," said stock agent Ross Chivers. "You can see the heartache there but those sheep now have no commercial value."[24] Some farmers begged for government help simply to slaughter their herds. Others took more extreme measures. According to Beyond Blue, an Australian mental health group, despairing farmers were by the drought's fifth year committing suicide at the rate of one every four days.[25]

If drought brought inconvenience, financial loss and individual tragedy to the developed world, in Africa it showed its power to shatter entire societies. Across the southern edge of the Sahara from Senegal to the Red Sea, an area known as the Sahel, drought has been nearly continuous since 1975. Rainfall over southern Africa has declined by a fifth over half a century. The volume of water flowing in African rivers has dropped by nearly the same amount in an even shorter time: since 1990.[26] Temperatures have risen nearly everywhere, with daily highs in Kenya's Rift Valley jumping a startling 3.5°C since 1985 alone. Famine and despair compound the continent's agonies.

Diplomats and aid agencies spent much of the new century's early years in a disheartening and largely futile struggle to pacify the chronically drought-stricken Darfur region of Sudan. Next door in Ethiopia and beyond it in Somalia, the worst drought in memory dried up even ponds that had held water for more than 50 years. Oxfam reported that some people had turned to drinking their own urine.

It was in Somalia where an intrepid staff reporter for the *Boston Globe* met Habiba Hassan, at the edge of a failed field of sorghum. "I am 70 years old now," she told John Donnelly, "and the temperatures are getting hotter and hotter as the years go by. [When crops fail] we cut down trees so we can make some money from charcoal, but those areas where we cut are turning to desert."[27]

After winter rains failed to arrive for a third year in Kenya to the south, newspapers wrote that gangs of thirsty monkeys had taken to hijacking produce trucks for their cargos of watermelons. Human families whose crops had repeatedly failed resorted to sending their daughters, many as young as 11, to work as prostitutes at the truck stops between Nairobi and Mombasa.

In Kenya's north, where no highways reach and nomadic herders from a variety of ethnic groups share an isolated range of open acacia scrub, the struggle to survive descended further still. There, summer temperatures at the ramshackle hamlet of Sambarwawa can reach 48°C, reducing the shallow creek that goes by the same name to a winding ditch. Still, water persists beneath the dry ground, and herders have traditionally dug boreholes to reach it. In what one local called "a sort of cafeteria system," different groups of herders each occupy a stretch of riverbed to dig their holes, where their animals take turns to drink every four or five days. As drought deepened in late 2005, however, more and more herds arrived, and some boreholes began to dry up. By December that year, some 10,000 herders and 200,000 animals had descended on the dry creek bed. When one group tried to push past another to reach a disputed borehole, shooting broke out. By the time the firing stopped, seven people were dead. Before a squad of Kenyan police finally arrived a month later to restore order, four more gun battles had left at least two more victims dead and dozens wounded.

"It's survival of the fittest," lamented Richard Odingo, a Kenyan scientist who has researched the link between drought and violence in Africa. "The strongest survive."[28]

Beginning in the 1970s, heat waves in every region of the world became longer. Droughts in much of the world, and in particular its tropical and sub-tropical regions, have become more intense and last longer. The portion of the planet stricken at any one time has more than doubled, until by the beginning of the new century, nearly one-third of the world's land was typically in drought at any given time.[29] Rainfall declined steadily between 1948 and 2003 over Indonesia, equatorial central and western Africa, Central America, Southeast Asia and eastern Australia. Crucial winter rainfall over southwestern Australia dropped suddenly by about 15 percent in the mid 1970s and has never returned to former levels.[30]

The combination of rising temperatures and more intense, enduring droughts is no coincidence. In a perverse cycle, hot days are drier while dry days are hotter and both together tend to make hot, dry droughts last longer. "Higher temperatures increase evaporation," one cogent study explains.[31] "If precipitation doesn't soon replenish the lost moisture, soils grow drier. In drier soils, less solar energy is used up in evaporating water, meaning more is available to raise the temperature of the soil and overlying air, leading to even more desiccating conditions." Not only can that self-amplifying cycle extend and intensify droughts, but dry soils release little moisture into the air that might later fall back to Earth as precipitation. The scientists who reported for the Intergovernmental Panel on Climate Change (IPCC) determined that just such a vicious cycle likely contributed to the early-century droughts in Australia and Europe.[32]

✦

Droughts that devastate poor countrysides may seem remote in well-plumbed rich cities. But even there, an impact eventually shows up in the one place it can't be avoided: the food aisle. No weed, no frost, no genetically modified seed or conversion to biofuel poses anywhere so great a threat to the world's pantry as the simple accumulation of sunny days piled one on another for too many weeks on end.

The simultaneous droughts that struck several of the globe's most important agricultural regions early in this century had mutually reinforcing impacts far beyond the borders in which they occurred. As grain shrivelled on the stalk in the American Midwest, in Europe, China, Australia, India, North Africa and elsewhere, the world's harvest of staple cereals plunged, dropping in some cases by more than half. By the second half of the decade, successive years of declining harvests worldwide had reduced wheat stockpiles to their lowest levels in more than a quarter-century.[33] Only once between 1999 and 2006 did the world's farmers harvest enough grain from their desiccated fields to feed everyone on the planet. As stockpiles dwindled, grain prices rose, by 20 percent in 2006 alone.

The most productive grain-growing regions are in the centres of continents: Canada's Prairies, America's Midwest, Ukraine, and the interiors of Australia, France, Argentina and India. Remote from the moderating influence of oceans, these areas enjoy strong swings of temperature from season to season. This is especially important for growing wheat, which needs cool temperatures in winter to "vernalize," a metabolic stage that triggers the creation of seeds, and without which the plants grow like tall grass and don't produce grain. Wheat then needs hot, late summers to dry out its mature seed heads for harvest and storage. But remoteness from oceans also makes such regions more reliant on rain born of moisture evaporated from the soil. Consequently, when summer temperatures soar and soils dry out, wheat becomes more vulnerable to the self-amplifying cycle that extends drought.

This weather combination worries food forecasters deeply. According to one study published in 2002, should world agriculture continue on its present course, the decline in annual cereal harvests by 2025 would be equivalent to China's entire annual rice crop during the 1990s, or double the amount of wheat the United States produced each year during that decade.[34] Even a "moderate worsening" of trends in water supply, such as the exhaustion of water tables in key grain-growing areas of China and India, would push the world into a calamitous decline in harvests equivalent to the current cereal production of all of Africa plus western Asia.[35]

The droughts that shrivel harvests in the world's breadbaskets are having an even more dangerous effect. They are shrinking the breadbaskets themselves, transforming what are now arid but arable landscapes into raw deserts. Since the 1970s, the area lost annually to desert has more than doubled as farm and ranchland disappear in over 100 countries.[36] China is especially susceptible.

Following the Silk Road across Central Asia in the 13th century, Venetian traveller Marco Polo encountered a region of sand hills known locally as the Singing Dunes for the sound of their countless grains rustling in the wind. Emerging from these he became perhaps the first tourist to set eyes on the green oasis at Dunhuang, near China's far northwestern border, and its out-of-place new-moon-shaped lake. These days, Crescent Lake is among the most popular destinations for China's own tourists, mainly because they want to see this World Heritage Site before it dries up entirely. After surviving for centuries, Crescent Lake has in recent decades shrunk to one-third its former size.

The dry winds that give Dunhuang's dunes their voice blow east, drying out the soil of neighbouring Gansu province. As a result, an area of Gansu the size of Rhode Island, or two-thirds of Canada's Prince Edward Island, turns to desert every year. Over all of China, an area as big as Indiana has become desert since the middle of the last century. Dunes have swallowed up lakes, prairies, forests and villages, forcing tens of thousands of people to seek new homes. As happened in the Dust Bowl decade of the last century in North America, the wind picks up dry soil and carries it hundreds of miles, so that choking dust storms have become a regular feature of the weather forecast in Beijing. Sometimes they travel even farther. One such dirt cloud blew right across the Pacific in 2001, sprinkling millions of tons of China over North America from Vancouver to Florida.[37]

Africa's outlook is also dire. The UN secretariat that administers the international Convention to Combat Desertification warned in 2004 that fully two-thirds of that continent's arable land may turn to desert by 2025, a "creeping catastrophe" that might make vast swaths of the continent "uninhabitable."[38] Three years later, in 2007, it warned that more than 50 million people in sub-Saharan Africa and Central Asia would lose their homes and livelihoods to the conquering desert within a decade.[39] Southern Europe is on the UN Secretariat's endangered list as well, with recurrent droughts threatening to turn as much as one-third of Spain and large parts of southern Italy to desert. South America could lose one-fifth of its currently productive farmland.

Scenes like those in Gansu or along the Nairobi-Mombasa highway, where child prostitutes haunt the truck stops, preview a future of famine and large-scale human migration. Eric Odada, a Kenyan geochemist who studies how changing weather has affected Africa, anticipates a "doomsday" when "there will be mass migrations by people from Africa in search of food. Europe should be prepared. They should not think that the barrier between Morocco and Spain will stop people."[40]

Just as water is essential to human life, so its loss is the one calamity that even the most advanced civilizations cannot withstand. Mesopotamia's Akkadians, Arizona's Anasazi and the nameless humans who raised sheep and goats in the Sahara, leaving their art on rock walls when that present-day desert was a green savannah some

8,000 years ago, all foundered when a change in the weather dried up their fields. Could today's most powerful civilizations find themselves on the same list?

The poet Shelley certainly imagined one answer, inscribed on a broken colossus in the sands of a nameless desert: the empty boast "I am Ozymandias, king of kings. Look on my works, ye mighty, and despair."

# Chapter 3
## Curse of Plenty:
## Tempests, Floods and Rising Waves

On Canada's Atlantic coast lies a promontory that, in society and to-pography, can seem the very antithesis of British Columbia's Okanagan Valley. Whereas a deep freshwater lake splits that western valley, salt water all but surrounds New Brunswick's Acadian Peninsula. Roughly similar in size, the two are opposites in other ways. A magnet for set-tlers, the Okanagan strains to assimilate growth; the peninsula at the other end of the continent struggles to hold onto its people, culture and slender economy. While the Okanagan basks under a Mediterranean climate, the fishing villages that bead the Acadian Peninsula more often shiver in clinging mists and gales that blow off the Baie des Chaleurs to the west or the Gulf of St. Lawrence to the east. Even so, miles of sandy beaches, green hills and salt marshes flocked with wa-terfowl give the peninsula a distinctive beauty dear to the heart of its resilient French-speaking residents.

Jean-Daniel Haché is one of those. Born in 1966, the latest son in a family of fishermen whose forebears in Maritime Canada go back four centuries, Jean-Daniel has lived his entire life in the village of Le Goulet, near the Peninsula's eastern tip. As a youngster in the 1970s, he found childhood adventure among the seaside dunes that stood between the village and the sea. Rising to heights of seven metres, the shifting, green-fringed sand hills formed a bulwark as broad across as two football fields placed end-to-end between the main coast road and the sea. Their comforting presence gave the village welcome protection from the beating surf, occasional extreme tides and routine winter storms that roar in off the Gulf.

In 1994, turning 28 and with steady work as a deckhand in the prospering snow-crab fishery, Jean-Daniel decided that he and his girlfriend, Nadine Robichaud, needed a place of their own. He soon bought a beige mobile home on the ocean side of the main village road. Set on a sturdy concrete foundation close enough to the water for the young couple to hear the sound of surf breaking beyond the dunes, it was a romantic location for a first home. But soon the sound of the waves would acquire a more ominous note.

Dunes spend their existence running in place, individual grains of sand in frequent motion even as they creep more slowly downwind as a group. They can endure only where natural forces maintain a dynamic equilibrium, supplying, among other things, fresh sand to make up for what is blown away. For centuries, just such a balance preserved the dunes defending the Acadian Peninsula. In the decades since Jean-Daniel's youth, however, that balance shifted. With each passing year, winter storms brought the biggest waves and highest tides a little farther up the shore, deeper into the dunes. Much of the sand simply washed back into the sea. By the mid-1990s, the dunes that still remained were hillocks barely one-third their former heights.

During Jean-Daniel and Nadine's first winter in their new home, a particularly strong east wind drove the sea all the way through the last low dunes. For several hours salt water crept into their backyard before the falling tide bore the sea back out to the Gulf, taking with it still more of the dunes' vanishing sand. Over the winters that followed, other storms again brought small rivers of sea water snaking through the dunes. Even more often, water from the mobile home's shallow well tasted unmistakably of salt.

Winter can be brutal on the Acadian Peninsula, but the millennium opened with unseasonably mild weather across the continental northeast. Parts of New England broke all records for consecutive days without measurable snowfall. Then, nearly three weeks into the new year, winter arrived with breathtaking savagery. A storm front swept up the Atlantic coast from the Carolinas, bringing bone-chilling temperatures, blinding snow and hurricane-strength winds. The tempest reached Le Goulet on the afternoon of January 20.

With gales on the way, the local fishing fleet stayed in port. Jean-Daniel was at home, enjoying an unexpected afternoon off with Nadine and the couple's young son, three-year-old Mathieu. Around mid-afternoon, the first gusts of strong wind shook their home's thin walls. Shortly afterward, Jean-Daniel noticed the first tendrils of salt water creep out of the eroded dunes into the family's backyard.

In itself that sight was no longer especially alarming. But several forces would come together at Le Goulet that day to a greater degree than they ever had before. One was the sheer power of the storm, whose expanse of extremely low-pressure air actually lifted the surface of the Gulf of St. Lawrence by several centimetres. The same deep pressure trough was sucking in icy winds from the thicker air masses around it at speeds that reached 145 kilometres per hour, the range of a Category One hurricane. With waves in the Gulf cresting as high as three-storey buildings, the fast-moving system struck the peninsula just as the tide was also reaching maximum height. The storm surged into the degraded dunes with unprecedented fury.

Within half an hour of noticing the first water in his backyard, Jean-Daniel had a foot of ocean in his driveway. Wading through rising water, Nadine carried Mathieu to the family pickup, and the three fled in the gathering dusk, the vehicle's tires sending up a foaming wake as they gained the road. With his family safe and dry at Nadine's parents' home, which stands on higher ground, Jean-Daniel returned to check on theirs. "I came back around seven in the evening," he recalls, "but I couldn't reach the driveway." From where he was forced to pull up three houses away, the headlights of Jean-Daniel's truck shone on "water, everywhere, with currents that looked like rapids, with lots of waves, lots of moving ice. There wasn't any truck, even a four-by-four, that could make it through the main road. There was too much water, too much ice."[1]

Not until the tide peaked that night, between 11 and midnight, did the flood begin to recede.

Returning the next day, the couple still couldn't enter the driveway. The sea had receded but blocks of sea ice as big as kitchen tables and a metre thick lay scattered around their house like monstrous confetti, barring the way to the door. Jean-Daniel had to call in a construction loader to clear the yard. A thick rind of ice glazed the house's concrete foundation. Inside, salt water had filled the rooms a metre deep, damaging floors, furniture and appliances at a cost to repair of over $10,000.

Dirty weather hasn't coincided with high tides to strike Le Goulet with such fury again. But more recent gales have almost washed away the last of the dunes; those remaining are barely knee-high. The sand, salt marsh and beach that once protected Le Goulet from the Gulf have been reduced by nearly 25 percent. By the end of the decade, water was sloshing into a score of backyards every couple of months. "When there are storms the water comes in between me and the neighbours, and reaches almost to the main road," Jean-Daniel says. "That happens quite often." Salt is so persistent in the well water that the pipes and taps of his house have begun to rust. "I don't drink it any more. We have a dispenser and bottles, and we drink that water. We only use the well for washing, laundry."[2]

In the years since the storm of 2000, scientists using airborne lasers have surveyed the Acadian shore to a precision that reveals differences of elevation as slight as the breadth of a hand. They have compared the results both to historic records and to forward-looking models of the region's rising sea levels.[3] They predict that a similar storm will strike again at high tide any winter now, driving ahead of it a sea surge twice as high as the one that chased Jean-Daniel and Nadine from their home that year.

"It's just a matter of time," Jean-Daniel says with resignation. In 2006, the community became the first in Canada formally to accept

that some of its 1,000 residents would inevitably become climate refugees. The village council asked its provincial government to help move
30 families out of the path of rising oceans and away from wells routinely rendered undrinkable by salt water.

Storms come in families. Nor'easters like the one that battered
the Acadian Peninsula in 2000 are members of one family of seasonal, large-scale horizontal movements of air and moisture. Their
relatives include the gales that blow in from the North Atlantic to
batter western Europe; India's summer monsoons, which begin over
the Indian Ocean; wet fronts from the Pacific that cycle over western North America every few days during the fall and winter; and
the nearly daily downpours that drench many tropical zones during
the rainy seasons. Large continental land masses and broad areas of
warm ocean generate another family of storms, whose common ele-
ment is convection: the vertical movement of warm air. This can fuel
very local tornadoes and thunderstorms or, on a much vaster scale,
the tropical cyclones known as hurricanes in the western hemisphere
and as typhoons in the Far East. By either name, these last are the
undisputed monarchs of violent weather.

Fire destroys with unrivalled intensity, consuming what it touches
and leaving only dry ash behind. Few but the most violent tornadoes
and cyclones approach them in focused devastation. But whatever
lesser storms lack in intensity, they often more than make up in scale,
the largest making their impact felt over hundreds if not thousands
of kilometres. Taken together, storms of all types do the lion's share
of direct damage chalked up to natural disaster, with wind and floods
accounting for 71 percent of all fatalities[4] and as much as 90 percent
of economic losses.[5] Beyond the immediate toll on life and property,
storms often leave behind less obvious long-term consequences, from
fouled water supplies to (counter-intuitively) depleted water tables.

Weather is a determining influence on plants, wildlife and such
natural features as creeks, marshlands or even entire hillsides. When
the weather changes, so do they. Sometimes, like Le Goulet's dunes,

they may vanish entirely. Over every ocean and above every continent, stronger winds are bringing dramatically dirtier weather.

Less than five years after Jean-Daniel and Nadine fled their turn-of-the-millennium nor'easter, a much bigger tempest displaced numerous other Hachés and Robichauds, along with hundreds of thousands of other residents of the U.S. Gulf Coast. At dawn on August 29, 2005, Katrina, a Category Five hurricane, swept over the Louisiana marshes, home to nearly half a million "Cajuns" from the same 18th-century stock as Le Goulet's Acadians. A mountain of water, rising above the tops of utility poles, bore down on the neglected levees protecting the hastily and only partially evacuated city of New Orleans. By that afternoon, a toxic gumbo of sea water, sewage and chemicals from flooded industrial sites had submerged more than 80 percent of the city, flooding most completely its poorest, predominantly African-American wards.[6] Around the world, anyone with access to television watched in astonishment as a major city in the planet's most powerful country descended toward anarchy.

Tropical cyclones unleash more sheer violence than any other earthly force we are ever likely to experience. Even a run-of-the-mill hurricane (and Katrina was much more than that) mobilizes four times more energy than the entire human species does in a year: the equivalent of the nuclear bomb that exploded over Hiroshima going off every 20 seconds at the peak of the storm. And their toll is rising, not only in regions accustomed to hurricane-force storms, but also where cyclones have never before been seen.

In 2004, storm watchers in the southern hemisphere witnessed an event that went beyond their experience: the first confirmed hurricane-strength Atlantic cyclone in the southern hemisphere. Spawned by unusually warm late-summer water 1,000 kilometres off Brazil, the storm reached Category Two hurricane strength, with winds peaking above 180 kilometres per hour on March 26, before making landfall two days later on the coast of Santa Catarina state. Without any precedent to draw on, Brazil's meteorologists had no convention for naming such storms. Popularly, however, the first major southern

Atlantic cyclone became known as Hurricane Catarina, after the state in which it killed three people and did one-third of a billion dollars worth of damage.[7]

The next year, while the more famous Katrina dominated North American headlines, so many other storms gathered over the Atlantic that the World Meteorological Organization had to start a second time through the alphabet to identify them all. In October, Hurricane Stan swept across the Central American nation of Guatemala, saturating unstable slopes above the country's largest lake, Atitlan. School care-taker Rafael Estrada later described a noise "like a volcano" as torrents of liquid muck 12 metres deep swept down on his lakeside village of Panabaj. Mud buried the elderly man's sister, two nephews and at least two other relatives among an estimated 1,400 who died in minutes.[8]

The following year produced a relatively modest harvest of storms in the Atlantic. But in the western Pacific, the 2006 typhoon season began nearly two months earlier than normal, when the year's first cy-clone struck south China on May 18.[9] Three months later, more than 1.6 million people fled the central Chinese coast ahead of Typhoon Saomai. With winds of 270 kilometres per hour, that super-storm sank more than 1,000 ships and fishing boats, ripping many from moorings where they had sheltered in harbours, and destroyed some 50,000 homes.[10] Three weeks after Saomai, the central Pacific re-corded another unprecedented event: the region's first-ever Category Five cyclone. Typhoon Ioke battered Wake Island so severely that it knocked out weather sensors at the island's evacuated U.S. military base. The same storm season ended only after yet another typhoon, threatening the central Philippine province of Cebu, forced Asian leaders to cancel a summit meeting scheduled for that location.

"I am old enough to remember when typhoons that hit the coun-try toward the end of the year rarely ever made landfall," columnist Dan Mariano wrote in *The Manila Times*, the Philippine capital's oldest newspaper, after that last brush with disaster. "The explana-tion was that as the temperature began to drop sometime in October or November, the cold front from northern Asia prevented tropical cyclones from going beyond the central Philippines. Not anymore. For the first time in the country's recorded history, three 'super-typhoons' have hit the Philippines in a single year."[11]

Journalists weren't alone in concluding that something had changed. "The strength of typhoons is increasing," producing storms that last longer, travel farther and wreak greater devastation than those of the past, the head of China's Meteorological Administration asserted.[12] In the Philippines, records stretching back to 1960 show that the season with the most tropical cyclones, the strongest such storm ever observed, the deadliest single cyclone and the two most destructive of property, as well as the typhoon dropping the most rainfall over 24 hours, had all occurred in the years after 1990. Meteorologist Leoncio A. Amadore called the evidence "signals of a changing climate."[13]

The same signal is evident in the Atlantic. Weather records reveal that the number of storms in Katrina's exceptionally violent class has almost doubled in the last 30 years, from roughly 10 a year in the 1970s to about 18 a year since 1990. What's more, the most powerful storms have become even stronger, to the point that some scientists suggest they deserve an altogether new designation. The conventional scale for hurricanes has five categories, topping out with storms that sustain winds of over 250 kilometres per hour. A storm moves up a category as its winds increase in increments of about 32 kilometres per hour (at each increment, storm damage typically increases roughly one hundredfold).[14] In recent seasons, however, researchers have clocked mega-storms with winds as high as 320 kilometres per hour. "This is out of people's experience," admits climatologist Roger Pielke, Jr., of the University of Colorado. "There's a new definition of 'normal' now." Some argue the definition demands a new ranking: the Category Six super-monster storm.[15]

It shouldn't surprise us that the planet's most powerful storms are becoming even more violent. For all the damage they cause, cyclones are ignited by nothing more complicated than warm water. Warm seas heat the air above them; that heated air expands and rises, creating a vast low-pressure zone that sucks in more air like a gargantuan vacuum. That air warms in turn, expands, rises and continues the cycle. The warmer the ocean, the more powerful the suction and more violent the resulting storm. And the seas are heating up: temperatures recorded at depths down to 700 metres below the surface of the Atlantic Ocean and 100 metres below the Pacific have risen over the last four decades.[16]

Hurricanes inspire fear as well as awe. But other seasonal weather systems bred over the world's oceans are welcomed for the vital precipitation they bring to continental landscapes. None is counted on more heavily than the monsoon winds that in most years come to India, Bangladesh and Pakistan, with roll-on effects that reach from Vietnam to Iran. What is welcome in moderation, however, may prove devastating in excess.

Monsoon season in south Asia begins as a springtime accumulation of warm, wet air over the Indian Ocean. By April or May much higher temperatures over the sub-continent's land mass create a zone of lower pressure into which the relatively denser ocean air rushes. Splitting in two on India's southern cape, wet winds sweep along both coasts and into the interior, delivering daily and often torrential rains as the monsoons march north from June through September. Striking the wall of the Himalayas at the top of the Indian Peninsula, they normally turn west, wringing out the last of their rains over northern Pakistan. By October, the monsoons reverse course, retreating south ahead of stronger winds flowing out of Tibet.

The vast amount of water transported on the monsoon feeds some of the world's most important rivers: the Indus, which transits through disputed Kashmir in northern India on its way to Pakistan and the Arabian Sea; the Ganges, which also flows through India but empties into the Bay of Bengal on the east, at a delta that forms most of Bangladesh; the Brahmaputra, which turns the eastern corner of the Himalayas on its journey from Chinese Tibet through India's Assam province to merge with the Ganges in Bangladesh; the Irrawaddy, principal river of Myanmar (Burma); and the Mekong, which forms the border between Thailand and Laos before flowing through Cambodia and entering the South China Sea in south Vietnam. For one-third of the world's population, the monsoons are the primary source of water for everything from farming to industry to bathing.

Heavy monsoon rains that overflow drains and ditches, flooding streets and fields, are no surprise to most Indians. Even so, what descended on July 26, 2005 on Mumbai (Bombay), the country's largest city and commercial capital, shattered all expectations. Driving out for a meeting with associates in her advertising business that Tuesday afternoon, Anjali Krishnan found no particular reason for alarm in the heavy grey cloud blanketing the city. But after 90 minutes of negotiating traffic in heavy rain, she found herself immobilized in gridlock. Outside her car, the torrential rain was beginning to back up over the pavement. "For the next ten hours, 'til two in the morning on Wednesday, I was stranded in my car," Anjali recalled. "As the hours passed, I realized that Mumbai had been inundated, everything had come to a halt. There were power outages. The rain was slapping ferociously on the wind screen, the sky was inky black, there was darkness all around. At two a.m. I decided to begin walking home. Wading out through knee-deep water, I ran into some firemen who forbade me to walk further. Then I saw three girls stranded in the water. They said they had been walking for hours to get home, and were exhausted. I took them back into my car." An hour later, the four women set out again, holding hands for safety. By then, "the water was deep—black and greasy right up to our necks and swirled fast around our waists. There were broken bottles floating all around. I saw two Mercedes Benz cars and a Toyota Lexus floating in the water." Hours later, Anjali made it home safely.[17]

Others in the city were less lucky. The heaviest rainfall ever recorded in India had dropped nearly a metre of water on the low-lying coastal metropolis in a day. The deluge overwhelmed the city's antiquated and poorly maintained drainage system that struggles even with moderate downpours. Maharashtra State officials later tallied the deaths due to drowning, landslides, accidents and flood-related infections as having reached 546 within the city of Mumbai and close to 1,000 more in outlying areas.[18]

Yet what broke records in 2005 may soon be within the range of everyday weather. Researchers who reviewed half a century of records from across India discovered that while the average amount of rain arriving with the monsoons over any single year had not changed, days with light rain had become fewer, while both the number of days with heavy rainfall, and the magnitude of the rain they brought, had increased.[19] In other words, while India is getting no more rain in total, more of what it does get is coming in the kind of deluge that brought Mumbai to a standstill.

One implication of that trend bore down on the northwestern Indian city of Surat the year after the Mumbai flood. When days of torrential summer rain threatened to burst a major dam upstream from the city, operators had no choice but to open the dam's 21 sluice gates. The flash flood that bore down on Surat with little warning filled its streets to the ceilings of second-floor apartments. The torrent's sucking current collapsed an apartment building, killing 40 of the 120 people who died over three days. Weeks after the Surat calamity, the operators of a dam in eastern Maharashtra State, believing the normal monsoon season had passed and anticipating dry months ahead, filled their reservoir to the rim. Contrary to experience, however, that year's heaviest monsoon came in August. These operators too opened their dam's gates to release water. The resulting flood washed away 400 villages, killing 700 people. "Weird things are happening," observed Devendra Fadnavis, a legislator in the Maharashtra city of Nagpur. "Monsoons are hitting in the wrong place at the wrong time."[20]

The same is true where monsoons reach the end of their inland rush, in the mountains of Nepal. Sherbahadur Tamang recalled the terror that visited his village of Khetbari at the end of that same bizarre season: "During the night there was light rain but when we woke, its intensity increased. In an hour or so, the rain became so heavy that we could not see more than a foot or two in front of us. It was like a wall of water and it sounded like 10,000 lorries. It went on like that until midday. Then all the land started moving like a river." By the time Sherbahadur and his neighbours were able to survey the damage, the normally placid Jugedi stream had torn a gulley six times its usual 50-metre breadth through generations-old terraced fields and irrigation canals. Boulders and rubble lay where several houses had vanished.

"The rains are increasingly unpredictable," said another Nepali farmer. Tekmadur Majsi lost his land to an earlier river flood and now camps near a highway with 200 other climate refugees. "We always used to have a little rain each month," he said, "but now when there is rain it's very different. It's more concentrated and intense."[21]

We who live on North America's northwest coast sometimes also use the word "monsoon" to describe the relentless rain and frequent high winds that signal the end of our summer. Here too, old records are falling like wind-toppled cedars amid unsettling weather reversals.

The year 2006 opened on a monthly record of 29 days of rain for Washington State's Puget Sound and southeastern British Columbia. By summer the trend had reversed. Drought brought those improbable water shortages to the rainforest resort town of Tofino; temperatures in the sun-baked Okanagan and other interior valleys soared to record highs. The Fraser River fell to the lowest level on record.[22] Then came autumn, and the weather reversed itself again. Shortly after Thanksgiving, what's known as a "Pineapple Express," a river of particularly wet, warm air, roared in from the tropical Pacific to wring itself out on the coastal mountains.

British Columbian environment officials measured some of the heaviest rainfall ever in the coastal mountains, dropping a metre of water.[23] Runoff pushed a tributary of the Fraser River over its banks, forcing 200 families out of their homes. Of more direct significance to urbanites, the record rain also triggered dozens of landslides in the mountains north of the city of Vancouver. Torrents of liquefied soil carried thousands of tons of forest debris and fecal material from wildlife into three flooded valleys serving as regional water reservoirs. Authorities declared the tap water of Canada's third-largest metropolitan area unsafe for drinking, brushing teeth or washing food. Health officials advised two million residents to boil water before using it. The widest such advisory in the country's history lasted nearly two weeks.

Hardly had that storm passed inland than another followed it, and then a third. Powerful winds, rain, and wet, heavy snow brought down power lines, washed-out roads, closed airports, kept ferries in harbour, backed up drains and filled creeks to overflowing. Swollen rivers forced more evacuations and caused at least four deaths, including that of a 41-year-old Seattle woman trapped in a flooded basement. More than a million and a half others across the Pacific Northwest lost electrical power, in many cases for days, in what utility managers described as the area's widest blackouts in memory. Two floating bridges that serve parts of Seattle had to suspend operations for varying periods of time. A week before Christmas, the last blow brought down 1,000 trees in Vancouver's beloved Stanley Park.[24]

The rest of the winter brought record and near-record snow to British Columbia's interior. By the following spring, six months after the Fraser River had experienced its lowest flow on the books, the amount of water waiting in the mountains to melt and flow down the same river had work crews scrambling to raise dikes along its lower reaches.

The early winter storms that have lashed both Canadian coasts in the last decade have counterparts in the northeast Atlantic. Usually battering the British Isles before piling up and unloading their cargo of moisture on the Alps of central Europe, these winter gales can reach cyclone force, prompting the German weather service to give some of them names.

The winter that brought the sea into Le Goulet also unleashed a trio of powerful storms on Europe. Two, dubbed Lothar and Martin by the Germans, struck France in quick succession on December 26 and 27. Rain, snow and hurricane-force winds of up to 180 kilometres per hour left more than 3.5 million French households in the dark

and hundreds of rural villages without drinking water. The gales top-
pled an estimated 300 million trees, including some at the château of
Versailles, which had weathered centuries of previous storms. Gusts
sent half a dozen stone pinnacles atop the Cathedral of Notre Dame
in Paris crashing down through its lead roof. Eighty-eight people died
in France, and scores more from Spain to Denmark. Economic damage from the three storms topped $20 billion. Speaking five years
before Katrina, a shaken chief of the French national power utility
called the storms' toll "without precedent in the world as far as a developed country is concerned."[25]

No precedent, perhaps, but close parallels are likely to become
increasingly common. The portion of Britain's winter rain that fell in
intense downpours during strong storms roughly doubled between
1960 and the end of the 20th century. In Scotland, the number of days
witnessing torrential rain has *quadrupled*, and the amount of rain falling in total over an average winter has gone up by 60 percent.[26] The
month after the Scottish Environmental Protection Agency released
that finding, several parts of the nation experienced their wettest
November on record, with rainfall nearly twice the average.

In colder latitudes, winter gales that arrive late in the season often
pile rain on top of melting snow. The results may be felt long after the
storm itself has vanished, and hundreds of kilometres away.

Such was the case in Europe in 2005. Heavy spring rain falling
on Alpine snow first set off landslides that swept away rail lines and
highways in Austria. Then several of Europe's longest rivers, including
the Rhine, Danube and Elbe, burst their banks. In Poland, swollen
currents collapsed seven bridges. The same combination occurred the
following year, when the storied Danube rose to levels not seen in
over a century. Authorities in Romania were forced to breach a dam
and drown an area of farmland the size of metro Toronto, rather than
allow the flood to submerge urban areas downstream.

A dozen years earlier, I had flown into St. Louis, Missouri, after
a similar spring in the upper American Midwest. A wet autumn had

been followed by heavier winter snow than normal, then by unusually torrential spring rain. By July, flood disasters had been formally
declared in Minnesota, Wisconsin, Illinois, Missouri and Iowa.[27] As
the plane dropped below a layer of thick cloud, I caught my first sight
of what surveys would later confirm to be the greatest flood in the recorded history of the 4,000-mile Mississippi River. Silver-grey water,
smudged here and there with reddish-brown farm dirt and dotted
with green trees, peaked roofs, bulbous silos and occasional islands of
higher ground, seemed to stretch from horizon to horizon.

Fortunately, the St. Louis airport is built on high ground. I collected my light luggage, searched out my rental car and consulted a
map. According to a local paper, a small community named Portage
des Sioux remained above water just downstream from where
two other great rivers, the Missouri and the Illinois, flow into the
Mississippi, nearly doubling its volume. If the paper was right, the
rising water had turned it into an island, more than a kilometre from
the nearest "shore." After 45 minutes of poking around county roads,
I came to a makeshift landing where the rural blacktop disappeared
into the flood. Half a dozen narrow, flat-nosed boats with outboards
lay pulled up onto the asphalt. Perhaps I could cajole the first owner
who appeared into ferrying me out to Portage des Sioux.

This turned out to be Paul. In his fifties, tall, florid, with un-
washed grey hair and a two-day bristle, he wore a soiled work shirt,
jeans and rubber boots. He willingly agreed to run me out to Portage
in his "jack" boat.

There is something surreal about travelling across flooded countryside. Here you pass a half-submerged traffic light, there peer into
the second-storey bedroom windows of a farm house. Unmarked
hazards lurk beneath the turbid water or float free. In Missouri that
spring they included flotillas of natural gas tanks drifting on the slow
current, hissing explosive vapour through broken fittings, and files
of raised utility poles whose sagging copper cables came to within
half a metre of the water. These, Paul nonchalantly explained, were
still charged with electricity, local utilities having decided to leave the

power on so that places like Portage could continue to run pumps, refrigerators and water-treatment plants.

The reason for Paul's nonchalance came out along with a pint bottle of bourbon from a tackle box. After two decades of middle management in a St. Louis corporation, he'd quit his job, cashed his savings and sunk everything into the purchase of a marina on the Mississippi. His grand opening, as he told it, had coincided with the order from the U.S. Coast Guard closing the swollen river to all traffic. His docks and investment were now irretrievably submerged. "I'm going to lose everything," he said with as much bravado as he could muster, toasting the clouds with an unsteady hand.[28]

At nearly $30 billion,[29] the eventual economic losses for the Mississippi Valley as a whole would make Paul's misfortune look like the proverbial drop in a very dismal bucket.

John Palliser's corner of southern Alberta and Saskatchewan is usually the driest part of Canada. But in the spring of 2005, two weeks of rain and snow melting off the Rocky Mountains sent an unprecedented pulse of water sweeping eastward. The foothills town of High River, Alberta, was first to order residents living alongside the Highwood River out of their houses. A day later, water overflowed a reservoir into the Elbow River above Calgary, forcing more than 1,500 people in Canada's fourth-largest city from low-lying homes. Fifty vacationers who ignored police orders to abandon a campground south of the city had to be rescued by helicopter. Other evacuations followed the flood crest as it rolled downriver through Drumheller and Red Deer, Alberta, and then across the provincial border into Saskatchewan. "Everything is destroyed," said Daryl Leshko of Melville, Saskatchewan. "This was just, bang, and it was here. And you can't do a thing about it. Even if you had a pump, where are you going to pump it? There's water all around you."[30] In the judgement of Alberta's Environment Minister Guy Boutilier, it was the worst flood his province had seen in the two centuries since non-Aboriginal settlers began keeping records.

A year later the same dangerous combination of rain and snow in New Brunswick nearly swept away a structure as iconic to that province's English-speakers as the dunes of the Acadian coast are to its Francophones. It was a covered bridge, one of 64 architectural treasures from the late 19th and early 20th centuries that endure in the province. Built entirely of wood and covered for protection against the weather, the longest and best-known example spans the St. John River at the town of Hartland. Erected on several piers, it ordinarily sits four storeys above the river below.

In 2006, however, rain coinciding with an unusually strong January thaw broke up ice on the freshly frozen river and piled it up in a six-kilometre jam above and below the bridge. As the mass of crushed ice came within a couple of metres of the bridge bed, more rain threatened to float the ice high enough to tear the wooden span off its foundations and carry it downstream. Local citizens set up a vigil and television crews mounted cameras to monitor the gap between bridge and ice. Hartland's mayor, Neville Hargrove, fretted for the centrepiece of the small town's economy: "People come into town just to walk the bridge or drive the bridge or photograph the bridge. It would be just devastating if we lost it."[31]

The suspense was eventually relieved when the ice subsided and moved on. But winter rain is coming more often to the St. John River Valley, records show, raising the risk of another early breakup and a future ice jam.[32]

Summer monsoons in India and their autumn counterparts in the Pacific Northwest ride huge currents of moist air that flow thousands of miles from the open oceans to penetrate deep into continental land masses. North Atlantic gales and their more powerful tropical counterparts, hurricanes and typhoons, spin out their fury across hundreds of miles of sea and shore. The storms that raced across southern Ontario in early August 2006 were on a different scale. Like condensed hurricanes, tornadoes are spawned by the convection of heated air. But their destructive power is focused into a tendril of sucking destruction across a few metres to a kilometre or more. Afterwards, one block of houses may stand untouched while those across the street are reduced to matchsticks.

After a week in which the combination of heat and humidity repeatedly reached 42°C on southern Ontario's humidex scale, dozens of tornadoes and hundreds of thunderstorms, some with winds of more than 120 kilometres per hour, formed an almost solid line across Canada's most densely populated region. Where they touched down, they damaged buildings from Windsor to Ottawa, left hundreds of thousands without power and terrified many more.

Among them was a friend of mine. Judy Carr is a British Columbian bookkeeper who makes her summer home at a lakeside RV park north of Toronto, close to her daughter and grandchildren. One evening in August 2006 she had retreated to the air-conditioned comfort of her tidy mobile home's living room to watch television. "Around nine I heard some thunder. I thought I'd go out and take down my canopy." She had just started to roll up the new blue-and-white canvas awning over her deck when "the wind started to pick up and within seconds I just heard this huge *rip* and I was holding onto the down-pole. It had just ripped right off across the top where it meets the trailer." Along with the wind came driving rain. "I went inside and sat on the toilet because it was the only room that didn't have windows. The trailer shook just like you'd shake a box. I could hear stuff outside that shouldn't be moving crashing and banging around. It was so violent for about ten minutes that I really thought the trailer was going to go over."[33] Farther east a full-fledged tornado pulled several railway cars off their tracks. "I watched it happen," an awed eyewitness told a local television crew. "It slowly went through the trees and then the two cars slowly left the track. It was like a train whistle coming in and then it got so loud, it just went *bam* and things were blowing in and breaking windows."[34]

Canada experiences more tornadoes than any country in the world outside the United States, mostly in Ontario and the three Prairie provinces. But America, land of Kansas and *The Wizard of*

Oz, remains the tornado champion, with some 1,200 reported each year. A few are like the monster that marched across southeastern Nebraska one early-summer afternoon in 2004. Reaching wind speeds of over 330 kilometres per hour, the storm ravaged a path two kilometres wide across half a dozen rural counties, destroying 158 houses and the entire village of Hallam. So complete was its destruction that the first emergency crews to respond to 911 calls were unable to locate what remained of the little hamlet.[35]

Sisters Gail Easton and Becky Simpson, along with Becky's daughter, Stephani Rust, took shelter in the bathtub in Gail's house. "The wind pounded the walls and the walls vibrated like the back side of a drum," Stephani later told a reporter.[36] Then the tornado lifted her aunt's house off its foundation and blew it apart, leaving the two women and girl unharmed under the open sky.

Even thunderstorms can kill. Lauren Fannin and Lindsey Harp, the first a 25-year-old pharmacy student and the second a recently graduated nurse the same age, spent the last Friday evening of their lives out with friends in Lexington, Kentucky. Early on the morning of Saturday, September 23, 2006, they took a taxi back to Lauren's apartment near the hillside campus of the University of Kentucky. In the week that had just ended, a series of thunderstorms trailing torrential rains had swept up the Mississippi Valley. As the two young women neared their destination, heavy rain lashed the car windows and sparkled in the streetlights.

They were less than a block from Lauren's front door when a policeman blocked their way. Water sheeting off the huge expanse of parking lot around Commonwealth Stadium, home to the University of Kentucky's beloved Wildcats football team, funnelled into the street ahead, turning it into a raging river. Officer T. J. Doyle ordered the cab to turn back. Undaunted, the women got out to complete their journey through knee-high water on foot. As Officer Doyle recalled later, he was watching the taxi head back the way it had come when he heard a cry. Turning, he saw that Lauren had reached safe ground but that Lindsey was struggling in the current. Lauren turned back into the flood to help her friend. Moments later first one and then the other seemed to slip and then vanish where the dark water swirled into a culvert. Their battered bodies were found the next morning in a drainage creek a kilometre downstream.[37]

Extreme by the standards of the last century, storms like those that terrified Judy Carr and gave Stephani Rust a story to tell her grandchildren are becoming routine in this one. More rain is falling over the continental centre, with most of that increase recorded over the Mississippi Valley. The concentration of precipitation into the kind of torrential event that killed Lauren Fannin and Lindsey Harp has jumped twice as fast, by 14 percent over the continental United States as a whole and by 25 percent over the eastern seaboard and mountains.

Atlantic hurricanes and Pacific typhoons; summer monsoons in India; winter gales in Europe; mid-continental line squalls and tornadoes: everywhere, storms are amping up. Some of these weather phenomena deliver the lion's share of the water that certain regions of the world count on for the entire year. In many of those, the absolute volume of rainfall is rising; in others, the same volume is arriving in more concentrated deliveries.

Floods kill thousands of people each year and destroy the homes or livelihoods of millions more. The toll on all counts is rising. According to the UN, the decade between 1970 and 1979 saw 1,110 natural disasters, the great majority weather-related, affecting 740 million people and doing $150 billion in total damage. By the 1990s, all three measures of storm destruction roughly tripled: 2,742 events affected more than two billion people and inflicted $725 billion in losses. By the new century, tolls equivalent to the entire decade of the 1970s were being recorded in a single year. In 2002, 734 million people were affected by weather disasters; storms in 2004 did $155 billion worth of damage. With a single hurricane accounting for $134 billion in losses, 2005 was the most economically disastrous weather year in human history, with material damage worldwide topping a quarter of a trillion dollars.[38] Of the 12 most costly catastrophes recorded in the United States up to that year, 10 were storms. Eight had occurred within the four most recent years.[39]

Floods are dramatic, even photogenic in their way. They may also mete out a swift mortality. But their effects aren't all immediate, or fully reported. Many take weeks or years to appear.

Floods overwhelm primitive latrines and sophisticated sewers with undifferentiated ease, mixing human waste together with chemicals from submerged kitchens and inundated industries, petro-fuels from vehicles and service stations, and pathogens shed by rotting corpses, both animal and human. When they retreat, they leave behind a thick scum of toxic muck, stagnant ponds attractive to mosquitoes, waterlogged buildings and possessions that quickly become nurseries for moulds. Thousands of houses survived Hurricane Katrina's initial assault only to be condemned later when fungi blossomed behind saturated wallboard. Allie Deger, who joined other Habitat for Humanity volunteers to help clear away debris seven months after that storm, described what she saw: "The toxic air smelled like sulphur and what I can only imagine as rotting animals. When the wind blew, fragments of molded fiberglass were visible."[40] Four months after the hurricane's winds had blown past, death rates in New Orleans were still nearly 50 percent higher than before the storm, and would stay that way for many months more.[41]

Deger at least was able to go about her task garbed in full-body overalls, respirator, goggles, gloves and hard hat. And when flood waters finally ebbed in central Europe after inundations there early in the new century, mass vaccination campaigns helped populations avoid epidemics of hepatitis.[42] Those left to clean up after deluges in developing countries are seldom so well equipped. Epidemics of cholera, malaria, hemorrhagic fever and "river blindness" caused by a water-borne parasite have followed floods in Africa and Latin America. Coping with the aftermath weighs on the spirit of survivors: suicide rates jump in the four years following major floods. The World Health Organization in 2006 blamed 150,000 additional deaths a year on increasingly frequent weather calamities, mainly floods.[43]

In river lowlands, natural floods have historically helped to recharge underground water tables. Where that is the case in developed countries, efforts expended in the past century to contain flooding within dikes have had double-edged consequences. Where dikes or levees have held back floods, little water has reached these important underground reserves. When levees fail, the water that does soak into the earth is often badly polluted. But in some circumstances, even the impression of abundant water may prove illusory.

Paradoxically, intense precipitation may leave *less* water stored in reservoirs and underground for use in other seasons. When rain falls too fast or coincides with melting snow, it may quickly fill surface reservoirs to the brim, forcing operators, like those upstream from Surat, to spill the excess. A comparable dynamic may keep the rain from percolating into underground aquifers. "You can have more rain falling," notes hydrologist Diana Allen, "but less of it is getting into the ground."[44] Surface soils can absorb rainfall only so fast. Light drizzle that soaks in slowly over time is able to trickle farther down to recharge water tables. Heavy rain saturates the top few centimetres of earth in the first minutes of a storm, preventing later drops from soaking in. Instead, that water simply runs off into creeks or drains, aggravating erosion, bearing pollutants and clogging streams with mud; sometimes, saturated soil breaks loose into a landslide.

There is another dimension to the change in these seasonal storms, hinted at in the freakishly early thaw that sent six kilometres of ice piling up on Hartland's covered bridge and in the unusually late monsoon that struck India's Maharashtra State later the same year. Not only are seasons becoming more extreme, but the differences among the seasons themselves appear to be breaking down.

Wanjohi "Edward" Ndegwa is a lucky man. When most of Kenya withers under relentless drought, his own close-set rows of cow-peas, cabbage, kale and arrowroot shine a healthy green against the soil. The one-acre patch of land he tills is never dry. Why? Because Wanjohi waters it with sewage. Wiry and slight at 55, he's a "squatter," vernacular for what aid groups call "residents of an informal settlement," on the fringes of Nairobi. His fresh greens find a ready market in a city where few of an estimated 3.5 million people possess refrigeration. He knows his produce may be contaminated, but he says, "As a farmer, you can't think about the germs. You think about the yield."[45]

He's much better off than most of Kenya's farmers. The seasonal rains on which the majority rely have become unpredictable in recent decades, he says. In his youth, the country counted on two rainy seasons: a longer, cool one from April to June and a shorter, warm one between October and December. Now, "the short rainy season has disappeared completely, and we have a long rainy season and a *long* dry season only." Worse, the dry season seems to be getting longer every year. Farmers without his access to sewage water have lost not only crops but also livestock, as sheep, cows and goats either died or were slaughtered for lack of fodder. "People who rely on rain are very badly off."

Wanjohe's experience is widely shared in other developing countries, where the reliability of seasonal rainfall may be a matter of life and death. Tearfund, a church-supported British aid group, polled associated congregations in several African and Latin American countries, asking how their local weather was changing. "Rainfall is becoming erratic," a Malawian reported. "Many years ago, October was the month when rains would come. Now it has changed to December and it is never consistent. Farmers tend to be at a loss when to plant."[46]

"Seasons have been very irregular and there are no precise times for planting as there used to be," agreed someone from Rwanda. "Crop yield has been reduced drastically, sometimes resulting in total crop failure."

"In the past," a Honduran correspondent told Tearfund, "the two seasons of the year could be distinguished quite clearly. Nowadays it is difficult to distinguish. The growing season has varied by about a month compared with five years ago. The time for sowing crops used to be in June. Sowing now takes place at the end of July. In spite of this, some crops have still been ruined. There are municipalities where they have been unable to harvest at all for three years due to drought." When wet weather does arrive, "rains come together at one time, causing floods. The time lapse between floods has shortened from five years to one year. Storms are more frequent."[47]

Humans aren't the only ones who suffer when seasons change their temper. The rains that historically watered Honduran crops during the summer also came to Costa Rica nearby. That small nation's impressive ecological wealth and numerous protected areas have made it popular among North American tourists. A favourite destination is Corcovado National Park, whose rainforest is home to all four of Costa Rica's native monkey species: dark-furred howlers, white-bibbed capuchins, nimble russet squirrels and long-limbed spider monkeys. In early 2006, however, biologists were horrified to discover many of these, along with scores of toucans, macaws, deer and sloths, dead or dying. Distressed scientists and park staff collected the corpses of four dead monkeys and rescued three more that were barely alive, shivering, lethargic and too weak to climb for food. They blamed the animals' state on drenching weeks of autumn rainfall, twice as heavy and far longer than normal. Heavy rain prevents some trees from bearing fruit and causes other fruit to fall before it ripens. It also discourages foraging. The same season had also been abnormally cold for the tropical region. Weakened by hunger, the monkeys that died may finally have succumbed to hypothermia. "Monkeys need sun to dry off," said ecologist Ronald Sánchez Porras. "When it rains like this, it's impossible."[48]

Canadians, far better equipped than either rainforest monkeys or Developing World subsistence farmers to cope, have nonetheless been similarly surprised by the increasing vagary of the seasons. In particular, several winters in the new century have featured extended periods of abnormally balmy weather. After one such extended reprieve from the normal winter chill had produced the warmest temperatures on record for three consecutive months, from November 2001 into January 2002, Environment Canada's David Phillips admitted that even he was at a loss to explain what was going on. "We just can't go back in the weather files and find this. Maybe the X-files, but not the weather files. I mean, this is so bizarre it really almost defies explanation."

Revisiting the subject several years later, Phillips had changed his mind. "I've had almost that 'walk in the blizzard' kind of thing," he told me in his cramped office in Environment Canada's north Toronto headquarters. "For thirty-five years I have always said, 'The past is a guide to the future.' I don't believe that any more. Here in Ontario, farmers are saying to me, 'What will I do next year? What will I plant?' I tell them, look at the last five years to tell you what you should do, don't look at the last hundred years.

"What Ontario farmers have seen in the last five years is the wettest beginning to a growing season ever; they've seen two of the driest years ever, back-to-back; they've seen a winter that was almost cancelled followed by the coldest May on record, which for a farmer is crippling—if you don't get your crop in in May, you don't get it in. You also had the single driest growing season, the hottest growing season and the hottest, sweatiest and dirtiest summer on record. I'm talking to a group of farmers in Stratford. They've had probably the best growing season on record this year [2006], but the worst harvest season. So all that money they counted in their pockets on Labour Day has evaporated by Remembrance Day [November 11] because they couldn't harvest the product.

"Their grandparents never faced this kind of variability, these swings back and forth, these flip-flops. We've always known the *weather* was unpredictable. Now the *climate* has become unpredictable."[49]

Blame for the spate of floods in recent years can't be laid entirely on a changing climate. Human choices alter how landscapes cope with natural events such as heavy rain and, in regions where it snows, spring melt. Unrestrained logging that stripped the absorptive capacity of hillsides very likely contributed to the tragic landslides in the Philippines, Guatemala and elsewhere. Mumbai's municipal government had dithered over planned improvements to its antiquated drainage system. Levees constrict the natural flood plains of the Mississippi, the Fraser and many European rivers, forcing flood waters to run high between artificially raised banks until those give way and the floods reclaim the "protected" land behind them.

Even so, landscaping can't account for changes in rainfall over half a century, nor for the extra heat and moisture becoming available as "fuel" for storm systems, whether those are localized thunderstorms or monster typhoons as wide as medium-size countries. Far less for the steady rise of sea levels and accelerated erosion of shorelines from New Brunswick's Acadian coast to the Florida Peninsula, from San Francisco Bay to virtually the entire tragic nation of Bangladesh.

Wherever you live, wherever you look, the winds moving over the face of the Earth are picking up, and blowing in change.

# Chapter 4
## Planet on Defrost:
## A World without Ice and Snow

Some 600 kilometres north of Winnipeg, Manitoba, about halfway between the 49$^{th}$ parallel and the shore of Hudson Bay and not far from the province's border with Ontario, lies Island Lake. Its name describes it well: a rough crescent of steel blue scattered with green, lying in a part of the boreal forest where land and water share the earth's surface with rough equality. Toward the lake's western end, set among a maze of small islands and inlets, a narrow finger of continental land pushes north, pinched almost into an island itself in a couple of places. This is St. Theresa Point. At its northern tip is a community of the same name. Jack Wood, a retired school administrator, has lived there his entire life, going on seven decades.

He remembers the winters of his youth. By Christmas the water in Island Lake was frozen a metre deep in what he calls "blue ice," water frozen so hard and clear that it retained the colour of the lake below and sky above.

Each December in those days, heavy equipment would roll in to begin clearing the "ice road." Scraped from frozen muskeg and lakes, the seasonal road winds over 300 kilometres north from the nearest all-weather highway to connect the communities of Garden Hill and God's Lake, Wasagamack and Shamattawa, and eventually

St. Theresa Point, to the outside world. It used to get to St. Theresa Point in time for New Year's. For the next 10 or 11 weeks, usually until late March, St. Theresa Point's residents made the most of their only opportunity of the year to drive out to the city or bring anything back by surface transport, hauling in gasoline for boats and diesel for the community generator, plywood and plumbing for new houses, a pump for the water system or new washers for the laundromat, in short almost everything they expected to need in the year to come. Once the road melted back into bog and lake, the villagers had to fly in whatever they had forgotten or run out of. Whatever was too big or heavy for a small float plane to transport, they would do without.

Wood is an elder and former chief of the St. Theresa Point First Nation. For years, he oversaw the road's construction. The ideal weather for building it, he explained, is when "it turns cold and the permafrost sets in. If it's thick enough, we're not too worried about how much snow's coming down, we'll doze that snow out. But if it's warm and then it snows, it creates insulation for the ground and that thickness of frost doesn't set in. If there's not enough permafrost, the graders can go down in the muskeg. Even the ice, if it snows early, snows heavy, it creates slush ice, eh? You're not getting that blue ice. Blue ice is very strong; slush ice breaks down."[1]

Since the mid-1990s, Wood has seen "very, very, very drastic changes" in the early winter weather. Heavy snow comes early, hard frost late. As a result, the ice road has been reaching St. Theresa Point later and melting earlier each year, its overall season shortening. "Normally we're up about the first week of January at the latest," he said, a few days after that date had passed without a hard frost. "Right now, they're targeting the end of the month for traffic." Because of slush ice on the lakes and thin frost on the muskeg, Wood expected that many shippers would, as in other recent seasons, load their trucks only half full to reduce weight. The price of the trip doesn't change; everything that comes in just costs more. Worse, Wood pointed out, "you double your number of trips, you double your time-line. Sometimes you can't get all of it in."

By the first decade of the new century, the ice-road season had dwindled to under six weeks. Fewer than 42 days to deliver over a narrow, winding two-lane (at best) track everything that several hundred families might need or want for 11 months. Sometimes, the clock runs out and the road melts before everything gets in. After one curtailed season in mid-decade, St. Theresa Point's gas station ran out of fuel a week before the following Christmas. With over a month before the ice road might re-open, emergency deliveries arrived by air. But the price for a litre of regular unleaded spiralled north of $2.25. "I put in 40 dollars, and I'm not even getting five gallons," Wood grumbled.

Others in St. Theresa Point suffered worse than inconvenience. One year a man died when his dozer went through the ice trying to finish the road. When the road melted again before transport trucks could deliver needed building materials, construction of half a dozen new houses came to a halt. Left empty for a season in a community where unemployment is high and alcohol and solvent abuse are chronic problems among the young, the half-finished houses were vandalized. "Then you have to order new windows," said Wood, whose term as chief included administering band housing. "And you might not get them." For the more than half of the families in the village who get by on welfare, losing the chance to make the 12-hour drive south to Winnipeg to stock up on groceries at city prices means having to stretch a tight budget around carrots from the village store at a dollar a pound and hamburger at $16.

The change in the weather has had other effects. The community's economy relies heavily on the lakes and forest around it. Game—rabbits, bear and especially moose—are traditional fare and cheaper than food brought in from the south. But with less frost and more snow, the animals have changed their behaviour, making it difficult for hunters to find them. Moose in particular are struggling: more frequent falls of thick, heavy snow conceal the young twigs the animals eat through the winter. "Four or five feet of snow, it hinders their travel," Wood has observed. "They can't move around the way they used to. It's easier for predators to get at them." Trappers have noticed that the fur of mink, beaver and muskrat isn't so thick as it used to be.

Scores of small hamlets across the Canadian north rely as St. Theresa Point does on annual ice roads, some 2,600 kilometres of them just in Manitoba. All are seeing the same meltdown of this crucial part of their transportation infrastructure. Not all are remote Aboriginal reserves. Resource development sites have also been affected. When their ice roads melted early in 2006, diamond miners in Nunavut and the Northwest Territories had received barely half the fuel, explosives and heavy equipment they had counted on for the busy summer ahead. Without those supplies, Nunavut's Jericho Diamond Mine was forced "to trim back mine development in order to conserve on fuel," its CEO conceded.[2]

Within a couple of decades, St. Theresa Point may demand a permanent road to the south. That might have some advantages, but it will cost the province more than $1.2 billion to build (at 2006 prices). And as a former educator, Wood worries about the social effect it will have on his people. Already, fewer youths can finish a sentence in their native Cree-Ojibwa language. The internet, he believes, is corroding the community's traditional culture even more than television did. "I often put my little granddaughter on my lap," he said as our conversation ended. "She's close to one, she doesn't talk yet. I ask her, 'What's going to happen to you?'"

The melting permafrost, whose loss threatens the ice roads to St. Theresa Point and other remote communities also threatens the stability of buildings, bridges, pipelines and roadways around the entire Arctic, from northern Quebec through Alaska and across the vast sweep of northern Russia. The implications of the disappearance of snow and ice, however, reach into some of the world's hottest and most teeming regions. And they touch every part of a country that has often been defined by its cold.

Voltaire, writing about the value of the northern half of North America in the 18th century, dismissed it as "*quelques arpents de* neige"—a few acres of snow. One of Canada's earliest artists, Cornelius Krieghoff, is best known for his 19th-century depictions of winter in Quebec. Our national game is ice hockey, closely followed in some age groups and provinces by curling. But the season that has characterized us is dwindling.

Not only were 11 of the years between 1995 and 2006 among the *warmest* 12 that mankind has recorded since we began keeping systematic records in 1850 (and the last of those the warmest ever in the continental United States), but the number of frost days has declined sharply as well. Between 1951 and 2003, the number of cold nights, in particular, declined over more than three-quarters of the world's surface.[3]

Anyone who has ever struggled out of a warm bed into the numbing darkness of a winter morning, scraped clear a car windshield that resembled centre ice or ground a grudging spark out of an engine kept above absolute zero only by a block heater may not think this is entirely a bad thing. And indeed, as the reality of a changing climate set in, farmers in much of the northern and parts of the southern hemisphere were checking the calendar and considering whether a longer growing season might allow them to grow different, more profitable crops, or perhaps even turn over more than one harvest in a year. While Jack Wood worried about his ice road, shippers on the Great Lakes and the rivers of Russia and northern Europe, for whom ice closes rather than opens the transportation season, considered the chances for additional trips. Highway crews hoped to get away with a bit less sand and salt. Visitors to a museum exhibit on climate change in Victoria, British Columbia, could even examine an animated map that showed them how their home heating bills might go down in the decades ahead (of course, it also showed how their air-conditioning costs might rise).

But for water, certain differences of degree are more important than others. The difference between the temperature at which moisture remains suspended in the air as water vapour and the slightly cooler one at which it forms droplets heavy enough to fall as rain, known as "dewpoint," is one such. Dewpoint varies, in part with the amount of water that any particular mass of air is capable of absorbing (which itself varies with the air's temperature). The temperature at which water turns to ice (or snow) or, going the other way, at which ice (or snow) turns back to water, is more constant: in nature, very close to 0°C.[4] A degree either way means the difference between frozen or liquid precipitation. It determines whether water remains in place as ice or snow—or flows downhill as fast as gravity will pull it along.

The world has already warmed by close to one degree Celsius since the Industrial Revolution a little more than two centuries ago. Wherever frozen water was already near the melting point, that small shift has huge consequences. The first is for the cryosphere, which comprises the frozen parts of our Earth: snow, permanently frozen soil (permafrost), Arctic and Antarctic ice-caps, mountain glaciers and ice sheets, seasonally frozen lakes. As the planet warms, the cryosphere retreats.

We are experiencing this retreat in our daily lives, on every continent, in ways that range from our choice of pastimes to the stability of our buildings to the price of carrots. Plants and animals, like Manitoba's moose, feel the impact too. By the end of the quarter-century or very shortly thereafter, the one degree of difference between -0.5°C and +0.5°C could erase from existence some of the greatest, and until now most durable, of the planet's physical features: the year-round ice-cap that covers most of the Arctic Ocean, much of the vast ice sheet that presently caps Greenland and many of the mountain-top glaciers at lower latitudes.

Long before then, the dwindling of the cryosphere will have had a profound effect on the great rivers that supply water to the western half of North America and others that do the same for more than half the world's present population.

As a child in Ontario, I used to toboggan with my brother at Hamilton's Chedoke public golf course and (as it was then) ski hill. The facility is set against the foot of the Niagara Escarpment, known locally as the

Hamilton Mountain. Grey limestone cliffs hedged with deciduous trees, bare and skeletal in winter, loom over a slope that, if hardly a mountain by most standards, nonetheless provided a gratifying burst of speed before your ride ran out at the bottom. There were tows for skiers and lights at the head of the hill for dark winter evenings. There was even a long, boxed wooden chute, glazed with ice, where you could start your toboggan run. On crisp nights when moonlight reduced the colours of the day to black and white on the unstained snow, you would dart from the chute into a spray of icy crystals coming over the front of your toboggan as you shrieked and rocketed through the night.

I visited there again recently. A small forest of sumac and scrub saplings had overgrown what used to be the top of the ski run. The armatures that held the ski tow were still there, green paint peeling from the rusted steel. Broken wooden steps, leading nowhere, mark where the vanished toboggan chute used to start. It was November, still early in the winter, but the facility was a ghost. It had closed in 2000.

Coralee Secore remembers those 20th-century winters as vividly as I. She's my age exactly and learned to ski at Chedoke. Now a district manager in Hamilton's Culture and Recreation Department, she was among those who decided to retire the ski tows at Chedoke (the toboggan chute had long been discontinued) after the winter of 2000 never even got cold enough for the facility to use its snow-making equipment. "Back in the 1960s," she said, recalling the era of our childhood excursions, "the season ran for 80 days, from before Christmas to the March break." By the end of the century, "the window was narrowing. It would be mid-January when we started, and we'd barely hold on to the last week of February to get in six weeks of [ski] lessons. It was only in the mid-'90s that we began to pay attention."[5] As the season dwindled, the $225,000 it cost to operate the ski tows became harder to justify, and then moot. Winter had left the park.

Its departure has affected other elements of the Ontario city's recreation program as well, Coralee told me. "We've had a big Winterfest event in the first week of February; the last six years we haven't had any snow for it. We've had to rethink what kind of event we have.

We're having trouble getting natural skating rinks up; we'll maybe get one up for a week or two."

Skating in the open air on natural ice is becoming a fading memory in much of the rest of southern Ontario as well. Metro Toronto's boroughs of Etobicoke and Scarborough abandoned their last natural rinks the same year Hamilton did. The City of Toronto ran its own for the last time in 2004. The disappearance of public open-air rinks prompted one stubborn and sentimental citizen to take matters into his own hands. Thomas Neal, a real-estate agent in the city's Beaches neighbourhood, made it his personal mission to keep a little ice on one rink in Glen Stewart Ravine. "We are a northern people, a northern culture," he explained. "Being Canadians, you want to skate." For four slushy winters in the new century he shovelled snow and faithfully flooded the ice each afternoon to give neighbourhood youngsters a taste of an iconic but fading pastime. In 2005, after working for a week to prepare the ice, Thomas managed to get his rink open for one day.[6]

Ever since the new millennium opened on three consecutive winter months of record mild temperatures, a country famous for ice and snow has been setting records for green winters. At Parry Sound, Ontario, where once in the early 1970s I hiked across foot-thick ice to check on a cottage at Christmas, by February of 2006, for the first time in local memory, the water had yet to freeze over. Later, Environment Canada confirmed that *this* was now the warmest winter ever, with temperatures on average nearly 4°C above historic norms. "Statistically, *in an unchanging climate* [emphasis added] Canada could expect a winter anomaly like this about every 100 years," the agency said.[7]

The following winter was more anomalous still. Across much of the middle of North America, the winter of 2006–2007 held off until well into January. In Ottawa, the world's second-coldest capital, the Rideau Canal, which the city touts as the world's longest skating rink in winter, failed to freeze well into the new year. Central Ontario's ski resorts left their seasonal employees on an extended and unwanted holiday. Along Lake Simcoe, ice-fishing huts remained ashore, the lake's water stubbornly liquid. The Ontario Federation of

Snowmobile Clubs told its members to leave their machines in the driveway: none of the province's public trails was open.

It was the same elsewhere. Some New Yorkers celebrated the first weekend of 2007 by taking in an outdoor cello concert in Central Park—the musicians in shirt-sleeves—while others boated on the park's pond or simply basked in the sun. The temperature, 71°F (21.6°C), blew away the previous high mark of 63°F (17°C), set more than half a century earlier. Not everyone was thrilled. At the Pine Hill Arms Hotel, near the foot of the Belleayre ski hill in the Catskills north of the city, owner Robert Konefal cursed the bare, green slopes. "I've been here for 32 years and this is the worst winter I've ever seen," he said. "I had three-day packages for New Year's Eve and in my main building every single room cancelled."[8]

Sheriff's Captain Kevin Caffery, of Buffalo, New York, used to spend many late winter afternoons chuttering over the shoreline of eastern Lake Erie in a helicopter, checking for stranded ice fishermen and rescuing many. Then in 2006, he made not a single rescue. There was no one to save. "The ice didn't freeze," he explained. In fact, after freezing over every winter between 1953 and 1998, the shallowest (and therefore most easily frozen) of the Great Lakes failed to freeze fully across in three of the subsequent nine winters. By early January, 2007, the water in the lake was a record 41°F (5°C), seven degrees Fahrenheit above historic normals for that date.

Mike Smith organizes and promotes an annual series of ice-fishing tournaments, sponsored by tackle-makers and outdoor equipment companies. His circuit boasts events from upstate New York to Minnesota. But after warm weather melted out two of his seven stops in 2007, he acknowledged that the climate for his sport had disappeared. The southern boundary of ice-fishing country, he explained, used to run through northern Illinois and Iowa as far as Montana. More recently, ice-fishing huts have generally been shore-bound anywhere south of Minneapolis-St. Paul. Half his sport's U.S. range has literally melted away. "Nobody ever remembered an entire ice belt with that poor ice."[9]

Michigan's Upper Peninsula, separated from the rest of the state by the Straits of Mackinac, is a place of rugged landscape and deep woods whose residents—who call themselves Yoopers, from the area's U.P. acronym—have long given winter a hairy-chested embrace. Hunting, snowmobiling and skiing are all popular there and are usually big contributors to the economy. Since the 1980s milder winters have raised January temperatures in the Houghton area by nearly 4°c and put less ice on the U.P.'s many small lakes. As the winter of 2006–2007 stubbornly refused to start, ski runs entered the new year streaked with brown, as empty as those farther east. With temperatures almost 5°c above freezing and less than one-quarter of the usual amount of snow recorded for the season so far (and most of that washed away by rain), trails that usually roared with convoys of snowmobiles lay bare and silent. Worse for the local economy, so did motels and restaurants that normally bustled with pre- and après-ski crowds. After a shortage of snow forced a popular inner-tube luge race through downtown Houghton to be cancelled, city fathers resorted to rationing what little snow was lying around, and trucking in more, to rescue its annual winter carnival. Jim Aho, whose snowmobile shop had plenty of machines to rent but no customers, declared the mild weather simply "terrible."[10]

On average over the last century, mid-winter snow covered nearly half the land in the northern hemisphere. In each decade over that century, however, snow vanished from three-quarters of a million square kilometres of North America—an area of snow roughly the size of New Brunswick disappearing every ten years.[11] Since 1950, three-quarters of the weather stations in the mountain areas of North America have reported less snow. Smaller snowbanks are not staying so long either. Canadian researchers have worked out that the ground in the western half of the country is snow-free for two weeks longer then was the case in 1955.[12]

Ski resorts and ice fishers in Canada's Maritime region have suffered the same complaints as their mid-continental counterparts. More than most observers, however, New Brunswick climatologist

Bill Richards has evidence to prove a longer-term trend is in play. He grew up on a farm at Oak Point along the Saint John River, about an hour south of the provincial capital. He remembers winters of his childhood when the big river iced up long before Christmas. He had long suspected that something was changing here too. He found proof in meticulous records, going back to 1825, of the dates on which the river first froze over and when the ice broke up.[13] Examining records from almost two centuries of winters, he said, "We can see a trend: there's more and more open water, about nine days a decade." In the first week of February 2006, he walked out onto a bridge over the river on the coldest day of that winter, to take a picture of the open water. "That had never happened before," he said. But it almost certainly will again. "By 2025," he told me, "the trend takes you down to zero. There will be no ice at all."[14]

Another way to look at this change in the weather is to think not about how cold or snowy a particular season gets, but about how long winter lasts. They still get enough of it in Alaska to know how to have a little fun with it. For nearly a century, the town of Nenana, on the Tanana River southwest of the capital, Fairbanks, has held an annual derby based on the exact time the river's ice will break up. With the advent of the internet, punters from around the world now wager on the minute and second that the ice will begin to move; in some years as much as $10 million ride on the winning moment. Each year the smart money moves earlier. The break-up in the first decade of the 21$^{st}$ century has come, on average, 10 days earlier than it did in 1950.

Other species are already responding to this "season creep." Sap in sugar maple trees, for instance, starts to run earlier than it used to. Rex Marsh has been tapping his family's Vermont sugar bush for six decades. When he was a young man, he'd begin sugaring-off on the first Tuesday in March. In 2005 and 2006 he drove his first taps in January. There's a name for this kind of observation: phenology, the study of the timing of recurring natural events. It has turned out to be remarkably revealing of changes in the seasonal calendar.

Scottish naturalists combed four decades of observations made of more than 500 different biological events marking the arrival of spring in northern Britain, from the appearance of butterflies to the nesting of birds and the hatching of aphids; three-quarters occur earlier now than they did 40 years ago. Researchers in Texas conducted a similar meta-analysis of phenological observation, but, being Texans, they did their study on a larger scale, covering over three times as many plant and animal species worldwide. They found that biological events timed to the change of season have crept ahead by more than two days per decade, or a week since 1975. They also found that individual species are migrating toward cooler places, either upward to higher altitudes, at a rate of several metres per decade, or north at an average speed of about six kilometres per decade.[15]

In vast areas of interior British Columbia, where Januaries no longer get cold enough, for long enough, to kill over-wintering pine bark beetles, living green forest has given way to dying reddish-brown. Unleashed in the billions, the bugs' rice-sized larvae are voraciously nibbling their way through an entire ecosystem. Without living trees to cut, the province's once-dominant lumber industry faces slow starvation. The beetle has meanwhile been spotted east of the Rocky Mountains, poised to extend its plague across the boreal forest.

A more frightening prospect is the number of human pathogens flourishing and extending their range in the absence of frost. Until recently, months of near- or sub-zero temperatures provided effective protection to temperate latitudes against the ticks that carry Lyme disease and the mosquitoes that spread malaria, dengue fever and encephalitis, among other vectors of disease. "The winter is the most wonderful thing that was ever invented for public health," says Harvard's Dr. Paul Epstein. "And we're losing it."[16]

Still, winter has a way of coming back with a vengeance. The strange dispensation from chill that lasted across most of central and eastern North America until early January, 2007, ended suddenly. Biting cold descended as far south as California, destroying a billion dollars' worth of citrus fruit still on the branches and dusting even Malibu with snow for the first time since 1964. Arctic air flowing south from Canada collided with a moist current rushing north from the tropical Pacific and Gulf of Mexico to create freezing rain and sleet from Texas to Maine. Ice-glazed electrical lines collapsed, throwing nearly one-third of a million houses and businesses into darkness; hundreds of miles of interstate and local highways were left impassable. Cold, unsafe emergency heating, fallen branches and dangerous driving conditions contributed to some 60 deaths. The same Arctic blast sent temperatures on the Canadian Prairies plummeting to −35°C in places and prompted the city of Toronto, so recently balmy, to declare a cold weather advisory.

Just as drier, longer droughts alternate in the new century with fiercer downpours when it does rain, an increasingly bipolar climate is bringing us both less winter in general and, when winter does assert itself, *more intense* winter cold and storms.

The winter that procrastinated over North America in late 2006 also dawdled in Europe. Through the warmest autumn on record, countries from Norway to the Mediterranean had basked in temperatures five degrees above 20th-century averages: 10 degrees above "normal" in Germany and Switzerland. Fruit and nut trees had burst into premature bloom. With destinations like Austria's Kitzbühel and France's Val d'Isère out of commission, the World Ski Federation had cancelled race dates from Italy to Norway.[17] In Russia, bears that would normally have been deep in hibernation awoke and ambled out of their dens in search of meals.[18] Then the most powerful north Atlantic cyclone in a decade—and one of the fiercest on record—swept down on the continent. The late January storm killed at least 41 people, left more than a million central European homes without power and made a shambles of Germany's vaunted national railway system.

A freak cold wave in early January, 2006, paralyzed transportation over most of Japan, dumping up to four metres of snow in some places and killing at least 57 people. As the storm moved on to China, temperatures there plummeted to −43°C, scores more died and 100,000 people were forced to flee houses that collapsed under the weight of snow. As the wave of Arctic air swept westward, at least 150 more people, most of them homeless or living in poor conditions, died of cold in Russia, Ukraine, Poland, Turkey and Germany. Even Delhi, the capital of India, experienced frost, a phenomenon not seen there in decades.

No one watches the weather more closely than a sailor. Being caught by surprise can mean the difference between living and dying. Captain Daniel Trottier of Cornwall, Ontario, has spent almost his entire life on ships. He first stepped aboard a vessel at the age of five, joining his father on the bridge of a laker. After studying navigation, he went to sea on his own at 18, first as a junior officer sailing tankers on the open ocean, then eventually earning a captain's rank. He has guided research vessels to Antarctica and into the Northwest Passage across the top of North America. Since 1990, he has worked the Great Lakes, becoming senior captain in the service that provides locally knowledgeable navigators to deep-sea ships travelling the St. Lawrence Seaway from the Atlantic to Thunder Bay.

Weather on the Lakes is a daily preoccupation, and Daniel has seen it change. "When I was young, Lake Superior was completely covered with ice [in winter]," he told me. "Now the big surface doesn't freeze over. Lake Huron used to be ice-covered from side to side; not any more."

But the most perplexing change, he says, is the "strange" behaviour of once-reliable seasons. In late 2005, for instance, "here in the St. Lawrence, eastern Lake Ontario and Montreal, early December was normal. But Niagara and the Welland Canal were completely frozen—we had 27 ships stuck up above [the canal]—up until the 17th or 18th of December. Then the weather changed to 57° Fahrenheit, and everything melted."[19]

This new unpredictability is of a piece with the increasingly erratic procession of dry and rainy seasons in the tropics. Everywhere, seasonal calendars are breaking down: neither African rain nor boreal cold is arriving on the familiar schedule of the past. Climatologists refer to this as "variability." It's what Andrew Weaver is describing when he envisions a marble racing up one side of a bowl, perhaps to inflict a severe drought or unusual February thaw, only to drop back and zip up the other side, there to unleash torrential rains or a sudden bitter frost out of season. As the marble's movements become wilder, the swings between hot and cold, wet and dry become more extreme, sudden and erratic. When this variability affects winter, it can disrupt far more than diamond-mining, seafaring and boozy winter break parties. From growing our food to moving goods around the continent, the growing unpredictability of weather exacts a high cost. "That's the stuff that doesn't kill you, but it destroys you," is how Environment Canada's David Phillips puts it.[20]

Unexpectedly severe cold commands our momentary attention, but it is a minor theme in the larger concert of changes taking place in the weather, a brief diversionary skirmish in winter's general retreat. While daily, weekly or even seasonal temperatures may swing up and down with increasing volatility, the dominant trend is one-way, and the result is inexorable pressure on the cryosphere, reaching into winter's most formidable redoubts.

One sunny April day in 1966, a footloose young Californian from Berkeley named Dennis Schmitt, living at the time in an Inuit community in Alaska, went for a walk on the ice of the frozen Bering Strait. The 19-year-old was filled with curiosity. With the ice spreading firm and continuous ahead of him, he kept on walking—and wound up hiking all the way across to what was then the Soviet Union, at the time locked deep in the Cold War with the West. Thrown briefly into jail for his exploit, the young American was soon released and returned home. But his enthusiasm for the North was undimmed. In the decades that followed, Schmitt became a semi-professional explorer and occasional adventure travel guide, making more than 100 other expeditions to both poles and supporting his wanderlust by lecturing about his experiences. In 2003 he claimed credit, with four companions, for discovering the northernmost scrap of land on the globe: a gravel bar only 40 metres long that cleared the frozen surface of the sea by less than the height of a short man, but which, at 83°42' North, was a full two "minutes" (about a mile) closer to the pole than the next-most-northerly contender for that distinction.

In 2005 Schmitt joined an adventure cruise that set out to retrace the voyage made a century earlier by Philippe, Duke of Orléans, and Jean Charcot, to survey the east coast of Greenland. At a point about halfway up the island's coast, just north of Scoresby Sound in an area known as Liverpool Land, their small vessel was nosing through icebergs to view what Charcot and the Duke had described, and Danish maps of the area still showed, as a rocky peninsula jutting out from the island's main mass. Instead of a solid peninsula, however, they found a medium-size rocky island, about seven kilometres long, separated from the rest of Greenland by a 200-metre channel of open water. "It was a shock," Schmitt recalled when we spoke. "I was disoriented at first. I thought we were some place other than where we thought we were." But it wasn't the group's navigation that was mistaken. It was the established assumption that land lay beneath a thick sheet of ice extending from the mainland to a higher point of land that earlier explorers took to be the tip of a peninsula. In the first decade of the new century the ice had vanished, and beneath it was a boisterous strait bobbing with icebergs that continued to break free from the stub of the former ice sheet about once an hour.

Dennis named the discovery Uunartoq Qeqertoq, "Warming Island" in Inuktitut. With the island's exposure, he says, the change in Greenland's weather "is undeniable, it's in your face, you can't get away from it."[21]

Nowhere are temperatures rising faster than at high latitudes of the northern hemisphere. The discovery of "new" islands along the ragged coastline of the Arctic Ocean is becoming almost commonplace. And Dennis Schmitt has no plans to repeat his adolescent adventure in the present century. "You couldn't do it," he told me. "You'd have to do it in a boat. The ice has retreated." With a rapidity that has stunned scientists, the Arctic is melting.

The ice-cap at the top of the world has waxed and waned for far longer than *Homo sapiens* has wandered the planet. During ice ages of the past it expanded south to blanket virtually all of Canada. In more distant eras it vanished entirely, leaving the Arctic coastline lapped, 50 million years ago, by something close to what today we would consider a tropical sea, complete with alligators and palm trees.[22] Even since the last glacial age began its retreat a mere 10,000 years ago, the ice covering the Arctic Ocean has contracted in the summer and expanded again in the winter. For most of that time, the ice that melted each summer generally reformed each winter, the whole mass staying relatively constant from year to year.

Some time in the early 1970s, that changed. Since then, more ocean has melted each summer than has refrozen each winter, annually reducing the expanse of year-round ice by an area the size of Lake Superior. The remaining ice melted from below, becoming thinner as well. Since the dawn of the new century, those changes have accelerated. In 2002, the biggest ice shelf along the northern coastline of Canada's Ellesmere Island, the Ward Hunt Ice Shelf, broke in two and began to disintegrate. Three years later another Ellesmere shelf did the same. Between the summers of 2004 and 2005 alone, an area as big as Texas—more than one-tenth of the entire ice-cap—melted away. Cracks began to appear in what was left. Scientists began to make book that the last of the Arctic's year-round sea ice would melt entirely before 2040, with some putting their money on a date as early as 2020.[23]

As dramatic as that would be, the sudden appearance of Dennis Schmitt's Warming Island may be the more ominous event. For one thing, there is much more ice on Greenland, where in places it lies two miles thick, than on the ocean, where it is seldom deeper than a few metres. Another is that even if the Arctic Ocean melts completely each summer, it will not change the level of the world's seas (in the same way that the level of a drink in a glass doesn't rise when the ice cubes floating in it melt). Greenland's ice sits on land, however; if it melts, it will run into the ocean. If all of it melts, the additional water could raise sea levels around the entire globe by up to six metres, the height of a two-storey building.

Not only is Greenland's ice melting, but like the Arctic Ocean, it is melting with increasing speed. This was confirmed in the middle of the decade by a variety of observations of the ice sheet's thickness, its weight and speed as glaciers slipped through valleys from the island's central plateau to the sea. Those measurements revealed that as average winter temperatures in parts of southern Greenland climbed above their 20th-century averages by as much as 5.5°C, many of the region's largest glaciers sped up. Some more than doubled their speed in just three years. The Kangerdlugssuaq Glacier, on the island's east coast, more or less stood still in 1996; 10 years later it was positively racing out to sea at 14 kilometres a year.[24] Other observations showed that the ice in southern Greenland was also losing mass (i.e., melting) more than twice as fast as scientists had previously believed.[25]

Two things seemed to be at work. First, as water on top of the glaciers melts, it trickles down through cracks and crevices in the ice to the bottom of the frozen mass. There, it spreads out along the rock, creating a lubricating layer that greases the glacier's progress downhill. Secondly, when an ice shelf floating on the sea at the mouth of a glacier breaks away, as the one at Warming Island did, its departure unplugs the opening, allowing the rest of the glacier upstream to pick up speed.

By the middle of the first decade of the new century, southern Greenland's ice was melting three times faster than it had been a decade earlier—and 20 percent faster than winter snowfall replenished it. Each year, more than 224 cubic kilometres of melted ice flowed as fresh water into the sea. That volume seemed small by some comparisons—equivalent to only about two and a half days' flow from the mouth of the Amazon River during its rainy season peak, for example—but large by others: enough to supply the city of Los Angeles' present-day thirst for two and a quarter centuries. And scientists saw alarming signs that the melt was accelerating. Pools of meltwater were seen over a larger expanse of Greenland's ice sheet in 2005 than ever before in the three decades since research began, with some places melting as late as December. The following spring, some research stations recorded air temperatures as much as 11°c higher than normal.[26] The rapid melting and glacier movement being seen in the south of the island seemed to be creeping north. "We may be very close to the threshold where the Greenland ice cap will melt irreversibly," says Tavi Murray, professor of glaciology at the University of Wales.[27]

As significant as that could prove over the long haul, what is happening to glaciers at lower latitudes will prove even more important to humanity over the next 25 years.

Perhaps one of the most talismanic of those is the improbable ice-cap atop Mount Kilimanjaro, less than 400 kilometres from the equator in east Africa. That peak has lost more than four-fifths of its ice and snow cover since 1912. "When I was a young boy in the village," recalled Philemon Ndesamburo, who now sits as the community of Moshi's member of Tanzania's parliament, "we seldom saw the whole of Mt. Kilimanjaro. Most of the time, the whole mountain was covered in snow and the ice-cap was so thick that the whole mountain would be engulfed in dense clouds for months." Nowadays the mountain is fully visible on almost any day of the year, and at the rate it is melting, the last of its ice will be gone by 2015.[28]

Then-and-now photographs as well as documented observations reveal the retreat of glaciers in virtually every other mountain range around the world as well. Just as daily temperatures don't move from summer heat to winter chill in a straight line, the glaciers' pull-back has proceeded in fits and starts—and occasional reverses. Researchers have documented melting by some mountain glaciers as far back as the 1800s, and advances by others in the past decade. Overall, however, the great majority of the world's sub-polar glaciers are undergoing progressive, irreversible and, in all likelihood, terminal meltdown. Europe's Alpine glaciers are half the size today that they were in the 19$^{th}$ century. Glaciers in the Tien Shan mountains between Russia and China dwindled by one-fifth over the last 40 years; so did those on the "roof of the world," in the Himalayan Mountains. Spain has seen half the glaciers in its Pyrenees vanish just since 1980. Venezuela boasted six Andean glaciers in 1972; it now has two. The Peruvian Andes altogether have lost one-quarter of their ice in the last 30 years.

And as demonstrated in Greenland and the Arctic Ocean, the melt appears to be speeding up. Peru's Quelccaya Ice-Cap, the biggest in the tropics, has been melting 10 times faster in the 21$^{st}$ century than it did between 1963 and 1983.[29] One of its largest subsidiary glaciers, the Qori Kalis, is expected to be gone by the new century's second decade.[30] Two-thirds of the Himalayan glaciers in Nepal, west China and northern India have also been melting faster in the new century than they did in the last.[31] Glaciers around the five-kilometre-high peak of New Guinea's Mount Jaya are melting 10 times faster in this century than in the last. Scientists who sampled 30 such mountain glaciers around the globe reported that, on average, the rate at which they were melting had tripled over the last 30 years.[32]

For many, the retreat of temperate and tropical glaciers has become the most visible manifestation of a changing climate. In the Alps, decaying glaciers have even spawned a novel form of tourism. Hundreds of gawkers have taken to congregating wherever melting ice threatens to trigger massive rock falls like the one that destroyed the Madonna, a popular feature of Switzerland's Eiger Mountain, in 2006. Another Swiss town, Gemsstock, hoping to preserve its popular local glacier a little longer, resorted to wrapping it in insulation during the summer. North American tourists were advised to visit Montana's Glacier National Park, which had lost more than 120 of its namesake ice fields by the dawn of the new century, before the couple of dozen that remained should vanish forever.

The aesthetic loss of these majestic white-capped peaks is lamentable in itself. A much bigger worry is the loss of the vital yet deeply under-appreciated role that mountain ice and snow play in providing hundreds of millions of people on every continent with a reliable supply of water.

Nature renews fresh water on a vast scale, but sporadically: rainstorms widely separated by dry spells, wet or snowy seasons set apart by rainless summer months. In western Canada, for example, between 80 and 90 percent of all precipitation falls between the late autumn and early spring. Yet we universally expect clean, fresh water 24/7. Even when demand goes up and down, as it does for agriculture and lawns, it's often out of synch with nature. Farming, which uses three to four times more water than everything else humanity does, demands it mostly in summer, when it is often least available.

Mountain ice and snow act as a bank to even out this imbalance of supply and demand. Water that falls as winter snow at high altitudes accumulates, either as snowpack or as glacial ice. Come warmer days in spring, the snow and ice begin to melt. They continue to melt slowly over the warm months that follow, releasing the water to flow down rivers from which we extract it to irrigate fields, water livestock or supply homes and businesses. Thus the rivers stay full, or at least flow, long after they might otherwise dry up for lack of recent rain.

This mountain "reservoir" is critically important both to humanity and to nature. By late summer, as much as 90 percent of the water flowing through some major rivers in western Canada, including the Athabasca, South Saskatchewan and Fraser, is meltwater released by upland snowpacks and mountain glaciers. The state of California banks as much water in winter snowpacks up and down the Sierras as it saves in all of its massive reservoirs combined. These high-altitude natural reservoirs temper seasonal imbalances in precipitation, to the benefit of billions of people and locally adapted wildlife around all of the world's great mountain ranges. During India's dry season between October and February, as much as 70 percent of the water flowing in its fabled Ganges, and more than half of that in other major rivers fed from the Himalayas, is melted snow and ice.

Now those picturesque mountaintop reservoirs are shrinking. As winters warm up, snow lines—the altitude of mountainside at which air chills enough for the moisture it releases to fall as snow—are also rising. That both diminishes the area where snow can accumulate and ensures that a larger share of precipitation arrives as rain rather than snow. Instead of being banked in frozen form, water that falls as rain immediately runs away into creeks and streams. As spring arrives earlier and sets in more quickly, rivers engorged by melting snow and late-winter precipitation falling as rain rather than snow, run high earlier in the season. Floods overwhelm levees and bridges built to withstand the more modest freshets of the past. But once that pulse of early meltwater and spring rain has coursed to the sea, much less remains frozen to flow later on. During the hot, dry months of late summer, rivers dwindle. We have seen exactly that in my province of British Columbia. The Fraser River, the largest North American river south of the Arctic Circle that still runs free without a major main-stem dam, started peaking a week earlier at the start of the new century than it did at the midpoint of the last, but in October 2006, stream gauges along its lower reaches reported the lowest flow ever recorded on the river.

Paradoxically, a succession of years of abnormally high glacial melt may have masked this critical shift. Over most of the world's mountain glaciers, warmer summers in the last century began liberating water that had been locked for centuries or longer in high-elevation ice fields to flow down mountain streams. With an effect like that of liquidating the principal of an investment account, the seasonal pulse of water over and above each year's precipitation income has given residents in many world regions the illusion that their rivers contain more water than the skies reliably deliver. Inevitably, however, the last water stored on the mountaintops will melt. Those rivers must fall back to whatever level nature's annual water income can sustain. In some places, that reversal has already occurred. Many of Canada's western rivers rose steadily through the first half of the last century, only to drop relentlessly in recent decades.[33]

Worse is in store. "Once the glaciers have melted," warns oceanographer Tim Barnett at the Scripps Institution of Oceanography, "there will be no replacement for the water they provide." Summertime water crises will become even commoner than they already are in northern China, in northwest India and Pakistan, in the southern Andes, and in the parts of Europe that rely on rivers—in all, affecting regions that are home to one-sixth of humanity and one-quarter of the global economy. "The prognosis," Barnett observes, "is clear and very dire."[34]

There was a particular chill for North Americans in the message. The two regions most vulnerable to the loss of the cryosphere's service as a water bank are also our two fastest-growing: America's glittering desert Southwest and Canada's Alberta. Later, we'll visit both at length.

We have many reasons to lament the loss of our big ice. Polar bears have become the poster-mammal for wildlife victims of climate change. As summer pack ice retreats, their nurseries are literally melting beneath them. In the Antarctic, tens of thousands of baby Adélie and Emperor penguins starved after the Ross Ice Shelf broke apart in 2002, causing giant icebergs to block their parents' access to the sea.

Gadfly explorer Dennis Schmitt imagines the day when an ocean once accessible only by dogsled, nuclear submarine or the most powerful of icebreakers becomes "a new Mediterranean." That may be premature, but a rush to exploit the resources beneath the newly open Arctic sea, and a burst of transport traffic through the long-sought polar shortcut from Europe to Asia, are on many minds. In 2007 Russia planted its flag on the seabed at the North Pole and Canada expanded its military presence in the high Arctic, as rivalry for the region intensified. "Both Russia and Canada assert policies holding navigable straits in the NSR [Northern Sea Route] and the Northwest Passage under their exclusive control," a Pentagon study noted. "The U.S. differs. As these routes become more available, conflicts are likely to arise."[35]

But neither the emotional tug of the extinction of another charismatic predator nor the addition of one more political flashpoint to the world's bulging inventory poses so great a threat to us as the less photogenic loss of ordinary winter snow and more modestly majestic mountain ice. It's the thought of what will happen to a billion people and one-quarter of the world economy when rivers go dry that ought, in Dr. Johnson's words, to "concentrate the mind wonderfully."

# Chapter 5
## Up in the Air:
### The Great Lakes' Uncertain Future

The arched sign over the high locked gate carries a single word: "Sanctuary." But the 800 acres of open hardwood forest beyond it are far from that. In fact, they're a sophisticated killing ground, where wealthy men pay to confine herds of white-tailed deer and flocks of wild turkeys for their exclusive hunting pleasure. The animals are kept in and trespassers out by tall double fences uneasily reminiscent of concentration-camp concertina wire.

Half a mile farther down the central Michigan county road, my host and guide, Tim Gratto, turns in at a second, unmarked gate. He leans out the window of his spotless new black SUV and swipes a pass card in front of a small box. The gate swings open, and we pass through. Seated behind us are an earnest, burly fellow named Greg Fox and a diplomatically attentive woman, Deborah Muchmore. Fox and Gratto work for Nestlé Waters North America Inc., a division of the global food giant; Muchmore is a minder from the company's public-relations firm. They are giving me a rare privilege for a writer in these parts: the opportunity to inspect ground zero in a heated battle between international corporate enterprise and local citizen activists. The stakes: millions of litres of pure, fresh spring water contained in the porous, sandy soil a hundred metres beneath our feet.

Through another double-gated set of fences we reach the heart of the Sanctuary. Tim pulls the big vehicle to a stop, and we climb down into the slightly other-worldly scene. It is very quiet. The November air is invigorating, a degree or so below freezing, even in the bright sun. Grey oak and maple trunks stand widely apart above a carpet of motley leaves. There is little undergrowth. Perhaps it obstructs the line of fire, or perhaps the deer have nibbled every shoot to the ground. A handsome buck with a wide rack of antlers gazes at us from a few hundred metres away, then moves off through the trees in elegant leaps.

Fox, Nestlé's midwestern resource manager, draws my attention to a grey stump, barely distinguishable from any other in the forest. I look more closely. It turns out to be several sections of weathered root arranged around the top of a steel pipe that disappears into the ground. It's one of several monitoring wells similarly concealed around the forest, he explains. Instruments deep inside it are constantly checking the level and quality of the water they're immersed in. Every week a technician comes out, opens the padlocked cap and reads the information stored in an electronic memory.

We climb back into the SUV and drive another few minutes, pulling up at last before a more obvious human presence in this captive forest: a neat cube of light brown stone, the size of a large utility shed, with a green metal roof. An L-shaped stone extension protects a large electrical transformer. The heavy steel door is locked. This and three identical buildings scattered about the rolling forest are the only outward signs that anything but hunting trophies is being harvested here.

The huts house Nestlé's most prized assets in Michigan: the production-well heads that allow the company to exercise the rights it has leased from the private club that owns the Sanctuary. Through each stone hut, state permits allow the company to pump as much as 100 gallons of water a minute out of the ground (although on the day I visited, it was only pumping about half that). A stainless-steel pipeline, one of the longest such on the planet, delivers the water to a plant 12 miles away at the town of Stanwood. There the water is micro-filtered, ozonated and packaged in plastic bottles for sale under the company's Ice Mountain brand across half a dozen upper-Midwest states, reaching stores as far afield as St. Louis and Buffalo.

Fox leads me away down a steep slope to a small lake. We reach the shore, where green sedges and brown bullrushes have created a moon-shaped marsh perhaps fifty metres long. Water seeps visibly from the foot of the hill and trickles into the lake. This natural spring, Fox explains, is a critical indicator of the aquifer's health. As long as it flows, he says, the company is confident that it is not withdrawing more water from the gravel hill than nature can spare. That's also important to Nestlé's marketing, he allows: "We couldn't label it 'spring water' if we caused these springs to dry up."[1]

As we drive back toward the main gate, Tim slows to point out an untidy mass of branches high in a tree. It's a bald eagle nest, he says. The company has a monitoring well close to the tree, but Gratto makes a point of telling me that it was installed while the eagles, a legally protected endangered species, were away from home. The company also buried cables away from the well, so that technicians could check its data from a distance. "It's all about being environmentally responsible," Nestlé's senior local manager tells me.[2]

He seems sincere. So does Greg Fox. But the stone and steel protecting Nestlé's production wells were not chosen for aesthetics only. The pocket blockhouses are bullet, fire and shrapnel-proof; eco-terrorists have attempted to fire-bomb other company installations nearby. And a more law-abiding group, organized as the Michigan Citizens for Water Conservation, has fought hard through the courts to roll back the state permit that allows Nestlé to take water from beneath the preserve. As both its moderate and extreme critics see it, Nestlé's withdrawals, amounting to a cubic kilometre of water every 14 months, are anything but "environmentally responsible."

The president of Michigan Citizens for Water Conservation is a fit-looking retired reference librarian named Terry Swier. I met her and her husband Gary, a former production manager for General

Motors, in the stunning new house they built a few years ago on the site of a cabin Swier inherited from her grandparents. Floor-to-ceiling windows look out over the restless surface of Horsehead Lake, another of the scores of water bodies splashed across this part of the state. The Swiers, too, are sincere—and deeply distrustful of Nestlé's assurance that its pumps have not hurt the area's surface water. Seven lakes and numerous small creeks surround the Sanctuary, Swier says: "We're all connected." She blames Nestlé directly for the decline of Dead Stream, which despite its dismal name has flowed vigorously out of the lake on the Sanctuary's land since before there were people here to drink from it.[3] After Nestlé switched on its pumps in 2002, she tells me, water once deep enough to float a canoe from bank to bank, a distance of perhaps 10 metres, fell to expose mudflats by 2004. By 2006, grasses and weeds grew where paddlers once floated.[4]

The Swiers believe that Nestlé's wells in fact threaten not only Dead Stream but also the wetland into which it flows, the Muskegon River beyond that, other local lakes and wildlife, and, by extension and precedent, the entire Great Lakes region. They point out that Ice Mountain water is shipped and sold outside the Lakes' basin, a one-way export that will never be returned. In Swier's view, the bottled trickle could easily become an unstoppable torrent threatening to drain the Lakes. "Water is for life; it's not for profit," she insists. "If you open it up to one company, does that open it up to other companies? How do you ever stop it?"

In 2002, a state court agreed that Nestlé had harmed Dead Stream and ordered the company to turn off its pumps. Nestlé appealed and won permission to keep pumping while the case proceeded, but it agreed outside court to limit its withdrawals to slightly more than half the amount the state agreed was sustainable. That compromise failed to appease Michigan Citizens for Water Conservation. "To be 'satisfied,'" said Terry Swier, "would be for them not to pump at all." By early 2007 the case had reached the state's Supreme Court and seemed destined, regardless of any ruling there, for the U.S. Supreme Court. Nestlé, in the meantime, had secured a new state permit to pump

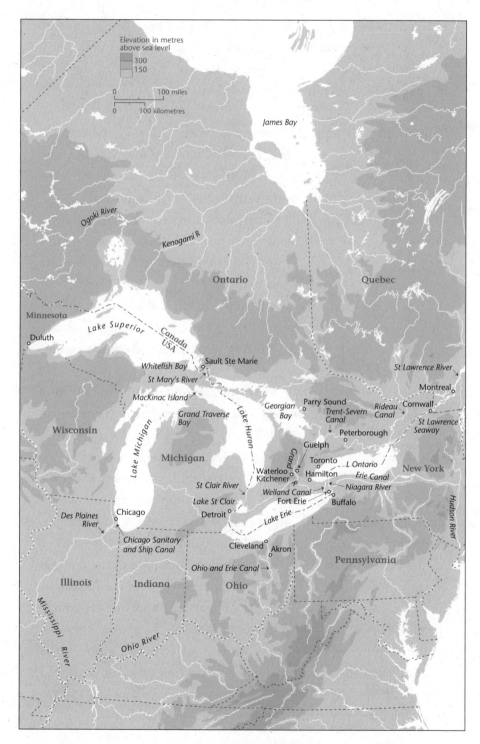

**Great Lakes region**

additional water for its Stanwood plant from a site a few kilometres from the preserve and was actively prospecting for further wells.[5]

"We'll continue to fight," Swier declared. "Because it's the right thing to do for our children's grandchildren."

Only Ontario is lapped by so many Great Lakes as the state of Michigan: four out of the five, as well as smaller Lake St. Clair. But seven more American states and Canada's Quebec also have a keen interest in the fate of the world's largest bodies of fresh water.

Indeed, the chain of lakes from Superior down through Michigan, Huron, Erie and Ontario constitutes one of the planet's most significant geographic features, longer end-to-end than Italy and at least as important to a continent's past and present. In North America, only the Mississippi and Colorado Rivers rival the Lakes' importance to human economies. The controversy over Nestlé's pumps resonates across the entire region. As growing communities encroach on natural watersheds, the quality of common tap water has come under suspicion even in many well-served places, contributing to the rising popularity of bottled drinking water. Nowhere has commercial response to that demand collided more violently with local and even national hostility than within the Great Lakes Basin.

For many who live around their shores, the Lakes anchor a sense of personal identity and justify uncompromising parochialism. Changes evident in the region's weather over recent decades, coinciding with expanding populations, arouse legitimate concern for the Lakes' future health. But reflexive opposition to the removal of any water under any conditions from anywhere in the Lakes' basin bespeaks selective amnesia. The Great Lakes are already among the most heavily engineered bodies of water on the planet. The slow, indecisive progress of *Michigan Citizens v. Nestlé Inc.* through the courts, meanwhile, brought attention to just how crowded, conflicted and jurisdictionally leaky is the social software of laws and institutions that attempts to manage these vital water bodies.

The stakes are as clear as spring water. In area, the five Great Lakes are as large as the state of Oregon. Together, they contain nearly one-fifth[6] of all the world's surface fresh water, a volume surpassed only by that of the polar ice-caps and Siberia's smaller (in surface area) but much deeper Lake Baikal.[7] Canada's share represents about 90 percent of all this country's fresh water; America's share is fully 95 percent of its. Forty-three million people live in the Great Lakes Basin or downstream from the Lakes in the St. Lawrence River Valley, including two of every three Canadians. Nearly 30 million of those people drink from the Lakes.[8] From Minnesota to upper New York State, the region's $2-trillion-a-year economy could rank as the third-largest in the world if it stood as a piece.[9] Every day, $750 million CDN worth of trade crosses between the two national shores.[10] Described by awed early explorers as "sweet seas," the Lakes' very greatness has invited their exploitation. There is simply so much water there that anyone looking for some can easily conclude that a little will hardly be missed.

That, certainly, was what business consultant John Febbraro thought in 1997, as he relaxed at his home in Sault Ste. Marie, Ontario, watching television. When an appeal for donations to aid the world's starving and frequently thirsty poor came on the screen, Febbraro thought at once of the broad expanse of Whitefish Bay outside his windows, and the even vaster body of Lake Superior beyond it. "They need water," was his thought, "and literally we look in our backyard and we have tons of it."[11] With the world's poor and thirsty, and his own potential profit, clearly in mind, he found that Ontario's laws at the time provided for the grant of a permit to withdraw water in bulk from a provincial lake. With a partner, he sketched out a plan to charter a tanker, sail it into the middle of Lake Superior, fill its hold with fresh water, and sail it out through the St. Lawrence Seaway to a thirsty world market. And in March 1998, the province of Ontario granted his small company, Nova Group, a permit to do exactly that: withdraw as much as 600,000 cubic metres[12] of water a year from the great lake for export to Asia.

Convinced that his own intentions were both compassionate and financially sound, he made no particular effort to conceal his venture. He was astonished, therefore, when word of the plan triggered a tsunami of outrage among environmentalists, in the leading media of two countries and on the floor of the Canadian House of Commons. Faced with a wall of public opposition and subject to intense pressure from the provincial government, he backed down. Nova surrendered its permit and, eventually, committed never to pursue the sensitive idea again. But once aired, the idea that the Great Lakes might be vulnerable to shipment overseas wouldn't go back in the box. Instead, it revived a debate among policy-makers that has flared up and died down repeatedly over the last century but has never been entirely extinguished.

Attempts have been made to put the issue to bed. As far back as 1909, the International Boundary Waters Treaty between Canada and the United States forbade either country to permit any withdrawal of water from their shared lakes and rivers that would alter the water bodies' level or flow. The treaty was silent, however, on projects like Febbraro's, which, by themselves, would have no measurable impact on the Lakes, even if their accumulation would.

As Peter Annin has retold the conflict in his finely detailed book, *The Great Lakes Water Wars*, a perceived triple threat from the United States breathed new life into the issue as the last century entered its final quarter. In 1976 the U.S. Army Corps of Engineers, at the request of several High Plains states, began a study of "adjacent" water sources that those states could tap into if the Ogallala Aquifer ever ran out. This heavily over-pumped aquifer extends from Texas to South Dakota. On the Corps' map, it's thus "adjacent" to Minnesota, whose shoreline lies along Lake Superior. Then in 1981, an audacious energy company conceived a plan to pump water out of Lake Superior as far as Wyoming, mix it with ground-up coal and pipe the resulting slurry back to Milwaukee and Duluth, where the coal would be settled out and used to fuel Midwestern power plants. Meeting much the same response as John Febrarro's brainstorm 17 years later, the idea was soon withdrawn.

Even with the coal-slurry pipeline off the table, and no Ogallala state actively seeking water from any adjacent area, a decision by the U.S. Supreme Court nonetheless kicked alarm for the Lakes up another notch in 1982. The case didn't deal with any direct threat to the Lakes. In fact, it involved a farmer who had challenged an order from the state of Nebraska to stop piping water from his property there to an adjoining acreage across the border in Colorado.[13] Nonetheless, the Court determined the law for the entire country, ruling that water in bulk was an "article of commerce," and that the U.S. constitutional protection of interstate commerce trumped any state law that sought to prohibit trade in it.

To the governors of the eight Great Lakes states, that looked alarmingly like a declaration of open season on the Lakes' water. Late that same year, they came together at Michigan's Mackinac Island to create a new forum for joint political action, the Council of Great Lakes Governors (into which they promptly invited the Canadian premiers of Ontario and Quebec as associate members). The Council's first act was to declare that no water would leave the Lakes without the sign-off of every one of the U.S. governors and Canadian premiers—and the two federal governments.

That declaration acquired more precise form three years later, when American and Canadian leaders signed on to a commitment to enshrine their agreed-on "principles for the management of Great Lakes water" in a new, basin-wide Great Lakes Charter.[14] It sought to preserve the Lakes' water and wildlife by compelling the states and provinces to manage them cooperatively as one ecosystem. Its American negotiators praised it for giving Great Lakes states a legal "process to say 'no'" to future water demands.[15]

But the Charter had two important flaws. One: while it required all states and provinces in the basin to seek the "consent and concurrence" of the others before green-lighting any "major" new water withdrawal on its territory, nothing in the Charter obliged them to abandon any project that other states or provinces objected to. The second flaw was even more profound: the entire Charter was suggestive only. Nothing bound the American states to make its provisions into law. Even 20 years after the governors signed the document, not all the states had yet turned their nominal commitments into legislation.

With those weaknesses in mind, delegates to Congress from the Great Lakes states took advantage of the periodic renewal of a federal law to fund water mains and sewers (and, not incidentally, to dispense lavish amounts of pork to home districts) to pursue a belts-and-suspenders strategy. They persuaded Congress in 1986 to tack on a two-page amendment that in plain terms prohibited the diversion of any water from the Great Lakes unless all eight Lake-state governors gave their approval.[16] That also sounded like a clear defence against any future threat to the Lakes. But top attorneys warned it would probably collapse under challenge. Its flaw? Lacking either a process for securing (or not) the governors' approval, or a standard by which such proposals might be judged, the new amendment could be struck down as indefensibly "arbitrary and capricious."[17]

That left the Lakes at the mercy of a non-binding Charter that would allow any state (or province) to approve whatever diversion it liked, and a U.S. statute that would probably collapse beneath the first lawsuit that blew up. Nonetheless, with no imminent threat on the horizon, Great Lakes politicians turned to other issues for the next decade—until John Febbraro, after watching a television appeal on behalf of the world's poor, looked out his window at Whitefish Bay. With one unexpected brainwave, the Sault businessman located in the Lakes' cobbled-together defences a loophole wide enough to sail a tanker ship through.

As the significance of his discovery sunk in, the governments of Ontario and Canada hastily introduced new legislation to impose unequivocal bans at both levels on the bulk removal of water not only from the Great Lakes but from any other watershed under their authority.[18] In early 1999, however, a confidential legal report warned the Council of Great Lakes Governors that such a "just say 'No'" approach would probably not stand the test of either U.S. constitutional or international trade law.

Two years of intense negotiations followed. Each of the 10 state and provincial governments had a different view of its stake. Ontario stood to feel the effect of any water withdrawals on the U.S. side, but as the owner of half the shoreline of four of the five lakes, it was also in a position to wield significant leverage. Quebec, by contrast, might value *le fleuve St.-Laurent* as central to its cultural identity, but its downstream location left it little to bargain with. Similarly, the significance of the stakes loomed larger to Michigan, all but surrounded by lake, than to Indiana or Pennsylvania, each with only small exposures to Lakes Michigan and Erie, respectively. When the governors and premiers convened again, in June 2001, to sign an Annex to the Charter, they had managed to agree only that each should apply the same "decision-making standard" to any future request to take more than 100,000 gallons a day (379 cubic metres, about one-third of Nestlé's daily Sanctuary withdrawal) from any of the Lakes. They gave their staff a further 36 months to work out how to make that standard both legally binding and legally defensible. Even so, Michigan negotiator Dennis Schornack promised that the new agreement would "put the kibosh on diversions to the Southwest."[19]

Thirty-seven months later, exhausted negotiators released the draft "decision-making standard" for public comment. Instead of a "just say 'No'" rejection of letting water leave the Lakes (legally indefensible in the United States), it adopted a policy that Peter Annin describes as "occasionally saying yes—as long as there's improvement to the Great Lakes ecosystem."[20] Any new or expanded withdrawal of Lakes water above a million gallons a day—a little more than one and a half Olympic-size swimming pools—would require the approval of every U.S. Lake-state governor.[21] It would also need to meet several stringent tests: that no other alternative be available, that most of the water diverted be returned to the Lakes and that a compensating "improvement" to the Lakes' ecosystem be undertaken in tandem with the withdrawal of water.

As might be expected from any compromise among so many players, affecting millions of individuals and hundreds of thousands of businesses, the draft met less than universal acclaim. On the American side of the Lakes, several interest groups raised objections. Farmers and a few industrial leaders warned that it would destroy jobs. Some environmentalists decried the loss of a state veto for future water withdrawals anywhere in the basin (only five of eight governors would need to approve). Others griped that the new text could make it easier to win approval for water diverted out of the basin than for water withdrawn and recirculated back into the Lakes.

In Canada, however, environmentalists and nationalists erupted in full cry against the document. In a lengthy critique commissioned by the University of Toronto's Munk Centre for International Studies, Alberta environmental writer Andrew Nikiforuk accused the U.S. states, in essence, of attempting to perpetrate a fraud: "Annex 2001 appears to be a regional compact dedicated to protecting the Great Lakes Basin. Yet in real terms it is a water taking permit system designed to minimize conflict among potential water takers."[22] Sara Ehrhardt, a spokeswoman on water for the hyper-nationalist Council of Canadians, a group ever eager to detect predatory American motives hidden in any cross-border accord, called the Annex "nothing more than a unilateral U.S. water grab … a permit to drain the Great Lakes dry." Far from a bulwark against future diversions, Ehrhardt saw the document itself as "the greatest threat facing the Great Lakes."[23]

It probably didn't help that the Annex Implementing Agreements were released into perhaps the most poisonous cross-border political atmosphere in thirty years: Canadians of many political points of view were horrified by the illegal U.S. invasion of Iraq. But in shrilly impugning American motives while preserving a wilful blindness to the realities of the U.S. legal system, the Annex's Canadian critics appeared petulant, parochial and deeply un-pragmatic. By insisting that only a complete ban on any further extraction of the Great Lakes' water could meet their minimum terms, they made the perfect the enemy of the good: a fruitless standard in any political arena.

With admirable doggedness, officials from both sides of the Lakes who had laboured to bring the Annex as far as it had come went back for one last try. In December 2005, the premiers and governors initialled the latest hope for a binding, comprehensive, binational, multi-jurisdictional agreement to protect the Great Lakes from runaway exploitation. Perhaps predictably, it contained even less protection than Canada's nationalists had earlier rejected.

The final-final draft of the compact on the Lakes committed all U.S. Great Lakes states to enact legislation that would:

+ include both ground and tributary water in defining the waters of the Great Lakes Basin;

+ notify other states and seek a non-binding "regional review" before approving new or expanded withdrawals of more than five million gallons a day of water for either diversion or "consumptive-use"[24] purposes;

+ ban *most* new diversions of water out of the Lakes' basin, with the exception, under certain circumstances, of supplies to public water systems in communities that straddle the divide between the Lakes' watershed and adjoining watersheds; and

+ allow water to be exported out of the basin in bottles 20 litres (5.7 gallons) or less in size.[25]

The terms of the final draft would have given Nestlé no reason to fear for its investment in central Michigan: neither the scale of the company's water withdrawals nor its shipments beyond the Great Lakes Basin would trigger the Annex's attention. Nor would future investors who proposed to withdraw even larger volumes of water be required to provide a compensating "improvement" to the Lakes' ecosystems.

After all that, do the legal levees around the Great Lakes hold figurative water? It's still hard to be entirely sure. The American states that signed the 2005 Annex entered a "compact" that could eventually open them to lawsuits if they breached its commitments. If the U.S. Congress one day endorses the deal, as some advocate, its assent would help forestall challenge under the Constitution's "interstate commerce" clause. Ontario and Quebec remain outside the compact, but they committed themselves to making their legislation mirror that of the American states. By mid-2007, the terms of the Annex had become law in only one state (Minnesota), although some state and provincial statutes already contained broadly comparable terms.

The author most familiar with this patchy and still only partly consummated plan to protect the Great Lakes hopes to see the Charter come into force. "As imperfect as it may be, it's the best [regional leaders] have been able to put forth," Peter Annin concludes. "That may, or may not, end up being enough. Regardless, something must be done in order to preserve one of the world's great treasures."[26]

Knee-jerk aqua-nationalism may have driven much of the Canadian antagonism to the Great Lakes Charter Annex. But on both sides of the Lakes another development early in the new century sharpened concern: the water in them seemed to be disappearing.

Most of the water in the Great Lakes has been there for thousands of years: it is what remains of the last ice sheet to cover North America. Only about one percent of the Lakes' volume is replenished each year by rain and snow. That's still a huge amount of water, and the Lakes' vast total volume provides an effective buffer against the inevitable variability of that inflow. Nevertheless, the Lakes have always gone up and down, over short cycles and longer ones. Snow that melts in spring and early summer feeds an annual peak that works its way down the chain from Superior to Ontario and slowly drains away, leaving the Lakes as much as 43 centimetres lower by autumn than they were in summer.

Observations over the past century and a half also reveal at least two cycles that return over periods of years: one reaching a peak roughly every 11 years, the other every three decades or so.[27] Lakes Michigan and Huron, which rise and fall in tandem, were low in the mid-1960s but rebounded to their highest levels in the last century by 1986. At my family's island cottage on Lake Huron, rising water twice forced us to relocate our dock to higher ground. Residents along the eastern shore of Lake Michigan suffered much worse, in some cases watching houses topple into the lake during the period of high water.

In 1998 the level of the three upper lakes began to drop again. Within a year, a 20-metre dock I had helped my father build, lugging boulders along the shore to protect it against the rising waves, barely reached the water. Hundreds of other cottagers and marinas around the Lakes faced the same dilemma, with many of the latter forced to pay for expensive dredging to stay in business. As Lake Huron dropped, so did Michigan beyond it. In Chicago, the falling water exposed century-old timber pilings that anchor the city's great curving breakwater, allowing airborne bacteria to attack the wood; nearly 60 metres of the crucial structure began to collapse.[28] Through most of the new century's first decade, three-quarters of the Great Lakes shipping fleet ran with holds only partly full, sacrificing $6,000 to $12,000 in trip revenue for every inch of draft (their depth below the water-line) they gave up to avoid grounding.[29]

Long-time observers of the Lakes shook their heads at the loss and inconvenience, shrugged and waited for the water to come back up as it always had in the past. But this time, the usual cycle failed to produce a rebound. A succession of dry seasons in the first few years of the new century put little water on the ground to flow into the upper Lakes.

At the Killarny Mountain Lodge and Outfitters on Georgian Bay, where his docks stand on solid granite that can't be dredged, owner Maurice West had to abandon a third of his moorings, giving up $40,000 in seasonal docking fees: "It's very disturbing, and not just from our personal business point of view," he said of the persistent low water, "but from an overall environmental point of view."[30]

Farther south, Rick Zanussi, a township councillor with an island cottage on Parry Sound, bemoaned the fact that "there are many areas we simply can't get to like we once did. The channels are too low."[31] Jim Doran, who bought a house on the shore of Lake St. Clair in 2001, had yet, five years later, to take his boat away from the dock at all. Instead, a rank expanse of garbage, weeds, bottles and dead fish marked his receding waterline. "It's not pretty and it smells," he fumed.[32] By 2007 Lake Superior was at a low point not seen since 1926.[33] Lakes Huron and Michigan had dropped more than a metre from their highs of 1986 and were half a metre lower than their average over the past century and a half.[34]

Disheartening and inconvenient as low water levels are to lakeside homeowners, they pose a more material threat to mariners. Early on a November evening, Captain Ed Harris drove through thickly falling snow down a rough, unlit forest track to an all-but-abandoned industrial wharf on the shore of Whitefish Bay. Burly, homespun and hospitable, Ed's a native of Indiana, and a graduate of the Great Lakes Maritime Academy, who explains his career very simply: "I always liked boats." After decades spent serving the U.S. Coast Guard, he's now in his early fifties, an independent contractor with a licence to navigate lakers and ocean-going "salties" anywhere in the St. Lawrence Seaway. His favorite trip, though, is the short seven-hour passage through the St. Mary's River between Lakes Superior and Huron.[35]

That night we would make the trip together aboard the Polish freighter *Odra*, carrying American wheat. There would be one lock to negotiate, at Sault Ste. Marie, then many miles of confined channel down to Lake Huron. "We're going to have less than a foot [of water] under the hull," Ed anticipated. The St. Mary's River has been the scene of numerous groundings since the Lakes began to drop.

A boat idled in the snow-filled night. A crewman handed me across a hump-backed steel deck to a dark wheelhouse. The boat was elderly and bare, the air heavy with the smell of diesel oil. Diodes glowing on a radio and the sweep of a radar screen provided the only light. As we entered the bay, waves slapped the hull and the radio came to life. "Tell those guys to use caution," the pilot already aboard the *Odra* for its Lake Superior crossing from Duluth advised. "It's just above freezing, and it could flash-freeze on the ladder." Twenty minutes later the running lights of a ship loomed suddenly in the darkness ahead. A floodlight blazed, and the small pilot boat put its nose into a battered black hull where a rope ladder hung down. With both vessels still making way, I scrambled up after Ed onto the larger ship. The pilot boat turned away into the night and we followed a sailor along wet deck plates and up several flights of interior stairs to the darkened bridge.

The pilot already aboard handed control of the bridge to Ed and went off to nap in a borrowed bunk. It was now Ed's job to direct this cumbersome mass of steel and inertia, a ship he had never seen before tonight, through the confines of the lock and the narrow St. Mary's River channel. The movements of a ship in close quarters depend as much on invisible forces around it—crosswinds and water currents—as on the turn of its wheel. Some vessels have twin screws or bow thrusters to make the job easier; this no-frills freighter had only its big single prop. Ed worked it like a *roué*, issuing a series of soft-spoken instructions to the crewman at the wheel: "Port five [degrees] ... Port 10 ... Midships." In the intimate darkness, his calm commands acquired the cadence of long ritual as he brought the huge ship in to kiss the quay above the lock. "Stop engine."

From the wharf below, a line handler called up through the falling snow. "Nasty weather! Whatever happened to that global warming? I was kind of looking forward to that."

The river beyond the lock was very dark. Dimly lit markers, spaced kilometres apart in the blackness, were the only streetlights. I could hear water splash against the shallow lip of the dredged channel. A depth sounder indicated less than half a metre of water beneath *Odra's* churning propeller. The only warning before the ship ran up on mud or rock would be a sucking sound as its worn hull forced water up against the bank. "I can't tell you how many times I've heard that," Ed admitted. "Working by radar and not seeing a thing. It's scarier than shit. That's when I don't like my job at all."

As we left the natural river and entered a long straightaway descriptively known as the Rock Cut, the radio crackled. A duty officer at the Coast Guard station back at the Sault advised Ed that the water in the Cut had dropped seven inches since we passed through the lock just 90 minutes earlier.

The reason had nothing to do with climate change. Rather, the hydroelectric generating plant at the head of the river had closed some of its gates, as it typically did at that late hour. The purpose was to back up water in Lake Superior to drive its turbines during the expected surge in demand for electricity the next morning. But the same gates also control the flow of water into the river below; when some are closed, the flow is reduced. I was reminded of a fact that often seems lost in the Lakes' passionate defense: that these are already some of the most heavily modified bodies of water in the world, helping Canada earn its ranking as the country diverting more water from its natural course than any other on Earth.[36]

Diversions of water from the Lakes began in 1819, with the construction of the Erie Canal from Lake Erie just south of Buffalo to the Hudson River. The first Welland Canal, linking Lakes Erie and Ontario, opened 10 years later. Four years after that, a canal linked Erie to the Ohio River, a tributary of the Mississippi. Over the rest of the 19th century, more canals were added, including the Trent-Severn, which joins Lakes Huron and Ontario, and the Rideau, linking Lake Ontario with the Ottawa River outside the Lakes' basin. Then in 1900, the city of Chicago opened up a channel from the south end of Lake Michigan to the Des Plaines River, another Mississippi tributary, in order to flush its modern new sewer system into that waterway rather than into the lake from which it drew drinking water (sewage entering Chicago's lake water intake had contributed to a typhoid epidemic in the city). The rest of the 20th century witnessed exploits of lake engineering on a much grander scale, mainly in Canada. Dredging in the early part of the century (and then again in the 1960s) deepened the St. Clair River, effectively widening the drain from Lake Huron into Lake Erie. Between 1939 and 1943, Ontario's public hydroelectric utility dammed two large rivers flowing into James Bay, the Ogoki and the Kenogami, redirecting their water south into Lake Superior. Then in the 1950s, a new and much larger Welland Canal was constructed to accommodate ocean-going freighters like the *Odra* as part of the international Great Lakes-St. Lawrence Seaway system.

By the dawn of the 21$^{st}$ century, the Great Lakes were gated and controlled virtually from top to bottom. Although the amount of water flowing through Chicago's Sanitary and Ship Canal (as its dual-purpose channel came to be known) has gone up and down over the years, it alone continues to drain more water out of Lake Michigan every two hours than John Febbraro's tankers would have been allowed to take from Lake Superior in a year. Ontario's Ogoki and Kenogami dams, meanwhile, divert nearly twice as much water into Lake Superior from Hudson Bay as Chicago's Sanitary and Ship Canal flushes from Lake Michigan. Other dams control how much water escapes from Lake Superior into Lake Huron and from Lake Erie into Lake Ontario (and of that amount, how much flows over Niagara Falls, through hydroelectric plants on the Niagara River, or through the Welland Canal), and then how much leaves Lake Ontario and enters the St. Lawrence River. Nearly a dozen more dams micromanage the water flowing through the river channels above and below the island city of Montreal. Nature may provide the Lakes an annual water budget, but humanity long ago assumed control over how it is spent.

Changing weather, however, will soon force all the Lakes' users to reconsider their courses. Before I left the *Odra*, I spent a little time with its Polish captain, Radostaw Sycz, in his office one deck below the bridge. A laptop computer sat on a non-skid pad below a large and incongruous sepia-tone print of a glamorous woman in vaguely Edwardian costume. Captain Sycz had been at sea for half his 48 years, visiting every ocean on the planet at least once, from the Falklands to the Bering Strait to the South Pacific. He's seen their weather change. "The wind blows more because the temperature is higher," he told me. "We can feel it. I can't remember winds so high as in the last five years. In the past it was easier to make forecasts: spring and autumn were windy but winter and summer were calmer. Now you can't recognize whether it's winter or not, because you can expect storms any time."[37]

Granted even that, the conditions his ship had encountered in his first voyage to the Great Lakes had shocked him. "Fifty-five knots

[100 kph] winds on Lake Ontario! Six-metre waves!" His brows lifted in astonishment. "The waves were more than our draft. I never expected it was possible."

The Great Lakes, and those who work or live around them, are witnessing all the weather changes we've examined. Their implications will become more profound as the century advances. No one knows that better than Linda Mortsch. Her childhood was spent near the banks of the St. Lawrence River, at Cornwall, in a house built in 1958 from lumber salvaged from a historic inn that was due to be submerged, along with half a dozen riverside villages, to make way for the St. Lawrence Seaway.[38] Today, she teaches geography at the University of Waterloo, investigating how the changing weather will affect the Great Lakes.[39]

Mortsch first walked me through the Lakes' historic water calendar. Typically, the year begins with most smaller lakes and rivers—and large expanses of the great ones—locked in ice. Snow covers the land. As spring comes, the snow and upland ice melt, releasing a vast pulse of fresh water to make its way down creeks, streams and rivers to the Lakes. Superior, the largest lake, receives the biggest pulse. As the winter's snowmelt flows in, the Lakes' levels rise, with Superior reaching its peak earliest and the lower lakes peaking progressively through the summer until the annual pulse of winter runoff reaches Lake Ontario, usually around Labour Day. As the spring pulse eventually passes into the St. Lawrence River on its way to the Atlantic, the Lakes are at their lowest in December and January, when the cycle begins again.

While that annual charge of fresh water makes its way through the Lakes, two other important things are happening, one at the surface and the other below. At the surface—not only of the Lakes themselves but over the entire landscape of the region—warm summer air draws up immense volumes of moisture through evaporation. Meanwhile, as water near the Lakes' surface warms under the summer sun, deeper, cooler water becomes immobilized, trapped in a process called "stratification." When that happens, water in the lower layer is no longer in contact with air. Over time, its oxygen can become exhausted. Fish die, literally drowning when the water no longer contains enough oxygen to keep them alive. Bacteria able to live without oxygen multiply, sometimes producing noxious gases in volumes big enough to "burp" to the surface.[40] Such so-called "dead zones" afflicted the shallowest lake, Erie, repeatedly in the 1960s and have re-formed in the new century. When autumn gales begin to churn the Lakes, the stratified layers usually break up, restoring oxygen to the depths.

Now this timeless rhythm is changing. Average air temperatures in the Great Lakes region rose by nearly a degree Celsius over the last hundred years, faster than the world average, with most of that increase just since 1985. Winter and spring have warmed even more, with highs in those seasons as much as 4°C above those of the last century. By 2003 places like Sault Ste. Marie and north-central Ontario's Kawartha Lakes were getting a month fewer days below freezing and nearly two months fewer of cold nights each winter than in 1950, but 30 *more* very hot days and nights each summer.[41] Like the first domino in the chain, this rising temperature has had a knock-on effect through the rest of the Lakes' annual cycle, some of it quite surprising.

"We're seeing springtime temperatures that are warmer and earlier," Mortsch says. "We're seeing plants leafing and demanding water earlier." Once summer hits, it now brings three more weeks of oppressive heat, with the mercury hovering above 32°C, than in the mid-20th century. Longer periods without any rain, interrupted by violent downpours, are bringing less rainfall altogether—in some parts of northwestern Ontario, less than half as much as in the 1970s.[42] The moisture imprisoned over summer in the muggy air is finally released through fall and winter, when it comes down now mainly as cold rain rather than snow. The new cycle ends with ice taking longer to form or failing to cover either upland streams or the main bodies of the Great Lakes.[43]

Paradoxically, the ice missing from the Lakes is largely responsible for some residents of the region getting *more* of a winter experience than they've been used to, not less. In October 2006, while most of the Northeast basked in one of the longest, mildest autumns on record, Buffalo and parts of southeastern Ontario were stunned by an overnight storm of thunder, lightning and wind that dropped as much as 60 centimetres of heavy, wet snow. More than 400,000 homes on both sides of the Niagara River went without power, some for days. Snowmobiles delivered emergency supplies to motorists stranded on the New York Thruway. Cross-border truck traffic backed up as crews struggled to reopen the strategic Peace Bridge crossing between Fort Erie and Buffalo.

Climate-change skeptics like tabloid blogger Matt Drudge pounced on the storm as evidence puncturing the scientific consensus that the globe was warming. But the opposite was closer to the truth. Lakes encased in a sheet of ice don't lose much to evaporation, whereas when they remain ice-free, water continues to escape into the air. That's particularly true late in the year, when the first winter blasts of dry Arctic air push south and blow eastward across lakes that are still comparatively warm. The air was dry to begin with. As it warms up over the lakes, its capacity to absorb and hold water vapour shoots up. Under these conditions water evaporates from open surfaces even faster than on a hot summer day when the muggy air is already saturated. Freshly loaded up on lake water, the same winds cross the coastline. Striking land surfaces that are colder than the lake behind them, the air quickly chills, wringing out its water as thick moist snow. "That's why you get snow belts in the lee of the Great Lakes," Mortsch explained.

The extra two weeks of open water on the Lakes each winter, especially when they are concentrated late in the year, create ideal conditions for such lake-effect blizzards. The answer to the Sault line-handler's question, shouted up through floating flakes in the lee of Lake Superior, had been all around him.

The counterintuitive snowfall in late 2006 didn't stay. Within two weeks Buffalo's streets were bare again. With less snow hanging around anywhere in the Lakes' basin, the yearly pulse of melting snow and ice starts earlier and carries less water into the Lakes. As a result, water levels peak earlier but lower than they once did. And once that pulse passes, the Lakes endure many more days of evaporation before ice lays a sheath over their excited molecules. "You end up with lower water levels at the low end," observes Mortsch.

Troublesome consequences rear their heads even before the Lakes drop to previously unseen lows in late autumn. "With warming, [lake water] stratification begins earlier and lasts longer," Mortsch has found, leaving more time for dead zones to develop and expand. Not only does warmer water run out of oxygen sooner, but it may also exceed the upper temperature limits that many marine species can tolerate. Trout, for example, prefer their water cold; few species can survive long in water above 18°C.[44] The American Union of Concerned Scientists has warned that most fishing streams south of the Lakes will lose their trout within the next few decades.[45]

And while summers in the region may be drier overall than in the past, hotter, more humid days produce more thunderstorms and heavy downpours that are equally hard on the environment. More than half the sewer systems in the Great Lakes are of decades-old designs that combine storm water and sanitary drains in the same tunnel, usually separating the two with a low wall. When heavy downpours overwhelm such systems, the storm water overtops the wall and sewage mixes with rainwater, usually to be discharged untreated into a river or lake. When many dry weeks precede a rain, a witches' brew of toxic compounds can build up on land: an excess of pesticides and fertilizer on fields and suburban lawns, lubricants and abraded tire material on streets and highways. A heavy drenching then flushes them all into streams in a single concentrated dose of mingled poisons. Compounding all these effects is simple mechanical erosion, whereby an increase in rain does a disproportionate degree of additional damage. According to one U.S. study, a storm that drops even 10 percent more rain than usual produces more than twice that percentage of additional erosion.[46]

By far the greatest threat to the Lakes, however, comes from the insidious amplification of evapotranspiration (ET). Evaporation already extracts more water from the Great Lakes than all our human diversions combined. Across Ontario, calculated losses to ET claim two-thirds of every centimetre of rain or snow the province receives. The water annually evaporated from Lakes Huron and Michigan is roughly 30 times what the Chicago Sanitary and Ship Canal drains. And ET is on the rise. Plants that become active earlier in the year, and stay active later, begin "breathing" heavily sooner, and do so longer. In some cases, higher temperature and air that is richer in carbon dioxide may also speed up plant transpiration, drawing additional moisture out of the soil and into the air. Scientists who monitored lakes in northwestern Ontario between 1970 and 1990 discovered that as temperatures rose by 1.6°C—more than twice the global average for that period—rainfall declined. But ET ballooned by 50 percent. Annual runoff into Lake Superior plummeted by almost two-thirds, from 40 centimetres to only about 15.[47] The average temperature of the water that remained in that lake rose by 2°C, nibbling away at the extent and duration of the ice that annually shielded it.[48]

If less water flows into the Great Lakes each spring, and more of it is drawn out by ET over longer ice-free seasons, exactly how much lower will the Lakes be at the end of each year? Linda Mortsch has worked with colleagues at Environment Canada and counterparts at the U.S. National Oceanic and Atmospheric Administration (NOAA), crunching numbers generated by the leading climate forecasts to see what they imply for the Lakes by the middle of this century. If she and her colleagues are correct, Lake Superior's seasonal low-water levels could by then fall 38 centimetres below present-day lows. Lake Ontario could drop more, losing 54 centimetres from present-day lows, with the deepest impact in the spring. But Lake Erie, already the shallowest of the five, could fall as much as 85 centimetres below its current low-water level. The flow in some channels between the Lakes, such as the St. Clair and Niagara rivers, could drop by one-quarter by mid-century.[49] Another study has suggested that by then, the St. Lawrence River at Montreal could in some late summers be at barely half its present volume.[50]

Although both those studies looked beyond our 25-year horizon, it's important to remember that they forecast averages. In the variable nature of real weather, certain seasons will deliver actual extremes within the forecast range long before the accumulation of such anomalies over decades changes the long-term average.

Mortsch, who has loved the Lakes ever since her childhood in Cornwall, fears equally for their future and for the millions who rely on them. "We'll have less hydro-power. There will be effects to navigation: shallower shipping channels and reduced access to the locks. Effects on recreational boaters: they get stranded, run aground, can't access their marinas. Issues of water quality and wetlands. All of those things arise out of one impact," she marvels. "And they all will be happening simultaneously."

Peter Annin draws a parallel between the Lakes and the Aral Sea, the huge salt lake in Central Asia that has been reduced to a brackish remnant of its former expanse, in less than 40 years, by ill-considered and rapacious human demands on its tributary rivers. His point is not that the Great Lakes are at immediate risk of the same fate, but rather that "People see how vast the Great Lakes are, and mistake that vastness for invincibility." We must remember, he says, that even "large lakes have limits."[51]

So do large countries. And small planets.

# Chapter 6
## Overdraft:
## In Arms over the Colorado River

I meet Florentino Flores on a warm morning in April. An open boat, scuffed with use and cradled on a trailer, sets his small house of unpainted adobe brick apart from the others like it on the quiet dirt street. A dismounted outboard motor lies on the ground near a tangle of nylon net trimmed with lead weights. A cat stalks out of sight behind one of the outdoor fridges that dominate the cluttered yard. He offers me a wooden chair in the welcome shade of a green canvas umbrella. A faint smell of fish and offal lingers in the dry air. Nearing 60 on the day we met, the hospitable Mexican has been a fisherman his entire life.

I've become acquainted with several fishermen over the years, well enough to know that it's never a soft life. For Florentino, who goes by the nickname Yorimuri, it has gotten harder every year. When he was a young man, he tells me, *humidades*—marshes—extended for miles on either side of the Colorado River main stem, approaching Durango, the rural community where he lives. Side channels ran deep enough that he could launch his boat within 20 kilometres of home. Fish schooled in numbers that made it common to return loaded down with sardines or a dozen 10-kilogram corvina. These days, the sardines have gone and the corvina, a cod-like fish once a staple of meals here at the top of the Gulf of California, are dwindling. "Now, I go all day and come back with one fish, and it's small, maybe two or three kilos," he complains. He has to travel farther too, hauling his trailer as far as 80 kilometres to find water deep enough to take his boat. "And the product sells for the same price as ever."[1]

But it's not the fish that he blames for his woes. It's the insatiable gringos an hour north. And the heedless government in faraway Mexico City that failed to prevent them from building so many dams on the upper Colorado, and so many canals taking its water away to their burgeoning cities, that little now reaches this once-productive delta. "With the years, the desert has come farther and farther, taking over the marshes," he tells me. "There is a catastrophe coming. In five, 10 years, it will be irreversible." He shrugs and pushes out his bristly moustache. "*Es un lástima que el govierno no escucho*" — "It's a pity the government didn't listen to us."

Forty minutes farther down the two-lane blacktop of Mexican federal Highway 5, I turn off on a road barely distinguishable from the surrounding stony desert. A few dozen compact houses, most of them single-storey brick structures plastered in white, run down a rocky slope under scattered pine and palo verde trees, their hard little leaves making wispy clouds around distinctive green trunks. The only other green in the strong afternoon sun comes from a few potted house plants. El Mayor Cucupá is the largest Mexican settlement of the indigenous people who once occupied the Colorado Delta all the way from here back up to Yuma, Arizona, 145 kilometres away to the northeast. Antonia Torres, a woman in her thirties, meets me outside a house where laundry hangs drying from a line. She calls for her grandmother, Inocencia González, and the two women take seats side-by-side on a wrought-iron garden bench. They offer me a white plastic lawn chair (minus the lawn), and Doña Inocencia, a woman in her 80s, tries to picture for me what the Colorado Delta was like when she was young.

The village was farther east from here, closer to where the river flowed. The river had water in it then, and the Cucupá, whose name means People of the River, fished for shrimp and corvina, sometimes catching the occasional cayman crocodile. Hand-dug wells gave them enough water to irrigate corn, squash, chile, cilantro and cabbage, and to keep herds of cattle. "It was like a garden here," she recalls. Then, in the mid-1960s, "as if from one day to the next, everything changed." The water in the river disappeared, sometimes ceasing to flow for months at a time. The wells dried up. With it went the Cucupá's traditional livelihood. Men who could went to work in the fields up toward the border or in construction. In the late 1970s the water unexpectedly came back, but in a brief flood that submerged old El Mayor, forcing its remaining families to relocate to this stony slope. "Everything was destroyed," Doña Inocencia says quietly. Then the water went away and everything dried up again.[2]

Once, the thick reed islands of the Laguna Salada—a large salt marsh west of the Colorado's main channel—teemed with fish, birds and amphibians. Now it is only hard-pan desert where even cactus struggles to survive. A shallow well and lengths of green plastic hose provide the houses of El Mayor with water for washing and a few houseplants; drinking water must be bought by the 20-litre bottle from the truck that comes every few days. Uprooted and deprived of their traditional living, the elderly woman tells me, the Cucupá have begun to turn on themselves: "Different groups fight and quarrel. But no one does anything."

Not far from El Mayor, another road, more dirt than stone, leads to an expanse of baked earth thinly peppered with the tiny leaves of some hardy ground cover. A few mesquite trees cast thin shade outside a cement-block house. Germán Muñoz sits on a cracked cement patio under a broad roof. He gestures me to the bench of a wooden picnic table. His parents farmed here in the 1950s and 1960s, he explains. Their 60 fertile hectares along the Rio Hardy, one of the old Colorado River's numberless side channels, gave them wheat, beans and corn, and provided pasture for cattle and a few horses. The Rio Hardy then was 100 metres wide, he says, and the water was "*dulce*," sweet.[3]

From under his brown ball cap, Germán's weathered eyes cast a troubled look out over the yard where his parents used to grow vegetables. The once-soft earth is baked now to the colour and texture of terracotta tile. As everywhere else in this dispirited region, the water that made the family's land bloom dwindled in the 1960s and early 1970s. When the snow disappeared each spring from the distant Sierras to the north, the river no longer rose in its banks. Sometimes, in seasons when it should have been at full flood, the river disappeared entirely. The land went dry. Salt water from the Gulf worked its way inland and poisoned the family's wells. The crops failed first. Soon there wasn't enough water to keep livestock alive.

On the day we speak, there is still a little liquid at the foot of Germán's barren domain. Four rough *campos turísticos* (rental camps) overlook a motionless channel, perhaps 10 metres wide. Soupy shallows reflect a cloudless blue sky, and birds flit daintily in search of insects. Across the sluggish surface, thick, olive-green shrubs hang over the far bank—invasive saltcedar that has pushed aside the native willow and papyrus reeds. Germán now ekes out a tenuous living for himself, his wife and his teenage son and daughter by renting the cottages out to vacationers from Mexicali, the bursting border city 80 kilometres to the north, or occasionally from over the border in the United States. The tepid liquid below the bank is no longer "sweet," however, nor is it even river water. It is agricultural sewage, drained off irrigated fields higher up the Delta and thickened with salts, manure and traces of fertilizer. And soon it too may disappear. American plans north of the border threaten to withhold water from the aquifer supplying Mexican irrigators. "If the American plan succeeds," Germán says, "the river will dry up. We'll have to leave, abandon this place. Who will buy it?"

About a million people live in booming Mexicali and its dusty working-class residential *colonias*. Nearly one-quarter of a million more live elsewhere in the Delta. Boxed in by the U.S. border to the north, the Gulf of California to the south, the forbidding red and black crags of the Sierra de Juarez to the west and the barren Altar Desert to the east, many of them nonetheless consider their lives a step up on the rest of Mexico. A vast Sony plant turning out colour television sets and circuit boards just off the highway south of town, with other factories that produce electronics, plastics and cement for export to the United States, gives Mexicali one of the lowest unemployment rates in Mexico. Outside the city, 12,000 irrigated hectares of industrial farmland—roughly the area of Hamilton, Ontario, or Tacoma, Washington—support thousands more jobs. Ranking the 10 best Mexican cities (out of 138) in which to live—by economic performance, safety and, strikingly, reliability of water supply—the financial newspaper *Expansión* in early 2007 put Mexicali in a respectable sixth place. Some migrants desperate enough to risk death by dehydration in the desert, abuse at the hands of criminal gangs and arrest by the U.S. Border Patrol, pass through the area on their illegal move toward America, but few start their journey here.[4]

If this is a Mexico that (mostly) works, its continuing viability depends heavily on its future supply of water. Some of that is drawn by canal from the remnants of the Colorado River after it crosses the American border; the rest is pumped from wells. The former has been much reduced over the last century; now new U.S. water projects threaten the second as well. That was too much for Baja California governor Eugenio Elorduy Walther, who angrily warned in March 2006 that the American plans risked causing "*la primera guerra del agua*"—the first war over water—between the two countries.[5]

The belief that wars over water are certain in the near future, strongly reflected in most discussions like this one, may reflect a little too much influence of Rachel Carson and not enough of Lao Tzu. But if water is likely to lead to war anywhere in North America, it is hard to find a better potential theatre than the Colorado River. The 2,330-kilometre river is the vital artery sustaining America's most envied states and fast-growing cities. More than 30 million people in the United States and Mexico count on the Colorado's water. In addition to Mexicali, they live in places like Denver, Las Vegas, Phoenix, Tucson, Los Angeles, San Diego and Tijuana.

Four-fifths of the river's water, however, is harvested for agriculture. The Colorado irrigates pasture land in Wyoming, the cotton rows that stretch implausibly across Arizona's Sonora Desert and

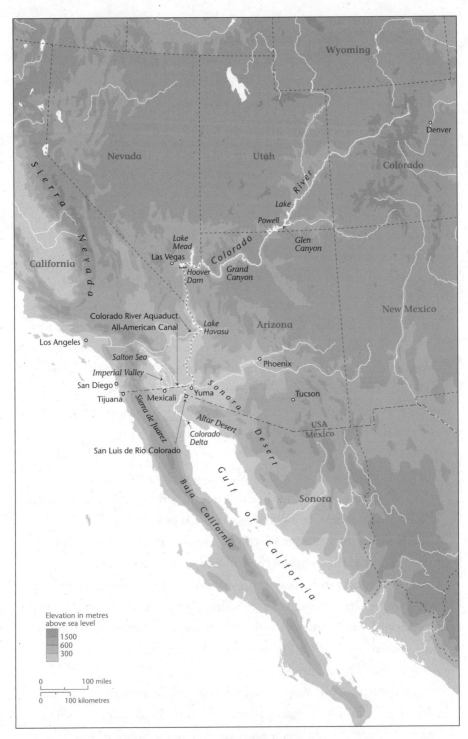

**Colorado River region**

California's Imperial Valley, the source of much of North America's mid-winter bounty of fresh vegetables. The last of these, a flat expanse of land lying below sea level in the extreme south of California, used to have another name more in keeping with its natural geography: *Valle de Muertos*, Valley of the Dead. Its transformation into what author Marc Reisner memorably termed a "Cadillac desert" is a testament to the enterprise, engineering and audacity (to say nothing of an abundance of greed and scallywags) that over the past century caused the Colorado to become perhaps the most litigated, as well as the most regulated, river in the world.[6]

The turn from the 19th to the 20th century in North America was an era of unbounded confidence in the human mission to conquer the wilderness, and of a related boom in speculative common-stock promotions designed at least nominally to finance that mission. The two came together in the Imperial Land Company. Land development syndicates, often closely tied to railroad construction, were riding a bull market as financiers acquired title to vast tracts of barely mapped wilderness seized from Native Americans and promptly resold it to white settlers migrating ever farther west in search of farmland.[7] U.S. government surveyors had crossed the *Valle de Muertos*, which they called the Colorado Desert, as early as the 1850s, marking out the southern border of California. Railway surveyors followed. Both found soil that might have held promise for cultivation had it not routinely broiled under summer temperatures above 42°C, or had it received more than eight centimetres of rain per year.

Late in the century, however, a winter of heavy snow in the Sierras brought the Valley of the Dead unexpectedly to life. Green plants and new shoots sprouted. Marshes appeared in its lowest areas and filled with birds. The transformation caught the eye of smooth-talking Denver businessman John Beatty and a surveyor named Charles Rockwood, who had previously laid out irrigation plans for Washington's Yakima Valley. "We knew," Rockwood wrote in a memoir, "that during the flood of the Colorado River in the year 1891 the overflow had found its way into this territory." Maps drawn by earlier surveyors showed that "not only was there in all probability a large area of fertile land in the valley, but that these lands lay below the Colorado River and could be irrigated from it."[8]

The following year, Rockwood took a new team of surveyors into the desert. He returned convinced that, "without a doubt, one of the most meritorious projects in the country would be bringing together the land of the Colorado Desert and the water of the Colorado River."[9] It took Rockwood (who eventually shed Beatty) another eight years to cobble together financing for his vision. But in December, 1900, the first earth was turned for what would become the Imperial Canal system. In less than 48 months, Colorado River water began to flow down 130 kilometres of main canal. Following a route laid out to take advantage of the natural contours of the land, much of the canal's length actually ran just south of the international border through Mexican territory. The route turned north, however, in time to irrigate the first 27,000 hectares of new farmland entirely on American soil. The *Valle de Muertos* was well on its way to becoming one of the continent's richest agricultural regions. By the turn of the 21st century, the Colorado River was watering an area of former desert twice the size of New York City. Industrial farms manned mainly by Mexicans harvested a billion dollars worth of cauliflower, carrots, broccoli, melons and other table produce, as well as hay, wheat, cotton and livestock, every year.

Since Rockwood's beginning, the rest of the Colorado has been transformed from a free river into one of the most intensely managed watercourses on the planet. Its most famous restraint, the Hoover Dam just south of Las Vegas, has attained iconic status for its scale and bold engineering. The immense reservoir behind it, Lake Mead, is nearly matched in volume by Lake Powell upriver, created by a dam near the Utah-Arizona border in 1963. In addition to those, 37 other dams, weirs and "control structures" block the Colorado between its source in Wyoming and its estuary in Mexico. Together, they have the capacity to hold back more than seven years of the river's annual flow.

The most elaborate of the many pipes that drain the river is the Central Arizona Project, which every second lifts the equivalent of five large tanker trucks of water straight up nearly a quarter of a kilometre over the Mohave Mountains at Lake Havasu and pumps it as far as Tucson, 540 kilometres away to the southeast (passing and serving Phoenix along the way). But by far the biggest gulp taken from the river is on the California side near Yuma, close to where Charles Rockwood sunk his original tap. The canals that run from there now supply not only the Imperial Valley but also half the water that keeps Los Angeles lush and most of what San Diego uses.

Conflict, mainly of the legal and political variety, has dogged this transformation at every step of the way. A series of lawsuits among investors helped stall the original scheme to develop the Imperial Valley. Others have erupted in every decade since. More, doubtless, are still to come.

The Hoover Dam still inspires awe: a vertiginous concrete plug four times higher than Niagara Falls. A memorial to the 96 lives lost in the dam's construction, embedded above it in the sheer rock wall of Black Canyon, evokes the ethos of its age. Sheaves of wheat sprout like wings from behind a naked male torso, whose arms stretch in benediction over a profile of the dam. A dedication reads: "They died to make the desert bloom." Turbines in the powerhouses far below and elsewhere along the river spin out 12 billion kilowatt-hours of electricity a year (about a third of what those on the Niagara River can produce). But it is the Colorado dams' success in bringing life to the desert that has turned the southwestern quarter of America from badlands to dreamland for so many.

Herbert Hoover, then Commerce Secretary of the United States, first proposed building the dam that bears his name in 1921. Businessmen and politicians in the seven states along the Colorado, asking themselves who would profit from the audacious project, quickly stumbled over the unsettled question of which of them owned what share of the river's water. As long as most of it had flowed unchecked from the mountains of Wyoming through the Grand Canyon to the Gulf of California, and the only diversion was just upstream from Mexico (about which none of them gave a damn anyway), the question hadn't been material. But with Hoover proposing to capture the river between Nevada and Arizona and extract electricity from it, the issue became pressing.

In January 1922, Hoover invited representatives from all seven Colorado Basin states to a lodge in New Mexico. It took him 11 months of talking to secure even the rough draft of a deal, but by November he was able to announce a basic agreement. Estimating the Colorado's average annual flow at 21.5 billion cubic metres (or 17.4 million acre-feet [AF], the usual measure in the western United States), Hoover's compromise awarded a total of 9.25 billion cubic metres (7.5 million AF) to the "lower" basin states of California, Arizona and Nevada and an equal amount to the "upper" basin states of Wyoming, Colorado, Utah and New Mexico. How the states in each basin would divide their respective shares was put off for future negotiation. At the last minute, the Americans also agreed to allow Mexico, which had not been invited to join the bargaining, to receive 1.85 billion cubic metres (1.5 million AF) of the river's water each year, roughly eight percent of its estimated flow.

This deal, known as the Colorado River Compact, has in the decades since acquired an authority approaching Mosaic Law among competing water interests in the American portion of the Colorado watershed. The numbers, as we'll see in a moment, turned out to be important. But in the immediate aftermath of Hoover's marathon bargaining session, politics dominated. As soon as the negotiators got back to their respective statehouses, the Compact began to crumble. After three years of wrangling, the four upper basin states came to terms on how to divide their share of the river. But Arizona, which claims nearly half the river's length as its northern and western frontiers, refused to close a deal with its lower-basin partners, especially thirsty California.

In the end, Congress had to bring the hammer down. In 1928 it passed a law that would activate the Compact as soon as six of the seven river states ratified it, effectively sidelining Arizona's protests. At the same time, Congress approved funding for Hoover's dam, others elsewhere on the river, aqueducts, and a new canal from Yuma to Los Angeles. Responding to frankly xenophobic lobbying from Southern California, however, Congress decreed that this new canal would run entirely north of the border. In recognition of that route, it would come to be called the All-American Canal. Eighty years later, those decisions haunt the Colorado, its many users and two nations.

Federal intervention didn't end friction over the river, even among Americans. Arizona, which continued to defy the Compact, twice came close to igniting a real shooting war over California's claim to the river. In 1928 and again in 1935, Arizona's governors called out the state's National Guard to erect machine guns on its bank of the Colorado in futile attempts to stop engineers from laying the groundwork for the Hoover Dam and later for the Parker Dam, designed to divert more water to Los Angeles. Lawyers for the state made repeated trips to the Supreme Court. It wasn't until March 1944, nearly 22 years after the Compact was first negotiated, that Arizona's legislature finally voted to accept it.

Just a month earlier, Mexico had also reluctantly agreed to the Compact's division of the Colorado. Moreover, in a concession its citizens may come to regret bitterly in the decades ahead, it agreed to accept a reduction in its "guarantee" of water in proportion to any future decline in the river's total flow. In putting his pen to a treaty "with respect to the waters of the Colorado," President Francisco Castillo Nájera tacitly conceded that while nature may once have borne 100 percent of the great river's water to Mexico, geography gave America the ability to stem its flow at any moment, while the imbalance of power between the two left him little choice but to be politely grateful for whatever dribbled through.

As dams multiplied on the upper river, however, the quality as well as quantity of water reaching the Delta declined to a point that tested even Mexican patience. Withdrawn as many as 18 times to irrigate fields, rinse bodies and flush toilets, then returned to the river, the liquid that reached the border had become so soiled, particularly from its last pass through Arizona's salty earth, that by 1960 farmers who applied it to crops in the Delta saw their plants shrivel and die. Then, in 1963, the gates on the huge new dam at Glen Canyon were closed to fill Lake Powell. Water levels in the river plummetted, and even though Mexico continued to receive its treaty-guaranteed flow, the concentration of salt in the water skyrocketed. "We were giving the [Mexican] farmers slow liquid death to pour on their fields," one American river official, cited in *Cadillac Desert*, admitted to Reisner.[10]

By the end of the 1960s, thousands of hectares of farmland around Mexicali had been rendered sterile. The local economy (far more reliant then than now on agriculture) neared collapse. Farmers rioted at the gates of the U.S. port of entry, burning hundreds of American visas to dramatize their anger. Finally, in 1973, 12 years after Mexico's first official protest on behalf of its beleaguered farmers, the United States agreed in an addendum to the 1944 treaty to ensure that the water reaching Mexico would be at least as pure as that drawn off to the Imperial Valley.

Mexico had not been passive itself in exploiting the river. In 1950 it built its own dam, *presa Morales*, just south of Yuma. The Morales Dam was and is meant to capture Mexico's share of the Colorado's water for delivery to Mexicali (and now Tijuana as well) and to farmers in the northern Delta. But it is there, still 145 kilometres from the sea, that a deeper problem with Herbert Hoover's achievement comes stubbornly to the surface. His estimate of the Colorado's average annual flow, the key number on which the multi-state river Compact, the international treaty with Mexico and the whole vast array of dams, canals, aqueducts and pumps were later commissioned, turns out to be simply wrong. It greatly overestimated how much water would flow down the Colorado over the course of the 20th century. Worse, that embedded error is widening as the weather changes in the current century.

Some of the original mistake may have been a fudge to make the numbers work diplomatically. When Hoover and his counterparts spent the summer of 1922 haggling over how to allot roughly 21.5 billion cubic metres (17.4 million AF) per year of river water, they claimed to rely on records kept over the previous 17 years (between

1905 and 1922) at Lee's Ferry, a landing on the riverbank just above the Grand Canyon. When the U.S. Geological Survey reviewed the same records much later, however, it found that what they actually show is an average flow during those years of only 19.9 billion cubic metres (16.1 million AF).[11] The difference (1.6 Bm³/1.3 MAF) is suggestively close to the volume of water (1.85 Bm³/1.5 MAF) that the negotiators decided at the last moment to award to Mexico.

Even if we set that discrepancy aside, there was a much bigger problem with the numbers Hoover's bunch used: the 17 years they sampled would turn out to be the wettest in the 20th century. Over the next 79 years, the Colorado would reach or exceed the anticipated "average" flow only 10 times. In the four decades after 1963, the river's real average flow was only 15.3 billion cubic metres (12.4 MAF), less than three-fifths of what the Compact allocated. Or to put it another way, Hoover and his buddies gave away at least 40 percent more water than really flows down the Colorado.

At first, this didn't matter much; none of the parties to the Compact except California was calling on its full entitlement. But as cities from Denver to Tijuana have grown, so have demands on the river. Every state along the Colorado came closer to extracting every litre of water the Compact allows, and the gap between what was assumed to be in the river and what is became apparent. It could also no longer be overlooked that Hoover's distribution of the Colorado's water had left nothing for the living river itself.

Thanks to the many large reservoirs that capture and store water from the few years of above-"average" precipitation, the states of the Southwest have managed to keep their hoses, car-washes and patio-spritzers from running dry. The same cannot be said for the river. While Lake Powell was filling in 1964, gauges at San Luis de Rio Colorado, a Mexican border town 50 kilometres south of Yuma and downstream from the Morales Dam, registered no water in the river at all from June until mid-October. The same thing happened the next year and again, for a shorter period, in 1966. In the late 1970s the river again went dry; on only four days between March and December 1978 did any water at all flow past San Luis.[12]

River deltas are, by definition, places created by water. In the summer of 1922, while Hoover was carving up the Colorado's water at his lodge in New Mexico, naturalist Aldo Leopold, sometimes described as the "father of modern ecology," was travelling its delta by canoe. Leopold describes what he saw:

> On the map the Delta was bisected by the river, but in fact the river was nowhere and everywhere, for he could not decide which of a hundred green lagoons offered the most pleasant and least reedy path to the Gulf. So he traveled them all, and so did we. He divided and rejoined, he twisted and turned, he meandered in awesome jungles, he all but ran in circles, he dallied with lovely groves, he got lost and was glad of it, and so were we.[13]

In Leopold's time, the Colorado Delta was a verdant patchwork of green and blue, half again as large as Florida's Everglades. Three hundred different species of birds lived there or passed through during their annual migrations. Shrimp, corvina and other marine life found a nursery in its marshes and coastal lagoons. Caymans and leopards capped its elaborate marine and terrestrial food chain.

Today the Delta is very different. "Since the last century, we've gotten one percent of all the water that would have come in the past," says Alejandro Olivera, a director of Greenpeace Mexico and a campaigner on the Delta's behalf.[14] Water is now difficult to find. Gravel wasteland thinly grown with salt pine, mesquite, palo verde and willow has replaced most of Leopold's green lagoons. Rubbish, brought here because dumping it is cheaper than paying local refuse fees, blows and drifts in the dry hollow of former river channels. Sometimes people burn their garbage, and the fire spreads quickly into the dry scrub, blackening branches and littering ashes over hundreds of metres. Where water exists beneath the surface, it is now frequently seawater, pushing ever farther inland as the freshwater aquifer fails to recharge.

The wetlands that survive on waste water from farms around Mexicali and southern Arizona are less than one-tenth of what once flourished. The caymans and leopards are on the brink of extinction, the resident waterfowl endangered and the flocks of migratory geese and ducks either vastly reduced or relocated. Ironically, many of the birds now stop instead at the Salton Sea, California's largest salt lake, created when a massive flood on the Colorado ruptured Rockwood's first canal in 1905, causing the river to spill for the next two years into the lowest reaches of the former *Valle de Muertos*.

Not only is the Delta dying, but it is disappearing as well. As sediment that used to flow down the river collects instead at the bottom of upstream reservoirs, surf at the Delta margins is washing it away faster than it is accreting.

Working my way east from Mexicali on a four-lane highway that parallels the U.S. border a few miles to the north, I drive for an hour past industrial cropland and dusty towns dominated by farm equipment and truck-repair shops. As I approach San Luis de Rio Colorado, the highway climbs onto a long, modern bridge. A sign tells me I'm crossing the Rio Colorado, but all I can see beyond the guardrails is scrub. Over the bridge I find a street that leads north two short blocks to where a strip of bare red dirt follows the fence along the U.S. border, here a bleak, graffiti-scrawled barrier of corrugated steel six metres high, topped with floodlights. I turn left, back toward the river. The lane along the border ends where saltcedar grows up a dusty bank armoured with broken concrete. Leaving my car, I pick my way down the bank and step onto grey sand.

I walk out onto the bed of the Colorado River. Midway between its banks I stop. I look up to where the snow must be melting in the Sierras beyond Yuma, then back south to where the Delta waits, as it always does, for the spring flood. I see the tracks of vehicles and footprints in the sand, a rusting muffler, but not a drop of water. I see the ghost of a river.

The American Southwest continues to add subdivisions, shopping centres and industries while the Colorado River continues to drop.[15] The two trends are on an apparent collision course, imperilling not only the Delta but also the whole glittering structure erected on Hoover's flawed, if not fraudulent, accounting. Reisner's Cadillac is in the role of Thelma and Louise's Thunderbird, with the dry, empty canyon playing itself.

Take the highway south from Phoenix and you first cross a desert where spiky yucca shimmer in the heat above bare gravel. Then you come to Maricopa. As you approach the bursting bedroom community, a cluster of coloured banners, in moist shades of green, blue and light yellow, draw the eye to billboards inviting you to inspect the latest dream houses available "from the low $200's." The desert ends at a four-metre masonry wall the same dun colour as the sand. Above it peak the rooftops of new two-storey houses. The tallest points in town seem to be the huge American flags that flutter here and there against the sky. The effect weirdly recalls a stockaded fort from an old western movie.

Between 1990 and 2000, Arizona's population grew by 40 percent, three times the U.S. national average. The pace of development was in step with that of the rest of the American Southwest. Colorado's population soared by almost one-third in the 1990s. Its biggest city, Denver, expects two million more residents by 2020 and plans to build a pipeline like Arizona's to the Colorado River to put water in their taps. Utah sees its population doubling over the next 40 years and wants to put its own pipe into Lake Powell to serve the additional households. California expects to add 14 million people by 2030, increasing its thirst for water by 40 percent. Las Vegas, home to 70 percent of Nevada's population, claims to be the fastest-growing urban area in the United States.[16]

Many of the new houses being added everywhere are also larger than the dream homes of the past, and use more water. Per-capita water use in Southern California went from 160 gallons (650 litres) a day in the early 1990s to 200 gallons (760 litres) early in the new century. Along with the new houses have come sprawling new office and industrial campuses, box stores, fashion malls and restaurants. They all use water too.

With warmer temperatures it's not only the people of the Southwest that are using more water. Plants transpire more actively too. Exposed reservoirs evaporate faster, losing seven percent more water for every extra degree of average air temperature. By the turn of the century, the Colorado was losing more water from its artificial lakes to the thirsty air than it delivered to Mexico.[17] By 2010, the trend suggested, the river's true average annual flow would sink to 7 billion cubic metres (6 million AF), less than one-third of the volume river states and Mexico believed themselves entitled to under the Compact.

The Southwest has seen recurring runs of years when precipitation has been far below what used to be considered average. Whether these constitute temporary dry spells or a new normal is hotly debated in the region. "'Drought' is a misnomer," says Mark Bird, a former water planner for the U.S. Department of the Interior who now teaches at the Community College of Las Vegas and campaigns for a revolution in the region's thinking about water. "This is permanent."[18]

It certainly looks that way at Lake Mead. Visiting Nevada to see for myself, I drove south out of Las Vegas, passing a bare, baked hillside where earth movers and surveyors were levelling million-dollar lots to expand the luxuriant "Lake Las Vegas" enclave that counts Céline Dion among its wealthy residents. Ten minutes farther on, I entered the Lake Mead National Recreation Area. The freshly paved two-lane highway twisted around hillsides the colour of brick, crossing bone-dry washes where posted warnings to beware of flash floods seemed incongruous. At a sign I turned off the highway toward Lake Mead Marina.

The parking lot immediately off the highway had a disused air. A notice indicated that it was for overflow accommodation only. Just beyond it, brown plants fringed a stony lip along the contour of the land in either direction. Patchy extensions to the paved roadway ran down a long slope of raw-looking sand and gravel to the distant water. I parked at the bottom and walked across tethered floats to the blue-painted buildings on barges that served as the marina office, store and restaurant. At my feet, fat grey catfish and striped bass glided languidly through clear, shallow water.

The store carried the usual marina assortment of fishing lures, boat gear, T-shirts, ice and beer. A petite woman in a sweater sitting behind the counter put down a local newspaper to talk to me. The stony edge up near the overflow parking lot, Kathy Sedlock told me, was Lake Mead's shoreline back in 1999 when she moved here from chilly Philadelphia. Since then the lake has dropped more than 27 metres. Every time it's dropped more than two or three metres, the marina that used to be steps away from the parking lot up by the highway has had to move farther down the hill. "I've worked here four years," she said. "It's moved 10 or 15 times." A long scree of broken rock, higher than the tallest sailboat at the docks, enclosed the marina. In the low January sun, it cast a lengthening shadow. It used to be the harbour breakwater, Kathy said, submerged except for a metre or so in the lake. She drew my eye to a structure that jutted out from the stony ridge far back up toward the highway; in the distance it looked like an extra-wide diving platform over a hillside of rocks and scrubby brush. "They used to fish from that," she marvelled.

The U.S. National Park Service has spent $21 million moving its own boat ramps, docks, sewage outlets and water intakes to follow the retreating lake. The Bureau of Reclamation acknowledges that years of drawing out more water than flows into Lake Mead and Lake Powell have left both giant reservoirs barely half full. Even that, Mark Bird argues, is misleading. The silt and sediment that no longer reach the Colorado Delta have been collecting at the bottom of the two giant reservoirs, along with sunken boats, lost lures, millions of beer cans, at least one aircraft and a few skeletons. The accumulation has significantly reduced the reservoirs' capacity to the point that, by 2006, Bird has calculated, Lake Mead was really only about 39 percent full of water; Powell, 37 percent.

It would take decades of above-average rain and snowfall to refill the great reservoirs, but they are nowhere in the forecast. With the Colorado River dwindling and cities counting on ever larger withdrawals to grow, some predict the taps will gush until they simply run dry. Bird, a frequent critic in print of the Southwest's water policies, believes that "a massive confluence of evidence points to a looming catastrophe." He foresees water bills jumping by half overnight, the same for hydroelectricity generated at Colorado dams and "a 50-percent increase in the cost of food grown in Southern California." He expects nothing less than the "economic collapse of California."[19]

Bird's a citizen-activist, the kind you often find across the barricades from bulldozers clearing the way for more houses or a new business. But even entities that have long regarded it as their mission to cheerlead for perpetual growth now admit that trouble looms. Four of the Colorado Basin's biggest water providers concluded after a study that their millions of customers face "recurrent drought" in which "conflict among existing and new water users will prove endemic."[20]

Brad Udall is a professor at the University of Colorado and an expert in assessing western water resources for the National Oceanic and Atmospheric Administration (NOAA). He compares the self-confident southwest to a certain celluloid star caught in what he calls a "Wile E. Coyote" moment. "You know, where he's off the edge of a cliff and dangling there before he plummets. The way it works, [the basin states] won't know they went over their allocation of water before they're well over it."[21]

When the taps do begin to gurgle and Southwesterners discover they have written cheques on an account the Colorado can no longer cash, they are unlikely to spare concern, much less additional water, for the river's perishing delta in Mexico. Indeed, the most energetic things the U.S. states were doing early in the new century to put that day off would have the certain if unintended effect of reducing even further the small amount of Colorado River water that still flowed south of the border.

Graders, dump-trucks and dozers growled out over the desert in June 2007 to begin a long-delayed project to twin the leaky old earth-and-gravel All-American Canal with a modern new channel.[22] One strand in a complex arrangement among San Diego County, Imperial

Valley irrigators, the water utility serving Los Angeles, the State of California and the U.S. Bureau of Reclamation, the idea is for San Diego to pay to replace the equivalent of 37 kilometres of the old canal (and 56 kilometres of one almost as old that serves Los Angeles), with a new channel of leakproof cement, receiving in exchange the water that presently seeps out of both canals—an estimated 96 million cubic metres (77,700 AF) a year, or about enough to supply 90,000 families at current California consumption rates—for the next century.[23] Through American eyes this is a straight-up case of saving water formerly "wasted" in order to avoid dimming the lights on the region's lifestyle. Or, as a boosterish description on the San Diego County Water Authority website put it, "avoid economically damaging reductions in water use."

The same argument is made to justify a separate plan to capture 74 million more cubic metres (60,000 AF) of water that now flows over the border. It involves another offset: in this, the Southern Nevada Water Authority (SNWA), which serves Las Vegas and suburbs, will pay for a reservoir to be built in Southern California near where the All-American Canal leaves the river. Presently, when farmers in southern Arizona and the Imperial Valley need extra water, they must call up operators at Lake Mead and ask for its release from the reservoir there. It takes the water three days to flow downriver to where it was requested. Sometimes it rains during that time, and the released water can't be used on already-wet crops. Nor can it be stored. Instead, it flows on to Mexico—in excess of the amount guaranteed to that country by treaty. The new reservoir will capture those "lost" releases for farmers to use later. In return, Nevada will get to withdraw a corresponding amount from Lake Mead for its own use. Another "leak" stopped. Or, as SNWA general manager Patricia Mulroy described it, another "efficiency measure" that will be "good for the entire river basin."[24]

A third American plan to squeeze more water from the river revives a scheme borne out of the salinity crisis of the 1960s and '70s. At that time, after guaranteeing to deliver water to Mexico no saltier than the water it sent its own farmers, the U.S. Bureau of Reclamation designed and eventually built a plant at Yuma to desalinate waste water recovered from irrigated areas of the (highly saline) southern Arizona desert. It hoped to use the desalted water to satisfy, at least in part, its treaty commitment to Mexico. Instead, when the plant was finally switched on in late 1991, the process was found to be much more expensive than predicted. A burst of relatively wet years reduced the need for the plant and, by coincidence, damaged several of its collection canals; it was mothballed. In this 21st century, however, the Colorado's flow has resumed its long-term decline and the value of water to the Bureau's U.S. clients has gone up. In early 2007 tests began to put the Yuma plant back into use. Yet more "wasted" water will be "recovered" and delivered to Mexico as part of its treaty-capped guarantee.

Except, of course, that none of the water has ever been truly "wasted." The agricultural runoff from Arizona's irrigated desert that was—and now once again is—to supply the Yuma desalinator flows over the border into Mexico's Sonora State. There it provides between two-thirds and three-quarters of the water sustaining the Delta's last surviving wetland of any size: the *Ciénega de Santa Clara*, a saltwater marsh three times the size of Manhattan that is home to herons, flycatchers, pelicans and more than 220 other bird species, many rare and endangered. *Birder's World Magazine* called the seasonal stopover for one-third of a million migrating ducks and geese a "world-class bird-watching marsh ... arguably the best wetland along the Colorado River."[25]

The water that leaks from the All-American Canal serves to recharge the Mexicali Aquifer. The leakage was expected when Congress voted to build the canal in 1928 and, in part, replaces the benefit of periodic natural floods such as the one that first drew Charles Rockwood to the *Valle de Muertos*. The occasional inadvertent release of water intended for Imperial Valley may exceed the terms of the 1944 treaty, but it certainly does not exceed the thirst of the Delta, whose rights to the river, if any, that treaty failed to consider.

A very little of the Colorado's water could go a long way toward bringing the Delta back to life. One expert working to save the remaining reed beds and native willow riverbanks believes that just the amount to be captured in the new Nevada-funded reservoir, about one percent of the revised predictions of river flow, would resuscitate the 145 kilometres of riverbank from San Luis de Rio Colorado to the sea.[26] Yet that would require not only concessions from the United States but also a binding commitment from the Mexican water managers at the Morales Dam to forego their present practice of capturing the occasional American water spill for the benefit of their subscribers in Mexicali and Tijuana. On neither count is there much reason for optimism.

"Mexican farmers have no legal rights to the leakage from the All-American Canal," the executive director of California's powerful Water Resources Control Board, Celeste Cantú, has insisted.[27] "That water belongs to the Imperial Irrigation District. We must protect that water and not let it go to waste."[28] J. C. Davis, a spokesman for the SNWA, explained to me that it would do no good to release the water his agency proposes to capture into the Delta, since "that inadvertent flow doesn't get to the Delta. It might, if the folks in Mexicali weren't just gobbling it up."[29] When the publicly owned Central Arizona Project (the agency that maintains the pumps at Lake Havasu) reviewed what it called the "critical" need to restore the Delta, it began, rather remarkably, with the precondition that "Basin states … should not contribute any additional Colorado River water" for the purpose.[30]

The situation bears multiple ironies. Another side to the All-American Canal agreement is that urban water consumers will pay to fallow fields in the Imperial Valley so that San Diego can use that water too. There will be funds to mitigate the loss of field runoff to the Salton Sea. When it was suggested that a little be spent to help restore the Delta, from whose lost water the Sea was created, Irrigation District director Lloyd Allen was indignant. "I would hate to see funds go to other places," he objected. "Like Mexico."[31]

Across the river, the Delta's last living saltwater marsh of any consequence is as much an accident of human engineering as the Salton Sea. The *Ciénega de Santa Clara* did not exist before irrigation water was brought to southern Arizona, and runoff from the fields there began to trickle over the border. As most native habitat farther south turned to desert, however, the Delta's wildlife has adapted, adopting the new, albeit artificial, saltwater marsh as a home. With much of their traditional economy destroyed or damaged by changes, so have some people. At Ejido Luis Encinas Johnson, the local farm cooperative operates a side business guiding birdwatchers and other ecotourists through the *Ciénega*.

America's plans to restart the Yuma desalinator now threaten that venture too. Juan Butrón is one of the founders of the enterprise. "I have to say it hurts when we go to the other side and see how much water, how much wealth they have there," he admits. "We only want what is fair, and I am afraid we will have to fight to get it."[32]

"Whisky is for drinking," Mark Twain once tartly observed. "Water is for fighting over." Juan Butron no more has an army to throw into battle than does Governor Elorduy, over the state line in Baja California. But water figures in a long history of conflict: the very word "rival" comes from a Latin root meaning "one who takes water from another's stream." One U.S. expert on water has documented more than a hundred instances of blood being shed for it over four millennia.[33] No wonder that "war over water" is such an insistent theme in so many discussions of this most strategic resource. It was Egyptian Minister of State for Foreign Affairs Boutros Boutros-Ghali, later to lead the United Nations as Secretary-General, who predicted in 1988 that "The next war in our region will be over the waters of the Nile, not politics."[34] (Of course, he spoke before George W. Bush took office.) Nearly two decades later, a panel of retired U.S. generals including General Anthony Zinni, charged by a Virginia consulting company with assessing the threat to America's security from climate change, identified conflict over water and other resources as the most destabilizing threat.[35] "We're going to have a war over water," flatly predicted Terry Root, a senior research biologist at Stanford University's Woods Institute for the Environment. "There's just not going to be enough water around for us to live with and provide for the natural environment."[36]

Good reasons exist for this apprehension. The U.S. National Intelligence Council is a CIA unit charged with long-range thinking. "By 2015," it observed in a report on emerging security threats, "nearly half the world's population—more than 3 billion people—will live in countries that are 'water stressed'—mostly in Africa, the Middle East, South Asia and northern China ... A number of developing countries will be unable to maintain their levels of irrigated agriculture ... Measures undertaken to increase water availability and to ease acute water shortages ... will not be sufficient to substantially change the outlook." Although water, the Council insisted, has not, in modern times, been the overt *casus belli* between nation-states, "as countries press against the limits of available water, the possibility of conflict will increase."[37] The odds of violence can only escalate where changing weather attacks traditional occupations, turns more farm land to desert, and exposes other areas to wildfire, gales and torrential rains.

Natural and political geography add to the risk of conflict. More than 260 rivers cross international borders, and one-half of the earth's land surface lies in watersheds that are shared, like the Colorado and Great Lakes basins, between two or more countries.[38] Forty percent of the world's people live in those regions, in dozens of countries that rely on the restraint or goodwill of upstream neighbours for a third or more of their water. Numerous authoritarian or military regimes depend, for two-thirds or more of their nation's water, on rivers that flow from elsewhere.

The Middle East, already seething with economic frustration, homegrown sectarian and political tensions, historic resentments and blowback from American military misadventure, is especially at risk. That is really nothing new. The oldest war from which history preserves a written armistice erupted in what is now Iraq, when the city-states of Lagash and Umma took up arms over the water of the Euphrates. The treaty in question (now lodged in the Louvre) failed to settle matters, and intermittent warfare continued for a century and a half.[39] That conflict flared up 5,100 years ago. In this century, one United Nations assessment recorded that "since 1950, approximately 80 percent of all violent disputes over water resources globally have occurred in the Middle East."[40]

A score of Middle Eastern countries, Israel among them, are among the world's most water-stressed nations. Indeed, according to the World Resources Institute, "the Near East 'ran out of water' in 1972, in the sense that since then the region has withdrawn more from its rivers and aquifers every year than is being replenished. Jordan and Yemen withdraw 30 percent more from groundwater supplies than is replenished every year, and Israel's annual use exceeds supply by 15 percent."[41]

Amplifying the potential for conflict, up to three-quarters of Israel's water is pumped from land seized from Palestinian or Syrian owners in the West Bank, Gaza and Golan Heights. Former Israeli prime minister Ariel Sharon remarked once that he believed Israel's diversion of the Jordan River in 1964 created the conditions that led to the Six Day War three years later. When, in 2002, Lebanon began pumping water from a spring on its own territory that happened also to feed a river that flows into the Sea of Galilee, Israel's largest surface source of fresh water, Sharon threatened military strikes to destroy the pump facility.[42] The attack did not happen then. But Israel did destroy the facility later, during its brief 2006 war against Hezbollah militants operating from southern Lebanon.

Other Middle Eastern leaders have made it similarly clear that they were prepared to go to war for water. The Nile, which flows through eight other countries, including Sudan and Ethiopia, before reaching Egypt, is effectively that country's only source of water, providing 97 percent of its supply. Shortly after a historic peace settlement with Israel at Camp David, Egypt's then-strongman Anwar Sadat declared, "The only matter that could take Egypt to war again is water."[43] Syria, whose army faced off with Iraq's during a 1975 confrontation over the Euphrates, has more recently taken issue with efforts by Turkey, its neighbour upstream, to divert at least a third (in dry years, even more) of the same river's water to expand that country's irrigated acreage.

Iran and Afghanistan have bickered for a century over the Helmand River,[44] whose intermittent flow sustains desperately poor farmers in both countries. Tensions rose there again with the return of dry conditions in 2006. Kazakhstan has objected to China's plans to divert additional water from the Ili River, as putting at risk Central Asia's fourth-largest lake, Balkash, which lies in Kazakh territory. If the Chinese proceed with their diversion, Kazakhstani scientist and government advisor Natalia Vorobeova has warned, "There'll be more desert. It will be just the same as around Aral. And Aral was less populated than here. This is a very populated area. Emigration will start, people will move. It will be a catastrophe."[45]

Pakistan has suffered as the Indus River, its most important source of surface water, fell in the new century to barely one-quarter of its earlier flows. The Indus is so heavily drawn down to irrigate Pakistani cotton and food-crop fields that, like the Colorado, it is often sucked dry long before it reaches the sea. But shortages have sharpened Pakistan's long-standing rivalry with India, which captures Indus water in upstream dams to generate electricity and extracts more to irrigate its own breadbasket in the Punjab. "A water war between India and Pakistan," leading Pakistani newspaper columnist Asif Mir has gloomy predicted, "is inevitable in the future."[46] Both potential belligerents have nuclear weapons.

Scores of other rivers are similarly subject to rising rival demands: the Brahmaputra, which flows from China into India and then into Bangladesh; the Ganges (India and Bangladesh again); and the Okavango (shared as a border between Angola and Namibia before it disappears into marshland in Botswana). In these and many other arenas, the coming storms, floods and megadroughts cannot help but exacerbate the friction from any upstream advantage-taking, imbalances of power, injury or injustice. But friction, even heavily salted with injury and injustice, does not lead inescapably to shooting war, as the calm prevailing at the mouth of the Colorado clearly demonstrates.

Water is only one of a scourge of other provocations in the Middle East's continuing nightmare. Elsewhere, nations drawn to war primarily over water may prove rarer than some fear. It is likely "only in a narrow set of circumstances," believes Thomas Homer-Dixon, a Canadian expert on conflict over resources. "The downstream country must be highly dependent on the water for its national well-being; the upstream country must be able to restrict the river's flow; there must be a history of antagonism between the two countries; and, most importantly, the downstream country must be militarily much stronger than the upstream country.

"There are, in fact, very few river basins around the world," Homer-Dixon adds, "where all these conditions hold."[47] His conditions for conflict can be found on the Jordan and the Nile, but not in other river basins such as those of the Indus or Euphrates. None of the rivers that entwine the Canada-U.S. border meets more than two of Homer-Dixon's tests. Nor does the Colorado.

Even so, every action begets its reaction, even if the consequences of coercion sometimes come in through a side door.

Before I left the Delta, I dropped into the tidy one-storey building occupied by the *Delegación Venustiano* Carranza municipal government. In an empty meeting room furnished with a bare desk and a few chairs, where a stack of brightly coloured piñata-style paper decorations left over from a town fiesta lay piled in the corner, I met Juan Jesús Muñiz Gutierrez, township secretary-treasurer and a biologist by training. *Muy macho* in polished cowboy boots and a large silver belt buckle, Muñiz answered my questions with a guarded but grave intensity. Thirty-five thousand people live in the 22 neighbourhoods the *Delegación* administers, he told me. "We depend absolutely on the river," he said. "Without water in the soil, there is no life for us."[48]

And if the water is taken away to irrigate San Diego's landscaping, I asked, what will people do then?

"There will be more illegals, or perhaps …"—his thick grey moustache twitched into a smile—"perhaps we'll have to go to Canada."

# Chapter 7

## Pumping Blind:
## Hidden Threat in the Foothills

He was a hard-boiled city cop. She was a tall, cool drink of water in a dress as green as summer. It was love at first sight. Then Muriel began to slip away. And Doug McNally needed to know why.

Or at least that's how Raymond Chandler might have told it. The truth is that as city cops go, McNally was more on the soft-boiled side, an open-minded liberal in a profession better known for toe-the-line thinking. And Muriel? She was a cool drink of water, all right, but you couldn't honestly call her tall. She was—and still is—just a lake. She lies enveloped in green boreal forest about 180 kilometres northeast of Edmonton, the Alberta capital, where McNally grew up and spent his police career. The rest of the story, however, has all the elements of pot-boiler fiction: love, then a vanishing act ... and a mystery.

Just into his forties in the early 1980s, McNally and his artist wife loved to take their teenage son and daughter out of the city whenever they could. But they had wearied of hauling a camper trailer from campground to campground. When they found an affordable lot for sale on a pristine lake far down a dirt road, it seemed like the perfect place to sink summer roots. Muriel Lake was about a four-hour drive from the city but a short hop into the town of Bonnyville for groceries. The lake wasn't too huge, perhaps eight kilometres long and six wide, but big enough to fish for pickerel or pike. When the breeze kicked up, waves broke close to the tree line, leaving just enough room for a crescent of sandy beach. And the cool water was so clear, McNally remembers, that "you could walk out to your neck and look down and tell if your toenails needed cleaning."[1]

The McNallys bought the property in the fall of 1984, cleared the brush by hand, and built a platform for their camper and, eventually, a cottage with a view out toward the sunset. But almost from the day they discovered her, Muriel began to draw away from them. Over the decade that followed, the water level dropped more than three metres. A shoal that ran just beneath the surface from the south shore emerged in time from the waves to form a peninsula of dry land that almost divided the lake in two. Trees sprouted there and grew into tall saplings. Muriel lost nearly half her volume, and the remaining water was no longer clear but murky with algae. The pike and pickerel all but disappeared; only suckers still took an angler's hook. The McNallys gained 60 metres of unwanted gravelly beach in front of their cottage deck.

By the early 1990s, McNally had climbed to the top of his profession as Edmonton's reform-minded Chief of Police, demonstrating a broad view of the social ills that fuel crime. But he still treasured his opportunities to escape to the lake he loved, and he couldn't let go of the mysterious loss of all that water. As he talked with a neighbour one day, they decided something had to be done. The two formed a cottagers' association with other property owners around the Lake to seek some answers. But as a trained investigator, McNally took up the case of Muriel's disappearance as a personal mission. He spent hours in municipal and provincial offices poring over files, examining correspondence relating to the lake and becoming increasingly frustrated with the evasive non-answers he often received. "We were just getting the royal runaround," he says. "I'd love to strap some of these guys to a polygraph. It would have been nice to be able to get a search warrant, but it wasn't a criminal matter." Instead he had to fall back on tools available to every citizen and what he calls the "trait of a good cop, persistence." He persuaded his fellow cottagers to hire a hydrologist to study Muriel's strange behaviour. The provincial Freedom of Information Act unlocked more of her secrets.[2]

In the end, McNally believes, he solved the mystery. But he never quite got his man. The reason is that no single culpable act had led to Muriel's disappearance. Rather, the now-retired top cop says, "I describe it as the perfect storm that hit the lake." The first blow landed as far back as the 1960s, when provincial authorities allowed water to be diverted from a nearby creek for irrigation, ignoring warnings that the decision could injure Muriel. Later, for a number of years into the early 1980s, the province once again overruled local protests to let an oil company withdraw water from the lake for drilling wells nearby. And then there has been the change in the weather: one dry year after another when, McNally says, "we literally weren't getting any runoff." Even some larger local rivers began to drop. Arguably a natural cause, the declining rainfall, he says, "has had a significant effect."

"It's still a beautiful lake," McNally says of Muriel today. "But there's a whole lot less of it. Will it ever come back? Who knows?" And, he believes, numerous other lakes and watersheds across the province have shared the same fate.

The evidence is strong. Breakneck development of what used to be called the "tar" sands of northern Alberta has ramped up demand for vast volumes of water to convert gluey bitumen into flowing synthetic crude oil. Already home to more than two-thirds of all the irrigated farmland in Canada, Alberta has set itself the goal of doubling the value of agriculture that irrigation supports. Cities like Calgary, Canada's second most important financial centre; Lethbridge, the fulcrum of Alberta's agri-biz in the province's south; and Fort McMurray, the service hub for oil sand development in the northeast, are all growing rapidly—the latter as fast as any city in America's sunbelt. But records also show that the water in virtually every one of Alberta's most important rivers is dropping. Some streams have lost even more of their volume than Muriel Lake over the course of the last century.

The ex-policeman, now retired again from a second career as CEO of Edmonton's largest charity, is neither a flighty alarmist nor a countercultural dissident. Nonetheless, he believes "some really serious questions need to be asked" about whether his province can continue tapping its water the way it has.

The short answer, many experts believe, is simply "No." Canada's most American-minded province by heritage and culture, and its second richest by dint of petroleum wealth, Alberta comes a close second after the U.S. Southwest in its calamitous depletion of water. Canada's driest province as well, Alberta gets less than 25 millimetres of rain over much of the territory east of its foothills in an average year. And the same "perfect storm" that emptied Muriel Lake is now gathering over the whole province.

The Muriel Lake cottagers' association hired hydrologist Bill Donahue. The young scientist was just completing his PhD at the University of Alberta under one of North America's leading watershed experts, a member of the U.S. Academy of Natural Sciences and veteran water wonk named David Schindler. Trained in "limnology," the science of inland waters, Schindler now lives north of Edmonton on the banks of the Lobstick River. Over the course of a decade, he had seen the water outside his windows dwindle from a stream that welcomed a canoe in mid-summer to a bed as dry at times as the last 100 miles of the mighty Colorado. Drawn by the mystery of Muriel's missing water, he and McNally expanded Donahue's research into a broader inquiry into what was happening to Alberta's major rivers.

What they found was unequivocal—and shocking. The water flowing down rivers in the north of the province in the course of a year had declined by 30 percent or more over the 20th century. Summertime flows in some southern rivers had dropped by more than *80 percent*. And the reasons? The same as with Muriel: human water extractions and alterations to the landscape, and a long-term shift toward drier, hotter, more drought-inducing weather. Like an accumulation of leaks in a rusty bucket, the pair wrote in 2006, those human actions and

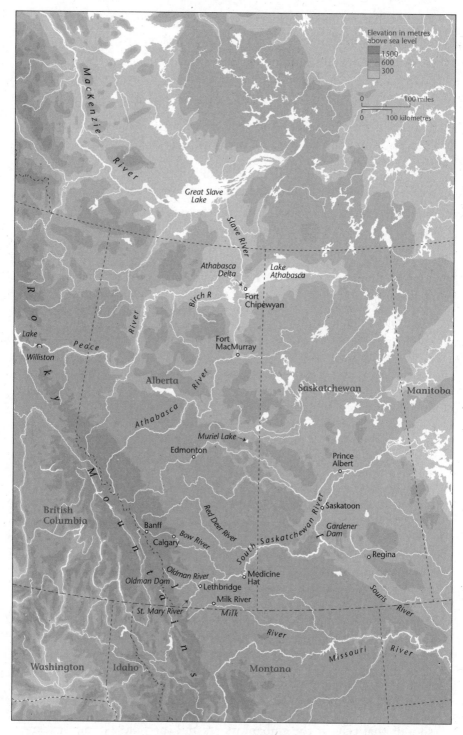

**Rocky Mountain rivers**

climatic changes had set Alberta on course for "an unprecedented water crisis" looming unavoidably "in the near future."[3]

Another group sounding the same alarm has been the Alberta
Institute of Agrologists, whose members are specialists in farming
science. They also have an intimate grasp of the importance of water
to a productive landscape. And they are worried. "Alberta is at a major crossroads," the Institute reported after studying the state of the
province's water supply in 2005. "The limit of available water has been
reached in a number of watersheds, is being approached in others, and
as growth continues, will be reached in Alberta's remaining watersheds."
Shortages, the Institute said, are both inevitable and "imminent."[4]

That impending crisis will, moreover, be felt far beyond Alberta's
borders. Some of the several rivers flowing out of the northern range
of the Rocky Mountains provide neighbouring Saskatchewan and
Manitoba with a large portion of their water supply. Others flow
north, nourishing wetlands as important to wildlife as the Colorado
Delta once was, and furnishing most of the water in the continent's
third-largest river, the Mackenzie.[5] At least one of Alberta's rivers also
flows south into Montana, where it has been the source of friction
between Canada and the United States in the past. In yet another
echo from the Southwest, the fear that thirsty Alberta may exhaust
some of those rivers entirely has prompted at least one downstream
politician, Northwest Territories legislator Michael Miltenberger, to
threaten a "water war" between the province and its neighbours.[6]

But rather like Wile E. Coyote hovering over the canyon in Brad
Udall's colourful simile, very few Albertans are yet aware of the long
plunge that lies before them.

Against the surrounding green velvet of the northern boreal plain,
veined with the dark blue of winding rivers, the huge open pits where
the continent's largest reserves of oil are being mined look like sca-
brous ulcers. Viewed from the air or through the satellite vision of
Google Earth, they seem deceptively small. The bright red power
shovels that claw at the embankments and the yellow dump trucks

that crawl along the excavated benches and ramps loaded with coal-black bitumen appear as toys in a child's sandbox. Only up close can you grasp the enormousness of the operations, with steel staircases that climb up the sides of the world's biggest trucks to deliver drivers to diminutive cabs perched at heights equivalent to those of third-storey balconies. With each trip from the pit, the trucks deliver 400 tons of tarry grit, enough to fill 20 regular dump trucks, to the gargantuan Erector set of hoppers, pipes, scaffolding, chimneys and steaming vents where oil is boiled off and piped into tanks. The cloying smell of petroleum vapour hangs in the air.[7]

Whatever their aesthetic shortcomings and mind-boggling distortions of scale, however, the half-dozen excavations 360 kilometres north of Edmonton are without a doubt the most economically significant and arguably most strategically important activities under way in Canada in the new century. Once regarded as little more than a promising geological curiosity, Alberta's "tar" sand—rechristened with the more user-friendly name "*oil* sand"—has, with rising world prices of crude, become the biggest, safest source of petroleum for a continent addicted to hydrocarbons. Covering an area the size of Florida, the three largest deposits of bitumen-containing sand are believed to hold eight times as much oil as lies beneath Saudi Arabia, and 80 percent of the entire world's "unconventional" (neither liquid nor gas) crude petroleum.[8]

Extraction doubled between 1995 and 2005, until the three largest mines near Fort McMurray and producers in the province's other oil sand areas were turning out more than one million barrels of raw oil a day. New mines and "upgrader" plants were expected to double that volume by 2010 and triple it by 2015 (by which time, roughly one barrel of crude oil in every four the continent produced would come from Alberta's mines rather than conventional wells).[9] With oil production in the United States continuing to fall and that country's military intervention to secure the Persian Gulf going badly, industry leaders in the petroleum capital of Houston met Canadian officials in early 2006 to argue for an even more ambitious goal: *quintupling* production from the oil sands by 2030.[10]

The rush to convert all that black gold into folding green turned Fort McMurray into an overheated boomtown, where the newest workers camped out in tents for lack of hotel rooms and even the McDonald's restaurants had to offer signing bonuses to attract counter staff. The billions of dollars being invested in additional mines not only fuelled Alberta's economy but sent spinoff benefits as far away as Newfoundland, where many of Fort McMurray's imported workers sent at least part of their paycheques back to families at home. The pell-mell pace of expansion produced inevitable controversy. Most of it centred on the very local concern that Fort McMurray's explosive growth was overwhelming local public services—and the global one that doubling or tripling oil sand development would also significantly raise Canadian releases of greenhouse gases, from both the production and the use of the resulting synthetic oil.

Both of those worries were justified. But they overlooked another impact, one with the potential not only to cause environmental damage more immediate than long-term change to the atmosphere, but also to hobble severely the hectic pace of the projected growth itself.

There are, essentially, two ways to get oil out of the sand with which it is mixed in such volume in northern Alberta. Both involve almost unimaginably vast quantities of water. In one, that water is heated to make steam, which is then injected into deep layers of sand, where it heats the embedded oil until it becomes liquid enough to flow into wells and be pumped to the surface. The other is to dig the sand from near the surface, truck it to an extraction plant, and mix it there with hot water and other emulsifiers to wash the oil out. In the first method, the water pumped underground stays there. In the second, the water can be reused, the industry says, as many as 17 times before it is reduced to a black broth too greasy to serve any further purpose and too toxic to release back to nature. Each of the surface mines has large "tailings" ponds where millions of gallons of this dirty liquid is stored while, operators hope, the toxic gunk in it settles to the bottom and water clean enough to release eventually rises to the top. Either way, however, it takes between two and four barrels of water to produce each barrel of crude.[11]

As much water is lost to this process every 24 hours as John Febbraro's ill-fated Nova Group proposed to extract over the course of an entire year from Lake Superior, minus the public outrage. If all the expanded production from the oil sands that is planned for up to 2015 is achieved, the "virtual" water content in the synthetic crude flowing south would fill a veritable fleet of *Exxon Valdezes* every day, the equivalent of one shipload of Canadian water departing every two and a half hours.

All of it, however, has to come from somewhere. Wells supply some. The various oil sands operators pumped about as much water out of the ground in 2005 as all of the province's municipalities combined: roughly one-quarter of all its withdrawals. But most of the water removed from circulation came out of the Athabasca River. It was for easy access to the largest river in northern Alberta that the first three large oil sand developments were located along the Athabasca's banks. Hundreds of metres of earth dikes are all that separate the mines' holding ponds from the living stream. Provincial permits allowed the mines to withdraw twice as much water from the river over a year as the city of Calgary used in the same time. According to the Pembina Institute, an environmental think-tank in Alberta, new mines that are expected to open by 2012 would increase withdrawals by half, bringing the annual total within range of the amount of water that Canada's biggest city, Toronto, uses each year.[12] By 2020, the same group predicted, as much as half the Athabasca's entire flow in some seasons might be tapped to keep oil flowing south.

In fairness, let's note that oil sands producers were spending millions of dollars to reduce their environmental footprints in a variety of ways. The oldest among them, Suncor, which pioneered production of synthetic crude from the oil sands in 1967, claimed to have reduced the amount of water needed to produce a barrel of oil by more than 30 percent between 2000 and 2004 alone.[13] Yet the worth of that improvement was bound to be lost in the multiplying demand for water from an industry contemplating doubling or tripling in size.

That prospect was especially troubling for one particular area downstream: an inland delta as magical still today as the Colorado's must have been in the days before Herbert Hoover gave away to the states upstream more water than the river possessed. Some 225 kilometres north from the gaping oil sand pits, the Athabasca loses itself in a watery labyrinth where, just as Aldo Leopold wrote of the southern delta, the river appears to be at once "nowhere and everywhere." A restless, shifting maze of marshes, reed beds, pools and sinuous river channels, some still active, others long ago abandoned and overgrown, this remote Eden at the western tip of Lake Athasbasca is, in fact, the junction of three important rivers. Here the Peace and Birch rivers also lose their separate identities, mingling their waters with the Athabasca's in a wetland nearly the size of Rhode Island before giving birth to the Slave River. That river winds and twists another 200 kilometres farther north to empty again into Great Slave Lake, from whose western end the Mackenzie River begins its journey to the Beaufort Sea.

The largest such inland delta on earth so far north (its only rival anywhere being tropical Africa's Okavango), the wetlands where the Peace and the Athabasca mingle provide one of North America's most important remaining nesting grounds for waterfowl. Naturalists estimate that half a million geese, ducks and swans stop here each spring on their way to summer homes even farther north in the Mackenzie lowlands. More than twice that number pause in the Delta each autumn, gathering strength before setting out on the long migratory flight over the inhospitable, human-inhabited regions farther south. Beaver, bison, moose, wolves and raptors also prosper here; Athabasca Delta muskrat pelts were once considered the benchmark of quality by fur traders for the Hudson Bay Company. In 1983 the United Nations Environment Programme (UNEP) designated the wetlands a World Heritage Site.

Yet even before the oil rush along the Athabasca, the Delta was feeling the distant touch of humanity's hand. In 1967 the province of British Columbia completed a hydroelectric dam on the headwaters of the Peace River and the next year began filling the huge reservoir behind it.[14] The capture of a year's worth of river flow was spread over three years, during which time water levels in the Athabasca Delta declined to the point at which some marshes were permanently converted to dry land, with willows and sedges replacing reeds and open water. In partial mitigation, local First Nations and the Canadian government built several weirs, low dams, to hold back some of the river's water. That helped, but it didn't entirely recreate the high summer flows of the past: that was now captured anew each spring in the mountains far to the west.

Then, over roughly the same time as at Muriel Lake, the water in the Delta began dropping again. Members of the local Chipewyan First Nation say that where the Delta borders Lake Athabasca, the water has dropped by three metres since the mid-1980s. From his home at Fort Chipewyan on the north shore of the lake, where it empties into Slave River, band councillor Allan Adam says, "You can walk all the way to the south shore with hip waders on—that's how shallow the water has gone."[15]

Whether the receding shoreline and drying Delta are a sign that the oil companies are taking too much water from the Athabasca is a difficult question. As at Muriel Lake, there may be more than one culprit at work. David Schindler and Bill Donahue's research has confirmed the Chipewyans' anecdotal impressions. Systematic observations taken over nearly half a century downstream from Fort McMurray show that summer flows in the Athabasca River actually increased between 1958 and 1975 but have been dropping steadily ever since; by mid-summer 2003, the river was nearly 20 percent lower than at the start of the record—and down by a full third from the mid-seventies peak. An even longer record, however, revealed that the Peace River's mid-summer flow through northern Alberta has dropped further still—by more than 40 percent since observations began in 1915—without any oil sand developments taking huge gulps from it.[16]

Some First Nations with territories downstream were unwilling to wait for a smoking gun to tie the decline in the quality as well as quantity of the water still flowing down the Athabasca to the oil sands development. In late 2006 the Dehcho, who live along the

Mackenzie, called for a moratorium on further oil sand development (the same group also opposed the planned construction of a pipeline that would deliver natural gas from the mouth of the Mackenzie to heat the water used to extract oil). The Delta-dwelling Athabasca Chipewyan, many of whose members have found work in the oil sand pits, lodged their protest by resigning from an environmental watchdog body whose other members, from the oil industry and government, the Chipewyan complained, were failing to respond to their concerns.

It was pouring rain as I turned off Alberta provincial Highway 3, east of the city of Lethbridge, onto the manicured grounds of the largest agricultural research station in Canada. I followed a paved drive past a modern red brick office tower. An eerie pinkish light shone through curtains of rain from the glass cube of a two-storey greenhouse. Water pooled on black asphalt and the green lawns beyond. Parking, I stepped out of the rental car and was instantly soaked. Breathing in the green smell of moist earth, I raced through puddles to the lobby and waited damply to meet Brent Paterson.

Courteous and self-contained, Paterson oversees the Alberta Irrigation Branch, ensuring the water supply for nearly three-quarters of all the irrigated acreage in Canada. It takes only a few minutes to discover a keen intelligence beneath his understated demeanour, somewhat longer to learn that he's so good at what he does that he spends part of his time advising places like Egypt on ways to restore land left poisoned by poor irrigation practices.

Alberta irrigates some 1.6 million acres of land, an area bigger than Prince Edward Island, almost all in the southern quarter of the province. From four percent of Alberta's cropland, irrigation coaxes harvests and livestock that earn an outsize share of its farm sales (more than 14 percent, about $1 billion per year at mid-decade).[17] It's not only that the extra water allows farmers to switch from traditional dry-land crops like wheat or barley to those earning three times as much per acre, like timothy hay for livestock fodder or beets for making sugar. Nearly as important is the *reliability* of water, which allows farmers to grow finicky plants, like potatoes, that require precise amounts of moisture at exactly the right time to meet the standard demanded by the even more finicky modern consumer. As a result, the irrigated four percent of Alberta's farmland supports nearly 20 percent of its agricultural employment.

A little past the research station on Highway 3, a vast, box-like processing plant turns local potatoes into 200 million pounds of McCain frozen french fries a year. More than 200 people work there.[18] "That plant," Paterson says, "is a direct result of irrigation." Other area plants freeze table vegetables, pack meat from cattle finished in local feedlots and even compress high-quality hay into bales that are shipped as far as Asia. For every additional dollar that irrigation brings to the farm gate, Paterson's agency claims, seven more flow to processors and their employees.[19]

Dashing back outside through the rain to the shelter of Paterson's spanking-clean new SUV, we set out to tour some of the plumbing that keeps that cash flowing. Paterson's agency maintains five big reservoirs on the main stems of Alberta rivers. All were brimming. At the Oldman Dam near Pincher Creek, water streamed out of the sluice gates and down a concrete spillway with a roar like that of a freight train. Where a lip at the bottom was meant to keep the current from scouring out the riverbed below, a cockscomb of whitewater rose to the height of a seven-storey building. The ground shook.

Far downstream, mud spattered Paterson's vehicle as we bounced to the end of a corduroyed side road. A long lake the same washed-out grey as the sky curled away from us around a dry yellow hillside. A few cottages dotted the shoreline, empty on this chilly day. This was Stafford Reservoir, one of 50 such seasonal "off-stream" storage pools, filled during the spring freshet and drawn down over the following summer (Stafford is an exception, kept at least partly full year-round to accommodate recreational uses). Together with main-stem reservoirs like the one on the Oldman River, they allow Paterson's agency to store some three billion cubic metres of water each spring, about one-tenth the volume of Lake Mead or twice what Mexico receives from the Colorado.

Rolling back toward the research station grounds, we crossed a canal in which brown water rippled within centimetres of the bridge-deck. Roughly 8,000 kilometres of such channels distribute water from the various on- and off-stream reservoirs to farmers, enough to carry a stream from Whitehorse in the Yukon Territory to Saint John, N.B., on the Bay of Fundy, and all the way back again. Paterson was proud of the fact that about a quarter of that distance had been converted from open canals to closed pipes in the last decade, reducing water lost to evaporation and saving acreage (farmers can plant over the buried pipelines). He hoped to double that percentage. Other changes have further reduced water waste. Farmers installed new irrigation equipment that uses nearly a third less water per acre than that used in the 1990s. At least one irrigation district had changed its price structure to encourage conservation. "Until recently, and still in some districts," Paterson explained, "if you paid $16 an acre for water, that essentially entitled you to an unlimited supply."[20] Now, any farmer who used more than 15 inches of water per acre paid a surcharge.

It was still raining when we pulled back into the parking lot near Paterson's office. "This is a very unusual year in a number of ways," he mused. Until the latest burst of heavy rainfall, "there was virtually no snowpack in the mountains; the snow moisture was very low. Farmers were seeding into very dry soil. If we hadn't gotten this precipitation, we would probably have drained the reservoirs dry by the end of the year." Yet little of the rain now falling would be saved for later. Having stored up every drop of springtime moisture in anticipation of a dry summer, the agency's reservoirs were nearly full by the time this week-long downpour began. The current rainfall quickly filled them the rest of the way, and most of what was still teeming from the skies would be spilled downstream. Despite appearances, Paterson said, there was no water to spare. "We have long lists of farmers interested in investing the dollars to irrigate," he said, "and we have lots of land to irrigate. Water is our limiting factor. We're telling them, 'There's no more.'"

Rather the opposite. If some others are right, southern Alberta's farmers are already in Wile E.'s position: using more water than their rivers can reliably provide and poised for a painful letdown.

Danielle Droitsch is a relative newcomer to Alberta. Raised in Washington, D.C., she first worked as a reporter. A story awakened her environmental conscience: a pulp and paper plant in North Carolina was fouling a river just before it flowed into Tennessee. "North Carolina got the jobs, Tennessee got the pollution," she remembers. Returning to school, she took a degree in environmental law and after graduation became a lobbyist on issues involving energy, clean air and nuclear power. She met a Canadian working in the U.S. capital, fell in love and married. When both became tired of D.C., Droitsch seized the chance in 2004 to become the sole employee of an Alberta offshoot of the American Riverkeeper movement (described in more detail in Chapter 11). The two moved to Canmore, a resort town east of Banff, where Droitsch is now, as she describes herself, "a steward for the river" that runs through the town: "Its eyes, ears and voice." As avidly as she has embraced the work, some of what she has seen has shocked her.[21]

Once free of the mountains, the Bow becomes one of the most important rivers in southern Alberta. It provides Calgarians with a treasured recreational corridor as well as most of their water. Farther east, it provides water for three of the largest irrigation districts in the province before merging with the Oldman as a tributary to the South Saskatchewan. Visiting the irrigation districts downstream in the summer of 2006, Droitsch says, she was astonished to discover that "the river was basically dewatered at the last diversion. I should have been swimming across the river. I could walk across, and it was up to my ankles." To the former environmental attorney, the sight was especially jarring. "I saw something that would be illegal in the United States," she says. "It would be illegal to dewater a river in the U.S."

She blames the Bow River's slow decline—over the past century its average summer flow has dropped by half—on the complacency of irrigators who have continued, in the face of decreased flows, to withdraw the same amount of water. "It's the frog in the boiling pot of water," she says. The gradual change in the temperature—or decline in river flow—that is to say, goes unnoticed until the frog is cooked. But the lesson, she adds, is also apparent: "We can't keep doing business the way we've been doing things."

It's a view David Schindler shares. Alberta, he argues, finds itself in exactly the same position as the Colorado states, having parcelled out more water than it has. "We're in this situation," he says, "because we've licensed too much water to agriculture." Annual permits to take water from at least one river, the Highwood (a tributary of the Bow southeast of Calgary), exceed what flows down that stream in most years. In the case of other rivers like the Bow and Oldman, summer flows have declined over time so that users who take only the volumes they are licensed to withdraw nonetheless leave little to carry on downstream. In the case of the South Saskatchewan, the water that reaches Saskatoon is now barely one-sixth of what got there a hundred years ago. "We need to take some back," Schindler contends, even if that means cutting off irrigation water to some farmers.[22]

In 2006, Alberta did halt new permits for water extraction from the South Saskatchewan. But giving any water back to the river was another matter. On the contrary: several irrigation districts that weren't already using every drop they were licensed to extract were busy planning new off-stream reservoirs that would allow them to do so. For his part, Brent Paterson hoped to find enough extra water through aggressive efficiency to expand irrigated acreage further. "We think there's another 10 or 15 percent that's possible," he told me.

"The wild card," he admitted, "is climate change."

In truth that card isn't so wild as it might seem. For several reasons the present century is almost certain to be drier than the last one. In all likelihood, much drier.

Evidence extracted from fossil algae and the rings of ancient trees, in which minute differences correspond to fluctuations in the weather of the past, indicates that the 20th century may have been the wettest in the southern Canadian Prairies in more than 500 years.[23] Earlier ages experienced frequent droughts that were longer and more severe than even those of the 1930s.[24] At the same time, changes over the 20th century were not for the wetter. In the Athabasca Delta, rain and snow declined by nearly a quarter between 1885 and 2003. Precipitation dropped by double digits in the southern Rockies, foothills and open prairie as well. With less water in riverbeds or falling from the sky, analysts calculated that rising temperatures would push up losses to ET from reservoirs, streams and soils by half in this century. The same heat has been stealing away the mountain ice that in the past kept water flowing down most Prairie rivers during the summer. The amount of water flowing from the glacier at the head of the Bow River, for example, has been in steady decline.[25]

"We may be looking at a triple whammy," Bill Donahue remarked, echoing Doug McNally's analogy of the perfect storm. "We don't think it's been nearly as bad as it can get."[26]

Alberta's looming crisis puts regions beyond the province at risk as well. They suffer the same vulnerability as Mexico, at the losing end of the Colorado. All the major rivers of the western Canadian Prairies arise in the Rocky Mountains and flow out from there to the east, north and south, giving Alberta the chance to tap their currents before anyone else.

An inter-provincial agreement dating to 1969 prohibits Alberta from taking more than half the water that flows annually down major rivers that cross into neighbouring Saskatchewan. Brent Paterson insists that in most years, the province extracts only about half its entitlement under the agreement. That may be true. But, much as happened under the Colorado Compact, Albertans are now moving to install additional storage reservoirs to take up the remaining water the agreement says is theirs. Downriver flows can then only decline.

How much water Alberta releases over a year tells only part of the story in any case. As a practical matter, it's only in the summer, when crops need water and shallow streams leave fish and other wildlife gasping, that the amount of water crossing the border becomes an issue. And that is when Alberta's irrigators often leave little in the river. As Danielle Droitsch puts it, "You can really damage a river during part of the year [under the agreement], as long as you let the water through at another time."

Compounding those factors is another problem: the farther Prairie rivers flow from the mountains, the more ET filches their contents. "The further away from the foothills you get, the greater the decline," says Bill Donahue. By the time the South Saskatchewan River reaches Saskatoon, for instance, barely 15 percent of the water that filled its banks a hundred years ago still flows there today. The South Saskatchewan is a major contributor to Lake Winnipeg, larger today than Lake Ontario. "Flows of water into Lake Winnipeg are way down," Donahue adds. "We're looking at substantial declines in the level of the lake."

If oil sands producers meet their most ambitious targets, the amount of water they withdraw from the Athabasca River may grow fivefold by 2030, even as Donahue's triple climate whammy decimates its natural flow. The combination of escalating withdrawals and a declining river can only leave less water to run downstream to the vast and productive inland Athabasca Delta and no less important wildlife habitat along the Mackenzie River.

Several rivers born on the eastern slope of the Rocky Mountains also cross the international border between Canada and the United States. Two are especially significant. One, the Milk, arises in the United States, crosses into Canada and then returns south. The other, the Souris, does the exact opposite, starting in Canada, entering the United States, then flowing north again back into Canada. In both cases, international agreements in the last century set out how much water each country might extract and how much it must let pass beyond its own border. Like good fences, these agreements were meant to make good neighbours by reducing the potential for mutual grievance. By and large they have, but trouble looms. Both rivers have been dropping. Often there is not enough water left in the streams for either country to keep commitments made in the past. Scientists who examined the trends early in the new century concluded that on the Milk River, "the U.S. share cannot be met at the Western Crossing and just barely so at the Eastern."[27] On the Souris: "on a number of recent occasions … the total discharge to U.S.A. has been substantially less than required by the Agreement." On neither river was there reason to expect an early reversal in that trend.

If there's a bear in the forest, you'd like to know two things: where he is right now, and what to do when he walks out of the trees and stares you in the face. On neither score has Alberta equipped itself especially well for a certain and imminent water shortage.

Weather stations across the province have continued to report the bare essentials of daily temperature and rain or snow. But decisions in the 1990s no longer to monitor winter snow and ice accumulation left critical gaps in forecasters' ability to picture declining rivers. In a particularly perverse decision, the provincial and federal governments put an end to year-round snow surveys in the mountain headwaters of many critical rivers, in favour of surveying only when the remote locations are free enough of snow to make access relatively easy. "We're monitoring for snowpack, we're just not doing it in the winter," Bill Donahue has griped. A monitoring station at the foot of the Athabasca Glacier—the largest ice field on the eastern slope of the Rocky Mountains and the source of the river that shares its name—was abandoned in 1997 and not reopened. To Donahue, such official incuriosity about where Alberta's future water will come from seems almost wilful: "The lack of data is being used now as an argument for not hindering development."

River advocates in the province's north and south bemoaned the absence of any enforceable threshold for pushing back against additional demands. "We're getting to levels [on the Athabasca] where we're going to lose habitat for fish," Karin Buss, a lawyer representing the Athabasca Chipewyan First Nation, has warned, and yet "there's no cut-off in sight" on the water that may be taken out of the river.[28] In southern Alberta, Danielle Droitsch has levelled much the same charge: "We're looking at significant reduction of flows in provincial rivers and they're going to get worse. I think we can meet a lot of human needs, *and* meet environmental benefits, *and* build growth *and* deal with climate change, *if* everyone gives a little. But we're not putting the system together that would address the problem. The government's not saying, 'Here's the backstop.'"[29]

Alberta has been an innovator in the past with water, building some of the continent's most efficient irrigation systems. Its citizens still have plenty of ideas. Free-market conservative Preston Manning has argued for one straightforward fix that would give every Albertan a strong incentive to use water more sparingly: charge all parties, including oil companies, the "full cost" of the water they individually consume. Practical Brent Paterson has contemplated all-weather diversion gates that would allow him to capture winter rains, rather than waiting on spring to fill Stafford Lake. Karin Buss has urged oil companies to build their own off-stream reservoirs and store water captured during the Athabasca's winter peak for use during its low summer flows. Agrologists have encouraged the province to buy back and retire outstanding water-withdrawal licences. One municipality has asked for permission to pipe water from the still relatively untapped Red Deer River overland more than 100 kilometres to a billion-dollar shopping mall and racetrack near Calgary. More radical notions have sought to curb growth itself. The Pembina Institute and the World Wildlife Fund have called for a halt to further expansion of oil sands production. Bill Donahue and David Schindler have gone so far as to recommend finding ways to cap the province's population.

Indecision cannot, in any case, go on long. "We can't afford to wait until demand exceeds supply and the problem is right in our face," Paterson observes. "If we're thinking about adding storage in the province, generally you're looking at least 20 years out from the time you begin to think more storage might be a good thing, until you start to fill the reservoir. Ignoring it won't make it go away."

"The worst-case scenario," says David Schindler, "is we could find ourselves in the same state as the Middle East: Iran and Iraq. That was the Garden of Eden. It's not the Garden of Eden anymore."[30]

# Chapter 8
## Outlook to 2030:
## Wild and Wilder

You expect a time machine to come with lots of blinking buttons, a fellow in a lab coat with wild hair and a big vault door to hold back the centuries. The real thing, when I encountered it, was a lot less outwardly impressive: just a smallish blue ship with a lumpy paint job, the smell of grease and salt hanging about, and an awkward-looking derrick of lattice steel rising up from its deck. Yet the 143-metre *JOIDES Resolution* was perhaps the scientific world's most successful terrestrial time machine ever. In more than 300 voyages, before being sent for refit in 2005, the drill vessel sent thousands of probes into the past, travelling from the latest few millennia into the distance of millions of years.

Built originally in Halifax to hunt for oil, the *Resolution* found her calling, instead, drilling the sea bottom for clues to prehistory. She searched for ancient avalanches on the submerged edges of continents and probed the formation of methane "ice" deep underwater. What brought her to a Canadian fjord north of Victoria was a peculiarity of geography that paleo-ecologist Richard Hebda and other local scientists knew might reveal far more than most places where the *Resolution* drilled sediment cores. The reason: worms—or, rather, their absence.

In even the most desolate-looking seabed elsewhere, primitive worms churn the top half-metre or so of mud and sand into undifferentiated goo as they search for food and partners in worm sex. Long, narrow and deep, Saanich Inlet shares a feature with only a few other spots on the planet: a shallow sill across its mouth keeps the tide from mixing oxygen into water any more than a few metres below the surface. At greater depths, the water has virtually no oxygen—and hence no worms. For Hebda, who specializes in reconstructing ecologies of the past, the absence of worms suggested that a scientific treasure might lie in the undisturbed mud. Like tree rings growing one outside the last, or seasons of snow building up into a frozen layer cake of ice in a Greenland glacier, he reasoned, anything that sank to the bottom of the inlet would just pile up, layer upon layer, season upon season, without being stirred into a timeless muddle.

The *Resolution* took a few hours to position itself over the deepest part of the fjord, then to drop its drill to the bottom. As the derrick rattled and clanked, digging deep into the soft muck below, Hebda waited impatiently on deck. Another Hamiltonian, with the look of a more intense Louis Del Grande, Hebda curates the earth history collections of the Royal British Columbia Museum in Victoria. Like a detective, he examines everything from pollen grains to volcanic ash, tree needles to insect shells, for clues to what weather, wildlife and vegetation were like in a particular place thousands of years ago. Harder sometimes than putting together the picture is knowing exactly when it was "taken" as those materials accumulated.

The turntable spinning the drill shaft turned to a stop. Cables high in the derrick tightened to lift the heavy pipe. When the last section lay on deck, a technician extracted a long, grey sausage of mud, about three inches thick. This he cut into shorter pieces about a metre long, which he laid out in order on a ribbed wooden tray. Retreating to the vessel's onboard lab, Hebda leaned over the glistening wet cylinder of history. His excitement mounted as he located what he'd been hoping for: finely separated layers, close-grained as the rings of a tree, where he could clearly distinguish the sunken detritus of one ancient season from that of the next.

The cores lifted from the Saanich Inlet would keep a score of scientists working for years to come. But Hebda had been reading the story they contained for less than four days when he came across something that astonished him. Examining a stretch of mud laid down around 11,000 years ago, he detected a startling shift. The pollen in earlier layers came from trees similar to those growing around the inlet today: cedar and hemlock. But then, in layers deposited only a couple of decades later, the evidence changed; pollen there came from the scrub alder that grows today only on high alpine slopes or in the sub-Arctic. Somehow, about the time that early human hunter-gatherers in the Middle East were domesticating the first farm animals, the climate of southern Vancouver Island suddenly switched from one very like that of the 20th century, with mild, moist winters and moderate dry summers, to weather more like that of inland mountain plateaus or windswept arctic tundra. And it had done so in less than 25 years. "Geologically speaking, that's an instantaneous change," Hebda explained. "It's scary."[1]

Hebda's work at the museum reflects his conviction that some discoveries demand the widest telling possible. His conversation becomes urgent when he struggles to convey the changeability of climates past and how quickly our weather may change again. He and other paleo-scientists have unearthed evidence of numerous climate upheavals like that sudden lurch 11,000 years ago.

Eventually, the Pacific Northwest coast warmed up, but it remained much drier than it has been in the recent past. Then it turned much wetter. Then it got colder again. While some weather patterns lasted several thousand years, others came and went within a generation. One sudden drought or cold spell (the clues are ambiguous; it may have been either or both) set in over 36 months, then lasted for decades. Trees on Vancouver Island almost stopped growing entirely.

It's likely that the same was true for the plants that fed local wildlife and early humans. Those people, Hebda believes, struggled to adapt to the constantly changing conditions. As the climate swung wildly from one extreme to the other, edible plants that were a staple for one generation vanished by the time the next came along. Game animals whose habits a young hunter had learned to anticipate disappeared from the forest before he could pass that knowledge on to his child. As Hebda imagines it: "What granddad learned and passed on to me was not useful any more. Those things didn't work any longer. I've got to figure it all out by myself." Under those conditions, he says, each new human generation "had to start all over again. You're constantly figuring it out, you don't have time to come up with things that are predictive, that help your children cope better than you did. You're stuck at the 'alpha' requirements of life, like feeding yourself. You've got no time for 'beta' activities. You're more concerned about whether you've get food or not."

Then, quite suddenly, things settled down. The climate of the Pacific Northwest stabilized in the moist, mild range that secured its twentieth-century reputation as our wet coast. *Homo sapiens* living there finally got a chance to build up some of those "beta" assets. "Four thousand years ago, stable climate arrives," Hebda deduces. "Now everything's predictable from one year to the next. I accumulate knowledge. It works the next year, and the next year; it works for the next generation. They're spending less time feeding themselves, clothing themselves, putting roofs over their heads. They're thinking. They're creating. What arrives is culture."

Earth's climate has changed repeatedly over the estimated five billion years of the planet's life. Eighty million years ago, what would become Canada's west coast was a tropical marshland of palm trees and long-necked water-dwelling dinosaurs. Days then were on average 7°c warmer than they are today. By 40 million years ago, the high Arctic was warm enough for creatures like alligators to survive the long winter darkness on what we now call Ellesmere Island. By 20 million years ago, temperatures had dropped to within a degree of today's, but the world was still a very different place. Enough water had evaporated from the oceans to leave the Mediterranean Sea a vast open valley. North America resembled the 20th century's Serengeti Plain, a vast, dry, open savannah where mice and snakes, small horse-like mammals and sabre-toothed cats roamed. In just the last two million years, the planet has been through four periods in which temperatures only 4 to 5°c lower than today's plunged the continent beneath sheets of ice more than a mile thick.[2]

Humankind missed most of those ups and downs. To put our brief 150,000-year experience on the planet into perspective, imagine that all the events of the last five billion years occupied every page of this book up to the very last word of the last sentence on the last page.[3] We've been around as a species for about the equivalent of the last three letters of that word. The history of all our combined civilizations, showing up just in time to catch the tail-end of the last ice age, would in this analogy occupy less than half the space of the period at the end of the sentence.

Even in that comparatively brief time, our world's climate has changed repeatedly, often abruptly. Another paleo-climatologist, Kendrick Taylor, who reconstructs the past from ice cores that he examines in his lab at the Desert Research Institute in Reno, Nevada, concluded that the change in the weather at the end of the last ice age struck with astonishing speed. "A large part of the change took less than 20 years," he wrote in *Scientific American*. Within the brief span of two decades, "the amount of snow deposited each year [in Greenland] doubled, average surface temperature increased by 5 to 10 degrees Celsius ... sea-ice decreased, atmospheric circulation patterns changed and the size of the world's wetlands increased." Much of the change, "including at least a 4-degree Celsius increase in the average annual air temperature, happened in *less than 10 years*."[4] For the early humans already expanding their settlements onto every continent at the time, "there was no warning. A threshold was crossed, and the climate in much of the world shifted abruptly from cold to warm."

On other occasions, the weather has switched suddenly between wet and dry. Around 10,500 years ago, just as Vancouver Island was warming up again after its sudden chilly spell, a change in the weather on the far side of the world brought heavy, wet monsoons to North Africa. From restless drifts of empty sand, the Sahara suddenly bloomed into green savannah. Elephants, rhinoceros and giraffes watered at pools nestling in the crescent arms of former dunes; hippos and crocodiles populated substantial rivers. People soon followed, establishing settlements. The wet spell lasted about 2,500 years before the weather changed again, returning the Sahara to its former, and current, state of permanent drought. Facing starvation, its people abandoned communities in which they had lived for over a thousand years and retreated to the Nile Valley, where their descendents eventually prospered again and built the pyramids.

A change in the other direction struck the northern Great Plains of North America much more recently. Central Nebraska is a region of rolling hills today, green in spring and brown in summer, where cattle graze around small ponds encircled by protective slopes. Warm, moist winds rolling up the middle of America from the Gulf of Mexico bring the rain that keeps the ponds reliably full. Look down on the same countryside from the air, however, and the wave-like lines of Nebraska's Sand Hills reveal their true identity: beneath the grass, these are sand dunes no different from the Sahara's. "Around a thousand years ago," says David Loope, a geoscientist at the University of Nebraska, "the wind shifted around and cut off the moisture supply."[5] For at least two centuries, no pasture, or anything much else, grew in this part of the plains. The sand hills drifted constantly as dry winds from the southwest in summer and the north in winter whistled over their crests. Anyone living there before the wind changed had to migrate elsewhere.

Humans have been forced repeatedly to adapt to abrupt alterations in climate. Not all societies succeeded so well as the Saharans-turned-Egyptians. Sharp changes in the weather have been linked to the collapse of several sophisticated and, for their time, dominant civilizations. Sudden drying has proven particularly chastening, contributing to collapses in Mesopotamia (the Akkadian empire around 2,200 BC), coastal Peru (the Moche about 600 AD), northern China and Mexico's Yucatan Peninsula (the Tang Dynasty and the Maya, respectively, both around 900 AD). The so-called "Little Ice Age" that began in the 13th century and lasted, with thaws and new chills, well into the 19<sup>th</sup>, froze rivers and harbours on both sides of the Atlantic, brought famine to two continents, provoked popular anger that fuelled decades of warfare, and entirely extinguished the Norse settlements in Greenland.

As cataclysmic as humans have found some of these shifts over the last few millennia, Earth's climate in that time has been—by geological standards—unusually stable. The average global temperature has wavered no more than one or two degrees Celsius. Many scientists believe, with Richard Hebda, that our species owes its general prosperity over that period precisely to the long stretch of relative calm. "We are the result of 4,000 years of climatic stability," Hebda says.

When he looks at today's weather, he gets an alarming sense of déjà vu. "Now we are at a point of environmental instability again, *way* greater than anything 4,000 years ago, an order of magnitude greater. We're into a time of intense and rapid ecological flux. It's beginning to happen. [Hurricane] Katrina's a classic example."[6]

Climate's marble is rolling faster and reaching farther up the bowl with each passing season. How close is it to the top? And what is the view over the edge?

Weather seems fickle and unpredictable, but in many respects it is like a machine: infinitely subtle, complex, possibly divine, but a machine nonetheless. And we know what makes it tick, even if we can't always predict when it will chime. Heat warms air and expands its molecules, creating the zones that weathercasters call "low-pressure." Air that's less dense is also lighter than the air around it, and so it rises; think of air going up a chimney or of the buoyancy that lifts hot-air balloons. Denser air from elsewhere rushes in to fill the vacated space, creating wind. Eventually, the rising air reaches a height where it is no longer lighter than the thinner air surrounding it. It stops rising and, like a welling spring, flows out in all directions. Such a high-altitude flow of air eventually finds a spot where cooler temperatures are creating an opposite vertical flow, a hole in the sky. The air pours back down through it to the surface of the earth, piling up to create a zone of high pressure before again flowing out in all directions. These flows then find yet other lows in the region and re-enter the cycle. Water gets caught up all along the way. Wherever air is relatively warm and under low pressure, the space between the atoms of its constituent gases expands, inviting molecules of $H_2O$ to pull away from soil, rivers, lakes and oceans (ET) and take up airborne residence as vapour. When air that has picked up moisture this way begins to cool and densify again, beyond a certain point it squeezes the water back into a liquid and we get precipitation.

What we call weather is the process we observe as these vast updrafts and plunging vortices, with their skirts of wind often hundreds of kilometres across, jostle and bump into one another overhead, alternately sucking water up into the sky and spitting it back out again. At any given time, about 50 of these great air drafts are active about the earth. Some are semi-permanent, others nomadic.[7] Some may be breaking loose from larger air masses, while others decay and dissolve into stronger currents around them. Powering this whole planetary game of bumper cars is heat.

The sun heats the earth unevenly: more by day than by night, more at the equator than at the poles, more on the side turned seasonally toward the sun than on the side turned away. As different parts of the earth warm and cool, the atmosphere responds. The sun's heat also warms the oceans, and, just as differences in pressure move the air, gradients of sea temperature and saltiness, aided by wind and tides, move the ocean around. In this great global circulation, heat is both the fuel and the product: as all these currents of air and water sweep around the planet, they broadly redistribute the greater incoming heat received at the tropics to the rest of the globe.

Imagine, for a moment, that we're sitting in the International Space Station, looking down at Earth and "seeing" the wind. We soon notice several fat, irregular and rather wobbly rings of air circling the planet below us, with three distinct bands between the equator and each pole.[8]

We see that one pair of these goes around the globe's waist like a double cummerbund, extending from each side of the equator to roughly 30° north and 30° south. Between these belts, around and on either side of the equator, where the sun heats the planet most, we notice a semi-permanent belt of vast upwellings of warm air. When that air reaches the upper atmosphere, it flows away either north or south. Reaching the northern (or southern) edge of the great global double cummerbund of wind, the air cools enough to sink back to the surface and slides back toward the equator. Looking closely, we might notice that this returning air, whether in the northern or the southern ring, almost always flows from east to west before it curls in toward the equator under what is called the "Coriolis effect." Old-time sailors knew these reliable breezes as "trade winds" and gratefully hitched a ride on them whenever they needed to cross an ocean; hurricanes and typhoons often follow the same track.

Continuing to look down from our seat in space, we see another set of rings, sitting around either pole almost like gigantic beanie hats. Here, things are driven by intense cold. At each pole, super-chilled air is flowing down from high in the atmosphere to the earth's surface, then spinning outward, once again following a westward track as it approaches the equator. By the time these winds cross the Arctic Circle or its Antarctic counterpart, they have begun to pick up heat from the ground. A little beyond those circles, the air becomes warm enough to rise and flow back toward whichever pole it came from. If we watch long enough, we may see one of these winds from the North Pole carry on farther south than usual, when Midwestern Americans shiver in a so-called "Arctic outbreak."

In between the polar beanie caps and the equatorial belts we've noticed, another pair of wind rings circles each hemisphere.[9] From our perch in space, we see that in these, the air flows essentially in reverse to that of the rings at either side, rather like a gear turning in opposition to its neighbours. Looking at this middle ring around the northern hemisphere, for example, we see that air along its southern edge is being pulled down toward the earth by the cool, sinking air of the equatorial ring. At the middle ring's other boundary, air rises, pulled up by the newly warmed winds of the northern beanie as they start their return journey to the pole. Within these middle bands, the wind over the ground is much more chaotic than that in the tropic or polar rings. Pushed by the rings' convective gearing, tugged by the rotational Coriolis effect, and slowed down by mountains and sur- face friction, winds here are more irregular and variable than they are in those heat- and cold-driven zones. Often they display the familiar O-shaped signature of large storms. Still, even these generally drift from west to east: the reason that residents of the temperate mid- latitudes refer to them as "prevailing" westerly winds.

If our "wind vision" is particularly acute, we may also detect something else: narrow rivers of very fast winds rushing along the boundary zones between the various belts that we first noticed. We see two of these in each hemisphere: a stronger one circling from west to east between the polar beanies and mid-latitude rings, and a weaker one going the other way between those mid-latitude rings and the equatorial cummerbunds. Over time, we may see these "jet streams" writhe and meander north and south, as the wobbly margins of the lower-level rings push them back and forth.[10]

Now suppose that in addition to wind vision, we're equipped with "heat" vision—and have quite a bit of time on our hands. As we sit in the Space Station enjoying our Tang, we notice something curi- ous in the Pacific Ocean. Every few years, a narrow band of water jutting west from South America suddenly becomes much warmer than the rest of the Ocean. When that happens, we see all the great latitudinal rings of wind bulge out and fall back in different places; the jet streams rushing in their valleys change course. On land, rain falls where it was lacking before and large green patches of ground turn brown. Listening to news from Earth, we hear people blaming these unusual downpours and droughts on "El Niño." After a while, the same patch of the Pacific turns unusually cold. All the patterns of wind, rain and drought change again, and now the news from Earth blames "La Niña."

If we hang out in space for 20 or 30 years, we eventually notice something else in the Pacific. A big area off the coast of China starts to get warmer than the rest of the ocean. Over many months, this warm patch bulges out east and north until it drifts away from the Chinese coast entirely and relocates south of Alaska. This pool of warm water persists for several decades, and while it does, we see patterns of wind and rain over North America like those that prevail during El Niño. In time the warm pool blends back into the surrounding ocean. This cycle takes place over a sufficiently prolonged period that few notice it—other than some scientists, who call it the Pacific Decadal Oscillation, PDO for short.

Imagine, finally, that we can peer into oceans and see the water within them move. We detect a giant, meandering "river" slithering like a huge snake around the entire globe. We catch it surfacing off the west coast of North America. From there, we watch it flow across the Pacific north of Australia into the Indian Ocean. We see it round Africa's Cape of Good Hope and run north, up the Atlantic, crossing from east to west to pick up warm water from the Gulf of Mexico before heading back toward Britain. In the course of its flow across the North Atlantic, we recognize what we know as the Gulf Stream, which is in fact but one stage in the longer, worldwide course this river takes. Somewhere between Scotland and Iceland, we see the stream cool off suddenly and sink fast into the ocean depths. Peering closely, however, we see it take a turn north of Iceland and slither south again, retracing its journey through the deeps, down the Atlantic, around Africa and finally traversing the North Pacific back to its starting point.[11] There are several names for this massive current, among them the Great Ocean Conveyor and the Thermohaline Circulation. As the first implies, it moves vast quantities of heat around the planet; the second suggests the differences of heat and saltiness (*halinos* meaning "of salt" in Greek)[12] that keep it going.

What our hypothetical perch in space has shown us is the basic drivetrain of the world's weather. Solar radiation provides the engine, heating up air and sea water near the equator. The high-level winds rushing north across the top of the cummerbund rings transfer that heat to the mid-latitudes, where it fuels the chain of alternating high- and low-pressure zones that march across our daily weather maps. Leftover heat pulls up the hems of the cold polar wind ring, dissipating the last of the equatorial warmth as that air makes its high-altitude ride back to the poles. The Great Ocean Conveyor serves the same purpose within the world's two biggest seas, continuously transporting heat from warmer to cooler parts. And, as with any complex system, a change in one place produces effects in superficially unrelated ones. In the case of climate, these long-distance linkages may span tens of thousands of miles. Climate scientists call them "tele-connections."

One of the most dramatic took place nearly 250 years ago. In June 1783, an Icelandic volcano named Laki began to erupt. Before it settled down, the most violent eruption of the last millennium expelled 12 cubic kilometres of lava and 100 million tons of sulphur dioxide and other toxic gases from the earth's core. Nine thousand Icelanders died at once. But huge volumes of debris also flowed into the atmosphere, much of it as sulphate aerosol, whose minute droplets scatter solar radiation back out to space. In a short time, Laki's exhaust had thus created a vast reflective ring around the northern hemisphere that prevented the sun's warmth from reaching the earth. That summer was the coldest in some parts of northern Europe in 500 years, according to tree rings. But that wasn't the limit of Laki's effects. In most summers, warm temperatures over the northern hemisphere lower the air pressure there. That attracts monsoon winds, bringing summer rain to southern Asia and northern Africa. But with the northern hemisphere unusually cool, there was less contrast in air pressure and the moist monsoons didn't come. Rather than receiving the normal daily drenching through late 1783, much of east Africa, Egypt, the Persian Gulf and India baked under cloudless skies. Harvests shrivelled. When the Nile failed the following year to produce its usual flood, one in six people living in its valley starved to death in ensuing famine, tele-victims of an Icelandic volcano they had never seen or, in all likelihood, even heard of.

Researchers in several countries have detected what they believe are modern counterparts of the Laki effect. Scientists at Australia's Commonwealth Scientific and Industrial Research Organisation believe that, in one case, the welcome rainfall that has come to northern Australia in recent decades may be owing to China's rising air pollution. In this tele-connection, aerosols emitted from Chinese smokestacks create clouds and block radiation as Laki's sulphates did, cooling the air.[13] Moisture-laden Pacific winds are deflected southward to Australia, where less polluted air is warmer and hence under relatively low pressure. As China succeeds in bringing its pollution under control, of course, a healthier future for its citizens could ironically mean a drier one for Australia's. That's very close to what Swiss climate scientist Martin Wild thinks has already happened in his country. Monitoring the sunlight that penetrated clouds, smog and airborne dust to reach Europe's surface, he found that after decreasing for 30 years between 1960 and 1990, it went up steadily for the next decade and a half. He put the effect down to the collapse of dirty heavy industry in the former Soviet Union.[14]

Another type of aerosol is what scientists call "black carbon" but the rest of us call "soot." It gets into the atmosphere from incompletely burned fuels (those black exhaust plumes from some truck engines) and burning forests. These particles absorb solar heat rather than reflecting it. Researchers in India, Israel and the United States have all found that soot clouds can reduce and relocate rainfall. Thick palls of smoke cast shadows that cool the land immediately beneath them dramatically, by as much as 26°C in extreme cases, reducing evaporation and thus the amount of moisture that enters the air. Even when sooty air becomes humid, the fine grains of carbon are too tiny to provide the "seed" around which water can condense into drops heavy enough to fall as rain; that effect reduces rainfall from even large clouds by up to half. By the time water droplets at last become heavy enough to fall, sooty clouds have often passed entirely over the places where rain used to land. Moisture that used to fall on India now rides dirty air all the way to Southeast Asia, where it rains with ferocious intensity.[15]

If burning forests create soot that redistributes the rain, living ones may have other climatic effects. Boreal forests in Canada, Alaska, Scandinavia and Russia get their distinctive piney scent from chemicals called monoterpenes. These turn out to have an effect much like that of sulphates: they bounce solar energy back up into space, helping to keep the planet's surface over those regions cooler than it would otherwise be. The transfer of heat energy from the air to molecules of water as they evaporate from forest foliage additionally cools leafy places. The water that trees "breathe" into the air also becomes available for rain when that air eventually cools down. For all these reasons, climate scientists have linked rampant deforestation in parts of Africa and South America to the decline in rainfall there.

A Brazilian researcher has unearthed what he contends is a forest tele-connection over a much larger distance. Until the latter part of the last century, Antonio Nobre believes, the huge volume of hot, damp air "exhaled" by the vast Amazon jungle created a constant upward convection current, rather like a huge chimney over northern Brazil. As warm air rose over the jungle, it created a region of low pressure that sucked in moist northeast trade winds from the mid-Atlantic Ocean. Those winds, he argues, also drew enormous quantities of heat off the surface of that ocean. In recent decades, however, widespread clearing of the Amazon forest has reduced ET there. The "draft" up the "chimney" is weaker, and so are the trade winds. More heat stays in the mid-Atlantic, fuelling more powerful hurricanes. If that is true, then at least a little of the tragedy of New Orleans may be tele-connected to deforestation in the Amazon.[16]

The connections and reconnections never end. For the researchers working them out, that's much of the fun. I imagine it must be like doing a crossword puzzle that expands as you approach its borders, revealing more clues and empty spaces for you to fill in. Fresh observations, records that now run over longer time periods, and the exploration of previously unexamined places—all the multiplying fruits of a spate of research in the last decade—suggest new climatic relations. They all, however, have one thing in common: they obey the well-proven, $2 + 2 = 4$ kind of physics that started with Archimedes and still applies every time an engineer designs a car. And the language researchers use to describe these new discoveries is usually that of mathematics, facilitated by computers.

Now you're in Greg Flato's world.

Flato remembers sitting on the back porch of his family's farm near Edmonton after supper, when, at the end of a hot August day, "like clockwork a thunderstorm rolls up. You can see it burbling around, and sometimes it'll come over you and sometimes it won't. And a mile away this guy's crop got wiped out because it hailed like crazy, and at your place you didn't get a drop of rain."[17] His view is limited these days to the drab parking lot outside his small office near the University of Victoria campus in British Columbia. But if anyone this side of heaven can claim plausibly to "hold the whole world in his hands," it's Flato. As manager of Canada's Centre for Climate Modelling and Analysis, he has the mission of capturing the sum of all the climate connections we know about in the equations of a single mathematical model.

"These aren't empirical models," he makes it a point to explain. "They're not based on some interpretation of what's happened in the past or extrapolation to the future. They're based on classical physics that's been known for a long time, like the Newtonian equations of motion, as applied to the atmosphere and the ocean.

"We don't approach it with some preconceived notion of what answer we want," he emphasizes. "That's the misconception people have, that we somehow adjust things to get what we want. But that's the whole point of the exercise: we want to know the answer as much as anyone else. So we have no reason to try to bias the outcome in some particular direction." At the same time, he adds, modellers take great care to test their mathematical representations against the real world. One way to do that is to set a model's "start" date at 1900 and see how closely its evolution tracks what we know of the last century's weather. Most leading models, including the one developed by the group Flato heads, show a coarse but unmistakable fidelity to the historic record.

As real world researchers identify new climate connections, modellers add more equations to capture those influences. "The main advances," Flato says, "have been [in] the way the ocean mixes things, the way clouds operate and the cooling effect of aerosols. The new version has three layers of soil. Moisture 'moves' between those layers. There are different kinds of plants. Their roots go down into these three [soil] layers. They intercept snow on their leaves, and the snow melts and drips to the ground."

Of the several dozen climate models developed around the world, a common problem is scale. Even the latest supercomputers strain under the load of the trillions of calculations required to render a single year of modelled time. Some modellers cope by surrendering resolution. The workhorse Canadian model, for instance, represents the globe in the equivalent of squares 400 kilometres across, roughly the distance between Toronto and Ottawa. A lot can happen in the weather between those two cities. In many models, entire hurricanes can get lost between the mapped grid points. Other models give up coverage. Higher-resolution ones have been constructed for smaller areas like the Great Lakes Basin.

These models give a picture of the last and present century that's fuzzy at best. Yet even a fuzzy photograph can reveal the key elements of the scene in view, and the models' resolution is rapidly improving. For its latest report on climate science, the IPCC ran 14 climate models through the 200-year period from 1900 to 2100 a total of 77 times.[18] The models broadly captured the observed fluctuations in global temperature over the first half of the last century. In the period since about 1970, however, their ability to match the real world has depended on the presence or absence of one key set of equations. When their calculations captured only the natural forces known to be at play in the atmosphere at the beginning of the last century, the modelled global temperatures through to the end of the 20th century were more or less in line with those of earlier decades (actually slightly cooler than at mid-century). Yet in the real world, temperatures had climbed steadily over the period since 1970. There's only one way to coax the same warming trend out of the leading climate models: you must include equations that represent the atmosphere's changing chemistry.

So let's talk about that.

◆

Like the rind enveloping an orange, layers of gas, together called the atmosphere, encase our planet. The layer we know best, because it's nearest the ground and contains most of the air, is the *troposphere*. Barely 14 kilometres deep at its thickest, it's the location of those broad belts and narrow jets of wind that we "saw" from space earlier. The troposphere is where we live, fly and watch the weather. But without the next layer beyond it, from about 15 to 50 kilometres above the surface—the *stratosphere*—we wouldn't be here. Nor, in all likelihood, would any other form of life. Gases there provide a chemical shield against the rigours of Earth's space environment, protecting the troposphere and the surface of the planet.

One way it does so is by acting as a global sunscreen. Stratospheric ozone, an oxygen compound ($O_3$), filters most of the cancer-causing ultraviolet waves out of the sun's light. It was largely to preserve the ozone's filtering effect that the world's countries acted in the 1980s to scrap the chlorofluorocarbon chemicals (CFCs) that were eroding it in the stratosphere. But ozone provides an even more fundamental protection. Without it, ultraviolet energy beating in from our favourite star might fracture the atomic bonds in molecules of water, reducing our lakes, rivers and oceans to clouds of elemental hydrogen and oxygen: the fate, scientists believe, that befell Venus, our dry and lifeless sister.

The third way the stratosphere makes life on Earth bearable is by maintaining the global temperature. We orbit too far away for the small sun's unaided radiance to keep our planet's surface above freezing. We keep warm only because so-called greenhouse gases (GHGs) in the stratosphere coddle us like a blanket. Of these, the most important are carbon dioxide ($CO_2$), methane ($CH_4$) and water vapour. They behave a little like a one-way heat trap: they allow much of the sun's radiant energy to pass through to heat the land below, but when a portion of that heat radiates back out toward space, the gas blanket reflects it down again, keeping it close to us. Without this effect, our planet would be at least 40°C colder, a frozen ball of rock and ice.

Artificial CFCs nibbled away at the ozone. But meanwhile, we're forcing the opposite change on GHGs: because of the pollution we generate, their concentration in the stratosphere is rising, and with it their insulating effect. Thus, as more and more heat is trapped in the atmosphere, we're also pouring on the gas that drives the weather.

Unless Newton's laws are rescinded, we therefore know with some certainty what the climate and weather will be like by the mid-2020s. The planet's average temperature will be about two-thirds of a degree Celsius warmer than it was during the last quarter of the last century—close to a full degree over land masses.[19] The extra heat pouring into the atmosphere, especially in the tropics, will expand the global cummerbunds of wind we "saw" from space, pushing their edges farther north and south. The middle bands will shift toward their poles. Familiar regional weather patterns will also move around, as high- and low-pressure zones relocate in response to different distributions of heat, moisture and various aerosols in the atmosphere. The air will hold more moisture altogether, cycling from the tropics through the great global bands of wind toward the high-latitude north and south.

A wetter world isn't wetter for everyone. Some parts will get less precipitation than before; others will experience more drying ET. The American Southwest can expect both, like two holes in the same bucket. In many areas, increased ET will offset any rise in precipitation, leaving more dryness overall. That describes much of the lower Mississippi Valley and the southeastern United States. Still, all the additional moisture cycling through the atmosphere has to come down somewhere, and many places will get more precipitation. Assuming no acceleration of the present rate of climate change, the IPCC forecasts in its most recent assessment that by mid-century "average annual river runoff and water availability are projected to increase by 10-40% at high latitudes ... and decrease by 10-30% over some dry regions at mid-latitudes."[20]

The IPCC, whose report is subject to revision by the governments that sponsor it, including those of Canada and the United States, is oddly coy about the exact location of the "line of zero change" in this continental redistribution—the frontier between the places getting wetter and those getting drier. One reference discloses only that it "is oriented more or less west-to-east and moves north from winter to summer." Another, that the wet side lies "poleward" from the 50th parallel. In his office down the corridor from Greg Flato's, Andrew Weaver made short work of the imprecision. Flipping through the international report's pages, he stopped at a coloured map of the world.[21] In shades from moist blue-grey to dry brick red, it showed where in the world we can expect more water, and where less, in winter and in summer.

"Draw a line at the 49th parallel," Weaver said. "There's more water above the line, less water below." Canada, already the most water-rich country per capita in the world, is going to get richer in the 21st century, perhaps as much as 40% richer (wetter) by mid-century. The United States' most booming regions, already on water overdraft, may lose nearly a third of the water they enjoy today.

No matter where we live, we can also expect that:

+ Storm tracks will shift toward the north over North America, Europe and Asia, and south in the southern hemisphere.[22] With them, precipitation will also move, roughly, toward the poles.

+ Bigger, windier storms will deliver heavier rain.

+ Despite heavier downpours when it rains, most places will also suffer more intense droughts.

+ Areas that are already dry now will become more so, especially in the sub-tropics (the bands of Earth's surface between latitude 30° and the mid-40's), including most of the continental United States, as the bands of hot air around the equator become warmer still and expand their range north and south.

+ More frequent, sweltering heat waves will stay longer, offering fewer cool nights for people, animals and plants to recover from sweaty daytime highs. Areas in the centre of the continent (southern Ontario, the Mississippi Valley) will suffer more than coastal areas.[23]

+ Many places will experience a greater number of high-humidex days, when hot air loads up with moisture but cannot cool down to the dew point that would release that captive humidity as rain.

+ Places where the growing season is limited by winter will enjoy more growing days, with fewer frost days.

+ Unfrozen lakes and rivers will lose more moisture to ET in winter.

+ Mild winters will see spells of extreme cold that damage crops left exposed without snow. With less snow on the ground, soils will freeze more deeply, later taking longer to thaw and increasing frost heave in areas that experience it.

+ There may be fewer tropical cyclones (the family of storms that includes hurricanes and typhoons), but those that do form will often be more destructive—stronger and wetter—than in the past.[24]

+ Weather will swing more wildly from one extreme to another, as the climate wobbles in response to the overall increase in energy and searches for a stable new equilibrium.

It's impossible to predict which face a changing climate will show us on any particular future date. What we know is that any of the above will become *likelier* than on any day in the past. Senior NASA climatologist James Hansen uses the analogy of dice. "Between 1951 and 1980," he explained once, "of the six sides of the dice only two were red, representing the probability of having an unusually warm season. By the first decade of the 21ˢᵗ century, four sides were red."[25] Perhaps the "red" side won't come up the next time the dice are thrown, or the time after that. But the more days that go by, the more the dice tumble, the more certain it becomes that one day will dawn red-hot.

Because of globe-straddling tele-connections in the climate's balancing act, it's also difficult to predict *where* some effects may appear. A relatively small adjustment in average air pressure in one area may, like Iceland's Laki, disable a familiar weather cycle that is a lifeline to millions half a continent away.

Probability and risk are the province of actuaries. These specialized statisticians act like casino card counters for the insurance industry, which bets its livelihood on the odds that individuals, properties and businesses will undergo harm. So it is striking that insurers and lenders have been in the vanguard of firms demanding more aggressive preparation for the rough weather ahead. More than a dozen of the world's biggest, including Bank of America, Munich Re and the Hongkong Shanghai Bank (HSBC)—hardly a bunch known for tree-hugging—cooperated with the United Nations Environment Programme (coordinator of the IPCC) in studying the rising damage from droughts, coastal storm-surges, hurricanes and floods. In 2006 this effort forecast that, "considerably before 2040," the increase in violent weather would incur worldwide losses of more than $1 trillion U.S. *in a single year.* Said Paul Clements-Hunt, who oversaw the research, "This is an unequivocal statement by 15 of the largest financial institutions: climate change is now certain."[26]

If there was no more room to doubt the reality of climate change, there was still a small chance that something other than human emission of GHGs was to blame. But even on that score, the odds were dwindling that another villain lurked in the clouds.

Energy from the sun keeps most of the planet's activity going, from the weather to the photosynthesis by which plants produce energy for themselves and virtually every other living thing.[27] So it was reasonable to wonder whether a change in our star's radiation might explain the change in the weather. Russian astronomer Khabibullo Abdusamatov noted that when the sun's habit of sending out flares from sunspots ceased for about 70 years in the 16th century, Europe became so cold that the Thames River and parts of the Baltic Sea froze over; Norse settlers had to abandon their colonies on Greenland. Abdusamatov predicted that the sun's flaring would, in fact, shortly settle down and that "Earth's global temperature [would] decline to a climatic minimum," an ice age, some time between 2055 and 2060.[28]

But there's no special reason to think sunspots are about to flare out for any extended period. And in any case, the amount of energy the sun releases may be less critical than the amount that reaches Earth's surface. According to NASA, clouds and airborne pollution reflect as much as 70 percent of the sun's energy back out to space, so that changes in cloud and smog cover would trump any small variation in the sun's radiance. For its part, the IPCC concluded that a downturn in radiance that might produce a new ice age isn't due in the well-established solar cycles for at least another 30,000 years, roughly twice the time that all of humanity's civilizations have been on the earth.

A different suggestion involving the sun has pertained to cosmic rays: radiation from deep space. According to this theory, cosmic rays penetrating the atmosphere play a role in helping water condense into cloud drops. When more rays reach the atmosphere, this theory holds, we get more clouds, which reflect sunlight and cool the earth beneath them. A Dane, Henrik Svensmark, contends that when the sun's radiation is strong, it deflects these rays, reducing the extent of cooling clouds. By contrast, he predicts, an anticipated decline in a well-known solar cycle will soon weaken the sun's radiation, allowing cosmic rays to come surging back and clouds to blossom. The trouble with this idea is that Svensmark has been unable, so far, to persuade many other scientists that clouds wax and wane with the strength of cosmic rays.

There is a more disturbing possibility than that the accepted forecast is too extreme. That is, that it may not be extreme enough.

The pace at which the weather changed over the last century, or even at which it revved up in the last three decades, is no guide to the speed with which it may change in the years ahead. In the short time between 2000 and 2005, researchers taking account of rapid warming during the 1990s had to raise by more than 20 percent their estimate of how much the globe had warmed during the 20th century, with the additional heating all coming in that final decade.[29]

Since the IPCC began issuing its state-of-the-science updates on the world's climate in 1990, time has offered a lengthening record by which to judge its earlier forecasts. Some changes fell within the forecast range. But when predictions erred, it was because they were too conservative, not too daring. A forecast that the world's average temperature would rise by between 0.15° and 0.3°c by 2005 was nearly right. Earth's temperatures actually rose by 0.33°c in that time.[30] The same 1990 report foresaw sea levels rising by two millimetres per year; in fact they rose much faster, by 3.3 millimetres annually.[31] That was largely owing to the fact that ice in the Arctic melted twice as quickly, and thirty years sooner, than the report's ice experts had predicted.[32] "Things are happening faster than we expected," conceded Patricia Romero Lankao, a scientist at the U.S. National Center for Atmospheric Research in Boulder, Colorado, who contributed to the ipcc report.[33]

By 2007, the scientific consensus predicted that Earth's temperature would rise by about one-fifth of a degree per decade in the early part of the new century. But that global average concealed sharp differences around the planet. While much of the southern ocean will warm by less than half a degree between now and the mid-2020s, continents in the north can look forward to average temperatures at least a full Celsius degree (1.8°F) higher than today's before 2030. Much higher temperatures are possible. The next few years may, in other words, be even hotter, stormier and rainier than the official world forecast, but they are very *unlikely* to be more temperate. Indeed, there were alarming signs that the climate marble might be about to go right over the rim of the bowl out into the atmospheric unknown.

Many scientists believe that the climate has already passed through a tipping point and that an avalanche of consequences is gathering speed around us. Lonnie Thompson, a glaciologist at Ohio State University, believes that the first pebbles in the avalanche got rolling half a century ago. "There are thresholds in the system," he said. "Warming around Earth's tropical belt is a signal that the climate has exceeded a critical threshold." As a sudden lurch in the climate from one state to another gathers speed "in the near future," he added, "there is the risk of changing the world as we know it to some form in which a lot of people on the planet will be put at risk."[34]

How close is the marble to the edge of the bowl? We can't know for sure, for at least two reasons. Our models are too coarse to produce a precise date, for one. We can't know either what choices we'll make in the critical next few years. Undeterred, the British in 2005 took a sporting run at a very similar question, asking hundreds of researchers around the world to help develop a strategy for "avoiding dangerous climate change."[35] Their inquiry tackled three critical unknowns: how quickly GHG concentrations will rise over the next several decades; how quickly any given increase would warm up the world; and how many additional degrees of average global warming it would take to produce a "dangerous" change in climate.

The answer to the last two questions worked out roughly to this: if $CO_2$ and its equivalents in the atmosphere reach as little as 400 ppm, the consequential warming could push the world into unpredictable and accelerating climate change.[36] The answer to the first question—how quickly we will allow GHGs to accumulate in the atmosphere—remains unknown, depending on our future choices. But even on the entirely unrealistic assumption that growth in global GHG emissions were arrested today, their concentration in the atmosphere was on track to pass that predicted tipping point as early as 2010.

In fewer than 10 years, we will be standing on a different planet.

Meanwhile, the rate and scale of climate change are slipping beyond our limited capacity to influence. Whether industrial emissions brought the atmosphere to its present heated state or something else did, that heat may now be triggering the first of a crescendo of reinforcing feedbacks that will push weather into a dangerously unstable new zone with no further human help. Evidence that this process has already begun appeared in 2007 when scientists at the U.S. National Oceanic and Atmospheric Administration (NOAA) determined that the increase in atmospheric concentrations of GHGs seemed greater than known human emissions alone could explain.[37] The rogue carbon dioxide in the atmosphere may have several possible sources, none comforting.

One is that the planet's forests, for eons a net "sink" of carbon (meaning that they absorbed more than they released) may have flipped over and are now contributing *more* $CO_2$ to the air than they take out of it. Biologists have been warning that exactly this might happen because of large-scale deforestation. As the unused parts of harvested trees decay or are burned in giant bonfires of "slash," they release to the atmosphere most of the carbon they contain. Meanwhile, fewer trees are left standing to re-absorb $CO_2$ from the air to build limbs and leaves. Increasingly frequent fires and proliferations of forest-killing pests further increase the amount of carbon freed to the atmosphere. No one has been certain when the switch would occur, only that when it did, the extra carbon released to the atmosphere could push warming up by another degree beyond the IPCC forecast.[38]

Another possibility is that carbon once locked up in soil and in permanently frozen vegetation may be leaking out to the atmosphere. This can happen in warm climates when the felling of trees exposes soils to biological decay, or simply when warmer temperatures hasten decomposition. Researchers were surprised to find that dirt in the U.K. had been releasing 13 million tons of carbon a year for the last quarter-century, more than offsetting the reduction in GHGs that the country's industry had accomplished over the same time.[39]

In colder regions, milder winters are allowing vast areas once permanently frozen to melt for the first time in millennia. Just as a package of frozen peas left on the counter will soon spoil, ancient moss and other plant material preserved in millions of acres of northern muskeg are now rotting and releasing carbon to the air. It would take only a small fraction of the carbon estimated to lie beneath northern bogs to outweigh by far the six or seven billion metric tons of carbon that humans put into the atmosphere every year.[40]

The same defrosted northern bogs could liberate an even greater danger. Methane, a combination of carbon and hydrogen ($CH_4$), is 23 times better at trapping heat than $CO_2$. Though fortunately far less common in the atmosphere, it's nevertheless next in line after $CO_2$ as a contributor to the greenhouse effect, responsible for about one-fifth of the planet's extra heat over the last century. Ronald Reagan, famously mocked in the 1980s for suggesting that cows cause global warming, has been partly vindicated: more than one-third of the excess methane comes from livestock and especially from flatulent, belching cattle.[41] Additional huge volumes of it are believed to lie trapped beneath the permafrost. Melting the north could have the effect of opening the freezer and letting out that gas as well.

An even bigger methane bomb may lie beneath the oceans. There, at depths usually below 300 metres, where the water is close to freezing, lie absolutely enormous volumes of methane congealed into a form variously known as methane "ice" or methane hydrate.[42] Vast beds of the stuff have been located in the Canadian Arctic, the Gulf of Mexico, west of Central America, around Japan and in the Black and Caspian Seas. Visionary energy companies hope to find a way to tap it as an energy source. But climatologists worry that the earth's rising temperature may get there first, melting the methane and releasing even more into the atmosphere. Just such a big "burp" has been surmised to be the cause of previous bouts of abrupt climate change. Rising temperatures have been detected in the oceans down to depths of 700 metres, well below where methane hydrates may already be defrosting.

Either carbon dioxide from the dirt or methane from the sea may explain how more GHGs have been entering the atmosphere. Another possibility is that lower volumes have been taken out. Throughout the last century's increase in those gases, nature has been scrubbing out of the atmosphere about half of what people have been dumping there. "The concern," Peter Cox, a climate scientist at Britain's Exeter University, has said, "is that climate change itself will affect the ability of the land to absorb our emissions."[43]

Deforestation isn't the only reason to suspect this (indeed, outside the tropics the world's forests were actually expanding as the millennium ticked over). It's also possible that after soaking up enormous quantities of humanity's exhaust $CO_2$ for the last century, the world's oceans have, at least in their upper regions, closest to the atmosphere, approached a stage of saturation at which they can absorb no more. Indeed, British researchers announced in 2007 that they had landed proof of just such an effect in the vast circumpolar Southern Ocean. "It's one of many feedbacks that we didn't expect to kick in until some way into the 21st century," admitted U.K. climate modeller Ian Totterdell.[44]

The oceans have been absorbing more than carbon dioxide. They have also been soaking up as much as four-fifths of the extra heat trapped inside the beefed-up greenhouse layer.[45] Now, that moderating effect may also be running its course. The warmer the upper layers of the sea become, the less easily they absorb additional heat. But heat has to go somewhere: what the oceans can no longer absorb must flow instead into the three great rolls of wind that circle each half of the globe, further amping up day-to-day weather and redrawing the familiar climate map.

The accelerating loss of mid-latitude snow, and of ice from the poles and mountaintops, is similarly ominous. Glistening white ice and snow reflect solar energy back into space in what is known as the "albedo" effect. But as the area of reflective white contracts, newly exposed expanses of darker sea and earth absorb greater amounts of solar energy, not only warming those areas but also hastening the melt of any remaining ice or snow. The difference is substantial: as much as 90 percent of the solar radiance falling on ice fields is bounced back; when the same energy falls on bare ground, as much as 90 percent of its heat is absorbed.[46]

Moisture liberated from melting ice and warmer seas by more energetic ET, meanwhile, increases the amount of water in the atmosphere. Water vapour is a potent GHG too. One study estimated that, in combination with the global decline in albedo, its increase in the atmosphere could "amplify the climate response to greenhouse gas forcing by a factor of 2.5."[47] Melting ice and a more humid climate, that is, might *more than double* the warming produced by other gases alone.

At least some of these feedbacks were certainly already at work when the new century began. As Arctic sea ice crumbled, the exposed water inevitably started to absorb more heat, hastening the end of the ice that remained. Others, like the release of deep-sea methane, might still be waiting to be triggered. They added to other threats hanging over a planet straining the limits of its biological carrying capacity. "Nature isn't linear," observed Jon Foley, a Wisconsin climatologist who joined several other experts to warn in 2001 that decades of human pressure on our habitat was leaving it susceptible to sudden catastrophic change.[48] "Sometimes you can push on a system and push, and finally you have the straw that breaks the camel's back."

This possibility has encouraged a chorus of gloomy outlooks for humanity's future. "Extreme pessimism seems to me the only rational stance," Britain's Astronomer Royal, Sir Martin Rees, succinctly told the 2002 World Economic Forum meeting in New York City.[49] James Lovelock, the scientist who coined the concept of "Gaia" to describe the earth as a single living organism, has predicted that "billions of humans will die, leaving a handful of diminished societies clinging to existence around a (balmy) Arctic Sea."[50]

In a scenario only slightly less bleak, consultants working for the U.S. Department of Defense contemplated the aftermath of an abrupt climate change they found "plausible" as early as 2010. As they imagined events, fresh water from melting Arctic ice would shut down the North Atlantic portion of the Great Ocean Conveyor, plunging northern Europe into a climate "more like Siberia's." Other regions would suffer and their governments tremble as various combinations of colder, windier, hotter and drier weather would reduce harvests and precipitate famine in Asia. Observing that historically, "every time there is a choice between starving and raiding, humans raid," the Pentagon's consultants forecast a sharp spike in hot conflicts. America, they predicted, would abandon its guarantee to Mexico of water from the Colorado River. The United States and Canada, rather than fight, would "become one."[51]

The Pentagon's scenario writers tapped into the same real science that 20th Century Fox exploited for its 2004 disaster flick *The Day After Tomorrow*. The Gulf Stream has, in fact, stopped on at least three previous occasions that we know of, most recently about 12,000 years ago, as the last ice age was ending. At that time, an ice dam over what is now Canada broke open, releasing unimaginably vast volumes of fresh water through the Hudson Strait into the North Atlantic. Measurements from deep-sea instruments show that the Gulf Stream has diminished over the last five decades, although the scientists who compiled the latest IPCC assessment gave it less than one chance in 10 of actually shutting down in the present century.

✦

In *Collapse*, his thought-provoking bestseller on why some societies fail while others prosper, geographer Jared Diamond compared the histories of Japan and Easter Island, each a small island with limited resources supporting a growing population.[52] Both peoples cut down increasingly large numbers of trees: in Japan as building materials and on Easter Island, at least in part, to erect the enormous statues for which it is still famous. In both places, the deforestation caused environmental harm; in particular, water became scarcer. Yet whereas the Japanese responded with strict rules to limit tree-cutting, the Easter Islanders chopped their trees down to the last one. Japan weathered its environmental crisis, continued to thrive and now sustains a population of 127 million. Its forests today occupy a proportion of its land area that is one of the world's highest. Easter Island's population, by contrast, crashed from tens of thousands of reasonably well-fed people to a few hundred semi-starving souls whose descendents have only in the last few decades reintroduced some trees to the island. The moral, Diamond points out, is that Japan recognized its danger and did something about it.

There has been some reason for optimism that industrial nations were ready to follow Japan's model and not Easter Island's. The European Union has set a target of cutting its GHGs by 2020 to nearly one-third below what they had been in 1990. China set a short-term goal of cutting its GHG emissions by 10 percent within five years. And in 2007, U.S. President George W. Bush reversed his long-standing dismissal of climate change to endorse setting global targets for GHG emission reductions by the end of his term. If that smacked of further delay, as some pointed out, California (with an economy larger than Canada's) and many more American states and its biggest cities were already setting their own courses to reduce emissions.

If these commitments are met, we may reasonably hope to duck climageddon. But not even an immediate and profound revolution in lifestyle is about to bring back the 20th century. Indeed, even if every plane were grounded, car parked and factory idled, and even if we cut our carbon emissions to zero instantly, weather would continue to become wilder and seasons less predictable for at least the next two and a half decades.

Why?

Because there is a lag between the moment that a dose of GHG leaves the smokestack and when it reaches the stratosphere and starts trapping heat. It takes more time for that heat to accumulate in the ocean, more still for the sea to release that energy into the hot cummerbund of equatorial wind that constitutes the first "gear" of the climate drivetrain. Only later still does that heat then amp up the violence of a tornado as it rips across Kansas or Ontario. Three decades or more will pass before the GHGs that we released up until yesterday stop pushing the climate marble farther up the side of the bowl. Indeed, had humanity entirely stopped releasing GHGs to the atmosphere as long ago as 2000, average global temperatures would still rise by another one-fifth of a degree (and local temperatures much more than that) from their levels in 2005 before things settled down sometime after 2025.[53]

In other words, unprecedented change in the weather is already in the bank. Areas on either side of the equator will become drier, those farther north, wetter. Some climate zones will disappear altogether. Storms everywhere will be worse, and the droughts between them, drier. Regional forecasts, however, vary.[54]

With its vast size and large equatorial expanse, Africa will become hotter sooner than many other places. Its subtropical regions, already dry, will heat more than moister tropical zones, parching further as ET quickens. Mediterranean Africa and the northern Sahara will get even less rain than now; areas in southern Africa that rely on winter rains will see those dwindle. East Africa will get more rain—but may lose much of it to rising evaporation.

Europe can look forward to warmer northern winters but also much hotter southern summers. Its north will get more violent storms with heavier rainfall; the centre, wetter winters along with drier, more drought-prone summers; and the Mediterranean south, both fewer rainy days and less rain overall.

Asia will warm up by more, and Central Asia from Tibet to Siberia by much more, than the globe as whole, apart from Southeast Asia, which will track the world average. Summer heat waves in China will become more common, more intense and longer, and winter cold snaps rarer. Precipitation will go up almost everywhere in most seasons of the year, but decline in summer in the already arid "Stans" of Central Asia. Recent record monsoons in India and along the Chinese coast are a foretaste of downpours to come. Likewise the more violent typhoons battering Taiwan, China, the Philippines and elsewhere in Southeast Asia.

Australia's early-century experience of searing summer heat and declining winter and spring rain will intensify over the coming decades. New Zealand, especially South Island, can look for stronger winds and more rain along its west coast.

Apart from the deep south, South America will heat up more than the world average. Central America, the Caribbean and the southern Andes will all get less rain and more ET, becoming drier in consequence. But rainfall will increase over central and northern Argentina and may do the same over Ecuador and northern Peru in the continental northwest. Eastern Brazil, already dry, will become more so. The Amazon's outlook is less certain, but climate forecasters at Britain's Hadley Centre predicted that by 2030 the vast, ecologically critical region would experience droughts like the record breaker it saw early in the new century, on average, one year out of two.[55]

"Civilization developed, and constructed extensive infrastructure, during a period of unusual climate stability," six of the United States' most prominent earth scientists reminded the developed world in a joint manifesto published in 2007. "That period is about to end."[56]

Of the new weather conditions, two are likeliest to provoke North American tensions. The first arises from the newly ice-free areas of the southern Arctic, where dark water warmed by 24-hour summer sunshine creates vast updrafts. These act like the former "chimney" over the Amazon, diverting water-laden winds that blow off the

Pacific to the north, away from the lower 48 United States. Rather than dumping snow on the Sierras of California, these now wring out their moisture over northern British Columbia and the Alaska Panhandle.

Much of North America will see more rain, but the greatest increases are likely to be concentrated in the extreme Northwest—northern British Columbia, Alaska and the Yukon—and far east around New England and the Maritimes. Southern British Columbia and Washington may get less rainfall over the course of a full year, but more winter rain that falls on snow to cause flooding. In the eastern shadow of the Rockies, Alberta and adjoining Montana can expect sharper differences between the seasons to overshadow any change in average annual precipitation: summers will continue to get drier, and winters, especially late winters, wetter.

In contrast—and this is the other great implication of climate change for North America—a broad slice across the American South and Southwest will see less precipitation overall.[57] This includes most places below a line that begins just north of San Francisco and runs southeast above New Orleans to southern Florida. The Colorado River states will lose still more of their winter snow; what little arrives will melt earlier. Of the additional precipitation that falls north of that line over the Great Plains, the Mississippi Valley and the mid-Atlantic seaboard, a large portion will arrive in drenching downpours that overwhelm soils, threaten embankments and scour stream beds. More active evaporation will claim a rising share of any portion collected in reservoirs and soils; those losses will increase on a gradient from north to south.

Whether water is life everlasting or just cause for war, an economic asset or a public trust, it is the essential prerequisite for everything else society might hope to enjoy. Here, then, are the two most freighted facts about the future of our continental climate. America is getting drier; its wealthiest and fastest-growing states, much drier. And Canada is getting wetter.

# Chapter 9

## Mirages:
## Taps for Big Plumbing

Dusk falls in the neon desert. At Sirens' Cove the pirates gird for battle. Lights glow aboard two faux galleons, permanently docked in opposing lagoons against the stucco arches of a vaguely Spanish colonial façade. Bare-chested buccaneers in bandanas and stage cutlasses appear at the rail and scramble up theatrically tattered rigging. Along the boardwalk, T-shirted tourists and sports-jacketed conventioneers press against rope handrails for a view of one of the most popular free shows in Las Vegas.

Up and down the fabled Strip, a kaleidoscope of other lights wink and flicker above crawling traffic. Beneath a silvery ovoid roof, a video wall advertises Apple Inc.'s latest i-products in spinning pastel green and pink. Across the Strip, lit windows glimmer against the dark bulk of the Wynn resort, looming behind its Mayan jungle and replica waterfall. Down the Strip, the illuminated fountains at the Bellagio's 10-acre lake subside from one of their periodic eruptions into a relatively modest chorus line of glowing spray. Farther on, a roller coaster twinkles between the cartoonish Manhattan towers of New York-New York. In the distance, an unearthly shaft of green light shoots skyward from the Luxor's black pyramid, as if signalling to space aliens that their suite is ready.

Back at the Cove, a detonation announces the start of the night's first battle. Rock-operatic music swells and mock cannons flash. Fireworks sparkle brilliantly against the broad wings of the Treasure Island resort hotel and casino towering above. Orange and yellow tongues of flame lick upward from the façade behind the ships, and the waters of the lagoon erupt with the impact of imaginary shells. On one vessel a crew of sirens, dressed in Bluebeard-themed bikinis and fishnet pantaloons, struts and preens. Its voluptuous captain introduces herself to the crowd as Cynnamon, although, she intones archly, "whatever seaman sails into my cove just calls me Cyn." Before the tease-and-grind dance show ends, Cyn's Sirens have successfully lured Captain Mack's Chippendale pirates from their galleon for what will plainly be a rousing bit of pillage post-finale. As the performers take a bow and vamp off the deck, an announcer reminds the crowd that the real treasure can, of course, be found inside.

It's precisely the kind of over-the-top tackiness that makes Las Vegas one of the planet's most visited and also reviled destinations. The civic come-on line—"What happens here, stays here"—is a sly wink to the city's well-nourished reputation as a kind of Disneyland for grownups, a pay-to-play paradise where the fantasies are X-rated but essentially harmless, and everyone gets to go home with nothing worse than a headache (although usually relieved of a considerable amount of personal treasure).[1]

Las Vegas' frank embrace of sanitized sin has perhaps made it all the easier for eco-moralists to single it out for loathing. To its many finger-wagging critics, the very idea of a resort in a desert, let alone one with waterfalls, dancing fountains and a cove big enough to host a pirate battle, is a felony against ecological ethics. California-based urban theorist Mike Davis calls the fastest-growing metropolis in the United States an avatar of "apocalyptic urbanism … aggressively turning its profligacy into a kind of environmental terrorism against its neighbors."[2]

Jaime Cruz politely begs to differ. Coming to the United States after graduating from university only to find that the engineering degree he earned in his native Peru was worthless in the land of op-portunity, Jaime made good in Las Vegas the old-fashioned way: he worked for it. He bussed tables at the opening of the Mirage in 1989, just as a new generation of mega-resorts began punting aside the old 99-cent buffets, offering celebrity chefs and $250 seats at the Cirque instead. Watching the in-house jobs board, Jaime eventually moved into facility maintenance. Compact, choosing words carefully and dressed for the executive suite in a dark suit and tie, Jaime is now director of environmental services for MGM Mirage, the $20 billion U.S. corporation that owns Treasure Island, New York-New York, the Mirage and Bellagio, among other properties.

He doesn't mince words. "We're not here to save the environment. That's not our job; that's not how we make our money; that's not what our shareholders give us jobs for," he told me. "Our product is the experience of Las Vegas. We're here to make the customer want to come back. Now, if we can do that smarter, keeping the environment in mind, then, of course, that is our job."[3]

Meeting me one morning by the side of Sirens' Cove, Jaime ex-plains one way he balances the two sides of his role. Most of the fresh water at our feet, enough to fill three Olympic-size pools, is being used for the second time, he tells me: it was earlier flushed down the drain above us in the hotel's 3,000 suites. Waste "grey" water from showers and tubs collects in tanks beneath a parking garage, mixing there with smaller amounts of runoff from landscape irriga-tion, the occasional rain drained from paved areas and undrinkable saline groundwater pumped from beneath the casino's footings. In a large, noisy room, pumps push the water through a bank of reverse-osmosis filters to scrub it clean enough for use in Sirens' Cove and the moat around the Mirage's faux volcano next door. And, Jaime boasted, that is very clean indeed: "We have swimmers in here, we can't put anything in that's not treated to the highest standards. Our recycled water is state-certified as better than bottled water." What happens in this corner of Las Vegas stays here in ways that few guests would imagine.

Having now lived in Vegas for 20 years, Jaime says local attitudes toward water have undergone a sea change. MGM is doing business differently. Thirsty turf on more than half its outdoor acreage has been replaced with desert-friendly "xeriscaping"[4] that uses two-thirds less water. Even that is drip-fed in accordance with temperature and humidity conditions, as broadcast daily from a weather station at the Bellagio.

Jaime is also proud to have reduced the use of water from guests' showers. As we walked past blinking slots and spot-lit blackjack tables like elevated putting greens, he explains how this has happened. Water is money in Las Vegas, but when a vendor showed up to pitch a showerhead he claimed could slash the amount dispensed every minute by 40 percent, from 2.5 gallons (industry standard for "low-flow" heads) to *one* and a half, "we were skeptical," Jaime recalls. "We said, 'Ow, that's gotta feel horrible!' Because until then, everything we had tried lowered the experience, and we didn't want that for our guests."

"The first thing I did," he says, "was try it myself. I didn't believe it. I thought, 'This has gotta be wrong, 'cause this feels really good.' So I stood there in my shower with a five-gallon paint bucket and timed one minute. Then I took an empty gallon container of milk and poured it into that and verified that it was one point five [gallons]." He solicited other executives to try the stingy head, making a point of including women: "I've been told that women appreciate showers more than men, in that they have longer hair and need to get the shampoo out." Only after it won their wholehearted approval, as well, was the device installed in Treasure Island—in a single room. "We put it in an unknown room, snuck it in, didn't tell anybody about it, fearing that somebody was going to complain and we'd go change it. No harm, no foul. But a month went by and no complaints. Then we did three or four more rooms. No complaints. Then we did one whole floor. I couldn't sleep that night." After the new heads passed that test as well, however, MGM installed them in nearly 45,000 suites. The amount of water they save in a month in just one of its resorts, the 5,000-room MGM Grand, would more than fill the Sirens' Cove.[5]

Las Vegas and its sprawling suburbs do offer much for an out-sider to fault. The 1.8 million people living there—seven-tenths of Nevada's population—use water twice as fast as other Americans, consuming 60 percent more even than those dwelling in Tucson, another desert city. Yet Las Vegas' profligacy is a mirage in more ways than one. Most of the waste takes place away from the Strip, which uses a lower share of city water—three percent of the total[6]—than many other cities' key industries. Even off the Strip, the region's thirst isn't quite what it seems. Las Vegas' bad rap from those who advocate for a lighter ecological footprint has obscured the impressive amount of ingenuity being deployed to keep the city's game afloat.

In west Las Vegas a landscaped embankment indistinguishable from those that surround gated neighbourhoods nearby encircles tile-roofed buildings and a covered reservoir that cleans up grey water collected from the surrounding houses in a process similar to the one at Sirens' Cove. Here, the recycled water is distributed to local parks and golf courses for irrigation. Bylaws throughout the valley prohibit water-guzzling grass from being planted in front of new homes (it's allowed in the back, where children might play). The region's water utility has spent $100 million U.S.[7] in getting the owners of older properties to replace turf with desert landscaping, an initiative that has seen the equivalent of 1,000 football[8] fields of grass dug up. A strict schedule dictates when and for how long homeowners may water the landscaping they do have. Daily patrols by "water cops" monitor compliance. While Nevadans still run far more through their taps than most people living where rain waters the shrubbery, consumption in the valley fell by one-sixth in the early years of the century, even while the number of people living there grew in nearly the same proportion.

Those steps have not solved the desert resort's water worries. Nine-tenths of its water comes from the Colorado River. Under an hour from the Strip, the "bathtub ring," as locals call the exposed rock around a shrunken Lake Mead, is a visible reminder of that river's decline. Various analysts forecast that Las Vegas may face shortages as early as 2010, or, if not then, by 2015. The Southern Nevada Water Authority (SNWA) assures its customers that it can push that crisis off until at least mid-century. The centrepiece of its strategy to keep the water flowing in Vegas' canals and faux lagoons was a highly provocative plan to extend two big pipes hundreds of miles to aquifers underlying the Utah border.

As uniquely cheesy as Las Vegas may be, away from the lights it is little different in economic imperatives and environmental overuse from any other North American city. The choices facing Southern Nevada—including whether to import distant well water or pursue the very long-odds alternative of capping pell-mell growth—await us all.

Almost everywhere, our multiplying numbers and expanding economies are on a collision course with the limits of water supply. Or, to be more exact, they are colliding with *conveniently available* water. As we discovered in earlier chapters, many places are getting more precipitation; on average, the globe is actually getting wetter. In the aggregate, viewed year-round and over the full cycle of such influences as El Niño, there's plenty of water. But as wet weather migrates about the planet, some of our most vibrant regions, including the American Southwest, are being left out to dry. Our species' problem isn't that we're running out of water altogether. It's that there may not be any where and when people need it.

It's a problem of distribution, both geographic and temporal. Water is available in the wrong place, or on the wrong occasion, or in the wrong form for our economic convenience. There's either too much water or too little, but seldom water in amounts Goldilocks would call "just right." Abundance flows where few of us choose to live; supplies are tight where we flock. Streams brim when fields are fallow, then go dry when crops are swelling.

It has, to a degree, ever been thus. But the gift of water from the sky, always capricious, is becoming more so as the globe's air currents bobble and rearrange themselves. Our problem of distribution is becoming more acute in both its dimensions. Moreover, we can't be quite sure how fast these changes are gaining on us or how turbulent they may become. Those with the longest perspective, like paleoclimatologist Richard Hebda, urge us, therefore, to build "resiliency" into whatever we might do. To equip ourselves for the widest conceivable range of future conditions with strategies and investments that will perform well in high water and low as well as during wild swings between the two.

The good news is that we have options. Vexing distribution is a much better problem to have than absolute shortage would be. It's a lot easier to live on an annual income of $200,000 paid all at once in December than on $100 paid every week through the year. But be it cash or water, we must bank it, managing within our means.

The menu of choices for budgeting through the uncertain weather ahead falls into two broad categories: *things* we can build and *activities* we can change. *Things* run the gamut of physical means to save and store water, from small solutions like new shower heads to extremely large ones like replications of Lake Mead. *Activities* are what we can do as individuals, companies, communities and nations to use water more efficiently, like letting our lawns go brown in August or choosing societally to pay more for the water we use.

In the remainder of this chapter, we'll take a look at *things*. We'll find that while much of what we've built in the past has been effective, it's also increasingly costly and poorly adapted to our future needs. The chapters that follow will examine some *activities* that might prove far more helpful than anything we can buy or construct. Preparations take time, and doing nothing is a choice, too: the worst one. We must favour the approaches likeliest to work for our own valleys, plains, coasts and communities, and begin to make them happen.

The estuary marshes that fringe the Bay of Fundy are as different from the deserts of southern Nevada as it is possible to imagine: cool, damp, green places with frequent fog and some of the highest tides in the world sweeping in twice a day. The indigenous people here took advantage of the lowest tides to build brush weirs that trapped fish swimming in on the highest ones. When the settlers who came to be known as Acadians arrived, among their first projects was altering this natural flow to better suit their farming economy.

They would enclose an estuary inside an earth and sod dike, penetrated by one or two wooden culverts. At the seaward end of the culverts they installed flapper gates, hinged at the top and opening out. At high tide the pressure of the sea kept the gates—known as *aboideaux*—shut, preventing salt water from flowing into the marshes. But when the tide fell, any fresh water that built up behind the dike could push the gates open and flow out. Over the course of a few years, the constant freshwater flow turned the former saltwater marshes behind these dikes into prime pastures.

The story of human society has largely been a story of plumbing. At the dawn of civilization, more than 6,000 years ago, ancient Egyptians used low dikes to capture the Nile's flood on their fields. Not long after, Mesopotamians in what is now Iraq built weirs and dug canals to divert water out of the Euphrates, irrigating their crops and draining the excess water back into the Tigris. Later, Persians excavated tunnels to convey water from distant hillside springs to their cities. Rome, in its turn, built stone aqueducts to transport water across entire river valleys to nourish fields, splash in fountains and supply houses with running water. Long before the Hoover Dam made the American desert bloom, Hopi and Anasazi societies diverted rivers through canals to their fields in what is now Arizona and New Mexico.[9] Central America's Mexica, the Andean Inca and societies across southern Asia tampered not only with water but with earth, sculpting hillsides into terraced shelves to conserve their water. In 2007 villagers in Alacahöyük, Turkey, returned to service a dam that had first been commissioned 3,246 years earlier by a king named Tudhaliyas, a Hittite monarch who had been forced by drought to import wheat from Egypt.[10]

Water wheels powered the earliest industry in Canada and the United States. The largest cities in Europe and eastern North

America owe much of their modern stature to having invested first in sewers and then in pipes to distribute clean water in the 19th and early 20th centuries. Wherever today's cities are growing, their governments put their highest priority, after roads and electricity, on delivering those same basic services.

Our species' inveterate redirection of water for its own convenience is as inherent a behaviour as it is for another habitual engineer: *Castor*, the beaver. Whether it has always been wise is another matter.

The 20th century may have witnessed the zenith of *Homo castor*'s accomplishment. Whether the water flowed on top of the ground, pooled invisibly beneath it or bubbled from a source far away, we reached out to seize it on an ever grander scale.

Where lakes were absent, we created them. North Americans were especially energetic, raising large dams on virtually every major river we could reach, often "taming" a single stream with multiple barriers. We redirected rivers from the Pacific to the Gulf of Mexico and others from Hudson Bay to the Atlantic. Europeans likewise dammed most of their rivers. Where they could afford to, nations in South America, Asia and Africa followed suit.

By the 21st century, humanity had barred the natural flow of six out of every 10 big rivers on earth. The world's reservoirs held more water than Lake Huron, roughly the amount our entire species uses each year.[11] China alone had built some 24,000 large dams.[12] The U.S. National Inventory of Dams listed 8,100 that are at least five storeys high; Canada claimed 850 more than nine storeys high, not including any being used to hold back mine tailings.[13] Estimates of the number of smaller dams dotting the continent run into the millions.[14] Dammed reservoirs provided water to one-third of the world's irrigated acreage and half the municipal water systems in North America.[15]

Natural or artificial, however, lakes are rarely sources of water themselves.[16] Rather, they're the banks that buffer the ups and downs of nature's water delivery. Saskatchewan has survived the plunge in summer water levels in rivers flowing out of Alberta because the

Gardner Dam captures enough of the South Saskatchewan River's spring freshet (in a lake named for native son and mid-20$^{th}$-century Prime Minister John Diefenbaker) to carry much of the province through the dry months that follow. Lakes Mead and Powell allow 30 million Americans in the Southwest to stretch the rain and snow that fall over the Colorado Basin in occasional wet years over several successive dry ones. Water banked in Egypt's Lake Nasser saw that country through a turn-of-the-century drought that brought famine and violence to the less fortunate Ethiopia, Somalia and Sudan. In 2006 China opened the floodgates of its recently completed (and still only partly filled) Three Gorges Dam on the Yangtze, releasing water from its reservoir to relieve regions downstream that were experiencing their lowest rainfall in a century and a quarter.

The ability to counter extreme swings in precipitation is becoming ever more valuable. It was for this reason that Tim Barnett and his colleagues at the Scripps Institution distinguished regions "where reservoir storage capacity is adequate" from those where it is not, which will find themselves increasingly vulnerable to shortages as springtime recedes and snow melts earlier. It's thanks to reservoirs that the Colorado River states, Manitoba (with dams on the Churchill River) and southern Ontario (with storage along the Grand River) are relatively immune today to this particular consequence of climate shift. Places lacking such storage, the Scripps team forecast, "will [encounter] regional water shortages ... within the next few decades."[17]

Many dams also generate energy. It was mainly to power wartime factories that Ontario reversed its Kenogami River and the United States dammed the Columbia in the 1940s. Hydroelectricity was the objective again later, when British Columbia dammed its portions of the Columbia and Peace rivers in the sixties, when Quebec did the same on several rivers flowing into James Bay in the seventies, and when China invested $25 billion in its Three Gorges, the biggest hydroelectric project in the world, beginning in the 1990s. In each case, the initial cost was enormous for its day. The price of the energy those projects generate, however, is relatively free of inflation and even declines, unlike fossil-fuelled power, as the original investment is paid down (and fuel prices rise). Larger reservoirs also offer economies of scale as they can create some power longer through dry spells. With very large reservoirs on two of its biggest rivers, British Columbia is especially resilient during shifts of rainfall north or south as El Niño alternates with La Niña.

The ability to manage the flow of water conveys additional advantages. In many places, dammed reservoirs restrain sudden bursts of runoff from heavy downpours or quickly melting snow, reducing the risk of flooding downstream. By controlling the amount of water released later on, they can also maintain river levels for the benefit of navigation and wildlife. An unrelated but perhaps more widely appreciated benefit is the recreation many artificial lakes provide. The Tennessee Valley Authority oversees 29 dams that offer the full suite of benefits; they brought electric light to seven Appalachian states and helped lift one of America's most neglected regions out of Depression-era poverty.

For all these reasons, large reservoirs continue to find advocates. Confronting California's disappearing snowpack, Governor Arnold Schwarzenegger asked his citizens in 2007 to approve a bond of $4.5 billion U.S. to construct two big new reservoirs in the north and south of the state.[18] Farmers in southern Alberta face the same climate threat. If they expect to keep harvesting water-sensitive spuds and table vegetables, Brent Paterson told me, they too may need more large dams on principal river courses. (Off-stream reservoirs like Stafford Lake are less controversial but are also less effective for capturing mid-winter rains.) Paterson and the Daminator have plenty of company. Both Quebec and neighbouring Newfoundland wish to add to their existing power dams on rivers between Hudson Bay and the Labrador coast. In fast-growing northeast Texas, utilities have mapped out four new reservoirs they hope to begin filling by 2030.[19]

Beyond North America, China has offered the countries of Southeast Asia up to $100 billion to build a series of dams on the Mekong River, mainly for irrigation.[20] India was at work on more than

450 dams of various sizes, mainly to store the extra rainwater falling during increasingly heavy monsoons for use during the hotter, drier seasons between them.[21] Planners in Turkey hoped not only to build hundreds of new dams but to connect them all with aqueducts and canals that would allow water to be directed from place to place almost anywhere in the country.[22] Climate researcher Hayley Fowler called for a similar campaign of reservoir-building in Britain, both to reduce flooding from the extreme multi-day rainstorms that have quadrupled in frequency over Scotland and to capture water to supply southern counties during increasingly dry summers.[23] Altogether, the World Wildlife Fund calculated that some 1,500 medium-size to very large dams were under construction around the world in the new century.[24]

Yet for all their utility, dams, especially big ones, carry enormous drawbacks. The toll on downstream habitat, grimly apparent in the Colorado Delta, ranks high amongst the environmental costs. Greater damage and dislocation occur upstream, where reservoirs invariably drown landscapes important to people and wildlife. That has long made dams the target of protest. Historically, some of the earliest dams in medieval England, built to power water wheels for mills, sparked protest from bargemen no longer able to navigate blocked streams. Early 20th-century naturalists who resisted a dam in California's Yosemite Valley lost that battle but forged the continent's first environmental movement.

Canada's record on this score over the last century was mostly discreditable. From Ontario's wartime reversal of the Kenogami River to British Columbia's post-war drive to capture energy from mountain streams, this country repeatedly flooded land that First Nations had occupied for centuries. Rarely did governments consult native communities due to be submerged. Never did they ask permission first.

In a conspicuously shameful episode, the British Columbia government turned over the Nechako River to the Aluminum Company of Canada (now Alcan) in 1950 to construct a dam that would provide power to an aluminum refinery at Kitimat, on the Pacific coast north of Vancouver. Neither company nor province bothered to inform the Cheslatta people living along the river that they were about to lose their homes until five days before the water began to rise behind the newly completed Kenney Dam. Not until the water had already claimed some buildings did representatives arrive to "negotiate" compensation and the band's relocation. "We were refugees in our own country," Chief Marvin Charlie recalled, decades after the expulsion. His people lost more than land and livelihood: worse, in some ways, was the violation of spirit and social fabric, as alcoholism, abuse and suicide soared.[25]

Similar injuries multiplied over the next half-century, as dams were raised on every continent. Over time it became much more difficult, at least in open societies, to flood places considered remote by the corporations, governments and cities that stood to benefit from dams, but where people facing inundation still lived. By century's end, opposition to such projects reached such an intensity that the World Bank, a major financier of dams in poor countries, joined with the World Conservation Union to commission an unprecedented assessment of the true costs and benefits of big dams. Its verdict, delivered in 2000, was harsh.

According to the World Commission on Dams, some 80 million people have been forced from their homes in the last half-century to accommodate reservoirs. And, in a sense, the dispossessed were the lucky ones: they lived. In 1978 Indian police killed four while firing on a crowd protesting the construction of a dam in Bihar State. In 1985 Guatemala's right-wing junta approved the murder of more than 375, mostly indigenous Achi women and children, in order to make room for the Chixoy Dam.[26]

The projects that displaced millions had almost invariably cost far more than expected or fell short of their promise: frequently both. Of 81 large projects the Commission analyzed, three-quarters had cost more than forecast, running over budget, on average, by more than half. Over two-thirds of reservoirs created mainly to deliver water had failed to produce as much of it as projected, with one in four of those unable to deliver even half of what was anticipated (although smaller reservoirs generally came closer than big ones).[27] And while many large dams built to make electricity benefitted the economies they served, the Commission found it impossible to say for sure whether those benefits outweighed the social and environmental costs. "Substantive evaluations," it observed, "are few in number, narrow in scope, [and] poorly integrated across impact categories."[28]

The World Commission on Dams was unique for its balanced membership of advocates and critics and for its global mandate. Its unanimous report was all the more persuasive in concluding that:

+ Large dams have "extensive impacts on rivers, watersheds and aquatic ecosystems—these impacts are more negative than positive and, in many cases, have led to irreversible loss of species and ecosystems.

+ "Efforts to date to counter the ecosystem impacts of large dams have met with limited success …

+ "Pervasive and systematic failure to assess the range of potential negative impacts and implement adequate mitigation … have led to the impoverishment and suffering of millions, giving rise to growing opposition to dams by affected communities worldwide.

+ "Since the environmental and social costs of large dams have been poorly accounted for in economic terms, the true profitability of these schemes remains elusive."[29]

Once built, at great expense, a dam is there for good. You can neither move it nor easily re-engineer it into a different configuration. If a changing climate diminishes the rainfall it was expected to capture, as appears to be happening for the vast reservoirs on the Colorado, it is too late to scale down construction. Conversely, if heavy downpours become more frequent or extreme than designers anticipated, a dam may fail to hold back the resulting flood, with potentially catastrophic consequences. Or, as in India, operators may have to release so much water in order to save the structure that disaster strikes downstream, anyway.

Less overtly calamitous than a dam break, evaporation poses a further threat to large open-air reservoirs as temperatures rise. ET already draws more water from reservoirs than people take from them for industrial and domestic consumption combined: an invisible annual loss worldwide equivalent to nearly half the volume of Lake Erie.[30] Lake Mead gives up three metres of its water every year to the dry desert air. In Oklahoma, ET has stolen every drop that once flowed into what maps still identify as the Optima Reservoir, even though it has dried up completely.[31]

What's the lesson? Yes, dammed reservoirs hold water, but they're also expensive in literally incalculable ways. Hydroelectric power may arguably produce fewer GHGs than some competing energy sources, but it is harsh on the environment in other respects.[32] And with ET exacting a daily penalty, an open reservoir is a losing proposition as a way to stockpile liquid assets.

Where we haven't drawn water from rivers or lakes, we've taken it from the ground. Shallow wells are as old as human settlements, often determining where villages developed and becoming their focal point. A well supplies water to the house in which I grew up; another serves my house today. In that, I am like roughly one in four British Columbians and one-half of humans around the globe.

Even so, the last century witnessed a rush of well drilling on a scale as unprecedented as its enthusiasm for dams. Several innovations drove the boom. First, mechanical drilling became more capable, making it possible to reach water deeper underground. Secondly, improved centrifugal pumps made it possible to pull water from the deeper aquifers the drills could now reach. And lastly, electricity reached rural areas, providing cheap and often heavily subsidized energy to run those pumps. Together, these developments sharply increased both the number of places where wells could be sunk and of farms and rural households that could afford them.

The attraction was obvious: once a well was dug, water was almost free; farmers could use it however they chose and in whatever quantities. Between the middle and the end of the 20th century, truly hundreds of millions of new wells went down worldwide. The number in India alone went from about one million in 1960 to 26 million at the end of the century. From those wells around the globe, enough water flowed each year to fill four Columbia Rivers.[33]

These flows of groundwater have kept two-thirds of the world's irrigated fields green. A single aquifer we've seen earlier, the giant Ogallala pool that runs from Texas to the Dakotas, has sustained one-fifth of all U.S. irrigation. Wells put water in one-third of Canadian homes, half the residences in the United States and Europe, and an even greater portion of those in China and India. In those developing states, the ability to water crops at any time freed millions of rural families from near-starvation, providing food security and even modest prosperity.

If all of this has seemed a little too much like a free lunch, the reason is that it has been. The underground pools into which all of these wells dip their straws are limited, just like ones above ground. Often, in fact, they're the same bodies: water masses that appear in some places as surface springs, rivers or lakes may extend underground for long distances beyond them. Powerful new pumps also reach deep waters that are separate from those on the surface, but their very separation means that these may not be recharged by rainwater or melting snow. Geological features that took eons to develop, these deep aquifers are effectively as finite as mineral ore: once mined out, they're gone for good.

Seldom is anyone sure precisely how large these underground pools are, how much water they hold or how fast even shallow aquifers refill from the surface. Often, all we know for certain is how far down the well the top of the water lies. We're like motorists driving a car out into the empty desert, foot to the floor, but without a gauge on the gas tank.

Las Vegas was one place with its pedal, in this analogy, planted firmly to the metal. Although nine-tenths of its water comes from the Colorado River, another tenth comes from underground. True,

Vegas is a city in a desert, but it was built over an oasis. The Spanish word *vegas* refers to the meadows that once bloomed a kilometre or so northwest of today's Sirens' Cove. The springs are still there. In places, salty groundwater lies so near the surface that buildings need sump pumps to keep their basements dry. Deeper aquifers are potable, and each year businesses, municipal wells and homeowners pump about 93 million cubic metres of water from them: roughly the amount that leaks from the All-American Canal each year. Nevada water engineers believe only about one-third of that is replaced by the rare flash floods that race out of the surrounding hills after rainstorms and soak away into the desert. They have made fitful attempts to close the gap for more than half a century, without success.[34]

The groundwater deep beneath the old oasis is dropping. The same has happened all across the continental Southwest and in scores of other places around the world. In the fastest-growing parts of southern Arizona between Phoenix and Tucson, water tables have receded more than 150 metres in the last seven decades, drying out the desert soil so thoroughly that like a giant mud-puddle, it has developed gargantuan fissures, many of them kilometres long. Booming Denver's water table is in geological free fall, dropping nine metres a year in the new century.[35] Wells in Kansas must go even deeper than those in Arizona to chase the receding High Plains Ogallala Aquifer, which replenishes in dry times at the barely measurable rate of 0.08 millimetres per year and refills by less than a centimetre per year even in wet seasons.[36] South of the Rio Grande, so much water has been mined from beneath Mexico City—once a lake—that the soil there has subsided into the vacated space; the city now sits about three storeys lower than it did a century ago.

All that said, cities and farmers in the western hemisphere have been pikers compared to their counterparts in Asia. At the turn of the century, the overdraft of groundwater in India and China had reached 10 times the United States' deficit.[37] Water tables beneath both countries' most productive grain-growing regions have dropped twice as far in three decades as the High Plains Aquifer has in five. As they fell, half of India's old hand-dug wells and even millions of new drilled ones stopped flowing; where owners of small farms had borrowed money to drill now-dry holes, social agencies reported a spate of farm suicides. Beneath China's capital of Beijing, wells must now go down a kilometre or more to find water. The coastal megatropolis of Shanghai, which began pumping water from beneath its own foundations in 1860, has experienced the same sinking feeling as Mexico City; it has spent $35 billion to repair damage from the combined effects of land subsidence and encroaching tides.[38]

The farmers, cities, states and nations pumping most strenuously risk doing so right up to the moment when the tank runs dry. When that moment will come for anyone is a guessing game. That it must is a geological near-certainty.

Hundreds of millions of people who were lifted out of desperate hunger by the late 20th-century rush to irrigate now face dropping back. "In essence," wrote Australian author, engineer and groundwater expert Lance Endersbee, "there has been an artificial stimulus of food production in many countries where groundwater enabled [harvests] to be raised well above sustainable levels. Countries have been borrowing water on credit, and effectively borrowing food on credit, neither of which can be repaid. It means that the world is facing an even more serious food crisis."[39]

In parts of India, where at least one farm in four relied on overtaxed wells, "groundwater supplies could be exhausted within the next five to 10 years," predicted Tushaar Shah, who heads a research station in Gujarat for the Stockholm-based International Water Management Institute. "When the balloon bursts, untold anarchy will be the lot of rural India."[40]

Yet farmers and urbanites everywhere continued to dip more straws into the tank. For every dry well abandoned in northern China at the end of the 20th century, drillers punched two new and deeper ones.[41] Increasingly high-tech India enlisted imagery from its growing satellite fleet to target tens of thousands of new wells on buried rivers.

✦

True to its character, Las Vegas made more extravagant plans. The SNWA proposed to spend $3.5 billion to pipe water more than 400 kilometres from wells beneath the state's thinly populated eastern frontier.[42] This scheme embodied all the most controversial elements of the third common way humans have historically obtained water: by getting it from somewhere else. Like the ancient Persians with their tunnels and Romans with their aqueducts, the Los Angelenos of the last century piped water in from the shadow of the Sierra Nevadas 480 kilometres north of Hollywood Boulevard. That scandal-shrouded undertaking turned the green Owens Valley into a place of whispering dust devils and stinging salt-flats and, much later, provided the plot for the *noir* drama *Chinatown*. Critics feared that Las Vegas' thirst now spelled the same fate for the Snake and Spring Valleys in eastern Nevada's White Pine County.

Patricia Mulroy, the SNWA's much-admired general manager, argued that those upland ranges held the only remaining water that could save Las Vegas from going dry. "We must have a backup supply to protect southern Nevada during a long and protracted drought," she told state legislators considering the plan in early 2007. "We must get it done by the middle of the next decade. We looked at everything. [A pipeline] is the only solution that can meet the time frame." The Authority insists that it will take only the sustainable pulse of new water that enters the ground with each year's spring rain and melting snow. It promises to begin pumping gingerly and to pull back if its withdrawals cause damage. "The days of Owens Valley are over," Mulroy testified. "Owens Valley happened when there were no environmental laws. Today it is very different."[43]

Perhaps. But naturalists like Nevada state biologist Jon Sjöberg point out that life in the arid valleys relies entirely on a few surface springs, the last vestiges of a lake that slowly evaporated and drained into the desert gravel after the continent's glaciers melted 10,000 years ago. The water trail through the area's fractured geology is complex and largely unmapped, making it difficult to predict how extractions in one place will affect springs elsewhere. Sjöberg has already had to break out buckets to rescue endangered fish from a spring that went dry after farmers began to pump water nearby. "We're in a constant crisis mode," he says, "running from one disaster with one species to another, trying to keep them from going extinct." The Authority's pumps, he fears, will push many more such vulnerable micro-habitats over the edge, endangering not only minnows but the entire food chain the remote springs support, from elk and bighorn sheep down to less charismatic creatures such as desert tortoise, sage grouse and pygmy rabbits. "It doesn't take much to affect them," he points out. "And that's where it kind of takes your breath away. You're looking at something happening on a landscape scale. We spend a lot of time just staring at the wall, going 'Oh shit, what do we do?'"[44]

The answer from his superiors in the state administration appeared to be "Not much." Nevada's then-Governor Kenneth Guinn ordered the state Department of Wildlife (Sjöberg's employer) to drop out of a study, run in cooperation with the federal U.S. Bureau of Land Management, that sought to determine how the SNWA's withdrawals might affect plants and animals on the surface. Nevada's State Engineer, whose responsibilities include ruling on how much water any industry in the state may pump out of the ground, declined to delay that decision until a second federal agency, the U.S. Geological Survey, should finish its tests, which were designed to reveal how much water was actually beneath Snake and Spring valleys. Many rural Nevadans were left highly skeptical of Pat Mulroy's assurance. Dean Baker, who ranches near Spring Valley, doubted that the Authority would be willing, once its billions were spent, to turn off its pumps if Spring Valley began to lose its namesake oases. "If they build that pipeline," Dean believed, "the urge will be overpowering to keep it full."[45]

Like dams, Nevada's pipeline threatens to cost too much and produce too little. Las Vegas wields overwhelming political power and unlimited money, whereas thinly populated White Pine County actually went broke early in the new century. Proponents argued that economic necessity compelled construction to begin before questions about the pipeline's impact could be fully answered. It was even uncertain whether the water being sought was really there to be had. But like a dam, once built, the pipeline would constitute an inflexible fact in the ground, demanding to be filled and resisting adaptation to future circumstances. Meanwhile, for the ranchers and pygmy rabbits of the Snake and Spring valleys, the prospective pipeline underscored the zero-sum arithmetic of water in a single basin: water removed cannot simultaneously serve its original ecological function.

Long-distance water transfers present additional risks. Once a continuous channel unites two water bodies, any harmful presence in one of them may contaminate the other. Just such a hazard compelled the U.S. Environmental Protection Agency (EPA) to spend $10 million to install a virtual "fence" in the Chicago Sanitary and Ship Canal to deter Asian Bighead carp from advancing into the Great Lakes.[46] Zebra mussels, which entered those Lakes in ballast water discharged by ocean-going freighters, had already travelled the other way through the Chicago channel, infesting northern stretches of the Mississippi.

For similar reasons, the unfortunately named Devil's Lake in North Dakota tormented Canada-U.S. relations around the turn of the century. The lake nearly tripled in extent during the 1990s, as the changing weather brought more rain to the upper Midwest. After the lake flooded several farms, schools and entire communities, North Dakota decided it was time to let some of the water out into the Sheyenne River, a tributary of the Red River that ultimately flows through Manitoba into Lake Winnipeg. The decision provoked near-hysteria among some Canadians who feared that (unspecified) organisms in the American water would threaten species north of the border. The kerfuffle was calmed only after the North Dakotans agreed to filter the water released and closely monitor its quality.

All these shortcomings have made large-scale river diversions and water transfer schemes even more controversial than dams in some parts of North America. We've seen earlier how the mere spectre of a pipeline from the Great Lakes to the thirsty Southwest has inspired decades of effort to frame toothy laws to prevent such an eventuality. Canada, as I noted before, has legislated a ban on the bulk transfer of water out of any river basins under federal rule. Still, many activists demand that bans on water diversion be made even more stringent. As evidence of the lingering threat, they point to a pair of visionary, even hallucinatory, schemes from the mid-20th century.

The first was conceived in the 1960s by a firm of California engineers. The North American Water and Power Alliance (NAWAPA) would have run artificial rivers over the length and half the breadth of the continent. It proposed to capture water that now flows into the Arctic Ocean down the Peace, Liard and other northern rivers. An assortment of tunnels, siphons and pumping stations, all on gargantuan scale, as well as natural waterways, would reroute the rivers' flow through the Rocky Mountain Trench (since that time partly flooded by British Columbia's Bennett Dam) to destinations as far apart as Duluth and the *Ciénega de Santa Clara*. The scheme promised to provide enough water to satisfy all the wannabe irrigators in Brent Paterson's inbox, secure the future of High Plains farmers and turn Mexico's northern deserts into a Chihuahuan version of the Imperial Valley.

A competing Canadian proposal came out of the fertile brain of Newfoundland engineer Tom Kierans. The GRAND (Great Recycling and Northern Development) Canal would first have enclosed James Bay, the southern extension of Hudson Bay, in a scaled-up version of the Acadian *aboideaux*, allowing the many rivers that flow into the shallow bay to create, over time, the world's largest artificial freshwater lake. A network of pumps, canals and reversed rivers (including Canada's Abitibi and Ottawa and portions of the Mississippi and Missouri in the United States) would have delivered water almost as far and wide as the rival American scheme.[47] First conceived in 1959, the supersize megaproject briefly enjoyed enough political oxygen to win high-profile endorsements in the 1980s from both Quebec Premier Robert Bourassa and Canadian Prime Minister Brian Mulroney.

Well into the new century, Kierans continued to defend his GRAND vision as an idea whose time would one day come. "In history," he told me from his home in St. John's, "we don't do things until the cost of *not* doing them is 10 times the cost of doing them. We just have to wait."[48] Virtually every other commentator on North America's water supply disagreed. Even enthusiastic engineers derided both blueprints for re-plumbing the continent as extreme examples of hubristic overreach.[49]

Yet schemes nearly as inflated were either on the drawing board or under way on other continents. Early in the new century, India's government approved a plan to divert the equivalent of nearly three Colorado Rivers from more than a dozen Himalayan tributaries of the Ganges and the equally important Brahmaputra River. The water would pour through a network of canals 12,000 kilometres long (roughly the distance from Vancouver to St. John's and back again) to replenish 17 depleted southern rivers and rescue millions of farm families whose drilled wells were going dry. Originally scheduled to deliver its first water by 2016 at a cost of somewhere between $70 and $200 billion, the plan was sent back for review, but not abandoned, after a change in government.

In late 2002 China began work on the first of three diversions from the Yangtze, in that country's south, to different points along the valley of the Huang He (Yellow) River in the north, where 130 cities face acute water shortages. The first phase of the $60 billion undertaking adapted stretches of the world's oldest canal, the 2,500-year-old Da Yunhe along China's eastern plain, to get water to modern Qingdao in time for it to host the aquatic events of the 2008 Olympics. Work was to begin on a middle route by 2010 and the entire scheme to be completed by mid-century.

Other large-scale water transfers continue to be proposed or undertaken on every other continent. As Australia's climate became increasingly dry, Queensland Premier Peter Beattie suggested building a 1,200-kilometre pipeline to carry water from Australia's Northern Peninsula, where precipitation had been rising, to the southern state capital. Across the continent, Western Australia contemplated a similar scheme to bring water from its wet north to Perth in the dry south.[50] In the same year, work continued on a combination of dams and tunnels to divert water from South Africa's northward-flowing Berg River south to fast-growing Cape Town. Brazil's President Luiz Inácio Lula da Silva pressed ahead with a plan to divert more than 10 times what Nevada draws from the Colorado out of his country's São Francisco River to an arid region known as the *sertão*.

Amid tension and crisis in the Middle East, delegates from Israel, Jordan and the Palestinian community managed to meet to discuss a proposal to rescue the dwindling Dead Sea. The Sea has dropped by more than 20 metres in the last half-century, as a result of over-extraction of fresh water from its main tributary, the Jordan River. The plan to refill it called for draining water from the Red Sea through a 180-kilometre canal; advocates suggested that as a bonus, the difference in altitude between the two seas (the Dead Sea is 400 metres lower) could be used to generate electricity.

Numerous smaller transfers continued to be proposed, planned or built closer to home. In the United States, various schemes on the drawing board would pump yet more water from the Ogallala Aquifer beneath the Texas Panhandle and pipe it hundreds of kilometres to maintain the lawns, car washes and religiously tended football fields of Dallas-Fort Worth; convey water out of a tributary of the Colorado named the Green River across the Continental Divide to Denver; and tap the declining Missouri River to supply communities across another continental divide in North Dakota. The last of these plans threatened to reawaken the dormant controversy with Canada over Devil's Lake. North Dakota's plans would move water—and conceivably aquatic organisms—from the watershed that drains into the Gulf of Mexico into rivers that flow through Lake Winnipeg, eventually to Hudson Bay.[51] Finally, the seven states of the Colorado Basin agreed on an anti-drought strategy that included "the addition of new sources of supply to the Colorado River Basin, including importation from outside the Basin." The bland reference was a wink and a nudge toward the Columbia River, one-half of whose immense volume (13 times the Colorado's) comes from Canada.

In Canada too, several smaller water-transfer schemes have been recently completed or are being contemplated. The brown hills of southeastern Alberta are deep in the triangle of territory that Captain John Palliser declared too dry to farm. Ever since the Irish-born adventurer surveyed the area in the mid-1800s, resilient homesteaders have been determined to prove him wrong. Harold Halverson is one of a group of ranchers and small farmers who successfully lobbied the provincial and federal governments to part with $23 million to bury 800 kilometres of pipe from near Lethbridge to 10 dozen farmsteads and 15 Hutterite communities close to the Saskatchewan border. Finished in 2006, the pipeline made "a fabulous difference" to families like his, Harold says. "It gives us satisfaction on the parched bald-headed prairie to have a little patch of green and a few shrubs. Mother can water her flowers. You've got water for domestic use and a few livestock, but there's not enough for large-scale irrigation."[52]

That limitation bothers Harold far less than the federal ban on transferring water between river basins. The prohibition prevented 80 more families just a few miles south of Harold's farm from joining his South East Alberta Water Co-op. The distant stream that supplies the Co-op's pipeline drains, ultimately, through the South Saskatchewan River to Hudson Bay; so does the land beneath its members' farms. Just a little farther south, however, any piped-in water that escaped from gardens or cattle troughs to percolate through the soil might eventually find its way into the Milk River, whose water flows into the Missouri on its way to the Gulf of Mexico. "They say we'll contaminate the Missouri system," Harold scoffs. "It's idiotic. You're dealing with a bunch of people in Ottawa who've never seen western Canada."

Be that as it may, communities in other parts of the Palliser Triangle envied the relief Harold and his neighbours secured. One petition before the Alberta government sought water from the Red Deer River, which flows through its namesake city, for irrigation and household use for several communities close to the Saskatchewan border. Other thirsty towns in neighbouring basins eyed the same river. So did the developers of a billion-dollar racetrack and destination mall north of Calgary, whose first intention had been to tap that city's Bow River before a moratorium on additional water-taking permits left them high and dry. Red Deer's leaders resisted every petition with the same argument: its citizens would soon need every drop in the river and no more was to spare.

In Southern Ontario, meanwhile, the Waterloo Region west of Toronto was also asking where its next drink would come from. With a booming economy underwritten by leading universities and several automotive plants, the old manufacturing cities of Kitchener, Guelph and Waterloo have become a consolidated sprawl of tract housing and box stores slowly colonizing former farmland. Faced with growing demand for water, the region put aside one tentative plan to pipe supplies 100 kilometres from Lake Huron but continued to work on a fall-back proposal to take water from Lake Erie. In a survey, residents expressed a clear preference for Huron's cleaner water, but regional planners feared resistance from environmentalists if they insisted on tapping that lake when Waterloo's treated waste flows down the Grand River into Erie. The fallback plan would, instead, take water from the lake to which the water will return.

The idea of water transfers arose even in Canada's wettest province. As the Okanagan Valley canvassed its options, a radical proposal surfaced now and again, a proposal to tunnel through the northern hills in order to divert water that now flows down the Shuswap River into the increasingly tapped-out Valley. Were it ever adopted, the diversion would also transfer water from the all-Canadian Fraser River into the cross-border Columbia.

If that concept and others seem implausible, keep in mind that many diversion schemes have languished for decades, dismissed as hare-brained, until political and economic change transformed them into contenders. The massive plan for dams that China has been pressing on its neighbours along the Mekong River was first imagined in the 1950s. North Dakota's diversions from the Missouri were first given legislative conception in 1944. And Brazil's project to transfer water from its São Francisco River dates all the way back to 1886. Hydrologist Mike Dettinger, who helped map the aquifers Las Vegas had in its crosshairs, got to the core of the matter: "Anything's possible if you have a big enough city at the other end of the pipe."[53]

Even so, *Homo castor*'s three top strategies for capturing water have clearly been reaching their limits. Dams and diversions bear drawbacks that many communities have found unacceptable. Tapping shallow groundwater jeopardizes wetlands and springs; drilling deeper invites over-reliance on a resource that will one day simply run out.

If traditional strategies can now produce little additional water, might there be other ways to "make" more? While a number of chemical reactions (including the combustion of gasoline in cars) produce $H_2O$ as a by-product, all begin with ingredients that are even scarcer than the water we might wish to create; they offer little prospect of providing meaningful new supplies. Unconventional sources of natural water may be worth exploring, however.

Wyoming committed over $9 million U.S. in 2005 to one technique that, despite decades of use, still has many skeptics. Known as "cloud seeding," this involves using aircraft or artillery shells to inject crystals of silver iodide or dry ice (frozen carbon dioxide) into the air to provide nuclei ("seeds") on which water molecules may form either drops of rain or snow crystals. Cloud seeding is widely practised in the American Southwest, where seven states have made it part of their plans to meet future water needs.[54] In Alberta as well as Texas and Oklahoma, clouds are seeded to trigger airborne moisture to fall as rain before it can form crop-damaging hail. In May 2006, the Beijing Weather Modification Office fired seven rockets loaded with silver iodide into the sky over the Chinese capital, taking credit for the heavy rainfall (the heaviest to date that year) that ensued.[55]

But making clouds turn to rain on demand is not quite the same thing as wringing more rain from them altogether. The U.S. National

Academy of Sciences has questioned the evidence behind the practice. "How much more snow actually falls on the ground?" asks Dr. Robert Serafin, a climate scientist with the U.S. National Center for Atmospheric Research in Boulder. "That's the bottom line. What if the cloud seeding isn't increasing snow-pack, but reducing it? There hasn't been statistically validated research."[56] Wyoming planned to collect data to determine whether its effort was effective.

A much older practice is extracting fresh water from salty. Ancient Greeks and Persians boiled sea water and collected potable water from the steam. The Royal Navy equipped its larger warships with stills for the same purpose early in the 20th century.[57] Two-thirds of today's desalination plants employ variations on the same theme. The rest use a variety of filters to strain molecules of water from salt and other contaminants. An estimated 11,000 plants using one technology or the other are pumping out water in more than 120 countries. At least half operate in the Persian Gulf or Israel,[58] but Spain, China, Australia, London's Thames Water Utilities and several small islands with rich tourist economies have also made large commitments to desalting sea water.

Despite all this activity, however, significant shortcomings limit desalination's promise for many water-stressed places. You need enormous amounts of energy either to boil water or to squeeze it through sub-microscopic holes. When you're done, you must dispose of large quantities—in some cases amounting to half the volume of the fresh water produced—of extremely concentrated residue, sometimes laden with chemicals used to help the process along and, with a high salt content, always corrosive. And, of course, you need large volumes of salt water to begin with. That's not a problem for coastal Israel, Florida or the Cayman Islands, but it is for arid inland areas (although some places far from oceans have ample supplies of saline groundwater).

Desalination might still provide water in volumes large and cheap enough to become a practical alternative to dams, diversions and drilled wells, at least for some. By 2006 the plants operating around the world were producing, collectively, nearly two-thirds as much water each year as flowed down the Colorado River. The cost of that water continued to drop, mainly as new technology reduced the amount of energy the process required. To extract from sea water the amount of fresh water a typical Canadian uses in a year would have cost between $7,400 and $10,000 in the 1950s.[59] By the early nineties that price had dropped to between $2,000 and $3,500. And by the mid-2000s a state-of-the-art plant in Israel claimed to do the job for about $940 CDN.[60] That compared favourably to the $2,590 that the city of Toronto, for example, charged to deliver the same volume of water to homes in 2007 and was even approaching the $896 that Vancouver charged for the same amount. It was, though, still far, far more than the $20 an Alberta farmer paid to receive the equivalent volume for irrigation.[61]

America's leading water analyst predicts that desalination's falling costs and growing availability will make long-distance water imports irrelevant for most coastal cities.[62] "NAWAPA," Berkeley-based scientist Peter Gleick told me, "will never be built. In the end desalination will be cheaper. Los Angeles will find desalination cheaper than moving water from northern California; it will never look at Canada."

It's a far cry from Sirens' Cove, but a gated compound on Annacis Island in the Fraser River south of Vancouver is a show-business star in its own right. A surprisingly tranquil campus of low administrative buildings, domed digesters and generic industrial enclosures served by a network of private roads and brightly lit service tunnels, the Greater Vancouver Regional District waste treatment facility, which treats 180 billion litres of sewage from the city and its suburbs every year, is a popular location for the city's busy movie industry. The 2004 Will Smith vehicle I, Robot shot scenes there. On the day I visited, another production had just packed away its cameras after transforming the facility's buildings into a prison for several weeks. Happily, film cannot capture the occasional pungent waft that reminds visitors of what really goes on here.

Alongside a roadway near the centre of the 128-acre facility, a mild-mannered engineer named Rob Andrews is dipping his toe into the same technological waters that Jaime Cruz works with at Treasure Island. In fact, you could say he's raising the stakes by extracting a potable liquid from the hard stuff: raw city sewage.

It was still an experiment on the day I dropped by. The larger plant around Andrews' small pilot project puts its raw material through three stages of treatment. The first separates liquid from solid waste, the second removes most biological contaminants. Andrews' pilot recycler taps about one percent of the liquid that emerges from the second process, already clearer and arguably cleaner than the murky water of the Fraser River beyond the plant gates. After a dosing with chemicals to coagulate microscopic solids, that water is filtered through fine sand in a two-storey open silo, then exposed to chlorine for 90 minutes as it slowly passes through a U-shaped black pipe a metre across. Out the other end comes enough clean, pure water to fill a tanker truck every hour.

"Can you drink it?" I asked.

"Didn't you notice how good the coffee was?" Andrews' straight face cracked into a smile. Actually, the water was being used only for wash-down and other jobs around the plant, not for coffee or any other direct human consumption. "That would be a pretty hard sell with the staff," Andrews admitted. Even so, he expected his plant's output to replace half the potable water the facility has previously purchased from a local utility, saving $600 a day, which would repay its cost within seven years. If it proved itself, however, the pilot was likely to be expanded long before then to produce more recycled water for sale to industries surrounding the treatment facility.[63]

It'll probably be long before Vancouverites find recycled water in their beloved lattes, but as we've seen in Las Vegas, the practice of using water more than once is increasingly commonplace. In the southern Okanagan Valley, the driest settled area in Canada, the wine and retirement community of Oliver boasts glowing green lawns around its small municipal airport—and fire hydrants painted a distinctive plum colour. The water that sweeps back and forth in cockscomb sprays over the airport's infield, like that in the distinctive hydrants, is recycled from town sewage and distributed through separate mains. Vallejo in central California has installed a similar system, as have the Phoenix suburbs of Mesa and Gilbert. Ski resorts near Flagstaff, Arizona, pipe treated waste water from the city for use in their snow-making machines; and no, it doesn't come out yellow.

Recycling the water content of sewage for drinking—"toilet to tap" as it's been called—has been tougher for consumers to accept. Beyond aesthetics, questions have been raised about whether state-of-the-art recycling technology adequately removes potent molecules that persist when pharmaceutical drugs are excreted in human waste. Voters in San Diego, Denver and the Australian town of Toowoomba have all, at various times, turned thumbs down on the suggestion.

But a growing number of communities that lack more palatable choices have swallowed hard and said "yes." Windhoek, the capital of Namibia, has reused highly treated recycled water mixed with fresh water for four decades. For the same length of time, Los Angeles County has injected water reclaimed from treated sewage into the ground, the combination of dilution in groundwater and long isolation from the air serving, the city hopes, to sanitize it further before it's pumped back up and used again. More than 500 other American cities draw municipal water from rivers downstream from where other communities release treated sewage, meaning that their residents too are drinking retreated, diluted waste water. By one estimate, as many as four million Americans occasionally drink 100 percent "pre-sipped" water, during periods of drought when the only liquid flowing in some of those streams is whatever was released from treatment plants.[64] In England, Essex and Suffolk counties have recycled sewage into tap water since early in the new century, and the Institute of Civil Engineers has been urging other parts of the country to do the same, as one way of preparing for a drier future.[65]

The same may be on tap for residents of Brisbane, whether or not their state builds its proposed northern pipeline. If drought persists, water analysts at the University of Queensland warned, drained reservoirs would soon leave the city with nothing to deliver but a 50:50 mix of water from a new desalination plant and water recycled from sewage. There was, Queensland's Premier Beattie warned, simply "no choice. It's a matter of life and death. You either drink water or you die."[66]

It wasn't something the city boasted about (unless you took "stays here" as a triple *entendre*), but Las Vegas led once again. Roughly 90 percent of the water flushed down sinks, tubs and toilets in southern Nevada eventually comes out of a tap another time. The Valley's treated waste water is pumped back into Lake Mead to mix with the virgin flow down the Colorado, eventually to be used again. In an accounting sleight of hand that would make a croupier proud, the SNWA calculates the difference between what it takes out and what it returns; only that amount is counted against its annual river entitlement.

Simply finding more water from somewhere, or constructing even larger reservoirs to hold it, represents the crudest possible way to prepare for the unprecedented shortages and unexpected surpluses that our changing weather holds in store. The water dilemmas we face everywhere in North America have as much to do with "when" and "where" or "what kind" as they do with "how much." As Las Vegas' accounting gimmick illustrates, there are more ways than one to think about even the last part of that problem. Let's look next for solutions that might be both more effective and much cheaper than any number of additional pipes, dams and wells.

# Chapter 10
## Green Inc.:
## Balancing Our Ecological Books

Late in the 1990s, I made a working visit by kayak to the outer edges of the Queen Charlotte Islands off Canada's west coast. One afternoon our little group landed on an island at the very margin of the continent. To the west, the next landfall was Japan. At our backs were trees as ancient as the Christian calendar, old-growth cedars that had escaped the chainsaw. And at our feet, scattered across the sea-washed gravel like the dry husks of some strange, five-armed cephalopod were dozens of salt-stained hockey gloves: flotsam from a shipping container, swept into the sea during a storm and broken open by the waves.[1]

The bell has rung on last century's people versus nature prizefight. People won. Nature, as a place innocent of humanity, has been conquered. The by-products of our industrial society have penetrated the deepest oceans, highest peaks and furthest poles in the form of rising ambient temperatures, scraps of plastic and an alphabet soup of chemicals. Our challenge now is to survive our own success. In a quiet corner of America's slowly rejuvenating rust belt, an unlikely pair of pioneers are blazing the way.

At the end of a four-hour drive from Buffalo along the American side of Lake Erie, I turned left at Cleveland and followed the interstate south toward Akron. Climbing gently past outcrops of grey limestone, the divided highway curled around the new development pushing westward: tracts of cookie-cutter housing, frontage roads lined with mid-price business hotels and big-box stores tilted heavily toward décor and electronics, leavened with theme restaurants. A city little different from any other prosperous mid-size community in 21st-century North America.

The freeway crested the hill. I followed an off-ramp to a stop sign where the scenery changed as suddenly as if I'd stepped from the carpeted casino at Treasure Island into the raw cement of a service corridor. Here the narrow blacktop was buckled from frost. A trucking yard crowded the ditch on one side. Past it was a clapboard tavern from an earlier era. A narrow bridge crossed a drainage canal, then another. I spotted the mailbox I was looking for and turned into a long driveway of rough gravel, framed by leafless autumn hardwoods. As the trees fell away, I glimpsed gunmetal water beyond a fringe of cattails. The drive ended at a tidy ranch-style house set in emerald lawn. A pair of farm dogs rushed to greet me. With them, in gumboots and work jackets, were the men I'd come to visit: Steve and Jerry Panzner, bankers.

The brothers have the round features and blunt independence of their German grandfather. Joseph Panzner came to North America shortly after the First World War and laboured to pull a working farm from the black muck of what was then known as the Copley Swamp. He buried clay tile and opened ditches to drain the land and make it dry enough to plough. For 70 years, the black peat soil produced onions, celery, cabbage and lettuce for the city down the road. By the 1990s, however, as Jerry hit his 40th birthday and Steve neared 50, the brothers could see the writing on the wall. Neighbours could truck celery from California and sell it for less than it cost the Panzners to grow it. The brothers had to pay their field hands even when there was nothing left at the end of the summer to pay themselves. They began to look for other options. Nearby farmers sold out to companies that dug up and sold the peat-rich topsoil, then began to mine the deeper sand and gravel. Steve and Jerry recoiled from doing that to land they loved. Then they learned about something new.

These days, they told me over fresh coffee and delivery pizza, "we farm in reverse." Ninety years after Grandfather Joseph grew callouses draining the swamp for the plough, his grandsons are turning his fields back into wetland—and being paid to do it. As one of numerous environmental benefits, water that for decades has rushed through the old farm network of tile and ditches into local canals that carried it away to a river—on some days enough to fill nearly 900 rail tank cars—now stays in the aquifer beneath Summit County.[2]

Where rows of carrots and onions once marched across the moist soil of one field, engineered terraces now host a succession of native plant communities leading down to a shallow pond where spotted turtles, almost extirpated in Ohio, are making a local comeback. In another former field, small creeks connect a chain of pools created with more amphibians in mind. The 15 or so species of sedge, rye and other fast-growing plants the brothers seeded have been joined by five times that number of wild volunteers. Along with turtles, mink have repopulated the surrounding woodland. Kestrels and goshawks hunt the jumping mice that thrive in the tall grasses. "We had two loons stay for about a month," Jerry said, beaming.

The brothers are having the time of their lives. "It's the neatest thing," Steve told me. "You go out there and you find a new orchid. Two years ago we got a bald eagle. It's like Wild Kingdom."

The U.S. federal law that has allowed the Panzners to give life back to their patch of Copley Swamp was signed by President George H. W. Bush and implemented by the Clinton administration. At its core is something called the "no net loss" wetlands rule. It requires that the loss to development of any wetlands under federal jurisdiction be mitigated by the creation or restoration of at least as much comparable wetland elsewhere. The more important innovation, perhaps, was that developers who didn't want to undertake the specialized task of recreating wild habitat themselves could pay others to do it for them. Supported by companion laws at the state level, the two rules created the conditions for a brand-new type of business: the "wetlands mitigation bank." Across the United States, more than 220 such banks were operating by 2002.[3]

Here's how they work. Investors acquire (or, like the Panzners, already own) land in a region whose natural landscapes are under pressure from development. The land must have a location, a topography, surroundings and soil similar to those a pristine wetland might occupy, most often found in marginal farm fields or barren former building sites. At his or her own expense, the investor-landowner sculpts the surface as necessary, connects the wetland to local natural water courses, and sows wild plants to create a marsh, fen or swamp (all subtly different). Once the new ecology is established, state biologists certify its quality and issue "credits" to the mitigation bank's owners for the acreage achieved (in Ohio, on a four-level scale of ascending value). Investors profit by selling their credits to developers who may "cash" them with federal and state environmental agencies to secure the right to build over otherwise protected wetlands elsewhere (Ohio's Department of Transportion bought many Panzner bank credits to build new highways for Akron's growing suburbs). The redemption ratio is designed to ensure that more "mitigation" wetland acreage is created than lost: as much as three times more in Ohio. Eventually, the created wetland is turned over to a custodian, often a park system, for perpetual preservation.[4]

The approach has had inevitable teething pains. Of a dozen first-generation wetland mitigation banks reviewed in Ohio, nearly half were judged "mostly unsuccessful," mainly because they failed to mimic the shallow water and periodic dry spells that characterize natural wetlands.[5] Only three received high marks for biological success, the Panzners' among them. "When people come here in 10 years," Steve predicted, "they're going to say, 'What a great wetland.' Not 'What a great *mitigation* wetland' but 'What a great *wetland.*'"

The Panzners have their own complaints. Criteria for certifying new wetland, they say, fail to recognize that "natural" conditions vary widely across the state. Worse for the siblings, after investing their savings to return the family land to its pre-farm condition, they say, state officials have been effusive in praise but slower to issue the credits they need to recoup their cost.

Those hiccups aside, wetland mitigation banking represents a daring and necessary new frontier in how North Americans manage land, water and the competition for space between urban development and nature. By encouraging rainwater to replenish the Copley Aquifer, the Panzners are helping put off the day when local wells run dry and the public demands more reservoirs. Water that seeps into or slowly off their land, rather than coursing out of ditches, is less likely to contribute to future floods on the Ohio or Mississippi. Endangered wildlife enjoys a permanent new home. The Panzners have also gained, as land that lost its economic value in one form recovers it in another. If the state straightens out its rule-bound bureaucracy, Steve Panzner says, he would be eager to restore more domesticated land to a state of nature. "I truly love doing this. It's like farming: it gets in your blood."

The conditions that will give our society its best shot at flourishing through the new climate's violent mood swings are evident. We must use less water whenever we can, extracting more work from every drop we do use. We must minimize our vulnerability to extremes of weather. To reduce our risk, we must "design in" flexibility and resilient adaptive capacity from the get-go. At every turn we should copy or employ the original and still best example of resilience to climate change: nature itself. And one more thing: any response that would prepare us adequately and in time for the turbulent weather ahead must surely find a way to work *with* the aspirations, psychology and economy of our society, rather than against them.

One morning in Las Vegas, I joined Dennis Gegen in his white employer-issue SUV as it rolled slowly through quiet residential streets several kilometres west of the gaudy Strip. A purple stopwatch hung from the rear-view mirror, a laptop computer was mounted below the dashboard, and a video camera lay between us. Gegen kept a sharp lookout along the paved gutter as he drove. "There's something," he muttered. Across the street a small creek rippled down beside the cement curb until it disappeared into a grate. He turned at the next intersection to follow the flow upstream. "If water leaves the yard," he said, "it's water waste."

That's the basic rule that the Las Vegas Water District's dozen "water cops" are out to enforce 24 hours a day, seven days a week. A native of Minnesota who moved to Vegas in 1994, Gegen has a background in landscaping. He knows you don't have to waste water to keep turf green in southern Nevada. The automated irrigation systems in this part of the city, where houses sell for $500,000 U.S. and up, are easily configured to water for only 15 minutes every three days: the maximum that the District allows for lawns. Sprinkler heads can adjust to water but a pie-slice of turf. There's no reason for water to run off onto the street.

Gegen followed the telltale trickle to the head of a cul-de-sac. In one yard water puddled in the flattened grass, overflowing in a rivulet that darkened the cement curb. Gegen stepped out of the truck, camera in hand. Murmuring into the built-in microphone, he documented in a time-stamped video record the broken sprinkler head that was the source of the problem. When a brisk knock brought no one to the front door, he made a quick note on a bright yellow plastic flag and spiked it into the lawn. The note gave the homeowner 48 hours to repair or replace the broken sprinkler.

Back in the truck, Gegen entered the address into his laptop. "We'll come back out in a couple days, see if it's fixed." If it's not, the "fee" (the District eschews the more punitive term "fine") for a first offence is $40 U.S. That doubles with each subsequent violation to a maximum of $640 for homeowners and $2,560 for commercial customers with larger service meters. "We've had people get eight, nine fees—$640, $640, $640—some people just don't get it," Gegen admitted. Most fix the problem after one or two escalating penalties. Even then, he and his colleagues keep a watch-list of former violators: "Once we send you a letter, you're in the system for 36 months. You're sort of on probation."[6]

Gegen insists it's not the violations that get his juices going, though. He's happier to see homeowners avoid watering altogether by replacing grass with more desert-tolerant xeriscaping or even artificial turf. In a carrot-and-stick approach, the SNWA will lower a household's water bill by two dollars for every square foot of lawn that's pulled out, up to $3,000 U.S.: about two-thirds the cost of a professional conversion. When we came to another house where half the yard was paved in artificial turf and water ran from the remaining natural grass, Gegen gets his camera out again. "Maybe one more violation will get him to do the rest," he quipped.

Environmentalists universally call on society to moderate its use of all resources, particularly water. Virtually every water utility also offers at least lip service to the same objective, although seldom with the vigour of Las Vegas' 24-hour waste patrols. Their efforts have met with some success: North Americans are making water work harder and go further than it did a quarter-century ago. Indeed even as the United States' population grew by 56 million and its economy by half in the two decades after 1985, its overall water consumption remained almost unchanged.[7] Canada's per-capita water consumption also dropped between 1980 and the start of the new century, but a doubling of our economy overrode improvements in water efficiency, with the result that our total water consumption went up by more than one-quarter over that time.[8]

There's little doubt that North Americans guzzle more water per throat, flush and shower than almost any other humans on Earth. Peter Gleick's Pacific Institute publishes a biennial collection of international water statistics as a reference. Its comparison of how much water different countries withdrew for domestic purposes in 2004 found Canadians near the top of the chart, at 767 litres a day each, about five and a half bathtubs full.[9] Americans were close behind, at 703 litres.[10] Strikingly, many other countries managed to satisfy both thirst and similar standards of sanitation and economic development with far less. The French used about 255 litres per person per day in houses and governmental institutions; Israelis, 282 litres; Czechs, 208;

Danes, a chiseling 112. Australia, despite its droughts, still found 381 litres a day for each of its 20 million people, while New Zealanders approached North American consumption at 745 litres a day. While less wealthy countries generally use less water, their withdrawals likewise cover a range and aren't always thrifty: Mexicans, for instance, withdrew nearly as much as Australians in 2004, at 375 litres per person. India's billion people, by contrast, used 142 litres—about one full North American bathtub of water—each per day. And China's 1.3 billion people got by on half that, barely 77 litres each per day.[11]

Local water utility managers loathe such comparisons. Weather, soil and land cover, they point out, all vary too widely from community to community for us to draw reliable conclusions from comparisons among the amounts of water they push through city mains to customers. Gardeners, for example, naturally use their hoses less in rainy places than in dry ones. Where soil is loamy, water lingers longer and must be replenished less often than where it's sandy. Even allowing for such differences, however, most North American communities could clearly use far less water than they do without sacrificing cleanliness, comfort or aesthetics.

We should do better even before water gets to our taps. In older North American cities and many developing countries, just patching leaks or replacing aged water mains could save staggering amounts of water. By one estimate, 40 percent of what Pakistan withdraws from the Indus River is lost before it's delivered to fields, homes or businesses.[12] Some Asian cities lose as much as 60 percent of the water in their mains to a combination of leaks, illegal connections and fraudulent metering.[13] Cities in richer countries may lose almost as much when their water systems are old. The Victorian-era pipes in London, England, waste about a third of that city's treated water supply.[14] In Canada, Hamilton has blamed leaking mains for the loss of more than one-quarter of the water the city treats.[15] Many other eastern North American cities, from Montreal to Savannah, could increase their water supplies to homes and business by as much as a third simply by securing the pipes that deliver it.[16]

More savings are available outdoors, where as much as 70 percent of the water used in neighbourhoods of single-family houses goes to keeping landscaping green, pools filled and cars washed. The utilities and governments that have been most successful at stretching North America's water resources have generally drawn from a common menu of tactics. The most popular are:

+ rebates paid in Toronto and many other cities to property owners for the purchase of water-conserving appliances like low-flow toilets (Las Vegas will even help you buy a cover for your swimming pool to control evaporation, which, in that climate, can extract a pool's entire volume of water over a year);

+ rebates to households for the purchase of cisterns or rain barrels to capture water for use in gardens;

+ free instruction or even individual expert advice on xeriscaping;

+ legal requirements to install low-flow toilets and shower heads in any house before it's sold (a more extreme step requires new houses to install only dual-flush toilets, which use less water for a No. 1 flush than for a No. 2.);

+ local bylaws that limit the extent of turf used in landscaping around new houses and businesses;

+ mandated weekly schedules to limit the watering of lawns and gardens; and

+ certification programs to identify low-water-use appliances.

Where they've been enacted, measures like these have often caused water use to drop dramatically. Las Vegas isn't the only desert city to have cut its water use while growing its population. Albuquerque did it too, implementing a comprehensive conservation plan in 1995 that incorporated several of the measures above; by 2005 water use there had dropped back to the 1985 level, despite the addition of 120,000 residents over two decades. Denmark's remarkably low water use per person results from a decade-long public campaign that tapped down consumption by nearly one-quarter.

While campaigns to promote conservation around the house receive the widest public attention, consumption there is typically but
a small fraction of what societies use. Much bigger potential savings
lie elsewhere.[17]

Globally, industry uses twice the water that homes, institutions
and offices combined do. Poor agricultural countries use less than 10
percent of their available water for industry; in North America, it's
about 50 percent, sometimes in surprising places.[18] The oil industry
injects millions of litres of highly pressurized water into the ground
to coax heavy crude from the sands of Alberta and natural gas from
limestone in northeast Texas (among many other places). In addition
to the vast amounts of water they use for processing, food packers
truck millions of additional litres of virtual water out of dry regions
like northern Mexico and Southern California in the form of watermelons, orange juice and other produce. Canadian federal statistics
indicate that one single industry alone, thermal power generation, extracts 64 percent of all the water removed from nature within our own
borders.[19] That may be so. But a significant omission in the reported
figure reveals a highly critical distinction in the way that industry uses
water, and how it might use less.

A little east of Toronto, eight large, grey, beehive-shaped buildings
file along the Lake Ontario shore. These contain the reactor chambers
in which radiation from pellets of uranium boils water into steam to
make 3,100 megawatts of electricity for Canada's most economically
vital region.[20] To do this, the Pickering Nuclear Generating Station, a
thermal plant of the kind Canada's statisticians had in mind, extracts
millions of litres of water a day from the lake. It also returns almost
all of that water straight back to the lake after using it briefly to cool
a much smaller amount of captive water that cycles endlessly through
the plant's turbines. The only difference in the returned water is that
it is a few degrees warmer than it was when it entered the plant.

Virtually all industries *use* water, but relatively few *consume* it in
the sense of removing it permanently from surface circulation or from
watersheds. Most are more like the Pickering power station. In effect

they only "borrow" water, use it to make something, and then release almost as much as they started with. In truth, industry's most crucial impact on water generally has far less to do with the quantity than with the *quality* of water it returns to nature. Yet, this impact is often more significant than a few degrees' change in temperature.

In many developing countries, industries release immense volumes of severely polluted waste water directly to the environment with little effective penalty. In China decades of pell-mell industrial progress have left less than half the river water drinkable, half the lakes badly polluted, and more than one-third of the groundwater contaminated.[21]

Much the same might have been said for parts of Europe and North America when I was born in the middle of the last century. Environmental laws enacted a generation ago did a great deal to eliminate the grossest excesses of pollution. I have witnessed the welcome regenesis of waterways in my childhood haunts near Hamilton. Optimists anticipate a similar ecological turnaround in China. Economists among them argue the existence of what they call a "Kuznets Curve"[22] relationship: that is, as a country develops economically, water waste and pollution first increase sharply, then level off, and eventually drop. And, in fact, China's government in 2007 launched a major national campaign to clean up its devastated air and water.

We are still taking the full inventory of our species' impact on our own habitat. Most of the laws enacted in the last century failed to take account of the many sophisticated molecules that form when human and animal pharmaceuticals break down. There is mounting evidence now that these can harm human and wild life (in particular, meddling with sexual development) and that new criteria need to be added to our standards for "clean" water.[23] While the process will be ongoing, industry in the developed world has, on the whole, greatly reduced both the sheer amount of water it needs to borrow and the amount of toxic residues it leaves behind when done.

Note why both these improvements happened: because the cost of disposing of dirty water went up—sharply. Public concern about pollution in the 1960s and '70s produced a generation of environmental laws that for the first time placed a price on the release of certain kinds, or excessive volumes, of pollutants into water, framed as fines for exceeding prescribed limits. When throwing away dirty water was no longer free, major water-polluting industries found it cheaper either to treat waste water before releasing it or to release less of it. Many discovered it was cheaper still to use the same water over and over again. As a result, the volume of water North American industries withdraw from nature for every dollar of economic value they create has declined steadily for decades, dropping by roughly half in the two decades after 1980.[24] America's industries used less water in 2000 than at any time in the previous half-century.[25] Over the same period, the quality of water in most of the continent's urban streams and lakes (those most vulnerable to industrial pollution) improved significantly.

By far the biggest guzzlers of the world's water are farms. Roughly 70 percent of all the water removed from rivers, wells and reservoirs and not returned winds up on fields or is fed to livestock. A full-grown cow slurps down a bathtub of water a day. Crops may need a lot or a little, or watering at particular times.[26] And efficiency of use varies hugely: the proportion of water sent to a field that reaches the roots of plants may be as much as 90 percent or as little as 25 percent, depending on the style of irrigation and the technology employed.

The North American farmers most frequently criticized for overusing water are those who live over the Ogallala Aquifer. From the Dakotas to North Texas, this vast underground storehouse of ancient water has been dropping for decades.

I meet Eddie Teeter by an open-sided equipment shed off a "farm-to-market" road north of Lubbock, Texas. Ruddy-faced and looking 10 years younger than his real age of 65, Eddie has farmed the area's red soil for 40 years and has worried the whole time about how long his water will last. The son of a Methodist preacher, he married into a farming family. When he wed, he recalls, "My in-laws said, 'I hope there's enough water for your children [to keep farming].'"[27] Today, his farm represents the state of the industry: 1,600 acres (650 hectares) planted mostly in cotton with a little corn, using the newest seeds genetically modified to resist pests and tolerate the chemicals he applies to keep down weeds. His huge, four-wheel-drive tractors can plow, seed or fertilize a 12-metre swath in a single pass. He says he wouldn't trade the way of life for any other, but he's not sanguine about its future. As everything about the business has scaled up, he told me, "You need to farm more land to make the same living. We're paying more for our production costs, but we're getting the same price as we did."

One of his biggest costs is water. Texas law gives him any his pumps can reach for free, but not the price of fetching it. Eddie's diesel and electric pumps have to pull it straight up 110 to 120 metres, and that distance has increased by four and a half metres in the time he's farmed. Meanwhile the price of energy keeps rising. By midway through the new century's first decade, he was paying eight to 10 dollars U.S. to pump 2.5 centimetres (one inch) of water over an acre of his fields. He needs 46 to 50 centimetres (18 to 20 inches) for each of his acres over a season, adding up to $320,000 poured into the dirt before he harvests a single bale of cotton. Running out of water won't drive farmers like him out of business, he predicts. The economics of getting it will.

Eddie and other farmers are fighting back, finding ways to use less. Some plow as little as possible, to expose less soil to evaporation. Others irrigate only on windless days. With 20 neighbours and the Texas Department of Agriculture, Eddie is part of an eight-year research project that measures almost everything he does on the land. Monitors record how much water his sprinklers deliver, the humidity in the air over his fields and the amount of moisture in the dirt. He keeps track of when and how he plows and at the end of the season will report how much his cotton sold for. "You can make three bales an acre or one bale an acre," he observes; the real question is which will produce the highest return for the investment. "In other words, what are we selling our water for?"

By the end of the exercise, he says, "We hope to come up with techniques and crops to be able to maintain an agricultural economy here." It may not be one that grows cotton or corn. Cattle feedlots, where thousands of animals are penned together as milk machines or for fattening before slaughter, are increasingly unwelcome in more densely settled areas. But in relatively wide-open north Texas, Eddie explains, "You can keep six thousand cows for the same water it takes you to grow a bale of cotton. And we'd be importing our water, from Illinois in the form of corn and as alfalfa from Colorado."

That's one answer. Forty minutes away Alan Birkenfeld has found another. Whereas Eddie and his neighbours have gone big, their field rows marching in disciplined monotony to the horizon, Alan has gone small, his windswept acreage looking more like the little house on the prairie with a satellite dish. Of his square-mile farm, he uses just three-quarters. Two hundred and fifty beef cattle and a similar number of sheep wander over green wheat pasture. Brown chickens and a few grey speckled guinea fowl ("to keep away the rattlesnakes") wander freely. The grazing animals control the same weeds Eddie buys herbicides to kill; what comes out their other end replaces chemical fertilizers. Alan uses his well water for growing wheat on just a quarter of his active land, irrigating any given acre in the spring of alternate years and shunning crops that need water during high summer. Instead of commodity cotton, he sells certified organic pasture-raised meat at a premium price by direct sale to consumers, shipping it frozen around Texas and beyond.[28]

Eddie Teeter's gross income, Alan concedes, is doubtless much larger than his own. "But we're keeping a lot more of our revenue. In terms of net income," he guesses, "we make as much with far less acreage." Most promising for Alan's future, while the big cotton and corn growers watch their wells and worry about the day the cost of pumping puts them out of business, the water table beneath his small farm is actually rising. Water in one well rose nine-tenths of a foot between 2004 and 2005 alone. Working the land his way, Alan tells me, "I think we're at a sustainable level."

Improvements to the water efficiency of our industrial processes, our cropping and livestock practices and our personal sanitation occur incrementally, in the small or large innovations each of us makes. They can't be centrally prescribed, any more than one device could solve every industry's pollution problem. At best they can be *motivated*.

So why are we so unmotivated to make our water last? Perhaps for the same reasons so many of us fail when we try to diet: we cheat. While praising water as "priceless" in the abstract, we value it at next to nothing at the tap. When we treat water that way, it's cheaper to let it leak from old pipes than to fix the holes.

Canada, having 10 times more water per citizen running over its surface or trickling beneath it than the United States has, is perhaps guiltier of this self-deception than any other country on earth. Charges from municipal utilities generally cover most or all of the day-to-day operating costs of delivering water and treating waste. They more rarely cover the capital costs of facilities and virtually never reflect the full cost of securing water for the future or ensuring that the environment remains able to absorb humanity's waste. Canadian farmers pay a minute fraction (about three percent) of what households pay for water. Many industries, including Alberta's oil extractors, pay nothing at all for even greater amounts of water than individual farmers use.

The United States is barely any better. Many of its cities, like Canada's, continue to provide water at flat "all-you-can-eat" rates that are below the cost of supply and delivery.[29] The large, publicly funded irrigation systems that keep the southwestern desert blooming give water away at between four and 23 cents on the dollar invested to build and operate them, with no allowance for securing future supply: a subsidy worth more than $2.7 billion per year in the new century.[30] The U.S. EPA has estimated that the cost of piping water to large-lot residential subdivisions amounts to a subsidy of $130,000 for every mile a given house lies from the water supply.[31]

Water that users extract from the ground themselves is valued even lower, free for the taking in most of North America. "If they own the land, they can take what they like, as much as they want," says Gwyn Graham, the provincial groundwater hydrologist for

British Columbia's chock-a-block Lower Mainland, where some municipal wells have run dry during recent dry summers. "Because it's groundwater, we don't charge for it."[32]

With characteristic bravado, Texas calls this the "right of capture," courts having held that in most circumstances, well-owners there may pump their neighbours' ground dry, as well as their own, without penalty or payment.[33]

In several U.S. states and Canadian provinces, you need a licence to extract extremely large volumes of water. Only a handful put a price on water actually withdrawn from a well on private land, and that's typically a nominal charge, selectively applied. Nova Scotia puts the highest value on its limited aquifers, charging up to $143.77 for a thousand cubic metres of groundwater: about what a typical urban Canadian uses for all purposes in four and a half years. Other jurisdictions, including California, Minnesota, Saskatchewan, Manitoba and Nunavut, charge large industrial water users a fee of between a penny and $12.53 CDN for the same volume.[34] In early 2007 Ontario announced its intention eventually to charge for large groundwater withdrawals, without revealing at what price.

We are an opportunistic species. Whenever we think we've found a free lunch, we chow down. Receiving water for next to nothing, we waste it with abandon. The malign consequences go beyond the mere squandering of a precious resource.

Nowhere more so than in agriculture. Subsidies of all sorts, including cheap water, encourage farmers to plant crops in places they're unsuited to and then douse them heavily with chemicals to keep them alive. After New Zealand stopped subsidizing its farmers, economist John Humphreys noted, "the use of fertilizer declined and there was a halt to land-clearing and over-stocking which had been responsible for widespread soil erosion."[35] Underpriced water, in particular, encourages overuse: the main reason, the same economist suggests, that one-quarter of America's irrigated farmland exhibits damaging concentrations of the mineral salts that build up when soils are watered to excess. In India, below-cost electricity has encouraged the over-pumping of wells that we saw earlier, as well as the over-cultivation of thirsty crops like sugar cane that aren't adapted to the climate there. Heavily water-subsidized vegetable farmers in Alberta and California take business away from their counterparts in places like Quebec and Ohio, who may grow those same crops without the need for irrigation.

In urban areas, undercharging for water at the tap hurts in three ways. Most obviously, it encourages waste. It also diverts public funds that might otherwise be spent to maintain and expand water supply systems. Beyond that, it *discourages* the pursuit of alternatives. As the *Sydney Morning Herald* pointed out in an editorial about Australia's response to deepening drought, "A key cause of the urban 'water shortage' is that artificially low prices for water have made alternative sources—including piping water from rural areas to the cities, better use of stormwater run-off and fixing leaking pipes, recycling and desalination—uneconomic."[36]

Our systemic dishonesty about the value of water is of a piece with the larger fraud we've perpetrated by failing to account in full for the myriad other services that natural ecosystems provide to our dollar economy. These range from the "free" fish in the ocean to the marsh-raised wild waterfowl that fill the larders in many northern communities; from the carbon dioxide that forests scrub out of the atmosphere to the forests' moist exhalations that cool the local environs before returning downwind as welcome rain. They include the waters bearing freighters through the Rock Cut south of Sault Ste. Marie and the crust of ice that shoulders the weight of winter traffic into St. Theresa Point. At the grandest scale, they embrace the vast planetary distillery and filtering system that cleanses our water.

Sixty percent of these critical services are now being over-exploited and run down, the UNEP found in its Millennium Assessment of the global ecosystem, *precisely because* they are undervalued in commerce. "Technology and knowledge can reduce considerably the human impact on ecosystems," the project's scientific board underscored in a statement. "They are unlikely to be deployed fully, however, until ecosystem services cease to be perceived as free and limitless, and their full value is taken into account."[37]

We dare not carry on this way. The health of our habitat must become as automatic and seamless a consideration in our economic decisions as the price of money (which affects everything from billion-dollar takeovers to personal credit-card spending). Far from segregating nature from human commerce, in other words, we must urgently reintegrate the two. Bringing natural services "onto the books" of our conventional economy would mean not only fully acknowledging their benefits, but also paying for their maintenance. It would give each of us a sharp new awareness of the load we place on the planet and an immediate reason to lighten it.

No device can accomplish this task better than a correctly set *price*. Price includes an entire chain of costs that go into a product's creation and supply, from raw materials to labour. There's more to getting a mango than a Macintosh apple to Toronto in January, so the mango costs more. Over time, multiple considerations have entered pricing: the cost of insuring the workers who make the product, the cost of taxes to pay for the roads over which it gets delivered, and so on. Increasingly, prices for some products, like electronics, also include costs of disposal. Certain social costs that should be included in prices aren't yet: in particular, the burdens borne by the "low-wage" societies that manufacture exports. Overall, however, the trend is in the right direction. But while we've made progress in integrating human social costs in prices, we've done extremely poorly at including nature's contribution.

A more inclusive price for water would dramatically change the incentives in the countless decisions we make in our daily lives. "If you want a clear signal with respect to the value of water sent every day, dozens of times a day, every time any one of us turns on a tap or any business or industry sticks a pipe into a river or reservoir," former national party leader Preston Manning argues, "there is absolutely no substitute for a properly established pricing system." Manning has urged his home province of Alberta to adopt "full cost accounting and pricing" for every drop of water that oil sand developments, other industries, farmers and homeowners use.[38]

The power of pricing is direct: when something costs more, we use less of it, and our existing supply goes further. By one estimate, charging North Americans the full, real cost of water would help us *double* our use of current amounts without building a single new dam, drowning one more valley, digging any new wells, running another pipeline or draining anyone's field of springs.[39] Moreover, the prospect of paying the full cost for water in arid regions where populations already overwhelm supply would certainly help constrain more hectic growth. If house purchasers and business investors in the American Southwest, foothills Alberta or the Okanagan Valley had to bear the true cost of their water, some would probably settle elsewhere. Those who moved to water-stressed regions anyway would have to limit their demands upon existing services or foot the bill for less conventional supplies.

Even paying somewhat more but still less than full cost helps. One study in California found that farmers who paid even a partial price for water used 20 percent less than those who took it from a river for free. They also grew 20 percent larger crops. Farmers in northern Texas who don't pay directly for groundwater but must foot the bill for pumping it to the surface have been significantly faster to embrace water-saving practices than their counterparts in Montana, who receive heavily subsidized surface water at a flat rate. Another study found that a 10 percent hike in residential water rates cut consumption in homes by as much as 12 percent.[40]

There's an obvious practical objection to making water more expensive: it flies against our pernicious love of an apparently free lunch, and against politics, which never tires of promising one. Nonetheless, a few places have begun to speak the unmentionable in public. Australia's Business Council has pointed out that if water prices in that drought-stricken continent rose by between 50 and 100 percent, a variety of alternative new supplies would become financially viable.[41] In the United States, city councils from San Diego to Seattle have adopted higher prices as elements in water conservation plans. Utah has embraced the same approach as state policy.[42]

Social critics object that letting costs determine the price of water will produce a world in which some cannot afford it. They argue, in effect, that to ensure that water reaches the poorest, even the richest should get it for a price far less than its value and their means justify. But how will providing water to the world's wealthy for next to nothing help deliver it to millions in poor countries who lack so much as a tap? As McGill economist William Watson notes, "The vast bulk of the benefits of free water go to the middle and upper classes. Most poor people don't have swimming pools to fill, cars to wash, lawns to water or fields to irrigate." There are better ways to ensure that even poor North Americans can afford to bathe and drink. "You could give them the money they needed," Watson suggests, as we do to ensure that the chronically destitute have food and shelter.[43] Simpler yet, most cities that already peg water bills to amounts used charge very modest rates for quantities sufficient for basic needs, but higher rates as consumption rises.

A more serious problem with charging in full for water is the difficulty of determining exactly what that full cost really is. We've avoided owning up to our appropriation of natural services for so long that we don't have enough reference points from which to calculate the economic value of snowbound water stored in mountain ranges or of bulrush marshes that metabolize some of the most noxious of our industrial wastes. When laws permit a municipality simply to stick a pipe into a lake, the cost of doing so may seem like zero.

But it isn't. At least some of the costs of removing water from ecosystems are readily apparent. They include the loss of plant and animal communities that once flourished in the withdrawn water as well as the economic activities (fishing, for instance) that those wildlife populations might have supported. Another loss is in the "opportunity cost" to humans who lose the use of flooded valleys where, for example, Aboriginal peoples might otherwise have pursued a traditional livelihood. And just as many businesses earmark funds for the maintenance or future replacement of capital equipment, a prudent water-pricing policy would involve calculating the cost of providing *tomorrow's* water, requiring us to compare the full relative costs of creating new reservoirs, building recycling plants or burying pipelines to distant lakes.

These are hardly straightforward sums, and many economists have recoiled from their complexities. Yet pioneering researchers at a few institutions have begun to establish benchmarks for a new economics of ecological services. The non-profit Canadian Boreal Initiative, for one, has estimated the dollar value of the vast arc of living conifer forest, muskeg, lakes and rivers that stretches from Alaska, around the south end of Hudson Bay, to Labrador. The Initiative's biologists and economists believe that the carbon the vast wilderness "sequesters" from the atmosphere, the oxygen it releases, the water it cleanses, and the biodiversity it preserves are worth about $448 billion a year to the world—more than 10 times the value of the oil, gas, diamonds and other resources extracted from it.[44]

Many communities are moving ahead, if in baby steps. To charge more for something, you first have to measure it. An easy first step is to install individual home water meters, still far from universal in the United States and Canada, without changing how consumers are billed for water. Places that do this have found that simply measuring something can help customers use less of it.

The town of Ladysmith, British Columbia, was founded shortly after the turn of the 20th century as a dormitory for miners digging coal from Vancouver Island's mountains. So some of its houses and water pipes are fairly old. More recently, its quaint charm and sheltered ocean views have attracted new settlers. Their growing numbers have added to the demand placed on those aging pipes and two small reservoir lakes above town. Then there's the weather: in the winter it rains a lot, but summers can be dry for weeks on end. In short, little Ladysmith faces the same water-budget problems as many much bigger places.

In the middle of the new century's first decade, the town took the giant step of installing water meters in every home. At first, residents fretted that this was a prelude to big hikes in water bills. But really, it helped the town engineer figure out where the water was actually going. It assisted his effort to locate leaking pipes and identify a few customers who were using water in inexplicable quantities, like the fellow who "air-conditioned" his apartment during July by leaving the cold water running in his shower while he was at work. Only after everyone in town had a year to see how their water use measured up did bills switch from a flat rate to metered charges. Then some households paid a little more than before, others a little less; overall, the change was well accepted. In the five years after installing meters, despite the fact that the town's population grew by over seven percent, its water use fell by 23.2 percent. Mayor Rob Hutchins called the device "the single most important tool to reduce consumption."[45]

For the same reason, a growing number of other cities across the continent are also installing meters in every home and business. And like Ladysmith, they typically find that meters encourage conservation even before rates are pegged to readings. Meters then allow utilities to charge rates that increase with the amount of water used, giving heavy consumers an incentive to cut back. Where water runs short only in certain seasons, meters allow for higher rates to be set during those months, encouraging short-term cutbacks. The latest generation of meters even does away with the need for large staffs of meter-readers: built-in wireless technology transmits readings to employees driving past on the street.

For elected leaders, though, raising the price of water looks like all stick and no carrot. In fact, trying to address most of our resource challenges through conservation only feels like trying to lose weight simply by cutting back on corn chips and beer, when really we'd be thinner *and* better satisfied if we changed our eating habits to whole-grain cereals and fruit and got a little more exercise. In the same way, simply turning down the tap on the water we use ignores the enormous potential to reward efficiency as well as to punish waste. Worse, it offers no incentive to overcome other sharp limitations of our existing infrastructure.

Up 'til now, we've managed water "vertically." Our houses, cities and most businesses are equipped with single-stream, source-to-sewer piping that obliges utilities to treat every drop of water to drinking standard, even when it's just going to wind up hosing down a garbage truck. Similarly, we collect every kind of wet waste, treat it exactly the same way, and then release it back to the environment. Thus we're spending more than necessary in treating more water than we need to treat (at both ends of the pipe), and we're making it unnecessarily difficult to use water more than once.

It's time to think outside the pipe. We need to move towards a more resilient model: "horizontal" plumbing that provides innumerable new opportunities for dispersed savings that *increase* rather than decrease convenience and allow innovators to *profit* as well as pay.

Such a system would recognize some basic principles.

+ *Quality*: Not every use requires potable water.

+ *Timing*: Not everyone needs the same amount of water all at once.

+ *Return*: Some uses of water produce a greater economic return than others.

+ *Nature*: The mechanical and chemical processes of natural ecosystems do many things—purifying water on a large scale, absorbing flood waters, storing water, metabolizing wastes— better and more cheaply than we can. We should let them.

+ *Diversity*: Many competing, concurrent solutions to the same problem will be inherently more resilient than any one-size-fits-all answer.

With their focus on function rather than on who owns the pipe, these principles can help us identify ways to extract the greatest possible value from every drop of water we consume, use the fewest drops for every task, leave more in rivers, lakes, wetlands and soil for other species, allow us to live better on what we do take and equip us better to respond smoothly to the changing weather. They open the door to the kind of creative solution that is taking root and wing in the restored Copley Swamp where Steve and Jerry Panzner "bank."

Nothing inspires innovation faster than a problem that can be solved profitably. The nascent commerce in eco-services is important in two critical ways. First, it takes a giant step toward acknowledging the notoriously "soft" contribution that natural ecosystems make to human welfare, in terms that the "hard" dollar economy can recognize. Second, it taps the creative genius of the marketplace rather than resisting it. These shifts in perspective point the way out of last century's expensive, rigid and cruelly destructive obsession with "big engineering," toward flexible, low-cost, ecologically light-footed, and even *profitable* solutions.

Unhappily, some of those who claim most assertively to be standing in defence of our planet's water stand in the way of the changes likeliest to preserve it. Well-meaning and well-funded social activists in Canada, the United States, Britain and elsewhere campaign energetically on behalf of three linked convictions: that water is a human right; that it must be preserved as a global public commons; and that it must be kept separate from the commercial economy by any means. The first of these assertions is well-intentioned, if not especially helpful. The second and third are worse than useless: they are actively destructive. Seen as a whole, this "rights-and-commons" approach would leave us paralyzed in the face of our changing circumstances. "Do nothing" risks becoming our default decision, at incalculable future cost.

Stoking unjustified fears, these voices have been especially strong in Canada, where they have suppressed even discussion, let alone the adoption, of the reforms necessary to secure our water supply. Their fullest expression appears in *Blue Gold: The Global Water Crisis and the Commodification of the World's Water Supply*, the widely circulated manifesto that Maude Barlow first released in 2001.[46] Versions of it have since been published in 40 countries. A career leftist who briefly advised Canada's Liberal Party on women's rights in the early 1980s, Barlow came to prominence as a fierce critic of North American free trade. Since failing to thwart continental commerce, she has portrayed the Council of Canadians, which she chairs, as the embodiment of Canadian patriotism, using the soapbox organization mainly to denounce business (she once greeted an anti-trade rally in Quebec City by shouting, "Welcome to the revolution!").

Her argument in *Blue Gold* proceeds from valid insights. It is hard to dispute that "nature, not man, is at the center of the universe."[47] Likewise, that aquifers will provide water reliably over the long haul only if "net extractions do not exceed recharge" is mathematically obvious.[48] And I would agree just as heartily that we need to temper every decision we make about water with consideration of its impact on our habitat, that we should restore rivers and wetlands to their natural ecological functions wherever we can and that most of our water problems are of our own making, "caused by economic values that encourage over consumption and grossly inefficient use of water."[49]

Such extremely flawed "economic values" concern me as well. The difference in our views comes down to this: whereas Barlow and company see the *economy* as the home of the problem (and wish to dismantle it for a remedy), I find the flaw in the economy's failure to capture the full *value* of water (and other ecological services) and the remedy in reforming the market, not repudiating it.

Barlow admonishes us to rekindle a "reverence" for water, something that surely could do no harm and perhaps some good. To that end, she urges society to declare water a human right from which "no one has the right to … profit" and to legislate that prohibition by outlawing any and all commerce in water.[50]

The campaign (much larger than Barlow's own) to declare water a human right possesses a facile virtue. Who could argue against the self-evident: that water is a *necessity* without which people can't enjoy any other rights? Yet a great deal of effort has been spent in international arenas debating whether the right to water is implied strongly enough in documents like the Universal Declaration of Human Rights or needs an explicit declaration of its own. UNEP, the World Conservation Union and scores of non-governmental organizations hold this second view. And yet, if merely declaring a right

272 ◆ CHRIS WOOD

were synonymous with its achievement, all the world's people would by now enjoy rewarding work, sufficient food and shelter, adequate medical attention and protection from arbitrary arrest. It is difficult to see how adding another good intention to the list will make those aspirations any more tangible to people in a Developing World shantytown or First World ghetto.

If effort spent on non-solutions is merely wasted, the activist agenda turns dangerous when it insists that the world's water can only be protected in the "global commons." The cry that water must remain "in the public trust" and strictly quarantined against "commodification" by the marketplace is heard from grassroots groups in the United States, Britain, India, Australia, Africa, Asia, Latin America and doubtless elsewhere, among whom Barlow is something of a folk hero. "Water is for life, it's not for profit," Terry Swier, the Michigan campaigner against bottled water, told me earnestly. "It's held in public trust for all of us."

This purported principle, in fact, confuses two quite distinct ideas. The first holds that water in nature—in lakes, rivers, underground aquifers or the oceans—is a public good that ought not to be appropriated as private property. With some exceptions, this is already essentially the case in North America and most of the rest of the world. The second idea, however, maintains that only public agencies—in a word, government—can be trusted to deliver, treat, protect or allocate it.

Government, as the agent of the public's collective interest, plainly bears a responsibility to protect natural water. The free-market United States claims just that role for its federal and state governments. Canada embeds it in the idea of Crown title. But governments set the context in many other areas in which we also insist on a high degree of individual choice. Legislators establish speed limits but don't tell us where to drive; the state polices sanitation at the slaughterhouse but doesn't package our meat or prepare our meals. We appreciate this distinction because it maximizes both our security and our freedom of choice. It's odd, therefore, that activists find it inconceivable with respect to water.

The effort to demonize private water services is driven as much by politicized public-sector unions as by the desire to ensure adequate supplies of safe water. Barlow's anti-business Council of Canadians frequently shares a stage (and occasionally court costs) with the Canadian Union of Public Employees, many of whose members staff public water systems across the country. Yet the assumption that only public management (and, less openly stated, collective bargaining) can provide secure drinking water is debatable.

Evidence suggests that cronyism, corruption, inertia and a reluctance to invest have left public water systems in many fast-growing cities in chronic disrepair, often unable to serve the very poor whose interests social activists claim to have at heart.[51] "Public water systems ... are a disaster in almost every developing country," observes William Reilly, a former head of the U.S. EPA who later chaired the board of the World Wildlife Fund. "They're overstaffed; they have a huge amount of leakage; they don't put money back into improving the system; they are corrupt."[52] When a private operator takes over and expands a decrepit public system, existing customers often do pay more for their water. But those who receive tap water for the first time in poor neighbourhoods typically pay far less than before and enjoy greater convenience. It's true that some privatizations of public water systems have gone spectacularly badly, but in France private water companies have functioned smoothly for more than a century.

The more seriously flawed activist conviction holds it "sacred" that water "belongs to the earth and all species" in the global commons, and must never be regarded as private property.[53] This is a deadly piety. It is precisely because their fate was left to the commons that the passenger pigeon, once the most populous bird in North America, no longer darkens its skies. In the same moral ether, the world's fishing fleets have ravaged its oceans to the point that every marine species of any significance to humanity now teeters over the same abyss into which Canada drove its cod in the last century. Left in the commons, productive assets are subject to everyone's exploitation and no one's protection. "People say you can't put a price tag on the priceless," remarks ecologist Gretchen Daily. "I agree—nature is priceless. But if we don't [put a price on it], it's like an all-you-can-eat buffet: People go whole hog and it's gone."[54]

Those who advocate the public commons and a human right to water are correct that water runs through us all. It infuses every aspect of economic, social and cultural life and every hour of the day. *For this very reason*, neither government, no matter how powerful and intrusive, nor any self-appointed overseer from "civil society," can possibly ensure its wise use. Only we ourselves can do that, through the decisions we make in our homes, fields, office cubicles, plant floors, schools and shopping malls or wherever else we spend our time. It's what we each do daily *in the marketplace* that will determine whether collectively we protect our water and the natural systems that provide it, or despoil both.

Once we shed the fear of mentioning water and markets in the same breath, a panoply of inexpensive, effective and adaptive solutions begin to recommend themselves.

By legislation in most Canadian provinces and under the legal doctrine of "reserved right" in the United States, governments hold an underlying title to water in nature. Individuals, communities or companies take water out of nature only under some form of concession (specific or general) from the state. Such concessions take a variety of forms, and the legal traditions to which they conform in the eastern states and provinces differ from those in the West. In most jurisdictions, however, water rights go with particular pieces of land and cannot be severed from them. Thickets of legal complexities discourage someone with the right to use a particular water source from easily transferring that right to someone who could put it to a more productive purpose.

An exception to the Canadian rule exists in southern Alberta. There, as in other provinces west of Ontario and states west of Texas, rights to surface water are organized around the legal principle known as "prior appropriation." This rule of first-come, first-served awards water rights on the basis of seniority. Historically, as settlers arrived, whoever first removed a certain amount of water from a given stretch of river (typically, a farm, ranch or mine) secured title to that amount in perpetuity. Anyone who came along later might also take what he needed from the same stretch of river, and also secure a permanent right to that amount, so long as he didn't prevent those with "senior" title from taking their accustomed amounts. If water ran low, those with "junior" rights went without. With the coming of more settlers, governments eventually limited new appropriations and assigned specific volumes to old ones (although in parts of the United States, disputes over entitlements have occupied the courts for decades), but the seniority system remained intact.[55] In Canada, water rights under this system are attached to, and generally can't be dissociated from, title to particular parcels of land. In much of the western United States, the right is regarded in law as personal property that can be sold or traded separately from the land that gave rise to it.

In the late 1900s, Alberta made a limited change that brought its laws closer to those in the western United States. Under the watchful eye of provincial regulators, water rights in a single river basin—the South Saskatchewan, where droughts are common and virtually all available water is already allocated—could now be severed from the land to which they were originally issued, and sold. One of the first to take advantage of this new freedom was Brian Arnold.

A farm boy who grew up to become a heavy-equipment salesman, Brian developed a romantic yen in the 1990s to get back on the land and raise buffalo. In 1999, just as Alberta was amending its water law, he acquired seven and a half sections of short-grass prairie overlooking the Saskatchewan River not far from Medicine Hat, deep in Palliser's Triangle. Along with the land came a junior right to extract more than 600 acre-feet of water per year from the river. Brian planned to get a few buffalo, raise the animals as a hobby on one of his new sections, and sell off the rest. He didn't need all that water. Moreover, as he explained it, "I live on top of the valley. It's 300 feet down to the Saskatchewan River. It's not very economical to pump it up."[56]

Meanwhile, 120 kilometres west, near the town of Taber, second-generation farmers Casey and Kyle Gouw were looking to expand their father's successful business, growing grain and vegetables along a bend in the Oldman River, a tributary of the Saskatchewan. Proudly boasting that they own "the only successful onion business in Alberta," the Gouws grow, store, pack and wholesale table onions that are sold all over western Canada. The only thing holding back the advance of their neat green rows of onions was lack of water.

The Alberta Environment Department put Brian in touch with Casey and Kyle, and in 2004 the part-time buffalo rancher sold his un-employed water rights (minus a portion the new law set aside for river flow) to the onion growers, for nearly $60,000. The deal was a win for both sides. Its benefit to the Alberta farm economy typified what the province's nascent water market has achieved more generally.

Economist Lorraine Nicol studied informal sales among more than 200 irrigators during a drought early in the new century. In gen-eral, her investigation revealed, water moved from farms with less efficient irrigation equipment to those with more efficient gear.[57] She also found that "water moved to higher-value uses, away from barley, wheat, forage, to potatoes, sugar beets and specialty crops." In other words, the market allocated the limited amount of water available for agriculture in a dry year to farms on which it would produce the most valuable yields.

Other parts of the world have reached the same conclusion. Australia, facing the most severe water shortages in the developed world, began to encourage markets in irrigation water in the 1980s. As in Alberta, sales generally moved water from less to more efficient uses, from lower- to higher-value crops.[58] The ability to sell any water they *don't* use has also encouraged farmers to invest in new, more ef-ficient irrigation technology. In a pattern that fits Brian Arnold's sale to the Gouw brothers, moreover, water has moved from non-commer-cial "hobby" farms to commercial farms.[59]

Chile freed its farmers to trade water in 1981, with reforms that detached water rights from land titles. Its experience has been more uneven, in part a reflection of its long, skinny geography, with many disconnected and relatively short rivers running quickly into the Pacific. In the few valleys with well-developed canals and clear arrangements for executing trades and settling disputes, however, water has once again moved from lower-value corn and cattle farming into higher-value fruit and grape cultivation. Growing Chilean cities can buy additional water more cheaply than they'd be able to if they had to acquire land, either for the attached water rights or to build new reservoirs.

In most American states, water rights still adhere to land title, although once owners acquire properties with water below, they may often use that water however they like. In Michigan, the owners of the Sanctuary are legally entitled to sell the groundwater beneath it to Nestlé's bottling plant (within state limits on the total volume withdrawn). In wide-open Texas, takeover tycoon T. Boone Pickens has acquired several derelict ranches in his state's Panhandle and announced the intention (strongly opposed by many North Texans) to pump Ogallala water from beneath the fallow fields for sale to booming Dallas, 500 kilometres away. But legal uncertainties, political opposition and the availability, in normal times, of ample supplies of subsidized water from public systems have all impeded the development of truly competitive and open water markets even in some states that have encouraged them.

In California a series of droughts have increased pressure to shift water from irrigated agriculture to growing cities, but attempts to harness markets to that end have had only stuttering success. Like other places where extensive canal networks make it easy to exchange water within irrigation districts, informal short-term sales among farmers have become common. But permanent transfers of water out of farming to urban use have been rare. Several factors stand in the way. The ambiguity of farmers' legal rights to sell the water they've been using leaves many afraid that if they try to sell it, governments will revoke their title. A complex state water law, with elements of both prior appropriation and riparian systems, further complicates sales between properties, as do multiple state and federal oversight agencies that must sign off on large transactions.

A more seamless market in bulk water has operated in northern Colorado for five decades. It was made possible by one of the last century's most Herculean exercises in big engineering, the Colorado-

Big Thompson Project: a chain of dams, canals, pumping stations, siphons and half a dozen tunnels up to 20 kilometres long that convey water from the upper reaches of the Colorado River across and under the Continental Divide to the eastern slope of the Rocky Mountains. The amount of water flowing through those pipes and siphons varies from year to year, depending mainly on winter snowfall on the western side of the range. But whatever the amount, the available water is always divided at the start of the growing season into 310,000 equal shares, matching the maximum number of acre-feet of water the system was designed to deliver. In a departure from much of the West, where legal practice allows those with senior licences to extract their full entitlement of water before junior licences are served (and perhaps left without water entirely), every Colorado-Big Thompson shareholder gets exactly the same volume of water as any other: typically, about four-fifths of an acre-foot per share. The shares are fully transferable, on bases either short-term or permanent. Some years, as much as one-third of the water the system delivers changes hands. Over the decades about 30 percent has been sold out of agriculture to municipal systems, with some towns buying shares then leasing them back to farmers for periods of time.

What can we learn from these working experiments in harnessing the power of market choice to the goal of making water go further? First, perhaps, that water markets don't arise spontaneously and, hence, are at low risk of breaking out of any regulatory cage to unexpectedly engulf every drop of the planet's supply. Several elements need to be present for them to work.

- Rights to water offered for sale or lease must be clear and legally defensible. What's being conveyed isn't necessarily outright *ownership* of the water, but there must at least be the secure right to *use* it, just as a rental agreement conveys the right to use but not own a building. Equally, the right should be unambiguously transferable.

- Water rights must be detached from any particular parcel of land and made available for a variety of purposes over a wider area.

+ There must be a convenient, economical way to get the water from vendor to buyer. Water is simply too heavy to move very far in large volumes unless it can *flow* where you want it to go: a practical requirement that limits the scale of markets.

+ "Transaction costs" must be kept low: buyers and sellers should be able to find one another easily and execute trades with a minimum of red tape. Australia's public water exchanges lower the costs; California's bureaucracy raises them.

Where these conditions exist, markets have advantages that will become increasingly desirable as the weather changes. In growing food, which is the human activity that uses by far the largest amount of water, markets direct water to the most efficient, productive users. They do this automatically, flexibly and free of government's slow-moving, politicized hand.

Successful markets that make every drop of water go further ought to convey a simpler but equally important additional lesson to their critics: that buying and selling water need not, by itself, produce the nightmarish consequences anti-business activists perennially invoke against it. Prominent among these is the alarm that if water is bought and sold, only wealthy corporations will have access, leaving the ecosystem out to dry. This has turned out not to be true.

Permission to trade privately in water rights can coexist in perfect harmony with public protection of water in the environment. Indeed, it must. The underlying public-trust title that governments hold to natural water implies a responsibility to protect the amount that nature requires to function. In Alberta, in fact, the same 1999 law that liberated markets also provides the opportunity for the public to claw back water previously granted: whenever a volume of water is traded under the new rules, the province retains the right to demand that up to 10 percent be returned to "in-stream" flows. Perhaps the percentage might be higher, but the precedent is established. Before inaugurating a water market in Australia, state governments there capped the maximum amount of water that might be withdrawn from the Murray-Darling Basin, and as drought bit deeper into the rivers' flow in 2007, officials threatened to ban withdrawals for irrigation entirely.

Still, Barlow asks, "Who will buy [water] for the environment?"[60] Simple: those who care. That's a positive advantage for nature that the "commons" can't deliver. If the first responsibility of the state is security, that must surely include its natural security. Governments can, should and do protect large, rare or relatively intact ecosystems where they can. In practice, though, they don't like to seize private property to create parks or to take back water previously ceded. Particularly in developing countries, they also resist assuming ongoing costs, with the result that the "protection" they provide remote wildernesses is often more rhetorical than real. In an open market, by contrast, the same donors who cheerfully raise money to fly pop singers to Newfoundland for photo-ops with seals are free to secure water for salmon streams too.

Many do already, sheltering a variety of natural habitats in ways just as durable as any government's political commitment. Ducks Unlimited has been doing this for decades, protecting more than 200,000 hectares of wetland in Canada and the United States either through direct ownership (mostly in Canada) or through conservation easements from private landowners (mostly in the United States).[61] The Oregon Water Trust and Environmental Defense Fund have followed a similar model to overcome government inertia and secure private water rights for "in-stream flow" on West Coast salmon rivers. In British Columbia, The Land Conservancy, modelled on Britain's National Trust, adopts stream-side habitats among other ecologically vulnerable properties; by 2007 it had taken on the protection of nearly 35,000 hectares of land and wetland in perpetuity.

In the same way, pragmatic ecologists are now beginning to reclaim on the open market a measure of the water that governments acting for the "public trust" have diverted over the decades from the Colorado Delta. It may as yet be only the proverbial drop in the bucket, but about 40 kilometres south of where I stood on dry sand at mid-"stream" in the Colorado, greener vegetation and an occasional damp track in the sand mark where the U.S.-based Sonoran

Institute and Mexico's non-profit Pronatura environmental organization are re-establishing a stretch of the river's native willow and cottonwood.[62] Making that demonstration possible, project director Francisco Zamora Arroyo told me, is the purchase from Mexican irrigators of rights to 750 acre-feet of water per year. That water will reliably sustain a small patch of marshland and 10 hectares of native trees. It's a start that Zamora hopes will inspire other Delta farmers to sell him more water in the future. "It makes a difference when people can come to the site. They see it's not just about ecological benefit, they see some social benefit to having a really nice river for their families."[63]

Even though the initial instalment is only about one-fiftieth of what the Colorado needs to keep a trickle in its bed year-round, the success has given Zamora a new hope that is independent of whether or not Americans to the north (or Mexico's distant federal government) choose to help the river. "If each farmer is willing to provide a little bit of water," the persuasive geographer told me, "I think it's feasible to get a base flow in Mexico. I'm still optimistic."[64]

Moving volumes of water of the same standard to its most valuable end-use is one thing. Another order of sophistication engages market incentives to improve the *quality* of water. Look at what they're doing along Ontario's South Nation River.

That slow-moving stream rises close to the St. Lawrence River near the town of Brockville and winds north through the province's intensely farmed eastern corner for 175 kilometres, emptying at last into the Ottawa River downstream from Canada's capital. Along the way, it flows through fields of wheat and soybeans, corn, and a growing number of dairy cattle. The water that drains from those fields into the languid river is loaded far beyond provincial guidelines with phosphorus, a constituent of fertilizer also found in animal and human waste. Getting the pollution down poses a problem, however. Requiring the valley's dozen or so modern municipal and industrial waste treatment facilities to reduce further the relatively small amounts of phosphorus they release now would make little change in what reaches the river, at very considerable expense. Most of the phosphorus getting into the stream comes from hundreds of "non-point"[65] farm sources.

So Ontario's government instituted a pioneering pilot program like the United States' wetland mitigation scheme. It allows existing and would-be polluters to work together to roll back the phosphorus they release at the lowest possible cost and on a schedule that makes most sense to the valley's 125,000 residents. It works like this: if a major polluter—a municipal sewage plant or one of the region's large dairies, for instance—wants to expand, raising the likelihood that more phosphorus will get into the South Nation River, it must either engineer a system to ensure that *none* does, or pay farmers to make improvements to their cattle barns and dairy sheds that have the effect of cutting by *four times* the amount of new pollution their own expansion may produce.[66] Instead of merely protecting the river against *additional* pollution, the exchange serves to *reduce* the pollution it receives. Communities and industry save about $800 for every kilogram of new phosphorus they release (the difference between the $2,000 it would cost to prevent that kilo's release and the $1,200 it costs to contain four kilos on a farm). Farmers are paid half the cost of improving their operations, up to $250,000 in some cases.

Playing the role of arms-length matchmaker is the South Nation River Conservation Authority, a provincially constituted non-profit agency with the job of caring for the river. "In the last seven years," says Ronda Boutz, who puts the two sides together, "we've always had more [farm] requests than we have [polluter] funding." Meanwhile, every waste treatment expansion in the South Nation Valley in that time has paid to reduce phosphorus rather than simply to hold the line.[67]

That's one way to "trade" in water quality. Australia has explored others. Under an umbrella scheme seeded with $5 million AUS from the national government, the southeastern states of Victoria and New South Wales instituted several market-type initiatives that, in different ways, pay private landowners to change how they manage their properties in order to improve river water.

In one scheme, the New South Wales government brokered a deal between 600 irrigators on the Macquarie River and landowners upstream to replant bare land in native trees. The irrigators pay the landowners an annual fee for the "transpiration services" the trees provide by holding rainfall in the soil and returning moisture to the air. That reduces the amount of water that percolates through the area's saline soil, picking up salt as it goes and later poisoning irrigated fields downstream.[68] Moisture returned to the air may fall again later as pure rain. Another initiative invited landowners in Victoria state to bid on a variety of land-management activities, including reforestation with native trees, that would improve local stream water and meet other ecological goals. The state's environment department calculated which bids offered the most benefits at the lowest price, then contracted 31 landowners to deliver those "environmental outcomes" for up to a decade, in most cases accomplishing more than one goal at a cost as low as one-seventh that of conventional grants.[69]

Those schemes in Ontario and Australia were both trials. When New York City appointed a forward-thinking bureaucrat named Al Appleton as its Water and Sewer Commissioner in the early 1990s, it took a much more daring step.

At the time Appleton settled into his new job supplying water and sewer services to eight million people, the Big Apple was in trouble. New federal rules required the city to bring its municipal water up to a quality that engineers said New York could only achieve by investing $6.4 billion in a massive new filtration plant that would cost another $320,000 a year to operate. Appleton thought there might be a better answer: pay the farmers and other landowners in the Catskill Mountains, where most of New York's water is collected, to manage the land in ways that reduced erosion, improved natural filtering and brought the city's water back up to federal standards without the need for a new plant. That turned out to cost less than $1 billion and had additional benefits for upstate residents, such as reviving water quality in local trout streams.

Now retired from his city post, Appleton has become a passionate advocate for closing the gap between markets and the ecological assets and liabilities usually left off the balance sheet. "Regulation exists," he says, "because the market hasn't figured out how to deal with externalities." If we start recognizing that a healthy habitat provides a service to our species, he argues, then we will find "less costly and coercive ways to protect the environment than command-and-control government oversight." The key, he says, is a new perspective on nature: "The environment is traditionally seen as a *cost* center. It's actually a *profit* center. We just don't have the mechanism to capture that profit."[70]

Earlier, we visited the Vancouver waste treatment plant on Annacis Island, where recycled sewage now supplies a portion of the plant's own water requirement while reducing waste released to the Fraser River. Another possible use for that reclaimed sewage water lies all around the sprawling facility. Rob Andrews hopes eventually to scale up his recycling trial and sell its product to some of the numerous industries nearby that need water, but not necessarily water suitable for drinking.

Every community has countless such requirements, from car washes and laundromats to metal-working shops that use water to cool industrial lathes. Some need their water as steaming hot as they can get it, others like it ice-cold. What's a contaminant in one application may not be for another. Metal shops, for example, can tolerate trace chemicals and some bacteria in the water they use; plant nurseries need water free of chemicals but don't mind the odd microbe. Heavy-duty air conditioning equipment that sprays water to cool down refrigerant coils can accept many kinds of chemicals or bacteria, but not dissolved minerals that build up on surfaces and reduce efficiency. The variations are endless. The common feature is that relatively few businesses need water that has been expensively treated to drinkable purity. In many cases, they may need just the quality of water that the business next door considers waste—and flushes down the sewer to be treated at a public waste facility.

Markets in rural areas can direct untreated irrigation water to its most productive local use. Urban industries could discover comparable rewards in trading water of varying *qualities*. The benefits would be multiple: reduced demand both for new water and for water treatment as more waste gets promptly recycled as a resource, with corresponding savings to the taxpayers who generally foot the bill at both ends of the pipe; less waste for the environment to absorb; price incentives to companies to buy cheaper, less clean water more exactly suited to their real needs; *and* new revenue opportunities for businesses that can sell "waste" streams they previously had to pay public systems to treat unnecessarily.

One of North America's brightest futurists is Amory Lovins, who, with another pioneering green entrepreneur named Paul Hawken, first advocated dispersed networks of small-scale energy producers as an alternative to big centralized power plants. Lovins' Rocky Mountain Institute in rural Colorado has applied the same thinking to water, finding that our needs aren't always for *more*. In reality our requirements are often as much about timing and the quality of water as about how much we need. Future cities, one study concluded, should, therefore, encourage as many connections among water consumers as possible, so that buyers and sellers could "match the varying characteristics of water required by quantity, quality (biological, chemical, physical), level of reliability, etc."[71]

The marketplace is the most flexible problem-solving institution we know of. Adopting and adapting it to the smarter use of water veers away both from the centralized, one-size-fits-all frame of last century's "big engineering" and from the equally outdated eco-Marxism that sets disciples of *Blue Gold* on course toward a tragedy of the commons. It directs us instead toward a liberating ecology of persistent innovation in which a diversity of solutions can prosper.

So far in this chapter, we've been concerned mainly to make water go further when supplies run low. How should we cope when we get *too much* water? Can we store surpluses for times of drought in less disruptive ways than by building more giant reservoirs?

Indeed.

At first glance, the Silver Ridge housing development in Maple Ridge, east of Vancouver, looks like any other hillside of upscale single-family houses attractively finished in fieldstone. What a casual eye misses are the many special features designed to help seasonal monsoons soak into the ground, rather than race down into nearby creeks or into the sensitive wetland at the foot of the hill. Its winding streets are narrower than normal, both to slow traffic and to reduce the area of impermeable surface. When it rains, gutters direct run-off from the pavement to a number of small parks planted in native shrubs and flowers. There, the water can collect and seep into the earth in hollows artfully recreated with local rock, old tree stumps and gravel to resemble natural stream beds. Lawns conceal an extra thickness of absorbent topsoil covering rock-filled pits that capture more rainwater. While adding little to construction costs, these details helped the developer scoot through municipal environmental checks in record time. They also provided a "green" boast to its marketing plan: after houses in the project's first phase sold out quickly, the same features were adopted for subsequent phases.

The landscaping employed in Maple Ridge and a small but growing number of other communities in the Pacific Northwest reflects a philosophy akin to xeriscaping in the dry Southwest, adapted to conditions on the rain coast. Rather than running around nature, it mimics nature's own time-tested design. A few North American cities are mandating such designs in their local development guidelines. Adoption would be hastened, however, if the full cost of both alternatives—a few inches of additional topsoil, native plants and some rocks, as opposed to kilometres of drainpipe, downstream dikes and penalties for all of the environmental damage done by excessive run-off—were tacked on to development fees and house prices.

This can be substantial. Levees and dikes along riverbanks can cost millions of dollars per kilometre to erect; storm drains are comparably expensive to bury. Left off the books entirely are the costs we expect nature to absorb. Immense volumes of water sluicing off acres of impermeable shingles, pavement and cement, do uncalculated damage to creeks and riverbeds. Worse yet is the damage caused by many cities' reliance on combined storm and sanitary sewers. One study found that combined drains in just 20 cities on the Great Lakes, representing only about one-third of that region's people, pour close to 100 million cubic metres of sewage into the Lakes each year. That's enough raw waste to fill Toronto's Rogers Centre (formerly known as the SkyDome) to its retractable roof in sewage more than 62 *times*.[72] Tacking the cost of the consequential environmental damage onto sewer rates in those cities, or immediately raising rates enough to pay for new conventional sewers and treatment plants, would doubtless spur consideration of alternative strategies.

Some of those might adapt Al Appleton's dictum and reframe the liability of too much water in certain seasons as an asset in disguise. Large-scale reservoirs that fill entire valleys are not the only way to store these periodic surpluses for later months of water deficit. Two techniques deployed for centuries in some climates and abandoned only recently in North America are now novel to many modern city-dwellers. Known as "rain harvesting" and "active groundwater recharge," these can be practised apart or together, by households or entire cities, in versions both high-tech and low.

The first, collecting the water that falls free from the sky, requires only an old-fashioned rain barrel or more elaborate home cistern connected to a downspout from roof gutters. The city of Albuquerque provides a rebate to homeowners who install the first; Germany does the same for the latter. With modest filtering, rainwater can be made potable. By one count, as many as four in 10 South Australian houses rely on cisterns for drinking water.[73] Britain's largest food-service supply firm began harvesting rain in 2006 to wash its fleet of delivery vans; propelling the investment were expected savings of nearly $12,000 a year, enough to pay back the investment in as little as 36 months. In India, more than 20,000 villages harvest rain, often in nothing more complicated than plastic jugs. And analysts have calculated that even such supposedly water-stressed places as Kenya and Ethiopia get enough rain to support seven times their present populations, if they harvested more of it. North America, most of which receives plenty of rain, could dramatically reduce the need for reservoirs by persuading more households to store a little water of their own.

"Groundwater recharge" is engineer-speak for another way of following nature's model. Geology stores vast amounts of water underground. Rather than flooding more valleys to store surpluses above ground, leaving them vulnerable to evaporation, vandalism or worse, why not save them where nature does?[74]

One Ontario region has begun to do just that. From Hamilton, I drove through farmland that resembles the outskirts of Akron: acres of tract housing with themed names like Country Hill and Windflower Terraces, served by arteries of retail outlets weighted toward home improvement. Past an intersection boxed with new car dealerships still laying out sod, I followed a street up an elongated hill. At the crest a sign at a security gate identified the Mannheim Water Treatment Plant. Beyond the gate, tall white tanks stood near a low-rise industrial building.

To one side, the hilltop appeared to have been scooped out long before, leaving a basin of gravel slopes, scruffy meadow and reed-fringed ponds. Around this shallow bowl of land, a handful of windowless grey metal sheds stood a few hundred metres apart. An accommodating employee of the Waterloo Region Department of Water Services, Alex Lee, unlocked the nearest of these. Inside, a squared loop of blue-painted iron pipe, as thick as a good-size tree trunk, emerged from the floor at one end of the shed and, after passing an assortment of valves and gauges, went down into it again at the other. The little building throbbed with a deep vibration. Checking a digital display, Alex informed me that the building's high-speed pump was moving 30 litres of water per second *into* the ground.

The Waterloo region, he explained, has a provincial permit to take up to 55 million gallons a day of water from the Grand River, 10 kilometres away. On most days, especially in winter, it uses only about 40 to 50 million of these. This pump and others like it in the scattered sheds inject the rest into the aquifer below the hill. It will be drawn out later to meet peaks in demand, typically during hot summer afternoons. The porous sand and gravel act like any other reservoir, but without the attendant loss of water to evaporation or the headaches, political and otherwise, of yet another dam. When heavy rains flushed a pulse of contaminated water into the Grand River one recent summer, obliging municipalities including Waterloo to suspend withdrawals, Alex said, "we were good." The natural reservoir allowed his agency to deliver water without disruption while the river cleared.[75]

This kind of resilience has motivated a few other North American cities to adopt similar recharge operations. The Metropolitan Water District that supplies Los Angeles pumps treated waste water into underground aquifers. Arizona has put its depleted aquifers to use as storage vaults for surplus water it receives from the Colorado River. On the flat plain of the Fraser Delta, the Township of Langley puts rainwater harvesting and groundwater recharge together. The unincorporated township is on the fringe of the Greater Vancouver Regional District's vast network of mains fed from three big reservoirs north of Vancouver. The mains supply half the township's fast-growing population; municipal wells serve the rest. "We pay much less for our [ground] water than we do for GVRD water," admits water resources manager Brad Badelt. "It's a real economic incentive for us to keep relying on groundwater."[76] But the free lunch may be coming to an end: the aquifer beneath Langley is poorly mapped, and even as the new century has brought a building boom to the area, the water table has started dropping.

With that in mind, the township persuaded a forward-thinking house builder to add rain harvesting to the other progressive features (like high-efficiency toilets and beefed-up insulation) already planned for 85 new houses the builder intended to market as eco-friendly. With roofs of non-toxic material and downspouts that channel water through sand filters to a central collection point, Yorkson Village is designed to harvest winter rain and send it down a recharge well to the aquifer 30 metres below. "We'll watch it for five or so years and see how it compares to other sites," Badelt told me. If capturing rainwater helps to put off the day when Langley's reliance on Vancouver's big dams and expensive pipes must increase, future housing developments may be required to adopt the same features.

Harvesting water and saving it in the ground is neither new nor necessarily high-tech. Native Americans in what is now New Mexico diked their gardens to capture rain and melting snow, and layered pebbles on the soil to protect the harvested water from evaporating.[77] In modern India's rural Gujarat State, most villages rely on the government to truck in water for most of the year, but not the village of Rajsamadhiya. Once as dusty as the rest, it now boasts gardens, trees, ponds, brimming wells and rich fields. "We haven't had a water tanker come for more than 10 years," said Haradevsinh Hadeja. "We don't need them." This retired policeman persuaded his neighbours to redirect roof and street drains so that monsoon rain now flows into a chain of shallow ponds, where it remains long enough to soak into the soil. The hamlet's water supply has doubled. "There is no more rain than before. We just use it better," Haradevsinh said. "We don't let it wash away."[78]

All these examples illustrate that we have plenty of options, despite the stormy weather ahead. A problem-solving, tool-making animal, we've adapted uniquely to our ecological niche by growing enlarged brains and opposable thumbs. Our natural response to a challenge is to invent. Freed from the self-imposed fetters of "rights and commons" nostrums and motivated by greater honesty in the prices we pay for natural services, we have all the means, models and imagination we need to stretch our available water from one rainy day to the next with enough left over to protect our biological habitats. The fight is not to "commodify" water but to *value it*—along with the intact ecological systems that collect, purify and store it—unleashing our creativity through billions of individual daily decisions to find countless new ways of using it better.

# Chapter 11
## No Fear:
## Putting Canada's Water Up for Sale

An hour south of Lethbridge, Alberta, and 20 minutes north of the Montana border, the sky was a bowl of wet, grey cloud. Persistent drizzle speckled the windshield of my rented ride. For a hundred kilometres west to the Rockies and twice that many east to Medicine Hat, this usually dry country was awash in six days of uninterrupted rain. Where rivers had burst their banks, several towns were under evacuation notice. Others in flatter country had declared states of emergency after overloaded sewers had backed up into basements.

The wetness was an ironic counterpoint to my purpose there. I had come to find an artifact of Canadian-American history born in drought, an all-but-forgotten testament to the enmeshed nature of our two nations' relationship with each other and with water. Some people call it the Spite Ditch.

As one drives down Alberta Highway 4, Milk River is the last Canadian town before the border station at Coutts. It has a bank, a Chinese restaurant, and yellow and green grain elevators. A sculpted dinosaur guards a provincial welcome centre. At the first grain elevator I turned west, bumping over a braid of railroad sidings. The pavement soon petered out, and my rental bucketed over potholes in a gravel road that followed the bluffs along the river. I looked north.

Across the treeless rolling hills, green with rain, a darker streak made a conspicuously level line.

The car vibrated over the pipes of a cattle guard and I pulled to a stop. Outside, wind from the distant mountains put a bite into the cold rain. The ribs and scattered bones of a bovine carcass completed an atmosphere of loss and loneliness. I scrambled up a runnelled, grassy bank. Beyond it was an empty channel two metres deep. The crumbling embankment and its dry bed followed the land along the sidehill, coming from the direction of the river and passing north out of sight. *This surely must be the place*, I thought.

It's curious that Canadians are allowing the prairie to take back such a significant part of our history, according it less honour than the faux dinosaur back at the welcome centre. This crude trench on its cold, rain-swept hill was the physical "fact on the ground" that, on the cusp of the *last* new century, brought Teddy Roosevelt's chest-beating young America to the table to accept a treaty that is still lauded today as a model for cohabiting with a superpower.

Here is that story.

By 1900 plainsmen from Utah and the upper U.S. Midwest had begun settling the northern range: a high, dry table spreading east from the Rockies and divided at the 49$^{th}$ parallel between Canada, in what would become Alberta, and the infant state of Montana. On both sides of that invisible line, homesteaders relied for water on the seasonal flows of two main rivers. One, the St. Mary, arises high in the Montana Rockies and runs north into Canada, joining other streams to empty eventually into Hudson Bay. The other, the Milk, arises east of the St. Mary and much lower in Montana's foothills. It too flows into Canada. But there it diverges from its sister. After a while the Milk turns back south, re-entering eastern Montana ultimately to join the Missouri on a long, muddy journey to the Gulf of Mexico.

Another quality distinguishes the two rivers, or did when the pioneer ranchers first encountered them. The St. Mary, fed by melting mountain snow and ice fields, flowed strongly all summer long. The

Milk, which starts lower in the foothills, in the dry "rain shadow" zone where the mountains have wrung all the moisture from inflowing westerly winds, dried to a trickle six summers out of 10.

Ever enterprising, the Montanans had an answer for that—and an active delegation to Congress. In 1901 surveyors from the U.S. Department of the Interior began mapping an ambitious series of dams, canals and enormous iron siphons designed to remove most of the water from the St. Mary and divert it across several foothill ridges to the Milk. In the Montanans' minds, the Milk would then act as a natural canal to deliver water from the St. Mary, via Canada, back to thirsty ranches and farms in the eastern part of their own state.

When homesteaders north of 49 got wind of the project, hackles rose. Montana's diversion threatened to drain the St. Mary of water vital to the young Alberta economy. The Albertans appealed to their own national government. Ottawa asked Washington to stop the diversion. Washington refused.

There matters might have ended. But these northern ranchers, most of them Americans themselves until quite recently, weren't the kind to leave their fate to distant bureaucrats and politicians. Rejecting surrender, they consulted a map—and hatched a plan of their own. The Milk River runs north of the 49th parallel for nearly 250 kilometres. If the United States were going to steal water out of the St. Mary, these bold new Canadians would steal it right back again out of the Milk. They formed the Alberta Railway and Irrigation Company, raised some money and in 1903 sent mule teams, gangs of workers and steam shovels to the banks of the Milk River. A few miles upstream from the settlement of that name, they drove wooden piles into the riverbed to hold back a diversion weir. Then they began digging a ditch across the low green hills overlooking the river toward the distant northern valley where they planned a reservoir safely out of the reach of those covetous Montanans.

Back across the border, the cry went up that the Canadians, so recently cousins, were planning to spoil the American project out of spite, and the "A. R. & I. Canal" became the Spite Ditch. That's about when the Roosevelt Administration decided it had a situation on its hands. Serious negotiations followed and in 1909, four years after Alberta's recognition as a province, the two sides signed the landmark International Boundary Waters Treaty. It created an International Joint Commission (IJC) to adjudicate the Milk River dispute and similar disagreements that might erupt in the future.

Things worked out along the border. The Americans finished their diversion, complete with its astonishing siphons. The Albertans abandoned their weir and trench. As its first act, the Joint Commission split the rivers' combined water between the two countries, going by a formula that turned out to favour Canada by roughly 60:40. Nearly a century later, the siphons still suck the St. Mary up over the foothills and dump it into the Milk. Thus fortified, the Milk River flows summer-long, and people on both sides of the 49th benefit. And the present-day IJC is still going strong: a venerable institution hailed over time as the granddaddy of all bi-national "dispute settlement mechanisms" to follow.

As a country searching, sometimes self-consciously, for a national mythology, it's odd that Canada has forgotten so completely the ditch in the hills that brought a bumptious America to heel. Back in the rental car, I rumbled over a few more cattle gates before a tuck in the hills opened up to reveal a house sheltered by maples and cottonwoods. An elderly man in suspenders and a plaid shirt answered the door. His name was Jay Snow. The land for miles around has been in his family since his grandfather, a Mormon, rode north from Utah.

I asked him about the ditch. He confirmed that I had found it. "But I take umbrage at the name," he said. "There was no spite involved. They were damn serious."[1]

We Canadians are still damn serious about "our" water. It's a source of pride for a national ego otherwise notoriously wracked by doubt. You could fit our population into greater Tokyo with futons to spare, our economy barely makes it over the threshold into the G8 and our undersea navy may famously be outnumbered by the toy submarines at the West Edmonton Mall. But when it comes to water, Canada is the 800-pound gorilla on the block. Few suggestions raise our temperature faster than that we should sell any of it, especially to America. And few beliefs are more deeply lodged in our collective subconscious than that one day Uncle Sam will insist that we do just that. That makes it a touchy topic. After one American expert spoke in favour of continental trade in water to an audience in Vancouver, he said afterward, only partly in jest, "I felt some need to leave the country very quickly."[2]

Left-leaning water activists work tirelessly to inflame Canadians against this "looming threat" from next door. "Canada is under pressure to sell water to the United States by pipeline or diversion," insists the Council of Canadians on its website.[3] Soon after the Canadian public elected a new Conservative government, Tony Clarke, a close Council ally with his own Ottawa-based think-tank, claimed that Prime Minister Stephen Harper's effort to repair relations with Washington, in fact, concealed "forces moving behind the scenes to turn on the taps for massive water exports to the United States."[4] In May of 2007, Maude Barlow herself appeared before Parliament's Standing Committee on International Trade to declare that it had become "obvious now that the United States is no longer thinking of the 'long term' when it comes to securing Canadian water … Canadian water is in their sights."[5]

Never mind that Canada's environment minister, John Baird, had stated plainly, only a month earlier, that "the Government of Canada has no intention of entering into negotiations, behind closed doors or otherwise, regarding bulk water exports."[6] In the aqua-nationalists' Orwellian world view, it remained an article of faith that "government leaders in Canada, the U.S. and Mexico [were] actively discussing bulk water export."[7]

In fact, the drumbeat that *the Americans are coming* for Canada's water crosses most of Canada's political divides. Peter Lougheed, the famously level-headed former premier of Alberta who, after leaving that office, later helped to negotiate free trade with the United

States, makes an odd bedfellow for Barlow's virulently anti-free trade Council. Nonetheless, he too believes that, "at some stage of the game, Washington is going to interpret the Free Trade Agreement and think they have a claim over our fresh water. It's coming."[8] When it does, "Canadians should be prepared to respond firmly with a forceful, 'No, we need it for ourselves.'"[9]

Even the generally pro-American and pro-market Alberta pundits Barry Cooper and David Bercuson have characterized any future dealings with the United States over water as a mugging. "A person dying of thirst with a loaded gun in the middle of a desert," the academic tag team wrote, "will waste little time trying to reason with another person, with bountiful supplies of water, who refuses to share that water but has no means to defend it."[10]

The suggestion of imminent ravishment plays to Canadians' chronic insecurity in the face of American power. But it also goads our latent patriotism: for many Canadians, especially those with deep roots on the continent, our country's countless waters are byways of identity. Images of *coureurs de bois* and the ghost of Tom Thomson hover in heroic soft-focus above the lakes of our collective subconscious. Margaret Atwood, our national poet-therapist, once identified near-drowning as a popular literary hazard through which survivors became authentic Canadians. Visitors to the Canadian pavilion at the Venice art *Biennale* in 2005 encountered a cascade on which projected images of water and blood ran together. According to Rebecca Belmore, the Ojibwa artist who created the work, this was a meditation on identity, conquest and "water as a saleable resource."[11] Lest any doubt linger about water's significance to our soul, the Canadian federal government maintains a website helpfully documenting historic, musical and poetic connections between water and the national identity.[12]

In truth, numerous other cultures have attachments to water at least as authentic and strong as ours. And we flatter ourselves in insisting that we possess an asset that America—*America!*—may wish to come after us for. Let's give ourselves a shake here: there is virtually no likelihood that the United States will suddenly decide to twist our tap and drain us dry. And despite that general truth, should a few local opportunities arise here and there to sell modest quantities of water to Americans, doing so wouldn't trigger the kind of continental demand for every drop of our water that activists invoke. Our water has, in fact, flowed south by truck and pipeline for years, and yet no stampede of NAFTA-quoting claimants has appeared at the border demanding to stick a pipe in Lake Athabasca.

There's more. If Americans or others do arrive at Canada's door with chequebooks and empty billycans, we shouldn't send them away. Not because they might be armed and desperate. But because the water that used to fall on other lands now falls on ours; because we can spare a little in ways that won't harm our environment (and that certainly make more ecological sense than pumping it into the ground to push out oil); and yes, because we can make money by doing so.

Probably few tourists wander far enough northwest off Las Vegas' Strip to find themselves at Boca Park, a cluster of white marble-clad designer outlets, home-fashion shops, cafés and restaurants catering to upscale consumers. Those few who do might be struck by the apparently spendthrift play of several outdoor fountains in the dry desert air. And if any were Canadians, they'd be more startled yet by the brass notice in front of each: "The water in this fountain is not from the State of Nevada or the Colorado River Basin. It is imported from northern states or Canada."

Boca Park happens to belong to the same wealthy Alberta family of property developers, the Ghermezians, as the West Edmonton Mall. When the retail developers opened their Las Vegas property in 2003, Nevada was in the middle of a historic drought, and local utilities refused to supply new water features. Reasoning that a shopping mecca with enough water to float its own fleet of submarines could spare enough to fill some modest fountains, the company acquired a 75,000-litre (20,000-gallon) milk truck and began driving it between Edmonton and Las Vegas once a week, transporting Alberta water to splash in the Nevada sun. Deliveries continued for the next four years.

Then they stopped. The weekly shipments of Alberta water to Nevada didn't end because Canadians objected (most didn't know). They ended because of economics. Boca Park's owners found it cheaper to contribute $11,750 to the fund that subsidizes conversion from grass to xeriscaping, in return for a hook-up to public mains, than to keep on trucking water from Canada.

Activists routinely assert that U.S. states are "looking toward Canada's water" as a "quick-fix solution" to regional water crises but rarely if ever identify the states in question.[13] Perhaps because none exist: no U.S. state agency or government to my knowledge has proposed importing water from Canada as a solution to its own shortage. Southern Nevada, the thirstiest part of the driest state of them all, has a detailed plan for supply that runs past the middle of the century. It includes various dams on the state's own rivers, purchases from farmers in Wyoming or Colorado "who might find it more attractive selling water to a city than growing alfalfa," as Pat Mulroy's deputy, Kay Brothers, told me, and, of course, that pipeline to Spring Valley. Canada is nowhere on the list of options.

In trying to prove that an American assault on Canada's water constitutes a clear and present danger, activists are especially fond of citing the unsustainable depletion of the Ogallala Aquifer and the sixties-era NAWAPA pipe dream.[14] But these are thin bogeymen. Texas, the Ogallala state with the largest population and the most money, has a number of plans to provide water to its fast-growing northern cities; none involves Canada. In North Texas water circles, laughed High Plains farmer (and leading local Republican) Eddie Teeter, no one talks about raiding Canada for its water. As for NAWAPA and its assorted near-cousins, they're extremely unlikely ever to be built. The IJC, itself the child of big engineering, made a detailed inquiry into the plausibility of various continental water transfer schemes and judged, "The era of major diversions in the United States and Canada has ended."[15]

The change of heart reflects no sudden surge of green values among water utilities. It's just that moving water any distance in any considerable volume is a hugely difficult and expensive way to solve the problem of supply. Try picking up a four-litre jug of milk and holding it by one hand outstretched from your body. Keep it there for a while and feel the burn. Liquid is heavy. Transporting it by truck or tanker quickly burns up more money in fuel than the water can be sold for. Tony Clarke asserted breezily that *"all it would take* is the construction of a network of new dams, reservoirs, canals, tunnels and pipelines [my emphasis]," to let Canadian water flow under its own gravity to the American Midwest, as if that were simple.[16] Little could be further from the truth.

In a remarkable, unpublicized study for the Canadian government, consultants Jim Bruce and Hans Martin, with others, examined how the changing climate and some other things might affect the flow of water across the Canada-U.S. border.[17] Among those other things was the export of water on a large scale. They concluded, in sum, that international trade in bulk water was simply not about to happen. For a good reason: "The economics of international bulk-water transmission are not very attractive, a fact that can be substantiated by observing that very little of it takes place anywhere in the world."[18]

It does happen in a small number of places. Tanker ships deliver water around islands in the Philippines as well as the Caribbean and Aegean seas; Lesotho sells water in bulk to South Africa. But other initiatives have failed. Britain contemplated tankering water from Norway to England during an early-century drought but eventually opted not to. Israel signed a deal with Turkey to import water, but logistic hurdles frustrated deliveries (among other things, no shipper would guarantee the quality of delivered water). Kuwait signed a similar deal to pipe water under the Persian Gulf from Iran, but America's invasion of Iraq interrupted the pipeline's construction.

New Mexico hydrologist and entrepreneur William Turner is one of North America's frankest advocates of treating water as a commercial good like any other. His Albuquerque-based WaterBank.com offers to match buyers and sellers anywhere in the world. Yet even he concedes, "Long distance bulk transport of water simply is not economically feasible."[19]

✦

Yet activists continue to ring the alarm that a slight Canadian mis-
step—in the sale of a single sip of our water—would be enough
instantly to "open the floodgates" to a rapacious America.[20] To
heighten our concern, the Council of Canadians and others throw
around authoritative-sounding citations from the text of international trade agreements. They interpret these snippets of the General
Agreement on Tariffs and Trade (GATT), the documents that created
the World Trade Organization (WTO) and the North American Free
Trade Agreement (NAFTA)[21] as implying the following:

a) that one commercial transaction in any volume of bulk water
   will legally transubstantiate all a country's water from being a
   natural "public good" (out of reach of predatory corporations)
   into a "commodity in commerce" (which those same corporations may demand at will);

b) that once any volume of water is allowed to leave Canada in bulk
   for the United States, that volume can never be reduced;

c) that once private business is permitted to play any role in the
   acquisition, treatment or delivery of water, Canadians will have
   no subsequent flexibility to favour Canadian businesses (or customers) over non-Canadian ones; and

d) that once any of the foregoing happens, American and possibly
   Mexican corporations can use NAFTA to hold Canada to a form
   of legal blackmail, obliging us to open up every creek to any foreign demand or pay billions of dollars in penalties.

These interpretations, derived from selective reading and a great deal
of alarmism, are, respectively: a) false, b) misleadingly incomplete, c)
true (but so what?) and d) wildly exaggerated. Let's put them under
the microscope in turn.

The first assertion—that a single drop of water entering commerce puts every lake in the land at risk—is both the furthest from
the facts and the most damaging, because it's employed so regularly

in Canada as to foreclose discussion of softer paths to water security that tap the creativity of the marketplace. In *Blue Gold*, Barlow begins the argument for this belief by pointing out that GATT provides "a definition of a 'good' which clearly lists 'water, including natural waters,' [while] NAFTA adds an explanatory note that 'ordinary natural water of all kinds' is included [on the same list]."[22] The list they're referring to, GATT's Harmonized Commodity Description and Coding System, is a standardized identification system designed to help the agreement's 150 members and their citizens' businesses keep track of trade in millions of different items with a minimum of confusion; it is not a list of anything that *must* be traded.[23] It does universally for goods what, for example, the International Standard Book Number (ISBN) system does for books. It provides a common reference base, but it doesn't require the sale of everything, any more than the ISBN system requires your bookseller to carry (or you to buy) every book with an ISBN.

Nonetheless, aqua-nationalists insist that the existence of such a list implies that once any water is traded, all of it must be. At the extreme, some say this means that all the water in Canada is already a commercial commodity. The Canadian Environmental Law Association, for one, has held that because Alberta sells irrigation water to commercial farms, water has already entered commerce in Canada and, therefore, "Americans can, indeed, 'turn on the taps' on Canadian water."[24] If this is, in fact, true, one must wonder what all the fuss is about: since the jig is up anyway, why bother resisting? Alternatively, if the jig is up and the feared horde of gun-toting, pipe-laying Americans hasn't materialized, why do aqua-nationalists still cry "wolf" at any whisper of water and sale in the same breath?

Numerous authorities argue persuasively that trade law, in fact, distinguishes clearly between water in the wild—in rivers, lakes or aquifers—and water that has been put up for sale, with different rules for each. As a Canadian government background paper on water law notes: "even if some water is extracted from its natural state to be made into a good (e.g., bottled water or as an ingredient in a beverage), the remaining water in the source from which that water was drawn still constitutes water in its natural state, and therefore is still not a good."[25] The NAFTA sustains this distinction. Before the trade agreement was signed, its three partner governments issued a common interpretation of its terms. "Water in its natural state," that statement read in part, "in lakes, rivers, reservoirs, aquifers, water basins and the like, is not a good or product, is not traded, and therefore is not and has never been subject to the terms of any trade agreement."[26] For particular clarity it also stated: "The NAFTA creates no rights to the natural water resources of any Party to the Agreement."

It is not only the Canadian, U.S. and Mexican governments that hold this view. James L. Huffman, the distinguished American expert in water law who felt a need to leave Canada briskly after raising the subject of water sales, has also said this: "My interpretation of NAFTA is that it clearly excludes water. Nobody in the United States, to my knowledge, has any idea that the agreement involves water."[27]

In short, the NAFTA "call" option by which aqua-nationalists contend that American states or foreign corporations could somehow compel unlimited access to all the water in Canada is, simply, a chimera. Like a televangelist's brimstone, it may shake open the pockets of the faithful, but it cannot be found on a map or, in this case, in the law.

The second assertion anti-trade water activists repeatedly make could be called the "one-way tap" claim. "If the export of water were to commence between NAFTA countries," *Blue Gold* insists, "the tap couldn't be turned off. Exports of water would be guaranteed to the level they had acquired over the preceding 36 months; the more water exported, the more water required to be exported. Even if new evidence were found that massive movements of water were harmful to the environment, these requirements would remain in place."[28] This contains both a distortion and an omission of what trade agreements actually say.

The distortion lies in the claim that NAFTA would prevent water exports, once undertaken, ever from being reduced in the future. Activists reach this conclusion by ignoring the text of the treaty, which says in plain words that "a Party may adopt or maintain a restriction ... with respect to the export of a good to the territory of another Party," so long as any reduction in shipments is proportional to the total amount of a good the exporting country produced.[29] Consider another commodity. Say the United States sold 90 million pounds of cleaned catfish to Canada in each of three succeeding years, an amount that is about 15 percent of its usual catfish harvest.[30] Then suppose that in the fourth year, disease swept America's catfish ponds. The United States could certainly reduce its fillet shipments to Canada, so long as they remained at 15 percent of the (reduced) American catch. Likewise, if Canada began to export "commercial" water to the United States and then reduced its own "harvest" of such water by one-third, it would be entitled without penalty to cut back shipments to the United States by an equal amount. The commitment to treat customers everywhere in North America equitably offends those who oppose free trade per se, but it can and should be defended as part of the moral foundation of a continental common market.

What activists also omit in decrying this purported "one-way tap" is that both the GATT/WTO and NAFTA clearly affirm member nations' rights to "protect human, animal or plant life or health," as long as the rules they create apply equally to domestic and foreign companies.[31] And reasonably so: why protect a lake from despoliation by foreigners only to allow your own citizens to ravage it instead?

The aqua-nationalists' not-so-latent desire to discriminate surfaces explicitly in their third charge against trade agreements: an attack on the principle of "National Treatment." This holds that once two countries open an industry to free trade, both nations' enterprises will be treated equally. As a consequence, Barlow complains, "if a municipality privatizes its water delivery service, it would be obliged to permit competitive bids from water service corporations of the other NAFTA countries."[32] Well, yes. That's the whole idea of free trade: to give *all* players access to the largest possible number of customers and suppliers. Canadians get the same benefit when they do business with the 93 percent of NAFTA customers who *aren't* in Canada.

The aqua-nationalist manifesto reads into National Treatment the further alarming claim that "if a Canadian company ... gained the right to export Canadian water, American multinationals would have the right to help themselves to as much Canadian water as they wished."[33] Wrong. To be clear: the principle is *equal* treatment, *not*, as Barlow and company routinely imply, favouritism for foreigners. National Treatment means that if a Canadian government were to auction a permit to withdraw water from a certain spring (as happens now routinely with oil and gas or mineral exploration rights), American companies would have the right to bid on that permit and expect equal treatment with Canadian competitors. The process couldn't be skewed to favour the homeboys. But so what? This is another moral foundation of fair as well as free trade, and again, it cuts both ways.

These inflammatory allegations obscure a protection embedded in National Treatment: it strongly reinforces the important principle that companies operating on foreign soil must comply with local laws as fully as any domestic firm. That is why when Wal-Mart opens a superstore in Brampton, it must obey the laws of Ontario, not those of Bentonville, Arkansas. In the same way, any laws Canada or its provinces might enact to protect the source of any water here would apply equally to foreign and to Canadian companies.[34] Once more, the only objection to this equitable treatment can be opposition in general to trade with the folks next door.

The last charge aqua-nationalists level at NAFTA has to do with what is known as its "Investor-State" clause.[35] This was meant to protect a business based in one NAFTA nation from having another country seize its investment without compensation. It allows a business in that situation to sue the country; a special tribunal then hears the case and renders a ruling, which may be appealed. From this, *Blue Gold* leaps to the astonishing assertion that "the very act of a government attempt to ban bulk water exports ... would trigger foreign investors' NAFTA rights, and they could demand financial compensation for lost opportunities."[36]

The clause has been controversial beyond the anti-trade left. Many people in all three NAFTA countries heartily dislike it. As an example of its supposed evils, Canadian activists point to the lawsuit that a California company, Sun Belt Water Inc., filed in 1999 against Canada. Earlier, Sun Belt and its Canadian partner (equipped with a valid provincial licence) had developed an agreement to ship water by tanker from Fanny Bay, a small community on the east coast of Vancouver Island, to Goleta, a seaside town west of Santa Barbara, California. Before the shipments could commence, and amid the furore over John Febbraro's highly publicized misadventure, British Columbia placed a moratorium on water exports. The company claimed it was owed $10 billion.[37] Yet, nearly 10 years after the suit was filed, the moratorium remained in place, no water was sailing south, and the suit had gone nowhere.[38] An independent expert on trade policy who reviewed the first 10 years of rulings under the contentious clause concluded that activists' fears that it would handcuff environmental-protection laws "have not been borne out."[39]

We know what is coming. Dry places at mid-latitudes are getting very much drier. Wet ones farther north are receiving even more water. By mid-century, as much as a third of the water that today falls over the southwestern United States may instead be falling over northwestern Canada. Comparable shifts are in the wind over every other continent. Among the losers in other hemispheres are billions of the world's most vulnerable human societies and threatened ecosystems.

Canadians represent less than one percent of humanity, living on a landscape that already contains nearly one-fifth of the world's water and that gets wetter by the day. Can we really stand by and watch others die of thirst? And will those others allow us that privilege? Andrew Nikiforuk, an ardent Canadian aqua-nationalist, has no mercy for residents of the pampered American Southwest when water shortages loom: "Tell them to move." But do we say the same to Mexicans who find they can no longer coax a crop from the baked earth when the last leak in the All-American Canal is cemented over? Or to farmers in Gujarat when their wells run dry? Or to nomads from Somalia when the monsoons fail? And in any case, move where? Toronto?

The inequities in climate's distribution of water are sharpening. When they strike the weakest, humanitarian crises may tug Canadians by the conscience into sharing some of "our" water with others. But physics erects limits to that help. We couldn't, even if we wished to, resolve the larger water challenges facing India, China or other vulnerable countries. On the other hand, with middle classes in those societies numbering in the hundreds of millions, the pressure to quench those markets' more refined thirsts will become overwhelming.

Whether water is to grace tables in Beijing or mist patios in San Diego, the urge Canadians will feel to sell a little of our water surplus to offset the rest of the world's diminishing account won't come from a roused America, armed, thirsty and dangerous. It will come from the growing sense of a missed opportunity. The state of Alaska has already declared its readiness to supply cities in the lower 48 or elsewhere with water harvested at river mouths. The state envisions tugboats trailing huge, waterproof bags filled with as much as 123,000 cubic metres of water (enough to supply 200 Los Angeles families with water for a year) for delivery anywhere in the world. A good deal of that water could come from rivers that start and grow large in British Columbia's mountains but happen to reach the sea after flowing for a few kilometres through Alaska's Panhandle. By law, the water that falls on northern British Columbia or the Yukon becomes Alaska's at the border. Canada could not object to Alaska's decision to sell it.

Denmark may be even better positioned to slake any future world thirst for bulk water. Its home territory is minute, but it manages Greenland, where scores of cubic kilometres of ice-cap are turning into torrents of pure fresh water each summer. Indeed, it might even be an environmental service to capture a little of it before it should enter the North Atlantic and endanger the salinity that keeps the

Great Ocean Conveyor circulating. And if there were a few Euros to be made in the bargain, well, *skoal!*

Vancouver entrepreneur Fred Paley is one of the few Canadian business people willing to float the idea of selling some of this country's water abroad. One company he founded, Global Resources, bottled and offered for sale bulk water from Sitka, Alaska.[40] "The need for pure drinking water continues to grow around the world," Paley told me. "In the future, as drinking water continues to be polluted around the world, and we're sitting here on all the water, do we say 'No'? I don't think from a humanitarian point of view we can. As a Canadian, I think as long as it's environmentally sound, we should be exporting water."[41]

For further proof that a little buying and selling of water over the border won't bring down the sky, you need to get out of committeerooms and let the Alberta wind ruffle your hair.

After parting from Jay Snow, I spent a little longer in the Milk River Valley. Twenty minutes farther on down the highway, I came to the Canada-U.S. border. The inspection post guarding the 49th parallel at Coutts, Alberta, and Sweetgrass, Montana, is an elegant, angular, stone-clad symbol to international cooperation. Opened not long after the terror attacks on New York and Washington, it was one of the first posts designed to accommodate both American and Canadian officials in a single building. After a few early hitches (the design was altered to allow armed U.S. agents to go to the bathroom without setting foot on Canadian soil, where their guns are prohibited), the unified facility seems to be working well.

Beneath the sagebrush that surrounds the post and the two small communities (combined population about 400) that its activity supports is a less obvious symbol of cross-border amity. There, for more than 40 years, a pipeline has carried water, withdrawn from the Alberta reach of the Milk River 11 kilometres north, past the Canadian hamlet of Coutts, to the Americans of Sweetgrass. In a typical month, 3,600 cubic metres flow down the pipe and over the border. In exchange, Sweetgrass' only governing body, its Sewer and Water Board, pays Coutts roughly $4,000. Whether this constitutes a sale is a matter of interpretation.

"We buy our water from Coutts," asserts Helen van Ruden, a frank, businesslike woman in chinos and jean shirt who works at the UPS forwarding warehouse on the U.S. side. "We have for as long as I've lived here. We pay per gallon. It's been great."[42]

Coutts Mayor Jamie Woodcock is a large fellow who staffs a much smaller UPS outpost on the Canadian side. He agrees that the arrangement works well. When Coutts had to upgrade its water treatment recently, Sweetgrass shared the cost through a hike in its water rate. But, he insists, "We don't sell it to them. We charge a fee for delivering and chlorination. We're not actually selling the water."[43]

What the original contract may say on the point is unknown. It's been lost for years.

Water carries no passport. It is never exclusively "ours" or "theirs." Like carbon and air, it's always passing through on its way to somewhere else. By virtue of that unavoidable truth, we Canadians delude ourselves in imagining that we can achieve our own water security in splendid isolation from our neighbours'. Again, the fear is not that going it alone would invite a stand-and-deliver ultimatum from a thirsty America (it wouldn't). It is simply that we will best protect the water that gives life to us both by acting together. The price of failure to do so is written in the loose sand and blackened marshes of the former Colorado Delta.

Water is a physical fact. Its challenges are always specific to the ground it flows over. Adversaries over water are usually neighbours; solutions require local compromise. The boundaries of the conflict are typically those of the watershed, the area within which all water passes to a common outlet. Within the natural frontiers described by elevation and physics, and heedless of our invisible lines, the river course connects a single, seamless biological habitat strung out along a chain of pools from its burbling beginnings to its easeful slide into the sea. Here, every human appropriation affects every other user (human and otherwise) not only downstream but often upstream as well. If we wish to adapt to the coming storms at the least financial and ecological cost, while giving ourselves the best chance to avoid conflict, we must start here: by allowing nature's geography to trump our imaginary one in shaping not only our physical infrastructure, but also our social and political infrastructures. Policy professionals call this idea "integrated watershed (or river basin) management."

Kindy Gosal is a policy pro with more dirty-fingernail experience than most. Raised from the age of six in the Kootenay Mountains of southeastern British Columbia, he became a forester, he says, "to get away from people." He discovered, instead, that most of what threatened the health of trees came not from the forest itself but from humans. Taking this knowledge abroad, he helped communities in Africa, Tibet and Japan manage crop and forest lands more sustainably—and realized that water was the thread connecting every activity that bore on social as well as forest health in those places. Now Gosal works with the Columbia Basin Trust, an organization funded indirectly by proceeds from the hydroelectric developments in that river basin with the intent of giving a stronger voice to its inhabitants.[44]

Gosal accepts that integrated watershed management has a wonky name. But he believes deeply in its intent: to ensure that the choices we make as individuals and societies account fully for their consequences for everyone and *everything* else. In the real world, that inclusive aspiration is quickly lost in the thicket of interests involved. In just the Canadian portion of the Columbia River Valley, Gosal tells me, no fewer than 19 federal and 17 provincial agencies—not including municipalities, First Nations and private landowners—have duties that affect water. "You have [communities with] responsibility to provide potable water," he observes, "but they can't prevent someone from putting in a pig farm."[45] What he calls "the essence" of integrated watershed management "is getting all the folks together who have some influence over watercourses, and the people that use the watercourse, so that you recognize what kind of activities are required to maintain the quantity and quality [of water] that we want."

The potential for conflict among fragmented authorities plagues politically divided river basins within and between nations around the world. So it is both striking and encouraging to find that in the last two decades, a common desire on both sides (or ends) of these shared streams has engendered a remarkable phenomenon: new entities concerned with entire watersheds have appeared on every continent. Advocates for these new river-basin scale entities must overcome both the reluctance of jaundiced taxpayers to fund new layers of government and the jealousies of existing institutions unwilling to cede jurisdiction. Yet, like water finding a way downhill, they continue to evolve. And like river basins themselves, they come on all scales. Some pioneering efforts have state backing and all the *gravitas* of the venerable IJC. Others are small, self-starting and, in an admirably 21st century way, viral.

The Riverkeeper movement is an example of this second type. First conceived by fishermen who were losing their livelihoods to development along the Hudson River, it involves "keepers" who recruit people with legal training and ecological zeal to act as attorneys for their watery "clients." These lawyers for the river monitor compliance with existing laws, press lawsuits if necessary and work toward changes in statute. The Bow Riverkeeper group, whose donors pay Danielle Droitsch's salary, is one of more than 100 such affiliates supporting riverkeepers, bay-keepers, lake-keepers and creek-keepers from Canada to Colombia and Australia, with 70 in the United States alone.[46]

At the other end of the scale are full-fledged international commissions. Since the 1990s, riparian states have created several such bodies to work out differences over the Danube (the world's most international river), the Rhine, the Mekong and other waterways.[47] In 2000 the European Union set a target of 2010 for implementing integrated watershed management plans on all of its member countries' major rivers.[48] The fitful evolution of the North American Great Lakes Charter has been a part of the same global movement. Perhaps ominously, no such organization exists to mediate competing demands on the Euphrates River from Turkey, Syria, Iraq and Iran.[49]

Representative bodies find it easier to bridge differences when rivers fall entirely within one jurisdiction. In France, six regional water parliaments, their boundaries based on watersheds, bring stakeholders together to decide what new infrastructures may be needed and to levy charges for water and waste disposal in order to finance them. The European Union, in which administrative and political integration has advanced faster than in North America, requires its member states to cooperate with its new water directive.[50]

In Canada, Ontario's decades-old, river-based Conservation Authorities have acquired additional authority to develop integrated plans for water management in their basins. One administers the phosphorus-trading scheme that reduces pollution in the South Nation River; another decides how much water Waterloo and its neighbours may take from, or must leave in, the Grand River. The Okanagan Valley's Water Stewardship Council, on which Deana Machin and Lorraine Bennest sit, is another step in the same direction.

The compelling case for managing migratory water on a watershed basis has even begun to overcome American touchiness about relinquishing sovereignty to foreign agents and Canadians' reciprocal distrust of U.S. motives. From the Rockies to the Atlantic, citizens of both nations are working to give structure and capacity to a new breed of institution that must work within, but also across, legal frontiers. In 2005 the IJC urged the governments of Canada and the United States to expand the role of existing binational regional advisory boards in the St. Croix, Rainy and Red river watersheds.[51] While the Canadian government was still studying that idea two years later, five Canadian Consular offices in U.S. cities in the Great Lakes Basin, acting together with several American think-tanks, invited a hundred elected officials, business and interest-group leaders from both countries to form "an ongoing network" for the discussion and solution of Great Lakes issues "in an integrated manner."[52] Aqua-nationalist attacks notwithstanding, the Great Lakes Charter also inches forward.

Large or small, however, these efforts displayed similar virtues and a common shortcoming: an abundance of dialogue but an absence of means to take hard decisions or compel even urgent action. British Columbia's Fraser Basin Council, for instance, has been praised as an international model of inclusiveness in the stewardship of temperate North America's last major free-flowing river. An independent charitable organization, it describes itself as "a catalyst for solving inter-jurisdictional issues, a conflict resolution agent, and a sustainability educator."[53] Notably, it is neither a decider nor a doer.

Marion Robinson manages the Council's activity in the still semi-rural stretch of river between the Coast Mountains and urban Vancouver. Home to tulip fields and condominiums, and lushly green at almost any season, the area is under strong pressure from development. In early 2007 as melting snowpacks sent a near-record freshet roaring downriver toward the lower Valley, the Council convened members of 30 local agencies to share their plans for the threatened flood. But it had no ability to compel any coordination among the hodge-podge of preparations. As a result, one agency's dikes directed the rising water away from the growing city of Chilliwack straight into the unguarded front yards of another low-lying community named Skway. "Information by itself," Robinson ruefully notes, "doesn't make decisions."[54]

Riverkeepers carry no warrant beyond the rights of any ordinary citizen to act under the law. Most international commissions (and all of those the IJC has sought to expand along the Canada-U.S.border) have even less authority: their influence is generally confined to the bully pulpit or to bringing rival parties together for good-faith discussion. As Danielle Droitsch tartly observes of her community's efforts to care for the Bow River, "there's no hammer" requiring good intentions to be turned into action.

"Canada's water crisis cannot be resolved via engineered solutions or more and better science," contend Oliver Brandes and Tony Maas, researchers at the University of Victoria who have been studying how ecosystems are governed around the world. If crisis is to be prevented, they believe, "new decision-making processes must evolve (or be created) specifically to fill the role."[55] Those processes, the pair add, must be governed by principles of sustainability that place nature's boundaries ahead of man's, acknowledge the full value of ecological services to the cash economy, and adopt "soft" engineering to buffer swings in water supply. For its part, the venerable ijc has committed its spinoff river boards to more neutral standards: "equality of membership [from Canada and the United States], joint fact-finding, science-based decision-making, and objective advice-giving to government."[56] But practical Danielle Droitsch and Marion Robinson put their fingers on the fatal weakness that lies behind such muscular statements of principle. When push comes to shove, most experiments in such "ecological governance" to date are impotent by design.

Yet the clock is ticking. The change in the weather—increasingly erratic, violent, alternately drenching and desiccating—is accelerating around us. Overhead, greenhouse gases will reach the trigger point for an unpredictable escalation of climate change in less than a decade. Any response, physical or institutional, will take at least that long to realize. Sooner rather than later, act we must.

If we are attentive, it may take but one or two devastating droughts and floods bearing Biblical comparison to persuade us that our old plumbing and practices are insufficient to the new extremes of "normal" weather. Cringe as we may from adding more dams and pipelines to our already over-engineered continent, we'll still need to find new places to store a little of the flood to drink (and grow and make things with) during the drought that is certain to follow. In the event, we may favour a few dams or pipes after all. But if we're honest about it, we'll find ways that are smarter, easier, kinder to the planet and, in the long run, cheaper to ourselves. Using landscaping rather than dikes to temper extremes of rainfall. Distributing our next big reservoir virtually among a thousand home cisterns or stashing it invisibly underground. Piping industrial zones for the commercial exchange of waste water. Protecting rivers by preserving (and re-establishing) wetlands that filter their living water. Even letting our beloved lawns go brown through August. Solutions to our avoidable water "crisis" are at every hand, within reach of each of us.

They are ready to be unleashed by one critical concession: a more candid accounting of nature's services to our market economy. Our most successful strategy will integrate our human industrial economy back into nature's biological one wherever possible, adopting and sharing the planet's own design for responsive, long-term resilience. Plainly we can do that most effectively if we respect nature's arena of action, the watershed. We must put differences across arbitrary borders into perspective against the larger stakes that we have in common. The biggest reason Canada's aqua-nationalists are wrong in their isolationism is, finally, this: we can only do what we need for ourselves by working, and acting, together with the neighbours.

The same, of course, is equally true for the neighbours. And surely two countries that agreed to settle their first water fight a century ago by the Churchillian method of "jaw, jaw, jaw" rather than "war, war, war" are capable of discovering (or inventing) mutually respectful and collaborative ways to adapt to the new weather sweeping down on us both.

The water that brought Montanans and Albertans toe-to-toe a century ago remains as vital as ever. The huge iron siphons that lift water out of the St. Mary River continue to serve their purpose, but they are now pitted with rust, leaky and long past retirement. Replacing them will cost more than $100 million. Meanwhile, a reservoir on Montana's stretch of the Milk River, downstream from Canada, has become so clogged with silt that it has lost one-third of its capacity for storing water. The spring freshet has also changed, in recent years arriving earlier and quickly rushing on by to leave Alberta fields baking by early summer. By July, farmers on both sides of the 49th parallel are biting their nails and hoping to coax their crops through to harvest.

Noting that Albertans have benefitted from the way things worked out on the Milk with those big siphons, Montana's government asked

Alberta's to kick in a little to the cost of their replacement. Alberta's government declined. Not far from the crumbling remains of the Spite Ditch, however, Ken Miller has more sympathy for his American neighbours. It was nearly five o'clock when I found Range Road 161, east of the town of Milk River. Prairie dogs skittered across the puddled gravel that led only to one house, a well-appointed ranch-style bridled in trees near the river plain. Ken invited me in for supper.

"I have friends and relatives on the other side," he told me over Canadian beef and California wine. "They're in a very difficult situation. They run out of water about half the years."[57] A trained economist who grows specialty grass seeds for golf courses and highway medians, Ken sees opportunity in the situation for people on both sides of the border. If the siphons are repaired, he envisions building a new reservoir at one of several suitable sites on the Milk's oxbow passage through Canada. That would allow more of the annual spring freshet to be captured and stored. "A storage facility," he argues, "is the only way to make the water pie bigger. It could make the difference for Milk River to live or die." And why not, he wonders, let Montanans help pay, in exchange for storing a portion of "their" water as well, to be released when it was needed?

I drove back to Lethbridge in the gathering dark of the late summer evening. Ken knew the odds were stacked against him. Dams, even small and beneficial ones, are out of fashion. Too many other Canadians view any truck or trade in water with Americans as near to treason. Swayed by half-truths and exaggerations, they'd rather play dog in the water trough than play well with others, even when the more cooperative course would be better for all. But something else stuck with me. "I have come to have a great respect for truth," Ken had said. "I think it will eventually come to the top." For years, many denied that the climate was behaving any differently from how it always had. For most North Americans, the evidence has become too great, too literally in our face, to disbelieve any longer.

The restless choreography of wind and wave, cloud and rain, is adjusting to a hotter beat, exploring new steps, touching down in unfamiliar places. The world's water is moving, too, and more; changing state in its excitement from ice to liquid, from liquid to vapour and back again to rain. We may face a dry spring, but chances are it will be followed by a soggy autumn. Earth isn't running out of water but, on any given day, *we* may. Whether that day constitutes a crisis will depend largely on what we do between now and then.

We can ignore the thunder in the distance or we can choose to prepare for the super-storms and hyper-droughts bearing down on us. We have time to get ready, if we start soon. But we must decide. Do we build more of the things we built in the past, aware of their rising price and diminishing return? Or do we open our imaginations to endless new alternatives to *more*—more water, and more of nature generally? Most urgently, can we accept what it means to say, "It's not *my* water, or *his*, or *hers*. It's *ours*"?

Let's use it wisely, together.

# Epilogue
## Future-Proof

The only certainty about what the world will look like a quarter of a century from now is that it won't look as it does today. Some things may be familiar to a visitor from the present; others will surely surprise. This book has nonetheless tried to cast forward what we *do* know about the weather ahead in hope that we in North America and, particularly, in Canada will choose to prepare ourselves to meet the future rather than wander blindly into the storm.

A great deal may happen between now and then that hasn't been part of this story. How animosities between Islam and the West will resolve—or not; whether we'll adjust our appetites to the planet's carrying capacity or have that adjustment forced upon us; when we will at last begin to wean ourselves from our addiction to hydrocarbons: all of these unknowns are beyond this book. It is enough to suggest that if we do make some of the changes it has identified, changes mainly in how we think about water, we will have more time and tools to devote to those other things.

With only the tiniest squint of optimism, here is a dispatch I can imagine filing from 2035:

> I am 82, nearly the age of my father when he died. I can sit
> in comfort at my desk, laptop open to write, a glass of fresh,

clean ice water at hand—more than I sometimes expected of this decade of my life. Canada is still one of the best countries on Earth in which to live. For all its challenges and flaws, the United States remains the globe's leading power, having proven itself once again more adaptable than its critics imagined.

To be sure, the last three decades haven't been an easy glide down a lazy river. The planet has weathered three transformations that have been felt in every country and community.

The first is the acceleration of climate change. The most dramatic sight has been the crumbling of polar ice. In 2032, for the first time in millions of years, the last year-round ice-pack in the Arctic Ocean broke apart; now only scattered icebergs offer dwindling shelter for the few polar bears still breeding in the wild. Although we've reduced our release of greenhouse gases, we've been frustrated by our failure to contain climate change. The costs of adapting to what NASA's James Hansen once warned us would be "a different planet" have risen exponentially.[1]

The second redefining development has been the unequivocal passing, early in the 'teens, of what energy analysts used to call "peak oil." Since then, oil's dwindling availability, strongly reinforced by the carbon taxes introduced in the second decade of the century, has spurred a radical reconfiguration of North American cities, business models and consumer lifestyles.

The third transformation has been social: the chasms among the "haves," the "have-somes" and the "have-nots" have deepened. Large parts of Africa followed Somalia into political regression and chaos, becoming fearsome no-go zones for outsiders. The rising cost of protecting (and often abandoning) coastlines, while adapting inland to new extremes of drought, has brought economic progress nearly to a halt in China, India and other large developing countries. Even here in the so-called First World, we have prospered largely by redefining our idea of progress: we now view it as a win that we are keeping one step ahead of our species' quickly evolving habitat.

In our western hemisphere, these three great changes have worked triple misery on the Caribbean. The Great Ocean Conveyor, which used to act like the radiator on a car, transporting heat away from the tropical oceans, has diminished by half since the last century. Northern Europe has benefitted, warming less than forecast. But the Conveyor's decline has left more heat trapped in the mid-Atlantic, spawning a vicious new sorority of Category Six hurricanes. Two years ago, Hurricane Hanna boasted wind speeds over 310 kilometres an hour, qualifying as the first Category Seven storm ever. Serial devastation from wind and rain, shrinking geography as the sea reclaims low-lying land, and the collapse of jet-charter tourism have reduced half a dozen Caribbean nations to little more than criminal statelets. Yacht harbours now shelter heavily armed small-boat pirates, preying on the cargo ships under sail that have also returned to the former Spanish Main.

Storm seas, constantly on the rise, have washed away coastal marshes, invaded cities and contaminated aquifers on all four continental coasts. North of Florida and the Gulf, the populated areas showing the most dramatic effects have been the Chesapeake and San Francisco bays, Canada's Maritimes and the Vancouver region. Less visible to most North Americans has been a wholesale transformation of the Arctic coastline, where beaches have given way to the waves, game animals have vanished and new species of plants have put down roots.

Last winter, the Rocky Mountains witnessed record-low snowpacks with hardly a wisp of white on any peaks south of Seattle. U.S. hydrologists forecast that the Colorado River will also hit new lows this summer. Across the continent, lashing rain has kept the Mississippi and other eastern rivers full.

The sudden spike in oil prices sparked an economic and political crisis in the late 'teens, but now North America has emerged from recession. Our new prosperity is buoyed by investment in urban infrastructure and the retooling of industry to profit from the new climate. Inescapable new realities forced citizens, governments and businesses into a period of deep soul-searching, from which has come what pundits jokingly dubbed the "double green revolution" that brought the environment fully into the dollar economy. Since the mid-twenties, the value and cost of services provided by our planetary ecosystems have been increasingly well established and integrated into every aspect of commercial and public accounting. Water prices have been leading indicators in this trend. Water for commerce, industry and agriculture is now priced near or close to "full replacement cost," as it is in most North American cities for home deliveries of any amounts above about 200 litres per person per day. These changes have triggered a surge in demand for low-water-use home appliances and industrial equipment.

A new regime of eco-payments in our economy means that my grandchildren pay less for products that contain less accumulated environmental impact. Industry pays for the eco-system services its processes require, embedding those costs in the price of products (motivating the most successful businesses to work ceaselessly to reduce them). As a result, spending patterns have changed. Buyers are drawn to features of design and durability that will keep them happy with their purchases for years. Throwaway "consumer" goods have almost vanished from shelves, priced out of the market by eco-charges. The higher price of the manufactured things that most people use only occasionally, such as power tools or vacation equipment, lies behind the current explosion of rental centres. We're seeing more social consuming: participation in popular group activities like dinner or hiking clubs that have replaced recreational shopping for many.

A city now includes the costs of the eco-services its citizens consume in any of a variety of public charges, from the nearly ubiquitous city-centre congestion fees, to water bills, property taxes and development permit fees. Tenants see the same charges on the individually metered utility bills that are mandatory now in most communities. The money from these levies, together with industrial eco-payments, flows to accredited eco-service providers, either locally or through the global eco-markets launched in the twenties in New York, London and other financial centres. It supports a burgeoning new economic sector. Wild-land management consortia, ecosystem "bio-neering" firms and habitat construction companies are booming.

In Canada, eco-payments have transformed the economies of many First Nations. Traditional territories whose only dollar value in the last century lay in extracting ores or lumber now earn saleable credits for their forests' oxygen-cleansing and carbon-fixing services. Several Nations have licensed pharmaceutical companies to prospect for cures in the biodiversity of northern muskeg swamps. In urban areas, employment in restoring and recreating ecosystems has more than offset the jobs lost in the retreat of big-box retailing. The number of cars on the road has plummeted, and many of the new green spaces occupy acreage once devoted to parking lots.

The few old-school environmentalists of my own age claim vindication that the environment is at last being properly valued. But they grieve (along with younger techno-Edeners) the ongoing cascade of extinctions, as scores of species lose their last fragments of habitat. The public mourning for these has produced contradictory responses. With each species that is extinguished, some people find less reason to go out of their way to save the next. "They're gone anyway," folks sometimes say. In the same way, Asian carp and other species once scorned as invasive "aliens" are being rehabilitated in public opinion these days as climate-change survivors. Non-profit stewardship groups and public environment agencies pay a premium for ecosystems that provide migration corridors for endangered species.

Almost every North American community now requires "green" street design and rain harvesting. Building codes insist on dual plumbing, with grey water collected for on-site or community reuse. Retrofitting a cistern in an older house has become as automatic a re-do as installing new kitchen counters. Montreal recently became the latest urban region to twin its entire water system for separate distribution of potable and "wash-down" water.

Air travel has become pricy, but those who do fly into North American cities no longer look down on industrial deserts of asphalt, concrete and tar-and-gravel roofing. Instead, they see kilometres of patchwork meadow: "green" roofs, planted with local grasses and shrubs. These reduce owners' heating and cooling costs and lessen flash runoff from rain. Some large factories have even turned their roofs into revenue opportunities, leasing them out to farmers for cultivation or qualifying for eco-payment credits. You can see cows grazing or grapes ripening above sprawling industrial complexes. Other businesses are locating where plumbing connections to "upstream" industries let them take advantage of lower-cost "used" water. Some have cut their ties to municipal mains entirely and provide their staff with premium bottled water for refreshment.

Stream-bed erosion and pollution from street runoff have been dramatically curtailed in most urban areas, despite increasingly heavy rain, without the need either to expand storm drains or to add municipal waste treatment plants. Those are now more often known as "recovery" facilities. At Annacis Island, a leader in the field, sanitary wastes are turned into saleable wash-down water with a residual byproduct of compost material. That, in turn, finds a ready market in the mitigation industry, where it is used to rehabilitate retired parking lots and other degraded landscapes into viable wetlands, meadows, savannahs and growing forests.

Thanks to these changes in streetscaping, building design, and home and commercial water use, no North American city has had to condemn a valley for new dammed storage in over a decade. The expanding reuse of water for landscaping and commercial purposes has allowed existing treatment plants in most cities to serve growing populations with ease. Many other cities have followed the lead of places like Waterloo and Tucson and now pump surplus rainwater underground for storage. In northeast Texas, tycoon T. G. Rezuly is promoting a two-way pipeline to the Panhandle, to deliver some of the water falling in record rainstorms over Dallas and Forth Worth to the emptier portions of the Ogallala Aquifer for safekeeping.

Challenges continue. Especially along the Eastern Seaboard and the Pacific Northwest, torrentially heavy rainfall has caused damaging floods over the last two and a half decades. Since the late 'teens, however, many watershed authorities have abandoned the endless quest to maintain and raise miles of dikes. Instead they have taken up a strategy the Netherlands pioneered early in the century: restoring natural floodplains where the occasional pulse of high water can stretch out and, as a bonus, soak into the ground to recharge water tables.[2]

The Great Lakes have fallen as far as a metre in some recent autumns. After several vessels went aground below Sault Ste. Marie and at the entrance to Saginaw Bay, lake shippers have been lobbying for new barriers at the outlets of Lake Superior and Huron; they hope to be able to dredge shipping channels deeper without draining the upper lakes. Opponents argue that the expense and environmental risk are unjustified because the Lakes have stopped falling; with all the green landscaping in Illinois, Michigan, Ontario and Ohio, more summer rainwater is being retained in soils and flowing to the lower lakes over subsequent weeks. Many areas of low shoreline have migrated permanently lakeward, however, as Lake Mead's experience has been replicated from Cornwall to Duluth. Eco-payments have encouraged many owners of less developed lakefront property to allow marshland to re-establish where shorelines are in retreat. For the first time in a century, an inventory of coastal Great Lake wetlands in 2029 recorded a net increase in area.

On sea coasts, the changing weather and rising oceans have wrought conspicuous losses. Shorefront property values in southern Florida and the U.S. Gulf of Mexico slumped after the landfall of devastating "Cat Six" hurricanes in the early 'teens and have not recovered, despite the billions of dollars invested in seawalls around areas like Palm Beach. After the destructive blow dealt by Hurricane Milly in 2011, New York launched a rush program of diking its boroughs, starting with Manhattan. The eventual completion of a new "super levee" around New Orleans in 2018 has preserved the core of that historic city. Elsewhere, states have begun a staged retreat from the Florida Keys and low-lying coasts as far west as Texas. Canada's Maritime Provinces have opted for a combination of retreat and selective diking, with Prince Edward Island receiving emergency funds from the federal government to defend Charlottetown, the "cradle of Confederation." On the west coast, the urban delta centred on Vancouver, with no land to spare, began a rush program to reinforce coastal and river dikes in 2014; it has so far weathered a series of record monsoons and high storm tides with only minor flooding.

The most general change historians note in the consumer experience is in the price of food. Full eco-costing, especially for water, has made highly prepared foods much more expensive than unprocessed grains, fruits and vegetables. The competing demand for corn and sugar cane for ethanol fuels has further escalated the price of some foods, especially sweeteners. Consumers have griped, but nutritionists credit the rising price of highly processed convenience foods for a corresponding decline in obesity over the last decade. Beef has soared in cost much more than chicken, pork and farm-raised fish. Agricultural economists say these price escalations have allowed farmers in drier parts of the High Plains and Canada's Palliser Triangle to invest in aquifer water storage, miserly drip irrigation and genetically modified low-moisture-tolerant seeds that have all helped growers maintain harvests during recurrent drought.

Higher water prices induced many farmers in the former Cadillac Desert to retire their fields and sell their water to cities. The fallowing of land, together with the spike in transportation costs, has reduced the abundance—and raised the price—of mid-winter produce in the north, centre and east of the continent. But the sacrifice of desert farming has meant that the continuing decline of the Colorado River hasn't yet spelled doom for Phoenix, Los Angeles or Las Vegas, although tourism to the last-named has suffered from the rising cost of air travel. After a decade of negotiation, three U.S. states agreed to build a massive desalination plant to supply water to Mexicali and Tijuana, in exchange for what is owed to Mexico from the Colorado River under the 1944 treaty. As part of the deal, both countries committed to supplying enough water to restore a year-round flow down the Colorado's entire length to the Gulf of California.

After the disastrous Iraq War and the cascade of international calamities in the decade that followed, Canadians began to reconsider the necessity and wisdom of keeping their distance from their southern neighbour. That shift in mood has fostered a renewed willingness to build common institutions. Our two nations and Mexico adopted common NAFTA standards of accounting for ecosystem services. Canada's old aqua-nationalist fear of being drained dry by the "one-way tap" has faded. Binational councils administer water-related activities in several major river basins from the Columbia to the St. Croix. These set annual limits on water withdrawals from their basins: the "cap" in the so-called "cap-and-trade" markets that have emerged in the areas of irrigation and industrial water. Most of these councils also accredit local wetlands, aquifer-recharge areas and flood zones to receive eco-payments, and oversee the regional eco-credit exchange. Several operate "water courts" to adjudicate complaints about water supply or quality.

As a result of all these innovations, no region of North America has suffered crippling water shortages. Europe, where many of these developments were well on their way sooner than they were here, has adapted with similar smoothness to the change in climate, having adjusted more easily, for certain, than it has dealt with waves of refugees from Africa, the Middle East and Central Asia. Likewise Australia, having moved before North America to adopt markets for irrigation water and invest in water-saving and recycling on a national scale, has prospered. And with its relatively small population, ample water and geographic insulation from the political turmoil of elsewhere, New Zealand ties Iceland as the world's most desirable place to live.

The North-South Canal has helped China's 1.6 billion people avoid mass starvation. Biologists now bicker over how far the canal's new value as an aquatic migration corridor offsets the extinction of species to which it contributed. The collapse of China's export trade in the 'teens led to a period of political instability, with thousands dying in protests. But by reorienting production to meet its own citizens' demands, the Chinese economy weathered its crisis. The country has enjoyed a new boom with the nuclear-powered revival of container shipping in the last few years.

India has not fared so well. It managed to avoid war with Pakistan over the Indus River, agreeing instead to a new river tribunal chaired by a neutral national (presently a Swede), with power to cap water withdrawals. But India's efforts to control the over-pumping of its groundwater have progressed poorly. The implementation of rural water harvesting has been more successful, widely credited with bringing an end to the succession of famines the country suffered in the twenties. The Northeast, however, has been wracked by unrest as it struggles to absorb refugees from devastated Bangladesh.

Latin America has followed much the same trajectory as China, suffering a troubled decade from the mid-teens to mid-twenties before a variety of initiatives set most of the continent back on a course toward relative economic progress.

International eco-payments that began to flow to Brazil have stemmed destruction of the Amazon rainforest. Environmental resistance gave way, though, to the construction of several new dams along the western Andes that will provide water storage to replace the lost mountain glaciers. Big engineering has also found a place in Mexico, which accepted a $40 billion loan from China to undertake its own "north-south" aqueduct. The first delivery of water flowed from the Yucatan to Guadalajara in 2031; an extension is now being built to carry water as far as Chihuahua in the country's far north.

The hubristic NAWAPA and GRAND Canal pipedreams look as anachronistic today as they did a quarter-century ago. Yet water exports have become a modest but profitable business. As China, India, Mexico and the water-stressed Middle East focused on securing sufficient domestic water supplies for agriculture and industry, the provision of good-quality drinking water has lagged. Alaska pioneered the export of estuary-captured fresh water in large towed bags for bottling at destination, making its first shipment to Mexico in 2012. Denmark followed, delivering glacial meltwater captured in a Greenland fjord to Portugal during a European drought a couple of years later. Russia has similarly captured estuary flow from several rivers, selling it to coastal China and giving it away to impoverished nations it wishes to influence. In the last decade, a handful of Canadian enterprises have received permits to capture water at the mouth of the Mackenzie and northern British Columbia's Nass and Stikine Rivers. The substantial payments these ventures promised to the First Nations whose territories lie upstream proved decisive in the overcoming of objections from aqua-nationalists living in southern cities. Canadian attempts to wheedle a share of the fees Alaska collects for water from the Yukon River, which grows large in this country, met rebuff.

The future is no surer than it ever was. We are still a long way from the end of the 21st century. Doomsayers still issue bleak forecasts. Clearly, the world's shorelines will continue to retreat inland as long as we can reasonably foresee. Also clearly, the world's "haves" and "have-somes" aren't going to mount any last-minute campaign to rescue the millions of "have-nots," whose fate seems likely to be one with that of the polar bears.

But we have arrived at the year 2035 with our human civilization intact. And our continent's economy today is more responsive to its impact on the environment than it has been at any time since before the Industrial Revolution. Not only did we get the water part right but, in doing so, we ended the estrangement of our species from nature. Let's celebrate 2034 as the first year in many when we used less of Gaia's bounty than our share of the planetary ecosystem produced. Our environmental account has returned, after many decades, to the black—or perhaps we should say, into the green.

Our part of the planet can claim, cautiously, to be mending.

The foregoing is, of course, purely a hopeful fiction. But it needn't be. We're already laying the foundations of that future.

Among many other places, those foundations have been poured along a stretch of reclaimed industrial waterfront in the capital of British Columbia. Late in 2007 the first of an anticipated 2,500 people moved into their new houses at a $600 million development designed from the sky down to be ready for tomorrow. Green plants cover the roofs at "Synergy" and "Balance," the first two of a planned score of residential, office, retail, hotel and light industrial buildings. Water collected from those roofs, from paved areas and from balconies, and recovered from the development's sewage, will be treated and used to irrigate gardens and fill the artificial creek and ponds that run down the centre of the complex. Dual-flush toilets, waterless urinals and low-water appliances will save as much water over the course of a year, as compared to the water requirements of conventional appliances, as the entire urban region uses on the hottest, driest day of summer.

Collectively, the buildings' occupants will save $150,000 a year in municipal fees by using neither city sewers nor storm drains.

The driving force behind the Dockside Green development was no eco-zealot or tree-hugging sentimentalist. It was an accountant. "I'm a capitalist," Joe van Bellingham, a bottom-line kind of guy, says without embarrassment. But as a disciple of Amory Lovins' "soft path," he works toward a bottom line with three parts: economic, environmental and social. The idea, Joe emphasizes, is not to score vague virtue points on the second two that will offset weaknesses in the hard numbers of the first. On the contrary, he says, "When you take a triple-bottom-line approach, the economics get stronger."[3]

The Victoria project and others he has completed in Calgary and Ottawa bear that out. Yes, his buildings cost three to eight percent more than his conventional competitors' to build. But construction, he points out, is only one of three big costs of a major urban development. Securing approvals to build, and marketing, eat up almost as much. "My costs of getting approvals are way less than other developers', and my costs of marketing are way less," he boasts. "'Future-proofing' is a way to distinguish the product." Eighty of Joe's first 95 condo units, in four buildings, sold out in three hours.

As a capitalist, Joe abhors subsidies, including the unacknowledged kind that our species extracts from the environment. Correspondingly, he's a fan of giving people the truth—and letting them take responsibility for what they do with it. At Dockside Green, every unit is individually metered, telling all occupants exactly how much heat, electricity and hot and cold water they're using and paying for. No one gets a free ride. "When you give people real data, they save energy because they can make decisions based on that data. Water is going to be a huge environmental issue: so charge more for high users and lower our property taxes. People are going to behave differently."

Joe admits this wasn't what they taught him in accounting school. "We didn't learn much about the environment except, 'Go out and do the minimum possible to avoid prosecution.' We were trained on a model that doesn't work." But, like so many others I've encountered on this book's journey, Joe van Bellingham has become a passionate evangelist for a model he believes *does* work. And he is winning converts. "This is just the way development should be done. The more people understand the economics, the more people are getting into it. The more we understand, the better we get at it and the more money we're going to make. I really think the private sector is going to jump on this and lead the market."

The weather is changing. Decades of climate denial and doubt are behind us. The details of the future remain, as always, a guess. But the broad outlines are clear enough to plan for. Joe left me with this: "We've got to really start thinking. We need to position ourselves for the future."

# "What Can I Do?"

What we do about water over the next few years is one of many problems we must confront without delay to keep our planet liveable. Here are some readily available choices that can help you, your family and your community ensure that the taps keep flowing.

## At Home

Check local sources, online and from your community utility or environmental offices, for the many ways of reducing your household's water demand. Look for existing rules about use, such as restrictions on or the assignment of watering days in summer. You may qualify for subsidies or incentives, for instance to install water-saving appliances. Examples of informational resources are Toronto's "Watersaver" site at http://www.toronto.ca/watereff/index.htm and Vancouver's equivalent at http://www.gvrd.bc.ca/water/residential-conservation -initiatives.htm.

As much as half the water you use in your lawn or garden may flow into the ground. If your area is dry in summer, consider xeriscaping. Local native plants that stay attractive after rainless weeks should be best for your conditions. Ask commercial greenhouses and community gardens for advice. If your locale is prone to intense downpours, landscape with those in mind. The right contouring, appropriate soil treatment and plants with lots of absorbency will reduce the amount that pools on the surface and runs off to flood gutters or worse. If your dwelling and local rules permit, consider installing a water tank or cistern to save the rain falling on your roof to water plants with later.

Inside, both high and low-end technology can help. When you can, choose high-efficiency appliances and the low-water settings on dishwashers and washing machines. Alternatively, repairing a running toilet or a dripping bath faucet may save as much. Twinning drains to collect grey water from sinks and showers for a second use probably only makes sense if you're building a new house or gutting an existing building.

Habits count too. If you have your own water meter, review your statements to see how much you're saving. At the store, pick products with less packaging and foods that are least processed: both packaging and industrial food preparation pile vast amounts of additional "virtual" water onto the ecological "cost" of products.

Buying bottled water isn't a great idea, chiefly because it leads to the accumulation of waste containers. If you live in North America, what's in your tap is in all likelihood just as safe to drink as what's in the bottle, and it's far cheaper. Even though it's improbable that buying bottled water will cause anyone else's tap to go dry, the economical and eco-kindly solution is to "bottle your own" from the tap at home.

## In Your Community

Most communities are facing a backlog of tens of billions of dollars that must be found and invested to repair, replace or extend the basic urban infrastructure, including water facilities.

Mandating green landscaping in every new and redeveloped street, and reusing waste water wherever possible, can sharply reduce the need for physical engineering while improving resilience to weather extremes, the health of wildlife and, often, a community's aesthetics. Separating potable and non-potable water supplies may not save money initially but may in some growing regions be the least expensive source of "new" water. Giving rivers more room to wander and parkland to flood now and again may be cheaper and more secure than constraining them inside dikes. In other places, desalination, recycling waste water and even a dam or pipeline may have decisive advantages. Each case will be different; keep an open mind.

Inform yourself about the source and management of your area's water. Decisions affecting future use are rarely made without repeated opportunities for public input and participation. Volunteer on local boards or write letters to your city council, legislative member or federal representative.

Support civic leaders who work to introduce water meters in every home. Support them again when they dare to propose progressive water rates that rise with household usage. If you've been doing the things above, you'll probably be among those who come out ahead! If your water comes from a well, don't assume that your supply is secure. Groundwater in many places comes from surface water; in the face of changing patterns of rainfall or evaporation, what happens above the ground will affect hidden aquifers as well. If your community hasn't mapped its groundwater or instituted a groundwater protection and recharge plan, stand by initiatives to do so.

Whatever your role in society, you have the opportunity to move minds in the right direction, starting with your own.

# Bibliography

Anielski, Mark and Sara Wilson. "Counting Canada's Natural Capital: Assessing the Real Value of Canada's Boreal Ecosystems." Ottawa: The Canadian Boreal Initiative, for the Pembina Institute, 2005.

Annin, Peter. *The Great Lakes Water Wars*. Washington, D.C.: Island Press, 2006.

Barlow, Maude. *Blue Gold: The Global Water Crisis and the Commodification of the World's Water Supply*. Rev. ed. Ottawa: Octopus Books, 2001. (Another version was published in paperback later: Barlow, Maude and Tony Clarke. *Blue Gold: The Battle against Corporate Theft of the World's Water*. Toronto: McClelland and Stewart, 2003.)

Brandes, Oliver M. and David B. Brooks. "At a Watershed: Ecological Governance and Sustainable Water Management in Canada." Victoria, B.C.: The POLIS Project on Ecological Governance, University of Victoria, 2005.

Brown, Lester. *Outgrowing the Earth: The Food Security Challenge in an Age of Falling Water Tables and Rising Temperatures*. New York: W.W. Norton, 2004.

Brubaker, Elizabeth. *Property Rights in the Defence of Nature*. Toronto: Earthscan Canada, 1995.

Bruce, James P., et al. "Climate Change Impacts on Boundary and Transboundary Water Management." Ottawa: Natural Resources Canada, 2003.

———. "Water Sector: Vulnerability and Adaptation to Climate Change." Ottawa: Climate Change Action Fund, 2000.

Cohen, Stewart, Denise Neilsen and Rachel Welbourn, eds. "Expanding the Dialogue on Climate Change and Water Management in the Okanagan Basin, British Columbia." Environment Canada and the University of British Columbia (Vancouver), 2004, http://www.ires.ubc.ca/downloads/publications/layout_Okanagan_final.pdf.

Daily, Gretchen C. and Katherine Ellison. *The New Economy of Nature: The Quest to Make Conservation Profitable*. Washington, D.C.: Island Press, 2002.

De Moor, André and Peter Calamai. "Subsidizing Unsustainable Development: Undermining the Earth with Public Funds." San Jose, Costa Rica: The Earth Council, 1997.

De Villiers, Marq. *Water: The Fate of Our Most Precious Resource*. Boston: Houghton Mifflin Company, 1999.

Ezcurra, Exequiel, ed. "Global Deserts Outlook." Nairobi: United Nations Environment Programme, 2006.

Gleick, Peter H., ed. *The World's Water 2004–2005: The Biennial Report on Freshwater Resources*. Washington, D.C.: Island Press, 2004.

*Intergovernmental Panel on Climate Change Fourth Assessment Report* (IPCC-4). Geneva: United Nations Environment Programme, 2007.

Irwin, Frances and Janet Ranganathan. *Restoring Nature's Capital: An Action Agenda to Sustain Ecosystem Services*. Washington, D.C.: World Resources Institute, 2007.

Jorgenson, Dale, R. Goettle, B. Hurd, and J. Smith. "U.S. Market Consequences of Global Climate Change." Arlington, VA: Pew Center on Global Climate Change, 2004.

Kling, George W., et al. *Confronting Climate Change in the Great Lakes Region: Impacts on Our Communities and Ecosystems*. Cambridge, MA: The Union of Concerned Scientists and The Ecological Society of America, 2003.

Poff, N. LeRoy, Mark M. Brinson and John W. Day, Jr. "Potential Impacts on Inland Freshwater and Coastal Wetland Ecosystems in the United States." Arlington, VA: Pew Center on Global Climate Change, 2002.

Postel, Sandra. *Pillar of Sand: Can the Irrigation Miracle Last?* New York: W.W. Norton, 1999.

*Preparing for Climate Change: Adapting to Impacts on British Columbia's Forest and Range Resources*. Victoria, B.C.: British Columbia Ministry of Forests and Range, 2006.

Reid, Walter V., ed. "Millennium Ecosystem Assessment." Geneva: United Nations Environment Programme (lead agency), 2005.

Reisner, Marc. *Cadillac Desert: The American West and Its Disappearing Water*. Rev. ed. New York: Penguin, 1993.

Roach, Rachel. "Dried Up, Drowned Out: Voices from the Developing World on a Changing Climate." Middlesex, U.K.: Tearfund, 2005.

Schellnhuber, Hans Joachim, ed.-in-chief. *Avoiding Dangerous Climate Change*. Cambridge, U.K.: Cambridge University Press, 2006.

Schubert, Renate, H.-J. Schellnhuber, N. Buchmann, A. Epiney, R. Griesshammer, M. Kulessa, D. Messner, S. Rahmtorf and J. Schmid. "Special Report: The Future Oceans—Warming Up, Rising High, Turning Sour." Berlin: German Advisory Council on Global Change, 2006.

Select Committee on Economic Affairs. "The Economics of Climate Change." 2nd Report of Session 2005–06. London: House of Lords, 2005.

Stern, Sir Nicholas. "Stern Review on the Economics of Climate Change." London: HM Treasury, 2006.

United Nations Development Programme, "Beyond Scarcity: Power, Poverty and the Global Water Crisis" (Human Development Report 2006). New York: Palgrave Macmillan, 2006. http://hdr.undp.org/hdr2006/pdfs/report/HDR06 -complete.pdf.

"Vulnerability and Adaptation to Climate Change in Europe (Technical Report No. 7/2005)." Copenhagen: European Environment Agency, 2005.

Wang, James and Bill Chameides. "Global Warming's Increasingly Visible Impacts." New York: Environmental Defense, 2005.

*Water, a Shared Responsibility (The 2nd United Nations World Water Development Report)*. Paris: World Water Assessment Programme, UNESCO, 2006.

# Notes

URLS cited in these Notes are up to date as of the time of this book's preparation for publication. Updates can be found at http://www.dryspringbook.com/notes.pdf.

## Prologue
### The Marble and the Bowl

1. "Drought to Shut Down Canadian Rain Forest Resort," Reuters (August 30, 2006), http://www.planetark.com/avantgo/dailynewsstory.cfm?newsid=37889.
2. Personal interview (October 13, 2006).
3. Annual rainfall 6.65 metres.
4. Personal interview (January 13, 1999).
5. Hans Joachim Schellnhuber, ed., *Avoiding Dangerous Climate Change* (Cambridge, U.K.: Cambridge University Press, 2006), p. 15.
6. Qur'an, Al-Anbiyaa', 21:30.
7. "Running Dry: The Humanitarian Impact of the Global Water Crisis," UN Office for the Coordination of Humanitarian Affairs (October 2006), http://www.irinnews.org/InDepthMain.aspx?InDepthId=13&ReportId=62312.
8. "Ecological Comparison of PC and Thin Client Desk Top Equipment" (Study), Fraunhofer-Institut für Umwelt-Sicherheits und Energietechnik (UMSICHT), Oberhausen (Germany) (December 18, 2006), p. 26, http://files.thinstore.com/Fraunhofer_Report.pdf.
9. Mark Charmer, "New Cars versus Old Cars: $CO_2$ versus Recycling" (blog), The Movement Design Bureau (London, U.K.) (March 27, 2007), http://movementbureau.blogs.com/projects/2007/03/new_cars_versus.html; Fiona Harvey, "Business and Water: Virtual Use Casts Light on Inequality," *Financial Times* (U.K.) (March 22, 2007), http://www.ft.com/reports/water2007.
10. "Canada's Oil Sands: Opportunities and Challenges to 2015," Energy Market Assessment, National Energy Board (Canada) (May 2004), http://www.neb-one.gc.ca/clf-nsi/rnrgynfmtn/nrgyrprt/lsnd/pprtntsndchllngs20152004/pprtntsndchllngs20152004-eng.pdf; Mary O'Driscoll, "Tar Sand Companies Try Balancing Oil Gains, Environmental Pains," *Energy and Environment*

*Magazine* (August 17, 2005), http://www.eenews.net/special_reports/tar _sands/; Stephen Leahy, "Canada: Oil Production Strains Parched Landscape," Inter Press News Service (July 21, 2006), http://www.corpwatch .org/article.php?id=13924.

11. That article was titled "The Future, Will It Work?" The answer was, more or less, "Don't bet on it." It won that year's Accenture Award for business journalism.

12. Pioneered by the pro-market non-profit Tax Foundation, based in Washington, D.C., the concept of Tax Freedom Day has been adopted in numerous other countries. In Canada, the date is calculated by the market-oriented Fraser Foundation.

13. Martin Hickman, "Earth's Ecological Debt Crisis: Mankind's 'Borrowing' from Nature Hits New Record," *The Independent* (London) (October 9, 2006), http://www.commondreams.org/headlines06/1009-03.htm.

14. The late Herbert Stein, a senior fellow at the American Enterprise Institute, claimed in, among other places, *Slate*, May 16, 1997, to have first uttered this widely quoted aphorism in the 1980s.

15. Gregg Easterbrook, "Case Closed: The Debate about Global Warming Is Over," The Brookings Institution (May 2006), http://www.brook.edu/views/ papers/easterbrook/20060517.htm.

16. In an online interview at http://www.alternet.org/story/31679/.

## Chapter 1
### Eden Ablaze: Why the World's Forests Are Burning

1. Protection Branch, "Fire Review Summary for Okanagan Mountain Fire (K50628)," B.C. Ministry of Forests (Summer 2003), http://bcwildfire.ca/ History/2003Review/Okanagan_Fire_Review_K50628.pdf.

2. Telephone interview (October 14, 2006).

3. Telephone interview (October 20, 2006).

4. "At Least 14 Killed in California Wildfires," cnn.com/US/ (October 27, 2003), http://www.cnn.com/2003/US/West/10/26/california.wildfire/index.html.

5. "Extreme Forest Fires in Portugal," Global Fire Monitoring Centre (GFMC) News (August 6, 2005), http://www.fire.uni-freiburg.de/ GFMCnew/2005/08/0806/20050806_port.htm.

6. Andres Darby, "Hobart Burns in Worst Ever Conditions," *The Age* (Melbourne) (October 13, 2006), http://www.theage.com.au/news/national/ hobart-burns-in-worst-ever-conditions/2006/10/12/1160246263509.html.

7. James Wang and Bill Chameides, "Global Warming's Increasingly Visible Impacts," Environmental Defense, New York (2005), p. 8, http://www .environmentaldefense.org/documents/4891_GlobalWarmingImpacts.pdf.

8. "Alaska on Fire: Record 6.5 Million Acres Burned," Alaska Fire Service, The Forestry Source (Society of American Foresters) (October 2004), http://www .fire.uni-freiburg.de/media/2004/news_20041026_us.htm.

9. Mike Tidwell and Ted Glick, "Fire and Heat," Truthout.org (August 17, 2006), http://www.truthout.org/cgi-bin/artman/exec/view.cgi/63/21888.

10. Eric Pape, "A European Sahara," *Newsweek International* (August 8, 2005), http://www.msnbc.msn.com/id/8770524/site/newsweek.

11. Ibid.

12. Bill Blakemore, "Is Global Warming Fueling Western Wildfires?" ABC News Internet Ventures (June 21, 2006), http://abcnews.go.com/GMA/GlobalWarming/story?id=2101402.

13. Rob Taylor, "World Faces Megafire Threat—Australian Expert," Reuters (January 22, 2007), http://www.planetark.com/dailynewsstory.cfm/newsid/39941/newsDate/22-Jan-2007/story.htm.

14. "Scripps-Led Study Shows Climate Warming to Shrink Key Water Supplies around the World" (press release), Scripps Institution of Oceanography (San Diego) (November 16, 2005).

15. Tidwell and Glick, "Fire and Heat."

16. Personal interview (July 21, 2006).

17. Personal interview (June 10, 2005).

18. Geoffrey Lean, "The Hungry Planet," *The Independent* (U.K.) (September 3, 2006), http://www.co.snohomish.wa.us/documents/County_Services/FocusOnFarming/hungryplanet.pdf.

19. Sandra Postel, *Pillar of Sand: Can the Irrigation Miracle Last?* (New York: W.W. Norton, 1999), p. 67.

20. Personal interview (June 10, 2005).

21. Vital Water Graphics, United Nations Environment Programme (Nairobi) (2002), http://www.unep.org/dewa/assessments/ecosystems/water/vitalwater/.

22. Oliver Brandes and Keith Ferguson, "The Future in Every Drop: The Benefits, Barriers and Practice of Urban Water Demand Management in Canada," POLIS Project on Ecological Governance, University of Victoria (May 2004), http://www.waterdsm.org/pdf/report3_full.pdf.

23. City Mayors Statistics, http://www.citymayors.com/statistics/us_cities_population.html.

24. Annual Rainfall for U.S. States: http://www.betweenwaters.com/etc/usrain.html.

25. Don Hinrichsen, "Freshwater: Lifeblood of the Planet," PeopleandPlanet.net (June 17, 2005), http://www.peopleandplanet.net/doc.php?id=671&section=14.

26. "Indicators of Climate Change for British Columbia," B.C. Ministry of Land, Water and Air Protection (2002), http://www.env.gov.bc.ca/air/climate/indicat/pdf/indcc.pdf.

27. Telephone interview (July 11, 2006).

28. Personal interview (June 10, 2005).

## Chapter 2
### Running Dry: Drought, Thirst and the Spread of Deserts

1. "2003 Farm and Ranch Irrigation Survey," National Agricultural Statistics Survey, U.S. Department of Agriculture (Washington, D.C.) (November 15, 2004), http://www.nass.U.S.a.gov/census/census02/fris/fris03.htm.

2. Personal interview (January 2, 2007).

3. "UN International Year of Deserts and Desertification Opens," Environmental News Service (New York) (January 2, 2005), http://www.ens-newswire.com/ens/jan2006/2006-01-02-09.asp.

4. Monica Davey, "Blistering Drought Ravages Farmland on Plains," New York Times (August 29, 2006), http://www.nytimes.com/2006/08/29/us/29drought.html?ex=1314504000&en=3651a0fcf5c73ff2&ei=5088&partner=rssnyt&emc=rss.

5. James MacPherson, "More Than 60% of U.S. in Drought," Associated Press (July 29, 2006), http://www.washingtonpost.com/wp-dyn/content/article/2006/07/29/AR2006072900414.html?nav=printbox.

6. Sarah Bush, "Texas Drought Hits Farmers Hard," KUT Radio/NPR (January 1, 2007), http://www.npr.org/templates/story/story.php?storyId=6705938.

7. Ibid.

8. Shaun McKinnon, "High Country Lacks Snowpack for First Time Since '30s," The Arizona Republic (March 3, 2006), http://www.azcentral.com/arizonarepublic/news/articles/0303drought-nosnow0303.html.

9. MacPherson, "More Than 60% of U.S. in Drought."

10. Jim Carlton and Lauren Etter, "Drought Wreaks Devastation in West, Southeast," The Wall Street Journal (June 26, 2007), A2; Adam Nossiter, "Drought Saps the Southeast, and Its Farmers," New York Times (July 4, 2007), http://www.nytimes.com/2007/07/04/us/04drought.html?ex=1341201600&en=a13d0df444e7fa4c&ei=5088&partner=rssnyt&.

11. James Wang and Bill Chameides, "Global Warming's Increasingly Visible Impacts," Environmental Defense, New York (2005), p. v, http://www.environmentaldefense.org/documents/4891_GlobalWarmingImpacts.pdf.

12. "Low Water Levels Starting to Affect Mississippi River," U.S. Water News Online (September 2006), http://www.uswaternews.com/archives/arcsupply/6lowxwate9.html.

13. Darcy Henton, "Crop Insurance to Pay Out Billions: Extreme Drought Resulted in Below-Average Crop Yields in Southern Prairies," The Ottawa Citizen (September 22, 2001), F8.

14. "Intergovernmental Panel on Climate Change Fourth Assessment Report" (IPCC-4), World Meteorological Organization (WMO) and United Nations Environment Programme (UNEP) (Geneva) (February 2007), p. 40, http://www.mnp.nl/ipcc/pages_media/FAR4docs/final%20pdfs%20of%20chapters%20WGIII/IPCC%20WGIII_TS%20final.pdf; "Climate Change Impacts Can Be Seen Today," Environmental Defense (November 11, 2006), http://www.environmentaldefense.org/article.cfm?contentID=4883.

15. Colin Woodard, "Europe's Scorching Summer," E: The Environmental Magazine (January-February 2004), http://www.emagazine.com/view/?1176&src.

16. Wang and Chameides, "Global Warming's Increasingly Visible Impacts," p. 7.

17. Defined as days with temperatures in the hottest 10 percent of all observations. Juliet Eilperin, "More Frequent Heat Waves Linked to Global Warming," Washington Post (August 4, 2006), http://www.washingtonpost.com/wp-dyn/content/article/2006/08/03/AR2006080301489.html.

18. "Drought in Europe," European Organisation for the Exploitation of Meteorological Satellites (March 7, 2006), http://www.eumetsat.int/Home/Main/Media/News/005280?l=en.

19. "One Third of China's Rural Residents Drink Unsafe Water," *People's Daily online* (December 29, 2005), http://english.people.com.cn/200512/29/eng20051229_231461.html.

20. Ben Blanchard, "China Grapples With Growing Water Shortages," Reuters (April 4, 2006), http://www.truthout.org/cgi-bin/artman/exec/view.cgi/59/18857.

21. "Australia a portal into global warming future," IOL (Independent Online), Cape Town (March 12, 2006), http://www.iol.co.za/index.php?set_id=14&click_id=143&art_id=qw1142153101793R131.

22. Justin North, "Dining in a Drought in Australia," *New York Times* (July 29, 2007), WK11.

23. Laurie Goering, "Thirsty Australia in Grip of Worst Drought on Record," *Chicago Tribune* (January 16, 2007), http://groups.google.com.pk/group/aus.invest/msg/464b059374c7947a.

24. Matthew Benns, "900 Sheep and Not One Bid: May As Well Give Them Away," *Sydney Morning Herald* (December 24, 2006), http://www.smh.com.au/news/environment/900-sheep-and-not-one-bid-may-as-well-give-them-away/2006/12/23/1166290788819.html.

25. Malcolm Burgess, "Australian Drought Driving Farmers to Desperation," Agence France-Press (October 17, 2006), http://www.terradaily.com/reports/Australian_Drought_Driving_Farmers_To_Desperation_999.html.

26. An average of 17 percent.

27. John Donnelly, "Drought Imperils Horn of Africa," *The Boston Globe* (February 20, 2006), http://www.boston.com/news/world/africa/articles/2006/02/20/drought_imperils_horn_of_africa/.

28. Odingo has also served as a vice-chairman of the IPCC. Ken Opala, "Climate Change Fuelling Conflicts," *The Nation* (Nairobi) (May 15, 2006), http://www.esnips.com/nsdoc/d9eea435-ec0a-4585-8da0-8abf45432d94.

29. After examining records from Canada, Europe, Asia, eastern Australia and western and southern Africa, researchers at the U.S. National Center for Atmospheric Research (NCAR) in Colorado calculated that over the last three decades the portion of the Earth affected by drought at any one time had risen from 15 to 30 percent. Asa Wahlquist, "Hot, Dry, Thirsty," *The Australian* (Sydney) (August 29, 2005).

30. IPCC-4, p. 715; Andréa Sardinha Taschetto and Matthew England, "An Analysis of Late 20th Century Trends in Australian Rainfall" (paper), Climate and Environmental Dynamics Laboratory (CEDL), University of New South Wales (Sydney) (2007), p. 60, http://web.maths.unsw.edu.au/~matthew/te_2007_ijc.pdf.

31. Wang and Chameides, "Global Warming's Increasingly Visible Impacts," p. 6.

32. IPCC-4, p. 54.

33. U.S. Department of Agriculture; the UN Food and Agriculture Organization; Kevin Morrison, "Grain Stockpiles at Lowest for 25 Years," *Financial Times*

(London) (October 12, 2006), http://www.ft.com/cms/s/0c021878-5a16
-11db-8f16-0000779e2340.html; Geoffrey Lean, "The Hungry Planet: As
Stocks Run Out and Harvests Fail, the World Faces Its Worst Crisis for 30
Years," *The Independent* (U.K.) (September 3, 2006), http://environment
.independent.co.uk/article1325467.ece.

34. Mark W. Rosegrant, Ximing Cai and Sarah A. Cline, "Global Water
Outlook: Averting an Impending Crisis," International Food Policy Research
Institute (Washington, D.C.) and International Water Management Institute
(Colombo, Sri Lanka) (September 2002), p. 15.

35. Ibid., p. 18.

36. United Nations Convention to Combat Desertification (UNCCD) (June 2004),
http://www.unccd.int/; Alexandra Olsen, "U.N. Conference Addresses
Drought, Creeping Deserts and Poverty," Associated Press (February 20,
2002), http://www.arabicnews.com/ansub/Daily/Day/020221/2002022128
.html.

37. Ibid.

38. Ibid.

39. Matt McGrath, "UN Issues Desertification Warning," BBC News (June 28,
2007), http://news.bbc.co.uk/go/pr/fr/-/2/hi/africa/6247802.stm.

40. "The Climate of Poverty: Facts, Fears and Hopes," Christian Aid (London)
(May 2006), http://www.christianaid.org.uk/Images/climate_of_poverty
_tcm15-21613.pdf.

**Chapter 3**
**Curse of Plenty: Tempests, Floods and Rising Waves**

1. Telephone interview (December 6, 2006) (author's translation from French).

2. "N.B. Ocean-Front Homes Being Flooded with Salt," CBC News (November
30, 2006), http://www.cbc.ca/canada/new-brunswick/story/2006/11/30/nb
-oceanhomes.html.

3. "Impacts of Sea-Level Rise and Climate Change on the Coastal Zone of
Southeastern New Brunswick," Environment Canada (2006), http://www
.adaptation.nrcan.gc.ca/projdb/final_coastal_e.php; telephone interview
(December 5, 2006).

4. "Risk Management: Baseline Document for Thematic Area No. 5"
(background document), Fourth World Water Forum, Mexico (2006), http://
www.worldwatercouncil.org/fileadmin/wwc/World_Water_Forum/WWF4/
Regional_process/Europe/Risk_management_doc.pdf.

5. "Natural Disasters Kill 25,000 Worldwide in 2001," Reuters (Munich)
(December 28, 2001), http://www.heatisonline.org/contentserver/
objecthandlers/index.cfm?ID=3851&Method=Full&PageCall=&Titl
e=2001%20Disaster%20Casualties%20Double%20Previous%20Year%20
&Cache=False.

6. "Hurricanes Katrina and Rita Storm Track Map and Animation," National
Aeronautics and Space Administration (October 13, 2005), http://www.nasa
.gov/vision/earth/lookingatearth/h2005_katrina.html.

7. Nick Nutall, "Extreme Weather Losses Soar to Record High for Insurance Industry," United Nations Environment Programme (UNEP) (Buenos Aires) (December 15, 2004), http://www.unep.org/Documents.Multilingual/ Default.asp?DocumentID=414&ArticleID=4682&l=en.

8. "1,400 Dead in One Guatemala Village as Stan Blasts Central America," CBC News (October 8, 2005), http://www.cbc.ca/world/story/2005/10/08/ Guatemala_floods20051008.html.

9. "Global Warming behind Killer Typhoon Season in China: Experts," Agence France-Presse (August 14, 2006), http://www.terradaily.com/ 2006/060814063655.3r7pfpz8.html.

10. "Typhoon Saomai Kills 105: 190 Missing," Associated Press (August 25, 2006), http://www.chinadaily.com.cn/china/2006-08/13/content_663530.htm.

11. Dan Mariano, "Captive to Extreme Weather Events," Manila Times (December 4, 2006), http://www.manilatimes.net/national/2006/dec/04/ yehey/opinion/20061204opi2.html.

12. "Global Warming behind Killer Typhoon Season."

13. "Crisis or Opportunity: Climate Change Impacts and the Philippines" (report), Greenpeace (Quezon City, Philippines) (November 3, 2005), http://www .greenpeace.org/seasia/en/asia-energy-revolution/climate-change/philippines -climate-impacts.

14. Bill Blakemore, "Category 6 Hurricanes? They've Already Happened," ABC News (May 21, 2006), http://abcnews.go.com/US/Science/story?id=1986862.

15. Ibid.

16. Mark Henderson, "New Proof That Man Has Caused Global Warming," The Times (London) (February 18, 2005), http://www.timesonline.co.uk/tol/news/ world/article516033.ece; IPCC-4, p. 47, http://ipcc-wg1.ucar.edu/wg1/Report/ AR4WG1_Pub_TS.pdf.

17. Anjali Krishnan, "Wading All Night through Mumbai," BBC News (July 28, 2005), http://news.bbc.co.uk/go/pr/fr/-/2/hi/south_asia/4724245.stm.

18. Justin Huggler, "Bombay Paralysed by Record Rainfall as Death Toll Rises," The Independent (U.K.) and Reuters (July 27, 2005), http://www.nzherald .co.nz/section/2/story.cfm?c_id=2&objectid=10338067.

19. David Biello, "When It Warms, It Pours: Climate Change Produces Fewer but More Extreme Monsoon Rains," Scientific American (November 30, 2006), http://www.sciam.com/article.cfm?articleID=3AF9F4CB-E7F2-99DF -3411CFE398433EC2.

20. Dave Amit, "India's Monsoon Rains Are Behaving Ever More Bizarrely," Reuters (November 14, 2006), http://community.livejournal.com/ twc_aficionados/tag/monsoons.

21. John Vidal, "Nepal's Farmers on the Front Line of Global Climate Change," The Guardian (U.K.) (December 2, 2006), http://www.guardian.co.uk/ christmasappeal2006/story/0,,1962372,00.html.

22. Jim Mattison, B.C. Water Comptroller and Assistant Deputy Minister for Water Stewardship, personal communication (September 26, 2006).

23. Scott Sutherland, "Intense Rainfall Most Ever Recorded as Storm Sweeps Southern B.C.," The Canadian Press (November 6, 2006), http://www .breitbart.com/article.php?id=cp_n110641A.xml&show_article=1.

24. "B.C.'s Stanley Park Loses 1,000 Trees after Storm," CTV.ca (December 19, 2006), http://www.ctv.ca/servlet/ArticleNews/story/CTVNews/20061219/stanley_park_061219/20061219/.

25. "Soldiers and Volunteers Join Storm Cleanup Effort in France," CNN (December 29, 1999), http://archives.cnn.com/1999/WORLD/europe/12/29/europe.storms.02/index.html; U. Ulbrich et al., "Three Extreme Storms over Europe in December 1999," Institute for Geophysical and Meteorological Studies, University of Koln (Germany) (March, 2001), http://www.uni-koeln.de/math-nat-fak/geomet/meteo/forschung/abstracts/ulbrich/ufkp_weather_artikel2001.pdf.

26. "'Extreme Rainfall' Incidents Increasing in Parts of United Kingdom" (news release), University of Newcastle upon Tyne (September 5, 2006), http://www.sciencedaily.com/releases/2006/09/060904143234.htm; "SEPA [Scottish Environment Protection Agency] Climate Fears for Scotland," BBC News (October 2, 2006), http://news.bbc.co.uk/1/hi/scotland/5400118.stm.

27. Chris Wood, "The Mississippi's Ruinous Deluge," Maclean's (July 26, 1993), p. 22.

28. Personal interview (July 13, 1993).

29. Neal Lott and Tom Ross, "Tracking and Evaluating U.S. Billion Dollar Weather Disasters 1980–2005" (data paper), National Climatic Data Center, U.S. National Oceanic and Atmospheric Administration (NOAA) (2006), http://www1.ncdc.noaa.gov/pub/data/papers/200686ams1.2nlfree.pdf.

30. "2,000 Ordered out of Flooded Areas," CBC News (June 18, 2005), http://www.cbc.ca/canada/story/2005/06/18/flooding050618.html.

31. Jane Armstrong, "Rising Ice Jam Threatens Historic Covered Bridge," Globe and Mail with Canadian Press (January 19, 2006), http://www.theglobeandmail.com/servlet/Page/document/v5/content/subscribe?user_URL=http://www.theglobeandmail.com%2Fservlet%2Fstory%2FRTGAM.20060119.wxbridge19%2FBNStory%2FNational%2F&ord=3750595&brand=theglobeandmail&redirect_reason=2&denial_reasons=1987581%3A4%3B&force_login=false.

32. Bill Richards, Environment Canada. Telephone interview (December 6, 2006).

33. Personal interview (December 5, 2006).

34. "Storms and Tornadoes Leave 150,000 without Power," CTV.ca News (August 3, 2006), http://www.ctv.ca/servlet/ArticleNews/story/CTVNews/20060803/storm_ontario_060803/20060803?hub=Canada.

35. Art Hovey, "Hallam's Heartbreak," Lincoln Journal Star (May 23, 2004), http://www.journalstar.com/articles/2005/02/01/top_story/10050007.txt.

36. Ibid.

37. Will Graves, "More Severe Weather Forecast for Midwest," Associated Press (Louisville, KY) (September 24, 2006), http://abcnews.go.com/US/wireStory?id=2484201; Dylan Lovan, "Midwest, South Clean Up after Big Storms," Associated Press (Louisville, KY) (September 26, 2006), http://www.usatoday.com/weather/stormcenter/2006-09-23-midwest-storms_x.htm; Sean Rose, "U.K. Pharmacy Student, Nursing School Graduate Drown in Lexington Flooding," University of Kentucky Kernel (Lexington, KY) (September 21, 2006), http://media.www.kykernel.com/media/storage/

paper305/news/2006/09/21/CampusNews/Breaking.News.Uk.Pharmacy
.Student.Nursing.School.Graduate.Drown.In.Lexington.Flo-2304412.shtml;
Jim Warren, "Women Died as One Tried to Save Friend," *Lexington Herald-Leader* (September 25, 2006).

38. Lott and Ross, "Tracking and Evaluating U.S. Billion Dollar Weather
Disasters, 1980–2005"; Jim Lobe, "Environment: 2005 Costliest Year for
Extreme Weather," IPS-Inter Press News Service (December 7, 2005), http://
ipsnews.net/news.asp?idnews=31316.

39. The exceptions were the terrorist attacks of 9/11 and an earthquake that struck
Los Angeles in 1994. Robert Litan, "Sharing and Reducing the Financial Risks
of Future 'Mega-Catastrophes'" (Paper, Issues in Economic Policy No. 4), The
Brookings Institution (Washington, D.C.) (March, 2006), http://www
.brookings.org/views/papers/200603_iiep_litan.htm; Lobe, "2005 Costliest
Year for Extreme Weather."

40. Allie Deger, "In New Orleans, A Second Freedom Ride," www.truthout.org
(April 4, 2006), http://www.truthout.org/cgi-bin/artman/exec/view.cgi/
59/18817.

41. Ed Stoddard, "Post-Katrina New Orleans Death Rate Shoots Up," Reuters
(Dallas) (June 21, 2007), http://today.reuters.com/news/articlenews
.aspx?type=topNews&storyid=2007-06-21T213730Z_01_N21396585
_RTRUKOC_0_US-USA-NEWORLEANS-DEATHRATE.xml.

42. Emma Young, "Flood-Stricken Czechs Plan Mass-Vaccination," NewScientist
.com (August 15, 2002), http://www.newscientist.com/article.ns?id=dn2682.

43. Juliet Eilperin, "Climate Shift Tied to 150,000 Fatalities: Most Victims Are Poor,
Study Says," *Washington Post* (November 17, 2005), http://www.washingtonpost
.com/wp-dyn/content/article/2005/11/16/AR2005111602197.html.

44. Department of Earth Sciences, Simon Fraser University, Burnaby, B.C.,
telephone interview (June 1, 2005).

45. Personal interview (March 19, 2006).

46. Rachel Roach, "Dried Up, Drowned Out: Voices from the Developing World
on a Changing Climate" (report), Tearfund (U.K.) (June 2005), http://www
.tearfund.org/webdocs/Website/Campaigning/Policy%20and%20research/
Driedupdrownedout.pdf.

47. Ibid.

48. Hillary Rosner, "Rain Forest Gets Too Much Rain, and Animals Pay the
Price," *New York Times* (March 7, 2006), http://www.nytimes.com/2006/
03/07/science/07costa.html?ex=1299387600&en=aee109a6d929c783&ei=5088
&partner=rssnyt&emc=rss.

49. Personal interview (November 10, 2006).

## Chapter 4
### Planet on Defrost: A World without Ice and Snow

1. Telephone interview (January 15, 2007).

2. Rachelle Younglai, "Arctic Ice Road Closes, Mines Face Shortage," Reuters
(March 22, 2006).

3. In research data, "very cold nights" has a specific meaning: nights during which temperatures fall in the bottom 10 percent of overnight lows for that location and date. IPCC-4, p. 40.

4. The salinity of the water can make a small difference; in the absence of any impurities water can actually be chilled in the lab to −42°C (−43.6°F) without freezing.

5. Telephone interview (December 5, 2006).

6. Leslie Scrivener, "On Melting Pond," *Toronto Star* (November 19, 2006), A4.

7. "Yes, It's Been the Warmest Canadian Winter on Record," CBC News (March 13, 2006), http://www.cbc.ca/canada/story/2006/03/13/warm-winter060313 .html.

8. "All Time High: 70 Degree Temps Blanket NYC," CBS New York (January 7, 2007), http://wcbstv.com/topstories/local_story_005210450.html.

9. Matt Higgins, "Outdoors: Warm Temperatures Chill the Ice Fishing Season," *New York Times* (January 10, 2007), http://select.nytimes.com/gst/abstract .html?res=F00F17FC39540C738DDDA80894DF404482&n=Top%2fNews %2fScience%2fTopics%2fIce.

10. Tim Jones, "Warm Weather Sends Chill through U.P.'s Tourist Industry," *Chicago Tribune* (January 12, 2007), http://forums.backpacker.com/eve/ forums/a/tpc/f/613107219/m/8391013232.

11. Pavel Ya. Groisman and David R. Easterling, "Variability and Trends of Total Precipitation and Snowfall over the United States and Canada," *Journal of Climate* (January 1994), http://ams.allenpress.com/perlserv/?request=get-abstract&doi =10.1175%2F1520-0442(1994)007%3C0184%3AVATOTP%3E2.0.CO%3B2.

12. James Bruce et al., "Climate Change Impacts on Boundary and Transboundary Water Management" (report), Natural Resources Canada (June 2003), http:// www.saskriverbasin.ca/Resources/Climatechangestudy/Final%20Report %20A458-402%20CCAF.pdf.

13. For much of that time, the information was used to plan log "drives" down the free-flowing river.

14. Telephone interview (December 6, 2006).

15. Alex Kirby, "Wildlife Seeks Cooler Climes," BBC News Online (January 1, 2003), http://news.bbc.co.uk/1/hi/sci/tech/2617139.stm.

16. "All Washed Up," *The Economist* (April 26, 2007), http://www.economist.com/ world/international/displaystory.cfm?story_id=8975357.

17. Roger Boyes and Joanna Bale, "Ski Resorts Left Hot and Bothered by Lack of Snow," *The Times* (London) (December 2, 2006), http://www.timesonline .co.uk/tol/sport/football/european_football/article1088390.ece.

18. "Warm Spell in Russia Wakes Up the Bears," Associated Press (January 18, 2007), http://www.livescience.com/animals/070118_ap_warm_bears.html.

19. Telephone interview (October 20, 2006).

20. Personal interview (November 10, 2006).

21. John Collins Rudolf, "The Warming of Greenland," *New York Times* (January 16, 2007), http://www.nytimes.com/2007/01/16/science/earth/16gree.html?ex =1326603600&en=b018c85a1b03d90f&ei=5090; telephone interview (January 18, 2007).

22. Seth Borenstein, "Scientiests Say Arctic Once Was Tropical," Associated Press (Washington, D.C.) (May 31, 2006), http://www.care2.com/c2c/groups/disc .html?gpp=714&pst=468256&archival=1&posts=2.

23. Deborah Zabarenko, "Arctic Ice Cap Melting 30 Years ahead of Forecast," Reuters (Washington, D.C.) (May 1, 2007), http://www.reuters.com/article/ scienceNews/idUSN0122477020070501.

24. "Greenland's Glaciers Are Slip-Sliding Away," Geophysical Research Letters (vol. 33, p. L03503, as noted in New Scientist (February 11, 2006), http:// environment.newscientist.com/channel/earth/mg18925383.500-greenlands -glaciers-are-slipsliding-away.html.

25. "Greenland's Water Loss Has Doubled in a Decade," New Scientist (February 25, 2006), p. 20, http://environment.newscientist.com/channel/earth/ mg18925405.200-greenlands-water-loss-has-doubled-in-a-decade.html.

26. Robert Lee Hotz, "Greenland's Ice Sheet Is Slip-Sliding Away," The Los Angeles Times (June 24, 2006), http://www.commondreams.org/ headlines06/0625-02.htm.

27. Geoffrey Lean, "The Big Thaw: Global Disaster Will Follow If the Ice Cap on Greenland Melts," The Independent (U.K.) (November 20, 2005), http://www .commondreams.org/headlines05/1120-03.htm.

28. "Mt. Kilimanjaro Is Melting to Its Death," East African Standard (Nairobi) (January 27, 2002), http://allafrica.com/stories/200201270228.html. "Kilimanjaro's Ice 'Archive,'" BBC News (October 18, 2002), http://news.bbc .co.uk/2/hi/science/nature/2337023.stm.

29. Rob Woolard, "Vanishing Glaciers Offer Clear Evidence of Climate Change: Scientists," Agence France-Presse (February 16, 2007), http://www.gulf-times .com/site/topics/article.asp?cu_no=2&item_no=133277&version=1 &template_id=43&parent_id=19.

30. Ibid.

31. "An Overview of Glaciers, Glacier Retreat and Subsequent Impacts in Nepal, India and China" (report), cited in "Water Crisis Looms as Himalayan Glaciers Retreat" (press release), World Wildlife Fund (March 2005), http://www .panda.org/news_facts/newsroom/press_releases/index.cfm?uNewsID=19111.

32. Catherine Brahic, "Melting of Mountain Glaciers Is Accelerating," NewScientist.com (January 30, 2007), http://environment.newscientist.com/ article/dn11064.

33. Described in more detail in Chapter 7.

34. Tim Barnett, J.C. Adam and D.P. Lettenmaier, "Potential Impacts of a Warming Climate on Water Availability in Snow-Dominated Regions," Nature (November 17, 2005), http://www.eldis.org/go/display/?id=18630 &type=Document.

35. Garrett Brass, ed., "The Arctic Ocean and Climate Change: A Scenario for the U.S. Navy" (Special Publication No. 02-1), United States Arctic Research Commission (2002), http://www.arctic.gov/files/climatechange.pdf.

Chapter 5
Up in the Air: The Great Lakes' Uncertain Future

1. Personal interview (November 3, 2006).
2. Personal interview (November 3, 2006).
3. Dead Stream's unfortunate name preceded its new notoriety and exaggerates its demise.
4. Personal interview (November 2, 2006).
5. "Supreme Court Asked to Rule in Nestle Case," *Muskegon Chronicle* (January 12, 2007).
6. 18 percent.
7. That volume is enough to submerge the lower 48 United States beneath 2.9 metres of water.
8. "Water: Vulnerable to Climate Change" (web documents), Environment Canada (May 18, 2006), http://www.ec.gc.ca/water/en/info/pubs/FS/e_FSA9.htm.
9. Peter Annin, *The Great Lakes Water Wars* (Washington, D.C.: Island Press, 2006), p. 53.
10. U.S. Embassy to Canada, http://ottawa.usembassy.gov/content/content.asp?section=can_usa&document=trade.
11. Annin, *The Great Lakes Water Wars*, p. 53.
12. 158 million U.S. gallons.
13. *Sporhase v. Nebraska Ex Rel. Douglas, 458 U.S. 941* (1982), http://caselaw.lp.findlaw.com/scripts/getcase.pl?court=US&vol=458&invol=941.
14. "The Great Lakes Charter: Principles for the Management of Great Lakes Water Resources" (Declaration), The Council of Great Lakes Governors (February 11, 1985). The Council's members are the governors of Illinois, Indiana, Michigan, Minnesota, New York, Ohio, Pennsylvania and Wisconsin. The Premiers of Ontario and Quebec are associate members. See http://www.cglg.org/pub/charter/index.html.
15. Ohio's Richard Bartz. Annin, *The Great Lakes Water Wars*, p. 74.
16. The amendment was to the U.S. Water Resources Development Act.
17. This construction is commonly invoked in U.S. courts to challenge and invalidate laws or regulations that meet the characterization.
18. The federal Canadian ban was eventually passed in December 2001, and replicated in every province except New Brunswick.
19. Annin, *The Great Lakes Water Wars*, p. 210.
20. Ibid., p. 216.
21. 3,785 cubic metres.
22. Andrew Nikiforuk, "Political Diversions: Annex 2001 and the Future of the Great Lakes" (report), The Munk Centre for International Studies, University of Toronto (June, 2004), http://www.powi.ca/pdfs/waterdiversion/nikiforuk_June2004.pdf.
23. Annin, *The Great Lakes Water Wars*, p. 220; Council of Canadians website, http://www.canadians.org.
24. Defined in the agreement as water lost to evaporation or by incorporation in a manufactured or agricultural product.

25. Something Ontario already allowed.

26. Annin, *The Great Lakes Water Wars*, p. 271.

27. "Great Lakes Water Levels" (data set), Great Lakes Environmental Research Laboratory, NOAA (February 2006), http://www.glerl.noaa.gov/data/now/wlevels/levels.html.

28. James Janega, "Great Lakes Drain Away," *Chicago Tribune* (September 3, 2006), A1.

29. Owen Heary, "Shallower Lake Erie Spells Deep Trouble," *Buffalo News* (August 29, 2006), http://www.greatlakesdirectory.org/on/082906_great_lakes.htm.

30. Adelle Larmour, "Water Levels Dredge Up Tourism Concersns [sic]," *Northern Ontario Business* (January 10, 2007), http://www.nob.on.ca/industry/energy/01-07-chicheemaun.asp.

31. Ibid.

32. "Changing Lake Levels Cause Problems for Boaters, Beachgoers," *Detroit Free Press* (August 27, 2006).

33. Jeff Alexander, "Lake Superior Closing in on Record Low Level," *Muskegon Chronicle* (Muskegon, MI) (October 3, 2006).

34. Jonathan Spicer, "Ships Run Aground as Great Lakes' Waters Drop," Reuters (July 3, 2006).

35. Personal interview (November 4, 2007).

36. "The North American Mosaic: A State of the Environment Report," North American Commission for Environmental Cooperation (Montreal) (2001), p. 26.

37. Personal interview (November 5, 2007).

38. Canadian critics of China's decision to relocate several cities in order to construct its Three Gorges Dam easily forget the villages drowned to create the St. Lawrence Seaway.

39. Telephone interview (December 13, 2006).

40. "Lake Erie Lakewide Management Plan Report," U.S. Environmental Protection Agency and Environment Canada (April 21, 2006), Section 11: "Significant Ongoing and Emerging Issues," http://epa.gov/greatlakes/lakeerie/2006update/Section_11.pdf.

41. Lucie Vincent and Éva Mekis, "Changes in Daily and Extreme Temperature and Precipitation Indices for Canada over the Twentieth Century," *Atmosphere-Ocean Journal* 44, 2 (June 2006), http://cmos.metapress.com/content/017157jp03w16698/.

42. Great Lakes Water Quality Board, "Climate Change and Water Quality in the Great Lakes Basin" (report), The International Joint Commission (IJC) (Ottawa and Washington, D.C.) (August 2003), http://www.ijc.org/php/publications/html/climate/index.html.

43. Ibid.

44. Geoffery E. Greene, "Land Use and Trout Streams," *Journal of Soil and Water Conservation* (July 1950), http://cwt33.ecology.uga.edu/publications/949.pdf.

45. George Kling et al., "Confronting Climate Change in the Great Lakes Region: Impacts on Our Communities and Ecosystems" (report), The Union of Concerned Scientists and the Ecological Society of America (April 2003), http://www.ucsusa.org/greatlakes/glchallengereport.html.

46. James Bruce et al., "Climate Change Impacts on Boundary and Transboundary Water Management" (report), Natural Resources Canada (June 2003), p. 11, http://www.saskriverbasin.ca/Resources/Climatechangestudy/Final %20Report%20A458-402%20CCAF.pdf.

47. Great Lakes Water Quality Board, "Climate Change and Water Quality in the Great Lakes Basin."

48. Dennis Cauchon, "The Case of the Disappearing Great Lake," USA Today (June 13, 2007), http://www.usatoday.com/news/nation/environment/ 2007-06-13-lake-superior_N.htm.

49. Mortsch. Telephone interview (December 13, 2006).

50. James Bruce et al., "Water Sector: Vulnerability and Adaptation to Climate Change" (report), Climate Change Action Fund (Ottawa) (June 2000), p. 46.

51. Annin, The Great Lakes Water Wars, p. 39.

**Chapter 6**
**Overdraft: In Arms over the Colorado River**

1. Personal interview (May 3, 2006).

2. Personal interview (May 3, 2006).

3. Personal interview (May 4, 2006).

4. The vast majority who try to enter the United States are from rural central and southern Mexico, with others from Central America.

5. Alejandro Abrego González, "Guerra por el agua entre México y EU [War for water between Mexico and United States]," Unomásuno (Mexico City) (March 18, 2006), p. 9 (author's translation from Spanish).

6. Marc P. Reisner, Cadillac Desert: The American West and Its Disappearing Water (New York: Viking Penguin, 1986).

7. To this day, a close reading of the title on many properties in western Canada and the United States will reveal that they once belonged—and some subsurface rights may still belong—to a land company associated with a railroad.

8. C. R. Rockwood, "Early History of Imperial County," in The History of Imperial County, California, ed. Finis C. Ferr (Berkeley: Elms and Franks, 1918), http://www.calarchives4u.com/history/imperial/1918-ch3.htm.

9. Ibid.

10. Reisner, Cadillac Desert, p. 7.

11. "Climatic Fluctuations, Drought, and Flow in the Colorado River Basin" (Fact Sheet 2004-3062), U.S. Geological Survey, Department of the Interior (August 2004), http://pubs.usgs.gov/fs/2004/3062/.

12. "Colorado River at Southerly International Boundary" (Table 09-5222.00 [metered daily mean river flows, January 1, 1950–April 30, 2007]), International Boundary and Water Commission United States and Mexico (2007), http://www.ibwc.state.gov/wad/ddqsibco.htm.

13. Aldo Leopold, *A Sand County Almanac: And Sketches Here and There* (New York: Oxford University Press, 1989), p. 128.

14. Saúl Sánchez Lemus, "La escasez de agua dulce en el delta del Río Colorado [Shortage of fresh water in the Colorado River delta]," ESMAS (Mexico City) (February 1, 2007) (author's translation from Spanish), http://www.esmas .com/noticierostelevisa/investigaciones/597094.html.

15. U.S. Geological Survey data show that the river's steady drop—despite a few seasons of unusual high flow—has continued more or less unbroken since 1890. The first five years of the 21$^{st}$ century were the lowest in the entire record. Between 2000 and 2003, the flow past Lee's Ferry was barely half what it was during the last century's Dust Bowl.

16. "Study Says California Will Need 40 Percent More Water in 25 Years," *U.S. Water News Online* (August 2005), http://www.uswaternews.com/archives/ arcsupply/5studsays8.html.

17. Dale Pontius, "Colorado River Basin Study" (report), Western Water Policy Review Advisory Commission (1997), https://repository.unm.edu/dspace/ bitstream/1928/2782/1/COLORADO.pdf; Bridget Kellogg, "The Dam Controversy," *Journal of Transnational Law and Policy* (Spring 2004), http:// www.law.fsu.edu/Journals/transnational/vol13_2/kellogg.pdf.

18. Personal interview (January 24, 2007).

19. Mark Bird, "A Water-Induced Economic Collapse of California?" *Water Conditioning and Purification* (October 2006), http://www.wcponline.com/ PDF/0610Bird.pdf.

20. "Behold the Incredible Shrinking Colorado River," MSNBC (February 22, 2007), http://www.msnbc.msn.com/id/17276693/.

21. Kirsten Brown, "Western States Must Fight Forest Fires, Drought with Long-Term Policy," *InfoZine* (Kansas City, MO) (September 26, 2006), http://www .infozine.com/news/stories/op/storiesView/sid/17951/.

22. Joyce Lobeck, "Work under Way on All American Canal," *Yuma Sun* (Yuma, Arizona) (June 30, 2007), http://www.yumasun.com/news/water_34985 ___article.html/canal_year.html.

23. Another part of the deal allows San Diego to pay Imperial Valley farmers to leave acreage fallow, freeing up irrigation water for that city to use.

24. "New Reservoir Will Funnel Colorado River Water to Nevada," Environmental News Service (December 20, 2006), http://ens-newswire.com/ ens/dec2006/2006-12-20-02.asp.

25. Charles Berman, "Paradox Rail: The Yuma Clapper Rail Is Thriving in Mexico in a Marsh Sustained by Water from the United States," *Birder's World Magazine* (June 2004), http://www.birdersworld.com/brd/default.aspx?c =a&id=302.

26. Francisco Zamora Arroyo of Tucson's Sonora Institute has estimated that 48,000 AF of water would restore a minimally functional river ecology from San Luis to the sea. Personal communication (February 5, 2007).

27. The California Water Resources Control Board is responsible for protecting and allocating all the water in the state.

28. Perlita R. Dicochea, "Historic Water Deal Triggers Worries along U.S.-Mexico Border," *La Prensa San Diego* (January 22, 2004), http://news.ncmonline.com/news/view_article.html?article_id=5489462 edo3a8d7b6e296a768c7fa1cc.

29. Telephone interview (December 21, 2006).

30. "Environmental Restoration in the Colorado River Delta" (report), Central Arizona Project (http://www.cap-az.com) (December 1, 2005), http://www.cap-az.com/docs/Enviro%20Rest%20Colo%20Rvr%20Delta.pdf.

31. Perlita R. Dicochea, "Water Transfer Not Enough, Water Conservation Is the Key," *La Prensa San Diego* (January 16, 2004), http://www.laprensa-sandiego.org/archieve/january04-16/water.htm.

32. Mort Rosenblum, "Colorado Delta Divide," Associated Press (May 20, 2001), http://archive.seacoastonline.com/2001news/5_20_w2.htm.

33. Peter H. Gleick, "Water Conflict Chronology," Pacific Institute for Studies in Development, Environment and Security (December 6, 2004), http://www.worldwater.org/chronology.html.

34. Marcel Kitissou, "Hydropolitics and Geopolitics: Transforming Conflict and Reshaping Cooperation in Africa," *Africa Notes* (November–December 2004), http://www.einaudi.cornell.edu/Africa/outreach/pdf/Hydropolitics_and_Geopolitics.

35. "Ex-Generals: Global Warming Threatens U.S. Security," The Associated Press (April 15, 2007), http://www.truthout.org/issues_06/041607EC.shtml.

36. Ibid.

37. "Global Trends 2015: A Dialogue about the Future with Non-Government Experts" (Paper NIC 2000–02), U.S. National Intelligence Council, Washington, D.C. (2000), http://www.loyola.edu/dept/politics/intel/globaltrends2015.pdf.

38. Integrated Regional Information Networks (IRIN), "Water is Running Out: How Inevitable Are International Conflicts?" (report), UN Office for the Coordination of Humanitarian Affairs (October 23, 2006), http://www.worldpress.org/Asia/2533.cfm.

39. Sandra Postel, *Pillar of Sand: Can the Irrigation Miracle Last?* (New York: W.W. Norton, 1999), p. 133.

40. IRIN, "Water Is Running Out."

41. Don Hinrichsen, "Freshwater: Lifeblood of the Planet."

42. Marie Therese, "You Can't Drink Mud and Salt: Hydropolitics and the Invasion of Lebanon," Newshounds.us (August 7, 2006), http://www.newshounds.us/2006/08/07/you_cant_drink_mud_and_salt_hydropolitics_and_the_invasion_of_lebanon.php. *See also* blogs at http://palestinianpundit.blogspot.com/2006/07/litani-of-sorrow.html and http://palestinianpundit.blogspot.com/2006/08/israeli-strikes-on-lebanese-watersheds.html.

43. Peter Gleick, "Water Conflict Chronology."

44. Bill Samii, "Iran/Afghanistan: Still No Resolution for Century-Old Water Dispute," Radio Free Europe/Radio Liberty (Prague) (September 7, 2005), http://www.rferl.org/featuresarticleprint/2005/09/bac55f18-bd4a-46b9-9f27-8078cb13bd8c.html.

45. "Chinese River Diversion Project Threatening Kazakhstan's Lake Balkhash," *AsiaNews* (Vatican City) (September 28, 2005), http://www.asianews.it/view .php?l=en&art=4215.

46. Asif J. Mir, "War over Water," *The Nation* (Islamabad) (June 15, 2005), http:// www.nation.com.pk/daily/june-2005/15/columns2.php.

47. Thomas Homer-Dixon, "The Myth of Global Water Wars," *Globe and Mail* (November 9, 1995), http://www.homerdixon.com/download/the_myth_of _global.pdf.

48. Personal interview (May 4, 2006).

## Chapter 7
## Pumping Blind: Hidden Threat in the Foothills

1. Telephone interviews (September 25, 2006, and November 27, 2006).

2. Formally the Freedom of Information and Protection of Privacy Act.

3. D. W. Schindler and W. F. Donahue, "An Impending Water Crisis in Canada's Western Prairie Provinces," *Proceedings of the National Academy of Sciences* (February 25, 2006), http://www.pnas.org/cgi/reprint/0601568103v1.pdf.

4. David Finlayson, "Shortages 'Imminent,' Agrologists Warn: Southern Irrigation, Northern Oil Sands Make Heavy Demands," *Edmonton Journal* (March 31, 2005), G8.

5. River Systems of the World: http://www.rev.net/~aloe/river/.

6. "Northern Water Wars Brewing, Predicts Miltenberger," CBC News (November 24, 2006), http://www.cbc.ca/canada/north/story/2006/11/24/ water-woes.html.

7. Mary O'Driscoll, "Tar Sand Companies Try Balancing Oil Gains, Environmental Pains," *Energy and Environment* (August 17, 2005), http://tech .groups.yahoo.com/group/energyresources/message/79794.

8. Bob Simon, "The Oil Sands of Alberta," CBS News (January 22, 2006), http:// www.cbsnews.com/stories/2006/01/20/60minutes/main1225184.shtml; Richard F. Meyer and Emil D. Attanasi, "Heavy Oil and Natural Bitumen—Strategic Petroleum Resources" (Fact Sheet 70-03), U.S. Geological Survey (August 2003), http://pubs.usgs.gov/fs/fs070-03/fs070-03.html.

9. Doug Struck, "Canada Pays Environmentally for U.S. Oil Thirst," *Washington Post* (May 31, 2006), http://www.washingtonpost.com/wp-dyn/content/ article/2006/05/30/AR2006053001429.html.

10. "U.S. Urges 'Fivefold Expansion' in Alberta Oilsands Production," CBC News (January 18, 2007), http://www.cbc.ca/canada/story/2007/01/17/oil-sands.html.

11. Compiled from various estimates: Dan Woynillowicz and Chris Severson-Baker, "Down to the Last Drop: The Athabasca River and Oil Sands" (Oil Sands Issue Paper No. 1), Pembina Institute, Calgary (March, 2006), http:// pubs.pembina.org/reports/LastDrop_Mar1606c.pdf; Schindler and Donahue, "An Impending Water Crisis in Canada's Western Prairie Provinces"; "Canada's Oil Sands: Opportunities and Challenges to 2015" (report), National Energy Board (Calgary) (May 2004), http://dsp-psd.pwgsc.gc.ca/Collection/ NE23-116-2004E.pdf.

12. Woynillowicz and Severson-Baker, "Down to the Last Drop."
13. Ibid.
14. B.C. Hydro website, http://www.bchydro.com/recreation/northern/ northern1199.html; "W. A. C. Bennett Dam," Wikipedia, http://en.wikipedia .org/wiki/Bennett_Dam.
15. "First Nations Call for Oilsands Moratorium," CBC News (January 31, 2007), http://www.polarisinstitute.org/first_nations_call_for_oilsands_moratorium.
16. Schindler and Donahue, "An Impending Water Crisis in Canada's Western Prairie Provinces."
17. Irrigation Water Management Study Steering Committee, "South Saskatchewan River Basin Irrigation into the 21st Century" (report), Alberta Irrigation Projects Association, Vol. 1 (2002), p. xv.
18. "McCain to Build French Fry Plant in Alberta," CBC News (January 8, 1999), http://www.cbc.ca/money/story/1999/01/08/mccain990108.html.
19. Annual Report, Alberta Irrigation Branch (Lethbridge, Alberta) (2004).
20. Personal interview (June 7, 2005).
21. Telephone interview (December 18, 2006).
22. Telephone interview (October 3, 2006).
23. "UCLA Study Explores Droughts in Canadian Prairies" (press release), Department of Geography, University of California, Los Angeles (July 24, 2003), http://www.eurekalert.org/pub_releases/2003-07/uoc--use071703.php.
24. Schindler and Donahue, "An Impending Water Crisis in Canada's Western Prairie Provinces."
25. Ibid.
26. Telephone interview (September 19, 2006).
27. The amount in question is 51,000 cubic metres (41 acre feet) per hour. The treaty provides for an alternative, in water-short years, of three-quarters of the "natural flow" of the river. But, the study's authors observed, "with climate change, the calculation of 'natural flow' remains difficult." James Bruce et al., "Climate Change Impacts on Boundary and Transboundary Water Management" (report), Natural Resources Canada (June 2003), http://www .saskriverbasin.ca/Resources/Climatechangestudy/Final%20Report%20A458 -402%20CCAF.pdf.
28. Bob Weber, "Officials Grilled on Oilsands Impact on Athabasca River," The Canadian Press (November 22, 2006), http://www.cbc.ca/cp/business/061122/ b112287A.html.
29. Telephone interview (December 18, 2006).
30. Bill Graveland, "Water Shortages, Climate Change Could Be Disastrous for Southern Alta: Expert," The Canadian Press (September 6, 2006), http://www .hamiltonspectator.com/business/agriculture/a090633A.html.

## Chapter 8
### Outlook to 2030: Wild and Wilder

1. Personal interview (August 20, 1996); telephone interviews (August 31, 2006, and February 15, 2007).

2. Royal British Columbia Museum, exhibit on changing climate, "Chronology of Prehistory," http://www.b17.com/family/lwp/chronology/prehistory.html.

3. Each letter, space or punctuation point would represent approximately 44,000 years of the world's existence.

4. Emphasis added. Kendrick Taylor, "Rapid Climate Change: New Evidence Shows That Earth's Climate Can Change Dramatically in Only a Decade," *Scientific American* (July/August 1999), http://www.americanscientist.org/template/AssetDetail/assetid/15750.

5. "Dunes Hint at Origins of Ancient American Drought," *New Scientist* (July 29, 2006), http://environment.newscientist.com/channel/earth/dn9635-dunes-hint-at-origins-of-ancient-american-drought.html.

6. Chris Wood, "Lessons from the Bottom of the Sea," *Maclean's* (September 2, 1996).

7. Keith C. Heidorn, "Air Masses: A Base for Weather Analysis," The Weather Doctor (website) (May 1, 2001), http://www.islandnet.com/~see/weather/elements/airmasses.htm.

8. These globe-straddling bands of wind are properly called the Hadley Cells: Wikepedia, Answers.com and Encyclopedia Britannica.

9. This middle Hadley Cell is also called the Ferrel Cell; ibid.

10. When weathercasters in the northern hemisphere talk about "the" jet stream, they're generally referring to the west-to-east flow between the polar and mid-latitude rings.

11. Victor S. Kennedy et al., "Coastal and Marine Ecosystems and Global Climate Change: Potential Effects on U.S. Resources" (report), Pew Center on Global Climate Change, Arlington, VA (August, 2003), http://www.pewclimate.org/global-warming-in-depth/all_reports/coastal_and_marine_ecosystems or full report (.pdf) at http://www.pewclimate.org/docUploads/marine_ecosystems.pdf.

12. Wikipedia, http://en.wiktionary.org/wiki/haline.

13. Judy Skatssoon, "Clearer Asian Skies May Worsen Drought," Australian Broadcasting Corporation (December 13, 2006), http://www.abc.net.au/science/news/stories/2006/1809721.htm.

14. Quirin Schiermeier, "Clear Skies End Global Dimming," *Nature* (online at Nature.com) (May 5, 2005), http://news.nature.com/news/2005/050502/050502-8.html and http://www.longpaddock.qld.gov.au/ClimateChanges/News/Archives/2005/May/10th/.

15. Michael Smith, "Pollution Drying Up Rainfall," UPI Science News (February 17, 2002), http://www.climateark.org/shared/reader/welcome.aspx?linkID=7932.

16. Geoffrey Lean, "A Disaster to Take Everyone's Breath Away," *The New Zealand Herald* (July 24, 2006), http://www.nzherald.co.nz/section/2/story.cfm?c_id=2&ObjectID=10392615.

17. Personal interview (December 19, 2006).

18. ipcc-4, p. 61 (Figure ts -22, caption).

19. Ibid., p. 69 (Figure ts -26) and p. 37. Based on ipcc estimate of recent warming of 0.27° per decade, over four decades 1980–2020.

20. Ibid., p. 7.
21. Ibid., p. 76 (Figure TS-30).
22. Ibid., p. 73.
23. Ibid., p. 71.
24. Ibid., p. 74.
25. James Hansen, "The Threat to the Planet," *New York Review of Books* 53, 12 (July 13, 2006), http://www.nybooks.com/articles/19131.
26. Daniel Wallis, "Disaster Losses May Top One Trillion Dollars Per Year by 2040," Reuters (Nairobi) (November 15, 2006), http://www.heatisonline.org/contentserver/objecthandlers/index.cfm?id=6133&method=full.
27. The enterprising exceptions are a few forms of life that draw energy from geothermal heat released deep in the sea.
28. "Russian Scientist Predicts Global Cooling," United Press International (Moscow) (August 25, 2006), http://www.upi.com/NewsTrack/Science/2006/08/25/russian_scientist_predicts_global_cooling/7556/.
29. IPCC-4, p. 36.
30. Sharon Begley, "Climate Pessimists Were Right," *The Wall Street Journal* (February 9, 2007), B1, http://www.uwlax.edu/faculty/knowles/eco346/Climate%20Pessimists%20Were%20Right.doc.
31. Ibid.
32. Deborah Zabarenko, "Arctic Ice Cap Melting 30 Years ahead of Forecast," Reuters (Washington, D.C.) (May 1, 2007), http://www.reuters.com/article/scienceNews/idUSN0122477020070501.
33. John Roach, "Grim Climate Predictions Not Exaggerated, Analysis Says," *National Geographic News* (February 1, 2007), http://news.nationalgeographic.com/news/2007/02/070201-global-warming.html; "Sea Level on the Rise: In Real and Virtual Worlds" (press release), Commonwealth Scientific and Industrial Research Organisation (CSIRO), Australia, Science Daily (February 5, 2007), http://www.sciencedaily.com/releases/2007/02/070204111703.htm.
34. Doug Struck, "Earth's Climate Warming Abruptly, Scientist Says," *Washington Post* (June 27, 2006), A3.
35. Hans Schellnhuber, ed., *Avoiding Dangerous Climate Change* (Cambridge: Cambridge University Press, 2006), http://www.defra.gov.uk/environment/climatechange/research/dangerous-cc/index.htm.
36. Peter Barrett, "What 3 Degrees of Global Warming Really Means," *Pacific Ecologist* (January 3, 2006), http://www.pacificecologist.org/archive/unchecked.html.
37. David Adam, "Surge in Carbon Levels Raises Fears of Runaway Warming," *The Guardian* (U.K.) (January 19, 2007), http://www.guardian.co.uk/environment/2007/jan/19/frontpagenews.climatechange.
38. "Feedback Loops in Global Climate Change Point to a Very Hot 21st Century" (press release), Lawrence Berkeley National Laboratory, *Science Daily* (May 22, 2006), http://www.sciencedaily.com/releases/2006/05/060522151248.htm.
39. Less than four percent of the carbon in the tundra would need to decay into carbon dioxide from its present chemical attachment to frozen organic matter for this to be the case. Peter Graff, "Global Warming Causes Soil to Release

Carbon: Study," Reuters (September 7, 2005), http://www.planetark.com/
dailynewsstory.cfm/newsid/32409/story.htm.

40. Bill Blakemore, "Could Global Warming Become a Runaway Train?" ABC
News (February 18, 2006), http://www.climateark.org/shared/reader/welcome
.aspx?linkID=52733.

41. "Harmful Environmental Effects of Livestock Production on the Planet
'Increasingly Serious,' Says Panel" (news release), Stanford University
(February 22, 2007), http://www.sciencedaily.com/releases/2007/02/
070220145244.htm.

42. Wikipedia, http://en.wikipedia.org/wiki/Methane_hydrate; "The Future of
Methane," University of California at San Diego (2002), http://earthguide
.ucsd.edu/virtualmuseum/climatechange2/11_3.shtml.

43. David Adam, "Surge in Carbon Levels Raises Fears of Runaway Warming."

44. Lewis Smith, "Rapid Rise in Global Warming Is Forecast," *The Times*
(London) (May 18, 2007), http://www.timesonline.co.uk/tol/news/uk/science/
article1805870.ece.

45. IPCC-4, p. 47.

46. Ibid., p. 43.

47. "U.S. Climate Action Report" (Third National Communication under the
U.N. Framework Convention on Climate Change), U.S. Department of State
(Washington, D.C.) (May, 2002), http://yosemite.epa.gov/oar/globalwarming
.nsf/UniqueKeyLookup/SHSU5BWHU6/$File/uscar.pdf.

48. "Accumulated Change Courts Ecosystem Catastrophe" (press release), Earth
Observatory, NASA (October 10, 2001), http://earthobservatory.nasa.gov/
Newsroom/MediaAlerts/2001/200110105252.html.

49. "World Forum Scientists: 'Climate Change Will Become a Security Issue,'"
CNN.com (February 2, 2002).

50. James Lovelock, "The Earth Is about to Catch a Morbid Fever That May Last
as Long as 100,000 Years," *The Independent* (U.K.) (January 16, 2006), http://
comment.independent.co.uk/commentators/article338830.ece.

51. Peter Schwartz and Doug Randall, "An Abrupt Climate Change Scenario
and Its Implications for the United States National Security" (report),
Environmental Defense (October, 2003), http://www.environmentaldefense
.org/documents/3566_AbruptClimateChange.pdf.

52. Jared Diamond, *Collapse: How Societies Choose to Fail or Succeed* (New York:
Viking Penguin, 2005), p. 79 ff, p. 277 ff.

53. IPCC-4, p. 69 (Figure TS-26).

54. Ibid., p. 847 ff (Chapter 11: Regional Climate Projections).

55. James Painter, "Amazon 'Faces More Deadly Droughts,'" BBC News (March 23,
2007), http://news.bbc.co.uk/2/hi/americas/6484073.stm.

56. Steve Connor, "The Earth Today Stands in Imminent Peril," *The Independent*
(U.K.) (June 18, 2007), http://environment.independent.co.uk/
climate_change/article2675747.ece.

57. Launce Rake, "Global Warming Will Strike Us First," *Las Vegas Sun*
(February 3, 2007), http://www.lasvegassun.com/sunbin/stories/
lv-other/2007/feb/03/566672794.html.

Chapter 9
Mirages: Taps for Big Plumbing

1. Technically, the City of Las Vegas is only a small part of the urban centre in Clark County that goes by that name. The famous Strip is actually in unincorporated Paradise Township.
2. Mike Davis, "House of Cards: Las Vegas—Too Many People in the Wrong Place, Celebrating Waste as a Way of Life," *Sierra Magazine* (November-December 1995), http://www.sierraclub.org/sierra/199511/vegas.asp.
3. Personal interview (January 22, 2007).
4. Landscaping with plants and horticultural techniques that require little or no irrigation.
5. Corporate release, MGM MIRAGE, Las Vegas (2006).
6. Southern Nevada Water Authority (SNWA). Personal interviews (January 23, 2007).
7. Bobby Magill, "Experts Call for Revision on Colorado River Plant," *The Daily Sentinel* (Salt Lake City, UT) (March 4, 2007), A1.
8. Regulation Canadian Football League playing field.
9. Rick Watson and Stan Morain, "Climate Variability and Water Management Strategies in Southwest Pueblo Cultures," *Acclimations* (Newsletter of the U.S. National Assessment of the Potential Consequences of Climate Variability and Change), U.S. Global Change Research Program (January-February, 2000), http://www.usgcrp.gov/usgcrp/Library/nationalassessment/newsletter/2000.02/Native.html.
10. Nicholas Cheviron, "3,000-Year-Old Dam Revives Farming in Turkish Village," Agence France-Presse (December 13, 2006), http://www.stonepages.com/news/archives/002192.html and http://www.turkishdailynews.com.tr/article.php?enewsid=61644.
11. World Commission on Dams, Dams and Development: *A New Framework for Decision-Making* (London: Earthscan Publications, 2000), p. 16.
12. "Large" means over 15 metres high. "Dam Facts and Figures: A Quick Guide to the World of Dams," World Wildlife Fund, http://www.panda.org/about_wwf/what_we_do/freshwater/our_solutions/policy_practice/dams_initiative/quick_facts/index.cfm.
13. "Major Dams of the United States," U.S. National Atlas website, http://nationalatlas.gov/mld/dams00x.html.
14. James G. Workman, "Deadbeat Dams: Perhaps It's Time to Pull the Plug," Property and Environment Research Center (Bozeman, MT), *Reports 24,* 4 (December, 2006), http://www.perc.org/perc.php?id=849.
15. World Commission on Dams, *Dams and Development*, p. 137.
16. The exceptions are a few spring-fed lakes such as exist in Florida.
17. Tim Barnett, J.C. Adam and D.P. Lettenmaier, "Potential Impacts of a Warming Climate on Water Availability in Snow-Dominated Regions," *Nature* (November 17, 2005), http://www.eldis.org/go/display/?id=18630&type=Document.
18. "Schwarzenegger Proposes $4.5 Billion for Water Storage," *U.S. Water News Online* (January 2007), http://www.uswaternews.com/archives/arcsupply/7schwprop1.html.

19. "Water Plan with New Reservoirs under Fire," *U.S. Water News Online* (April 2006), http://www.uswaternews.com/archives/arcconserv/6wateplan4.html; Jeff Prince, "Water, Water ... Where?" *Fort Worth Weekly* (October 11, 2006), http://www.fwweekly.com/content.asp?article=4264.

20. Lance Endersbee, "A Voyage of Discovery," *Executive Intelligence Review* (March 10, 2006), http://www.larouchepub.com/other/2006/3310endersbee _water.html.

21. Somini Sengupta, "Thirsty Giant: Often Parched, India Struggles to Tap the Monsoon," *New York Times* (October 1, 2006), http://www.nytimes.com/ 2006/10/01/world/asia/01india.html?ex=1317355200&en=95117551ebb265d6 &ei=5088&partner=rssnyt&emc=rss.

22. Ercan Yavuz, "[Turkish national waterworks authority] DSI's Water Survey: Turkey Is Running Out of Water," *Today's Zaman* (Ankara) (February 3, 2007), http://www.todayszaman.com/tz-web/detaylar.do?load=detay&link=10 1903&bolum=101.

23. "'Extreme Rainfall' Incidents Increasing in Parts of U. K." (press release), University of Newcastle upon Tyne (September 5, 2006), http://www.ncl.ac .uk/press.office/press.release/content.phtml?ref=1157358561.

24. "Dam Facts and Figures: A Quick Guide to the World of Dams," World Wildlife Fund (Switzerland) (November 13, 2005), http://www.panda.org/ about_wwf/what_we_do/freshwater/our_solutions/policy_practice/dams _initiative/quick_facts/index.cfm.

25. J. Douglas Porteous and Sandra E. Smith, *Domicide: The Global Destruction of Home* (Montreal: McGill-Queen's University Press, 2001), p. 147.

26. The World Commission on Dams, *Dams and Development*, p. 18.

27. Ibid., p. 31.

28. Ibid.

29. Ibid.

30. Evaporation, at ~230 km³, takes about half of Erie's ~484 km³ each year. Personal calculation from information at "Lake Erie Facts and Figures," Great Lakes Network, http://www.great-lakes.net/lakes/ref/eriefact.html, and "Industrial and Domestic Consumption Compared with Evaporation from Reservoirs," a graphic based on data from Igor A. Shiklomanov, State Hydrological Institute (St. Petersburg, Russia) and UNEP (1999), http://www .unep.org/dewa/assessments/ecosystems/water/vitalwater/15.htm.

31. "Droughts and Reservoirs: Finding Storage Space Underground" (press release), Geological Society of America (September 18, 2006), http://www .geosociety.org/news/pr/06-39.htm.

32. The claimed carbon benefit from hydro-electricity is strongly contested: warm reservoirs release large volumes of methane.

33. Endersbee, "A Voyage of Discovery."

34. "Nevada State Engineer Looks to Protect Main Aquifer from Over-Pumping," *U.S. Water News Online* (January 2005), http://www.uswaternews.com/ archives/arcconserv/5nevastat1.html.

35. "Growing toward More Efficient Water Use: Linking Development, Infrastructure and Drinking Water Policies" (report), U.S. Environmental

Protection Agency (EPA) (January 2006), http://www.epa.gov/smartgrowth/pdf/growing_water_use_efficiency.pdf.

36. "Low Aquifer Threatens Farming," *U.S. Water News Online* (September 2005), http://www.uswaternews.com/archives/arcsupply/5lowxaqui9.html.

37. Sandra Postel, *Pillar of Sand: Can the Irrigation Miracle Last?* (New York: W.W. Norton, 1999), p. 80.

38. Endersbee, "A Voyage of Discovery."

39. Ibid.

40. Fred Pearce, "Asian Farmers Sucking the Continent Dry," *New Scientist* (August 28, 2004), http://www.newscientist.com/article/dn6321-asian-farmers-sucking-the-continent-dry.html.

41. Lester R. Brown, *Eco-Economy: Building an Economy for the Earth* (New York: W.W. Norton, 2001), p. 146.

42. The plan proposes to withdraw 180,000 acre-feet of water a year, enough to flood a square kilometre of land to the depth equal to the length of two football fields.

43. In testimony to Nevada State Assembly Government Committee. "Southern Nevada Water Import Plan Pushed," Associated Press (February 22, 2007), http://www.kolotv.com/news/headlines/5990776.html.

44. Matt Jenkins, "Squeezing Water from a Stone," *High Country News* (September 19, 2005), http://www.hcn.org/servlets/hcn.Article?article_id=15778.

45. Ibid.

46. The "alien" carp was introduced into the American South in the 1970s by catfish farmers, escaped captivity during the 1993 Mississippi floods and subsequently prospered.

47. Lyndon H. LaRouche, Jr., "The Outline of NAWAPA" (concept document), Schiller Institute (Washington, D.C.) (January 1988), http://www.schillerinstitute.org/economy/phys_econ/phys_econ_nawapa_1983.html.

48. Telephone interview (May 11, 2005).

49. Tom Kierans, "GRAND Canal Project Summary," from Mr. Kierans' Great Recycling and Northern Development (GRAND) Canal Proposal website, http://ca.geocities.com/grandcanal2005/proposal.htm.

50. Alex Salmon, "Western Australia's Water Crisis," *Green Left Weekly* 615 (February 16, 2005), http://www.greenleft.org.au/2005/615/35415. "Barnett Resurrects Kimberly-Perth Canal Water Plant," Australian Broadcasting Corporation (ABC) (March 18, 2007), http://www.abc.net.au/news/stories/2007/03/18/1874522.htm.

51. Gordon Weixel, "Plan to Get Water to Red River Valley Endorsed," *Tribune Bismark* (North Dakota) (November 2, 2005), http://www.bismarcktribune.com/articles/2005/11/02/news/local/104852.txt.

52. Telephone interview (June 8, 2005).

53. Matt Jenkins, "Squeezing Water from a Stone."

54. Arizona, California, Colorado, Nevada, New Mexico, Utah and Wyoming. "Scientists Excited about Cloud-Seeding Project," Associated Press (December 19, 2005), http://www.usatoday.com/weather/research/2005-12-19-cloud-seeding_x.htm.

55. "China Makes Artificial Rain for Beijing," Associated Press (May 5, 2006), http://www.chinadaily.com.cn/china/2006-05/06/content_583222.htm.

56. Jerd Smith, "The West's Water Future May Float on Cloud Plan," *Rocky Mountain News* (Denver) (April 17, 2006), http://www.rockymountainnews.com/drmn/cda/article_print/0,1983,DRMN_15_4626968_ARTICLE-DETAIL-PRINT,00.html.

57. Fred Pearce, "Water, Water, Everywhere," *Prospect Magazine* (London) (May 2006), http://www.prospect-magazine.co.uk/article_details.php?id=7425.

58. U.S. National Research Council Committee on the Scientific Bases of Colorado River Basin Water Management, *Colorado River Basin Water Management: Evaluating and Adjusting to Hydroclimatic Variability* (Washington, D.C.: National Academies Press, 2007) [draft], p. 118.

59. For this comparison, estimated at 1,600 cubic metres of fresh water per Canadian per year. Mark Bird, "$000 Current Seawater Desalting Costs?" *Water Conditioning and Purification* (April 2005), p. 11.

60. Pearce, "Water, Water Everywhere."

61. I calculated these comparisons from pricing information publicly available online to citizens of these cities from their respective water utilities, with the exception of the pricing of Alberta's irrigation water, which I learned about from personal interviews with Brent Paterson, among others. Caution: these per-capita figures represent *all* the water Canadians use in any form, but most people use, and are billed for, only a small portion of that at home (my previous house, which was metered, used about 180 m³ per person a year). As a result, most of us actually paid far less for water at home than the amounts given. In Victoria, for instance, flat-rate residential customers in 2007 paid as little as $329 a year for as much water as they could run.

62. Gleick was lead author of "Water: The Potential Consequences of Climate Variability and Change for the Water Resources of the United States" (U.S. Global Change Research Program: September 2000), still the only comprehensive U.S. government-sponsored survey of the impact of climate change on American water resources. Telephone interview (June 14, 2005).

63. Personal interview (July 24, 2006).

64. Ian Gunn, "Drink Up and Don't Fear the 'Yuk' Factor," *New Zealand Herald* (February 16, 2007), http://www.nzherald.co.nz/section/1/story.cfm?c_id=1&objectid=10424218.

65. "'Recycle More Sewage,' Say Engineers," EDIE [Environmental Data Interactive Exchange] news centre (London) (October 18, 2006), http://www.edie.net/news/news_story.asp?id=12143.

66. "Queensland to Drink Waste Water," BBC News (January 29, 2007), http://news.bbc.co.uk/2/hi/asia-pacific/6308715.stm.

## Chapter 10
### Green Inc.: Balancing Our Ecological Books

1. One of the class of spineless animals that includes octopi and squid.

2. Personal interview (November 1, 2006).

3. "Mitigation Banking Fact Sheet," U.S. EPA website (June 2007), http://www
.epa.gov/owow/wetlands/facts/fact16.html.

4. Ohio Environmental Protection Agency (EPA) officials Ric Queen, John Mack.
Telephone interviews (October 11 and 17, 2006, respectively). Also:
http://www.dnr.state.oh.us/dnap/wetlands/banking/tabid/997/Default.aspx;
http://www.epa.gov/wetlandsmitigation/; and http://www.ramsar.org/forum/
forum_mitigation.htm.

5. Alice Kenny, "Ohio Study Shows Mitigation Banks Not Living Up to
Potential," Ecosystem Marketplace News (August 14, 2006), http://
ecosystemmarketplace.com/pages/article.news.php?component_id=4485
&component_version_id=6594&language_id=12.

6. Personal interviews (January 25, 2007).

7. U.S. Gross Domestic Product (GDP) was $25.4 trillion in 1985 and $37.2
trillion by 2005 (constant 2000 U.S. dollar basis). "What Was the GDP Then?"
Economic History Services, http://eh.net/hmit/gdp/.

8. Canada's water consumption rose by 25.7%. "Canada vs. the OECD: An
Environmental Comparison." OECD at http://www.environmentalindicators.
com and "Global Econ Data," EconStats.com at http://www.econstats.com/
weo/CV030V017.htm.

9. "Withdrawal" is a subtly different notion from "consumption," since some of
what is withdrawn may be returned, for example as treated sewage put back
into a river to be used again downstream.

10. Includes commercial and governmental users.

11. Adapted from Peter H. Gleick et al., The World's Water 2004–2005: The
Biennial Report on Freshwater Resources (Washington, D.C.: Island Press,
2004), p. 295 ff.

12. World Commission on Dams, Dams and Development: A New Framework for
Decision-Making (London: Earthscan Publications, 2000), p. 140.

13. Ibid., p. 158.

14. Goska Romanowicz, "Thames [Water Utilities Ltd.] Plans U.K.'s 'Biggest
Reservoir for 25 Years'," EDIE news centre (September 14, 2006), http://www
.edie.net/news/news_story.asp?id=11994.

15. Carmela Fragomeni, "Drip, Drip, Drip: City Disputes Study on Water
Use," The Hamilton Spectator (June 26, 2007), http://www.thespec.com/
article/211733.

16. "Growing toward More Efficient Water Use: Linking Development,
Infrastructure and Drinking Water Policies" (report), U.S. Environmental
Protection Agency (EPA) (January 2006), http://www.epa.gov/smartgrowth/
pdf/growing_water_use_efficiency.pdf.

17. Steven Renzetti, "Economic Instruments and Canadian Industrial Water Use,"
Canadian Water Resources Journal (2005), http://policyresearch.gc.ca/doclib/
SD_Steven_Renzetti.pdf; Steven Renzetti and Diane Dupont, "The Value of
Water in Manufacturing" (working paper), Centre for Social and Economic
Research on the Global Environment, University of East Anglia (2003), http://
www.uea.ac.uk/env/cserge/pub/wp/ecm/ecm_2003_03.pdf.

18. "Facts and Figures: Water Use," World Water Assessment Programme, People and the Planet, UNESCO (2003), http://www.unesco.org/water/iyfw2/water _use.shtml.

19. "How Do We Use It?" Environment Canada, http://www.ec.gc.ca/water/en/ info/facts/e_use.htm.

20. "Nuclear Power," Ontario Power Generation, http://www.opg.com/power/nuclear/.

21. "Report: China Faces Severe Water Shortages, Mounting Pollution," U.S. Water News Online (March 23, 2005), http://www.uswaternews.com/archives/ arcglobal/5chinface4.html.

22. Originally developed by Nobel-winning American economist Simon Kuznets to describe the relationship he perceived between economic development and income inequality.

23. John Miner, "Pesticides May Affect Penis Size," The London Free Press (Ontario) (April 29, 2006), http://lfpress.ca/newsstand/CityandRegion/ 2006/04/29/1556379-sun.html; Cornelia Dean, "Drugs Are in the Water: Does It Matter?" New York Times (April 3, 2007), http://www.nytimes .com/2007/04/03/science/earth/03water.html?ex=1184817600&en =f871f0eb61c758f1&ei=5070.

24. Gleick et al., "World's Water 2004–2005."

25. Excluding thermal power plants, U.S. industry accounted for only five percent of that country's total water use; Canadian manufacturers consumed a large share—14 percent—of this country's water. "How Do We Use It?" Environment Canada; "Estimated Use of Water in the United States 2000," United States Geological Survey, http://pubs.usgs.gov/circ/2004/circ1268/ htdocs/text-total.html; "Water Use in the United States," NationalAtlas, http://www.nationalatlas.gov/articles/water/a_wateruse.html#five.

26. Animal Improvement Program Laboratory, U.S. Department of Agriculture, http://aipl.arsU.S.a.gov.

27. Personal interview (April 28, 2006).

28. Personal interview (April 28, 2006).

29. "Water Performance and Challenges in OECD Countries," Organization for Economic Cooperation and Development (OECD), Paris (2003), http://www .oecd.org/dataoecd/12/38/2498050.pdf.

30. Daniel Griswold, "Wreaking Environmental Harm: Another Case against Farm Subsidies" (report), Property and Environmental Research Center (n.d.), http://www.perc.org/perc.php?subsection=5&id=756; Terry L. Anderson and Pamela S. Snyder, "Priming the Invisible Pump: Water Markets Emerge" (Policy Series PS-9), Property and Environmental Research Center (February, 1997), http://www.perc.org/perc.php?subsection=6&id=198; André de Moor and Peter Calamai, "Subsidizing Unsustainable Development: Undermining the Earth with Public Funds" (report), The Earth Council, San José, Costa Rica (1997), http://www.envict.org.au/file/Subsidizing%20Development.pdf.

31. When those costs are hidden in city-wide property taxes, the burden for servicing the new houses shifts to existing residents in denser neighbourhoods. EPA, "Growing Toward More Efficient Water Use."

32. Telephone interview (July 17, 2006).

33. Some exceptions have crept in where areas have established local groundwater districts under recent legislation.

34. Strangely enough, the two extremes can be found in the neighbouring provinces of Manitoba (low end of the range) and Saskatchewan (high). Randy Christensen and Simone Magwood, "Groundwater Pricing Policies in Canada" (report), Sierra Legal Defence Fund (February 9, 2005), http://www.sierralegal .org/reports/Groundwater%20Pricing%20Case%20Study2%20March%202005 .pdf.

35. Daniel Griswold, "Wreaking Environmental Harm."

36. Steve Burrell, "Higher Price Must Reflect True Cost of Water Supply," *Sydney Morning Herald* (October 23, 2006), http://www.smh.com.au/news/ scorchedearth/higher-price-must-reflect-true-cost-of-water-supply/2006/ 10/22/1161455611185.html.

37. "Living beyond Our Means" (statement from the directors), Millennium Ecosystem Assessment, UNEP (March 2005), http://www .millenniumassessment.org/documents/document.429.aspx.pdf.

38. Preston Manning, "Balancing the Ecological Budget: Marrying Environmental Stewardship and Economic Development," speech delivered to the Alberta Conservation Association, Sherwood Park, Alberta (January 24, 2007).

39. William Watson, "Water Shouldn't Be Free," *The Gazette* (Montreal) (September 11, 2000).

40. Anderson and Snyder, "Priming the Invisible Pump."

41. Burrell, "Higher Price Must Reflect True Cost of Water Supply."

42. Governor Jon Huntsman, "Nuclear Waste," http://www.utah.gov/governor/ environment.html.

43. Watson, "Water Shouldn't Be Free."

44. "Natural Wealth of the Mackenzie Region Close to $500 Billion, Says Report" (news release), Canadian Boreal Initiative (Ottawa) (January 31, 2007), http:// www.cpawsmb.org/news/newsitem.php?news=1060.

45. "Growing Ladysmith Using Way Less Water," *Cowichan Valley Citizen* (June 13, 2007), p. 3; personal interview (July 3, 2006).

46. Maude Barlow, *Blue Gold: The Global Water Crisis and the Commodification of the World's Water Supply* (Ottawa: Octopus Books, 2001).

47. Ibid., p. 57.

48. Ibid., p. 58.

49. Ibid.

50. Ibid., p. 59.

51. De Moor and Calamai, "Subsidizing Unsustainable Development." In the United States, the Congressional Accounting Office found that "public drinking water utilities are more likely than their privately owned counterparts to defer maintenance." Cited in EPA, "Growing toward More Efficient Water Use," p. 9, http://www.epa.gov/piedpage/water_efficiency.htm.

52. David Roberts, "Getting Fresh," Grist Environmental News and Commentary (June 30, 2006), http://www.grist.org/news/maindish/2006/06/30/roberts/ index.html.

53. Barlow, *Blue Gold*, p. 57.

54. Dave Brian Butvill, "A Famed Ecologist Wants to Put Price Tags on the Priceless," *Sierra* (July, 2004), http://www.sierraclub.org/sierra/200407/interview.asp.

55. East of Manitoba in Canada and east of Texas in the U.S., a different system applies. Known as "riparian" law, it grants an owner of property along a river bank (the "riparian" zone) the effectively unlimited right to take water from that river, along with the right to sue any owner upstream whose use negatively affects his or her own supply. Texas, states north of it and states on the west coast blend the two systems, as does Mississippi. Hawaii uses a riparian system; Alaska, prior appropriation.

56. Telephone interview (March 6, 2007).

57. Specifically, about half the sellers had "wheel-move" sprayer trains, and three-quarters of buyers used higher-efficiency pivot systems that released water close to the ground, losing far less to ET. Telephone interviews (June 4, 2005, and October 10, 2006); Lorraine Nicol, "Irrigation Water Markets in Southern Alberta" (MA thesis), Department of Economics, University of Lethbridge (2005), http://www.aipa.org/Adobe_Files/Value_of_Water/2005_04_Lorrain_Nichol_Thesis_Final.pdf.

58. Follow-up studies found that the emergence of water exchanges in both New South Wales and Victoria "significantly enhanced" the growth of temporary water markets. Henning Bjornlund, "Signs of Maturity in Australian Water Markets," *New Zealand Property Journal* (July 31, 2002), p. 46, cited in Nicol, "Irrigation Water Markets in Southern Alberta," p. 44.

59. Nicol, "Irrigation Water Markets in Southern Alberta"; Terry Anderson, "Markets and the Environment: Friends or Foes?" *Case Western Reserve Law Review* 55, 1 (Fall 2004), http://www.perc.org/perc.php?id=519; Terry L. Anderson, "The Rising Tide of Water Markets," paper delivered to Property Rights, Economics and Environment seminar at Aix-en-Provence, France (1998), http://www.environnement-propriete.org/english/1998/pdf_dowload/.anderson.pdf; Anderson and Snyder, "Priming the Invisible Pump."

60. Barlow, *Blue Gold*, p. 55.

61. "U.S. Habitat Conservation through Land Ownership and Conservation Easements" (factsheet), Ducks Unlimited (n.d.), http://www.ducks.org/media/conservation/conservation%20fact%20sheets/_documents/ConservationFactSheet.pdf.

62. Full disclosure: I am a small but regular donor to the Institute.

63. Telephone interview (February 5, 2007).

64. Francisco Zamora Arroyo et al., "Conservation Priorities in the Colorado River Delta: Mexico and the United States" (report), Sonoran Institute (Tucson) with partners (2005), http://sonoran.org/index.php?option=com_content&task=view&id=157&Itemid=204.

65. Environmental agencies use this term to mean both dispersed pollutants like those that run off a field into a river, and the miscellaneous leaks from plumbing joints, corroded pipes and careless oil changes in driveways and vacant lots. The opposite is a "point source," a large, clearly identified source of pollution such as a factory drain outfall.

66. The transaction achieves a net reduction of three kilos of phosphorus from older sources for every one that the new facility releases.

67. Telephone interview (March 7, 2005); personal interview (July 13, 2007).

68. "Developing Markets for Salinity Control" (factsheet), State Forests of NSW, Australia (n.d.), http://www.forest.nsw.gov.au/env_services/salinity_control/developing_markets/Developing_markets_fo_salinity_control.pdf, and a backgrounder at http://www.forest.nsw.gov.au/env_services/salinity_control/default.asp. See also James Salzman, "Creating Markets for Ecosystem Services: Notes From the Field," *New York University Law Review*, 80 (June 14, 2005): 870, http://www.law.nyu.edu/journals/lawreview/issues/vol80/no3/NYU302.pdf.

69. Ninety-seven percent achieved more than one ecological objective. "National Action Plan for Salinity and Water Quality" (report), Australian Government Natural Resource Management Team (February 2006), http://www.napswq.gov.au/.

70. Personal interview (July 6, 2006).

71. Richard Pinkham and Scott Chaplin, "21st Century Water Systems: Scenarios, Visions, and Drivers" (report), Rocky Mountain Institute, Snowmass, Colorado (1996), http://www.rmi.org/images/PDFs/Water/W99-21_21CentWaterSys.pdf.

72. Volume of Rogers Centre found at http://www.glasssteelandstone.com/CA/ON/TorontoSkyDome.html.

73. Nick Nutall, "Harvesting Rainfall a Key Climate Adaptation Opportunity for Africa," UNEP (Nairobi) (November 13, 2006), http://www.unep.org/Documents.Multilingual/Default.asp?ArticleID=5420&DocumentID=485&l=en.

74. In the United States reservoirs are regarded as prime terror targets.

75. Personal interview (November 9, 2006).

76. Personal interview (July 24, 2006).

77. Rick Watson and Stan Morain, "Climate Variability and Water Management Strategies in Southwest Pueblo Cultures," *Acclimations* (Newsletter of the U.S. National Assessment of the Potential Consequences of Climate Variability and Change) (January-February 2000), http://www.usgcrp.gov/usgcrp/Library/nationalassessment/newsletter/2000.02/Native.html.

78. Fred Pearce, "Earth: The Parched Planet," *New Scientist* (February 25, 2006), http://environment.newscientist.com/article/mg18925401.500.

## Chapter 11
## No Fear: Putting Canada's Water Up for Sale

1. Personal interview (June 8, 2005).

2. James Huffman, "NAFTA and Water: Dare We Talk about Water Markets?" in A. R. Riggs and Tom Velk, eds., *Beyond NAFTA: An Economic, Political and Sociological Perspective* (Vancouver: Fraser Institute, 1993), p. 97.

3. "Act for Canada's Water" (online brochure), Council of Canadians, http://www.canadians.org/water/documents/ACT_Canada_Water.pdf.

4. Tony Clarke, "Turning on Canada's Tap," *Canadian Dimension* (September/ October 2006), http://canadiandimension.com/articles/2006/09/07/646/. Clarke's think-tank is the Polaris Institute, http://www.polarisinstitute.org.

5. Maude Barlow, "Presentation on the SPP [Security and Prosperity Partnership] to the [House of Commons] International Trade Committee," The Council of Canadians (May 1, 2007), http://www.canadians.org/DI/documents/trade _committee_presentation_May107.pdf.

6. "Canada Has No Intention of Negotiating Bulk Water Exports" (press release), Office of the Minister of the Environment, Gatineau (April 13, 2007), http://www.ec.gc.ca/default.asp?lang=En&n=714D9AAE-1&news =B362E955-305B-49FB-BA8B-AD6292238387.

7. Council of Canadians website.

8. Telephone interview (July 8, 2005).

9. Steve Maich, "America's Thirsty," *Maclean's* (November 28, 2005), p. 26.

10. Barry Cooper and David Bercuson, "Fresh Water Resources Should Be Shared," *Calgary Herald* (April 18, 2001), p. A19.

11. Peter Goddard, "The Fountain of Truth," *Toronto Star* (June 12, 2005), p. C9.

12. "Water and Canadian Identity," Environment Canada (January 31, 2003), http://www.ec.gc.ca/water/en/culture/ident/e_ident.htm.

13. These words are from Maude Barlow and Tony Clarke, respectively.

14. Clarke, "Turning on Canada's Tap."

15. "Protection of the Waters of the Great Lakes: Final Report to the Governments of Canada and the United States," International Joint Commission (IJC) (2000), http://www.ijc.org/php/publications/html/ finalreport.html.

16. Clarke, "Turning on Canada's Tap."

17. James Bruce et al., "Climate Change Impacts on Boundary and Transboundary Water Management," (report), Natural Resources Canada (June 2003), http:// www.saskriverbasin.ca/Resources/Climatechangestudy/Final%20Report %20A458-402%20CCAF.pdf.

18. Ibid., p. 146.

19. "However," Turner adds, "if anyone wants it, WaterBank has sources." Telephone interview (June 3, 2005). William M. Turner, "The Commoditization and Marketing of Water," distributed at the Annual General Meeting of the Council of Canadians (July 5, 2001), http:// www.waterbank.com/Newsletters/nws35.html.

20. Or "commodify." The terms are touchstones of rights-and-commons rhetoric about water. As in, for example, "NAFTA ... could see water traded as a commodity, forever—with no chance to turn off the tap," in a letter from Council of Canadians national water campaigner Susan Howatt to *Port Hope Evening Guide* (Ontario) (April 30, 2007), which is posted on the Council's website, http://www.canadians.org/media/council/2007/30-Apr-07.html. Along with "open taps," "floodgates" also flow heavily through Council of Canadians communications. An earlier national water campaigner, Sara Ehrhardt, warned that if the Great Lakes Charter Annex were implemented, "the floodgates will be opened, and neither Canadian provinces nor the federal

government can stop the U.S. diversions." (Council of Canadians, "Feds Need to Enforce, Not Just Promote, Great Lakes Water Protection" [news release] [January 11, 2005].)

21. Respectively, the multilateral post-war GATT, the WTO that subsumed it in 1995 and the 1993 NAFTA (each of which the Council of Canadians cordially reviles for other reasons).

22. Maude Barlow, *Blue Gold: The Global Water Crisis and the Commodification of the World's Water Supply* (Ottawa: Octopus Books, 2001), p. 45.

23. The section in question is GATT Heading 22.01. A good explanation of its purpose is available online from the Joint Canada-Alberta government business advisory website at http://www.cbsc.org/servlet/ContentServer ?pagename=CBSC_AB%2Fdisplay&lang=en&cid=1084286449722 &c=GuideFactSheet.

24. Canadian Environmental Law Association, "NAFTA and Water Exports" (legal opinion), Ontario Ministry of Intergovernmental Affairs (1993), p. 2., cited in James Bruce et al., "Climate Change Impacts on Boundary and Transboundary Water Management," p. 144.

25. "An Act to Amend the International Boundary Waters Treaty Act: Questions and Answers," Foreign Affairs and International Trade Canada (Ottawa), http://geo.international.gc.ca/can-am/main/shared_env/q_a-en.asp.

26. "Prime Minister Announced NAFTA Improvements: Canada to Proceed with Agreement," Office of the Prime Minister (Ottawa) (December 2, 1993). "Canada Announces Intention to Proclaim NAFTA: U.S., Canada and Mexico Release Joint Statements on NAFTA," Office of the United States Trade Representative, Executive Office of the President (Washington, D.C.) (December 2, 1993), p. 2.

27. Huffman is an expert in U.S. constitutional and natural resources law, including water law. He is a former dean of the Lewis and Clark Law School in Portland, Oregon.

28. Barlow, *Blue Gold*, p. 46.

29. The baseline is the 36 months before any reduction takes effect. "Article 315: Other Export Measures," NAFTA (1993). Among many online sources for the full NAFTA text is http://www.sice.oas.org/Trade/NAFTA/naftatce.asp.

30. The U.S. harvests 600 million pounds of catfish a year.

31. GATT (General Agreement on Tariffs and Trade) Article XX (b) and (g), NAFTA Article 2101, incorporating these into the North American accord. For the relevant sections of the GATT, see http://www.wto.org/english/docs_e/ legal_e/gatt47_02_e.htm.

32. Barlow, *Blue Gold*, p. 45.

33. Ibid., p. 46.

34. This applies in British Columbia, for example, where Nestlé and local businesses must abide by the same rules for bottling spring water. If British Columbia obliged all, equally, to begin paying for that water (as it ought to), Nestlé could have no objection.

35. "Chapter 11: Investment," NAFTA (1993).

36. If the authors really believe this, it is curious that the Council of Canadians nonetheless continues to call on Parliament to take just such an action.

37. Ruth Walker, "Canada's Dry on Exporting Water," *The Christian Science Monitor* (June 15, 1998), http://www.csmonitor.com/1998/0615/061598.intl.intl.3.html. See also statement of claim at http://www.dfait-maeci.gc.ca/tna-nac/documents/Sunbelt.pdf.

38. B.C. eventually settled out of court with the Canadian partner, which had held a provincial license for the proposed withdrawal. Canada does not accept Sun Belt's standing to sue under Chapter 11. A Canadian government website notes that Sun Belt's claim was "received," but does not include it on a list of "active" cases: see http://www.dfait-maeci.gc.ca/tna-nac/gov-en.asp.

39. Maureen Appel Molot, "NAFTA Chapter 11: An Evolving Regime," in *Whose Rights? The NAFTA Chapter 11 Debate* (Ottawa: Centre for Trade Policy and Law, 2000), http://www.carleton.ca/ctpl/pdf/chapter_11_book/5_molot.pdf.

40. It was purchased in 2004 by a Nevada corporation, Nordic American Inc.

41. Telephone interview (May 16, 2005).

42. Personal interview (June 8, 2005).

43. Personal interview (June 8, 2005).

44. The Trust owes its funding to the B.C. government's belated recognition of the damage those developments did to river communities.

45. Telephone interview (February 12, 2007).

46. Robert F. Kennedy, Jr., and David Whiteside, "Riverkeeper Background" (backgrounder), Black Warrior Riverkeeper (2003), http://www.blackwarriorriver.org/library/waterkeeper%20history.htm.

47. Various treaties called into existence the Mekong River Commission, the International Commission for the Protection of the Rhine, the Danube Commission, and the Indus River Commission, among others.

48. "Towards Sustainable Water Management in the European Union" (staff working document), Commission of the European Communities (CEC), Brussels (March 22, 2007), http://www.internationalwaterlaw.org/intldocs/eu/WFD-Implementation-2007a.pdf.

49. Ali Akanda, Sarah Freeman and Maria Placht, "The Tigris-Euphrates River Basin: Mediating a Path towards Regional Water Stability," *The Fletcher School Journal for Issues Related to Southwest Asia and Islamic Civilization*, Tufts University (Spring 2007), http://fletcher.tufts.edu/al_nakhlah/archives/spring2007/placht-2.pdf.

50. "Towards Sustainable Water Management in the European Union," CEC.

51. These rivers drain parts, respectively, of: Maine and New Brunswick; Ontario and Minnesota; and Manitoba, North Dakota and Minnesota. "A Discussion Paper on the International Watersheds Initiative," International Joint Commission (IJC) (Ottawa and Washington, D.C.) (June 2005), www.ijc.org/php/publications/pdf/ID1582.pdf.

52. "LAKESNET 2007 Aims to Integrate Bilateral Discussion of Future of Great Lakes" (press release), Department of Foreign Affairs and International Trade (Ottawa) (January 29, 2007), http://geo.international.gc.ca/can-am/main/rightnav/lakenet-en.asp.

53. Fraser Basin Council, http://www.fraserbasin.bc.ca/about_us/faq.html.

54. Telephone interview (May 29, 2007).

55. Oliver Brandes and Tony Maas, "What We Govern and What Governs Us: Developing Sustainability in Canadian Water Management," POLIS Project on Ecological Governance, University of Victoria (June 2006).
56. "A Discussion Paper on the International Watersheds Initiative," IJC, p. 6.
57. Personal interview (June 8, 2005).

## Epilogue
## Future-Proof

1. Mary Miliken, "World Has Ten-Year Window to Act on Climate, Expert Says," Reuters (September 14, 2006), http://www.enn.com/top_stories/article/5054.
2. "Room for the River," Project Objectives, Netherlands, http://www.ruimtevoorderivier.nl/ (note English option).
3. Telephone interview (August 18, 2006).

# Acknowledgements

The author and publisher wish to express gratitude for permission to use the following material in this book:

Excerpt from Lester Brown's interview with Terrence McNally, reprinted from Alternet.org, © 2007 Independent Media Institute. Used with permission.

Excerpt from "Wading All Night through Mumbai" by Anjali Krishnan, adapted from BBC News at http://news.bbc.co.uk. Used with permission.

Excerpts from *Dried Up, Drowned Out: Voices from the Developing World on a Changing Climate* by Rachel Roach, © 2005 Tearfund. Used with permission.

Excerpts and material paraphrased from *The Great Lakes Water Wars*, © 2006 Peter Annin. Used with permission of Peter Annin and Island Press.

Excerpt from *A Sand County Almanac: And Sketches Here and There*, © 1992 Aldo Leopold. By permission of Oxford University Press.

Excerpt from *Dams and Development: A New Framework for Decision-Making*, © 2000 The World Commission on Dams. Reprinted with permission of Earthscan Publications.

# Index

# About the Author

Chris Wood is a veteran international journalist. In a career span-
ning four decades, he has penned thousands of magazine articles and
other stories, writing for the *Globe and Mail, Reader's Digest, The
Financial Post*, and more. He has written and produced prize-winning
documentaries for CBC radio. He has served on staff at *Maclean's* as a
Senior Writer, National and Business Editor, U.S.A. Correspondent,
B.C. and Pacific Rim Correspondent, and National Technology
Correspondent. "Melting Point," a feature he wrote for *The Walrus*
on the water crisis, won two Gold National Magazine Awards: for
Politics and Public Interest and for Science, Technology and the
Environment. A recipient of the highly competitive Investigative
Reporting Fellowship from *The Tyee* (http://thetyee.ca), he wrote
a multi-article exposé for the web-based publication about water in
British Columbia titled "Rough Weather Ahead." His most recent
book for the adult market, *Blockbusters and Trade Wars*, written
with co-author Peter S. Grant, about popular music, movies, books
and television, was shortlisted for the prestigious Donner Prize. His
Sirius Mystery series for teens (Raincoast), co-authored with Beverley
Wood, includes *The Golden Boy*, which was named an OLA Best Bet,
and *DogStar*, which was shortlisted for two awards. He makes his
home in the Cowichan Valley of Vancouver Island, where he is active
in local efforts to achieve a more sustainable community.